Lecture Notes in Computer Science   12805

Shigeru Yamashita · Tetsuo Yokoyama (Eds.)

Reversible Computation

13th International Conference, RC 2021
Virtual Event, July 7–8, 2021
Proceedings

Editors
Shigeru Yamashita (iD)
Ritsumeikan University
Kusatsu, Japan

Tetsuo Yokoyama (iD)
Nanzan University
Nagoya, Japan

ISSN 0302-9743   ISSN 1611-3349 (electronic)
Lecture Notes in Computer Science
ISBN 978-3-030-79836-9   ISBN 978-3-030-79837-6 (eBook)
https://doi.org/10.1007/978-3-030-79837-6

LNCS Sublibrary: SL2 – Programming and Software Engineering

This Springer imprint is published by the registered company Springer Nature Switzerland AG
The registered company address is: Gewerbestrasse 11, 6330 Cham, Switzerland

Preface

This volume contains the papers presented at the 13th Conference on Reversible Computation (RC 2021), held online (due to the COVID-19 pandemic) during July 7–8, 2021, and hosted by Nagoya University in Japan.

The RC conference brings together researchers from computer science, mathematics, engineering, and physics to discuss new developments and directions for future research in the emerging area of Reversible Computation. This includes, for example, reversible formal models, reversible programming languages, reversible circuits, and quantum computing.

The conference received 21 submissions from authors in 13 countries. After careful deliberations, the Program Committee selected 15 papers for presentation. In addition to these papers, this volume contains the three invited talks: "How Can We Construct Reversible Turing Machines in a Very Simple Reversible Cellular Automaton?" by Kenichi Morita (Hiroshima University, Japan), "Decision Diagrams and Reversible Computation" by Shin-ichi Minato (Kyoto University, Japan), and "Variational Quantum Eigensolver and Applications to Specific Optimization Problems" by Atsushi Matsuo (IBM Research - Tokyo, Japan).

When we started planning RC 2021, we thought the conference would be held in person. Unfortunately, the COVID-19 pandemic has been having a strong impact on society, and we decided to hold the conference online as with RC 2020. Of course, an online meeting makes interaction much more difficult in general. Nevertheless, we strongly believe that this online edition contributed to the research community like previous editions of the Conference on Reversible Computation.

The conference would not have been possible without the enthusiasm of the members of the Program Committee; their professionalism and their helpfulness were exemplary. For the work of the Program Committee and the compilation of the proceedings, the extremely useful EasyChair conference management system was employed. We thank Telecom Advanced Technology Research Support Center (SCAT) for their financial support, and we also thank the Graduate School of Informatics at Nagoya University, Japan, for providing various resources. Finally, we would like to thank all the authors for their submissions, their willingness to continue improving their papers, and their wonderful presentations during RC 2021.

May 2021

Shigeru Yamashita
Tetsuo Yokoyama

Organization

General Chair

Shoji Yuen   Nagoya University, Japan

Program Committee Chairs

Shigeru Yamashita   Ritsumeikan University, Japan
Tetsuo Yokoyama   Nanzan University, Japan

Steering Committee

Rolf Drechsler   University of Bremen, Germany
Robert Glück   University of Copenhagen, Denmark
Ivan Lanese   University of Bologna, Italy, and Inria, France
Irek Ulidowski   University of Leicester, UK
Robert Wille   Johannes Kepler University Linz, Austria

Program Committee

Gerhard Dueck   University of New Brunswick, Canada
Michael P. Frank   Sandia National Laboratories, USA
Robert Glück   University of Copenhagen, Denmark
Eva Graversen   Imperial College London, UK
James Hoey   University of Leicester, UK
Jarkko Kari   University of Turku, Finland
Jean Krivine   CNRS, France
Ivan Lanese   University of Bologna, Italy, and Inria, France
Martin Lukac   Nazarbayev University, Kazakhstan
Claudio Antares Mezzina Università di Urbino, Italy
Claudio Moraga   TU Dortmund, Germany
Keisuke Nakano   Tohoku University, Japan
Luca Paolini   Università degli Studi di Torino, Italy
Krzysztof Podlaski   University of Lodz, Poland
Mariusz Rawski   Warsaw University of Technology, Poland
Markus Schordan   Lawrence Livermore National Laboratory, USA
Mathias Soeken   École Polytechnique Fédérale de Lausanne,
              Switzerland
Milena Stankovic   University of Nis, Serbia
Himanshu Thapliyal   University of Kentucky, USA
Michael Kirkedal Thomsen University of Copenhagen, Denmark
Irek Ulidowski   University of Leicester, UK

| Rodney Van Meter | Keio University, Japan |
| Robert Wille | Johannes Kepler University Linz, Austria |

Additional Reviewers

Giovanni Fabbretti
Clément Aubert

Decision Diagrams and Reversible Computation (Abstract of Invited Talk)

Shin-ichi Minato

Graduate School of Informatics, Kyoto University, Kyoto 606-8501, Japan
minato@i.kyoto-u.ac.jp
http://www.lab2.kuis.kyoto-u.ac.jp/minato/

Abstract. Decision diagrams have attracted a great deal of attention for thirty years in computer science and technology, because those data structures are useful to efficiently manipulate many kinds of discrete structures, which are the fundamental mathematical models for solving various practical problems. Also for reversible computation systems, decision diagrams are sometimes used as key techniques for solving problems. In this invited talk, we overview the decision diagrams related to reversible computation. First we start with BDD and ZDD as classical models of logic and set. Next we review QMDD (Quantum Multiple-valued Decision Diagrams) and DDMF (Decision Diagrams for Matrix Functions) for dealing with special logic functions computed by quantum logic circuits. We then discuss πDD (Permutation Decision Diagrams) for manipulating permutation, which is closely related to reversible computation. We review some previous work on reversible circuit design using πDDs, and also show our recent work related to reversible computation.

Contents

Theory and Foundations

Circuit Synthesis

Invited Talks

How Can We Construct Reversible Turing Machines in a Very Simple Reversible Cellular Automaton?

Kenichi Morita$^{(\boxtimes)}$

Hiroshima University, Higashi-Hiroshima 739-8527, Japan
km@hiroshima-u.ac.jp

Abstract. A reversible cellular automaton (RCA) is an abstract spatiotemporal model of a reversible world. Using the framework of an RCA, we study the problem of how we can elegantly compose reversible computers from simple reversible microscopic operations. The CA model used here is an *elementary triangular partitioned CA* (ETPCA), whose spatial configurations evolve according to an extremely simple local transition function. We focus on the particular reversible ETPCA No. 0347, where 0347 is an ID number in the class of 256 ETPCAs. Based on our past studies, we explain that reversible Turing machines (RTMs) can be constructed in a systematic and hierarchical manner in this cellular space. Though ETPCA 0347 is an artificial CA model, this method gives a new vista to find a pathway from a reversible microscopic law to reversible computers. In particular, we shall see that RTMs can be easily realized in a unique method by using a *reversible logic element with memory* (RLEM) in the intermediate step of the pathway.

Keywords: Reversible cellular automaton · Elementary triangular partitioned cellular automaton · Reversible Turing machine · Reversible logic element with memory

1 Introduction

We investigate the problem of composing reversible Turing machines (RTMs), a model of reversible computers, from a simple reversible microscopic law. In particular, we study how simple the reversible microscopic law can be, and how elegantly RTMs are designed in a given environment. For this purpose, we use a reversible cellular automaton (RCA) as an abstract discrete model of a reversible world. Here, we consider a special type of an RCA called a reversible elementary triangular partitioned cellular automaton (ETPCA) having only four simple local transition rules. Thus, in this framework, the problem becomes how to construct RTMs using only such local transition rules.

However, since the local transition rules are so simple, it is difficult to directly design RTMs in this cellular space. One method of solving this problem is to

© Springer Nature Switzerland AG 2021
S. Yamashita and T. Yokoyama (Eds.): RC 2021, LNCS 12805, pp. 3–21, 2021.
https://doi.org/10.1007/978-3-030-79837-6_1

divide a pathway, which starts from a reversible microscopic law (i.e., local transition rules) and leads to reversible computers (i.e., RTMs), into several segments. Namely, we put several suitable conceptual levels on the pathway, and solve a subproblem in each level as in Fig. 1. Five levels are supposed here.

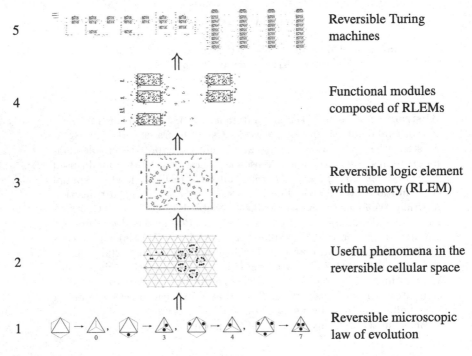

Fig. 1. A pathway from a reversible microscopic law to reversible computers

- Level 1: A reversible ETPCA, a model of a reversible world, is defined. Its local transition rules are considered as a microscopic law of evolution.
- Level 2: Various experiments in this cellular space are done to see how configurations evolve. By this, useful patterns and phenomena are found.
- Level 3: The phenomena found in the level 2 are used as gadgets to compose a logical primitive. Here, we make a reversible logic element with memory (RLEM), rather than a reversible logic gate, combining these gadgets.
- Level 4: Functional modules for RTMs are composed out of RLEMs. These modules are constructed easily and elegantly by using RLEMs.
- Level 5: RTMs are systematically built by assembling the functional modules created in the level 4, and then realized in the reversible cellular space.

In this way, we can construct RTMs from very simple local transition rules in a systematic and modularized method. Though ETPCA 0347 is an artificial CA model, it will give an insight to find a pathway even in a different situation.

In particular, we can see that it is important to give intermediate conceptual levels appropriately on the pathway to design reversible computers elegantly.

2   Reversible Cellular Automaton

In this section, using the framework of an RCA, a reversible microscopic law of evolution is given, which corresponds to the level 1 in Fig. 1. After a brief introduction to a CA and an RCA, we define a specific reversible ETPCA with the ID number 0347. Note that formal definitions on CA, ETPCA, and their reversibility are omitted here. See, e.g., [8] for their precise definitions.

2.1   Cellular Automaton and Its Reversibility

A *cellular automaton* (CA) is an abstract discrete model of spatiotemporal phenomena. It consists of an infinite number of identical finite automata called *cells* placed uniformly in the space. Each cell changes its state depending on the states of its neighbor cells using a *local function*, which is described by a set of local transition rules. Applying the local function to all the cells simultaneously, a *global function* that specifies the transition among *configurations* (i.e., whole states of the infinite cellular space) is obtained. Figure 2 shows a two-dimensional CA whose cells are square ones. In this figure each cell changes its state depending on the states of its five neighbor cells (including itself).

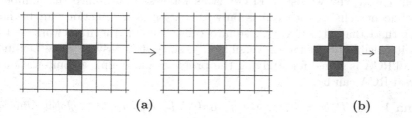

(a)   (b)

Fig. 2. Two-dimensional cellular automaton with square cells. **(a)** Its cellular space, and **(b)** its local transition rule

A *reversible cellular automaton* (RCA) is a CA whose global function is injective. Hence, there is no pair of distinct configurations that go to the same configuration by the global function. However, it is generally difficult to design an RCA if we use the standard framework of CAs. In particular, it is known that the problem whether the global function of a given two-dimensional CA is injective is undecidable [4]. In Sect. 2.2 we use a *partitioned CA* (PCA) [11], which is a subclass of the standard CA, for designing an RCA.

2.2   Triangular Partitioned Cellular Automaton (TPCA)

Hereafter, we use a *triangular partitioned cellular automaton* (TPCA) [3,9]. In a TPCA, a cell is an equilateral triangle, and is divided into three parts, each of which has its own state set. The next state of a cell is determined by the present states of the three adjacent parts of the neighbor cells (not by the whole states of the three adjacent cells) as shown in Fig. 3.

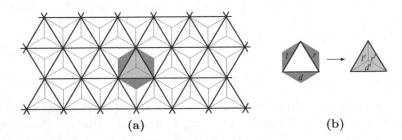

(a)   (b)

Fig. 3. Triangular partitioned cellular automaton. (a) Its cellular space, and (b) its local transition rule

A *local function* of a TPCA is defined by a set of local transition rules of the form shown in Fig. 3(b). Applying the local function to all the cells the *global function* of the TPCA is obtained.

The reason why we use a TPCA is as follows. First, since the number of edge-adjacent cells of each cell is only three, its local function can be much simpler than that of a CA with square cells. Second, the framework of PCA makes it feasible to design a reversible CA, since it is easy to show Lemma 1. Hence, TPCA is suited for studying the problem how simple a computationally universal RCA can be.

Lemma 1. *Let P be a PCA. Let f and F be its local and global functions, respectively. Then, F is injective if and only if f is injective.*

Note that this lemma was first shown in [11] for a one-dimensional PCA. The lemma for TPCA was given in [8].

2.3   Elementary Triangular Partitioned Cellular Automaton (ETPCA), in Particular, ETPCA 0347

An *elementary triangular partitioned cellular automaton* (ETPCA) is a subclass of a TPCA such that each part of a cell has the state set $\{0,1\}$, and its local function is *isotropic* (i.e., *rotation-symmetric*) [3,9].

Figure 4 shows the four local transition rules of an ETPCA with the ID number 0347, which is denoted by ETPCA 0347. Note that since an ETPCA is isotropic, local transition rules obtained by rotating both sides of the rules by a multiple of 60° are omitted here. Therefore, the local function is completely

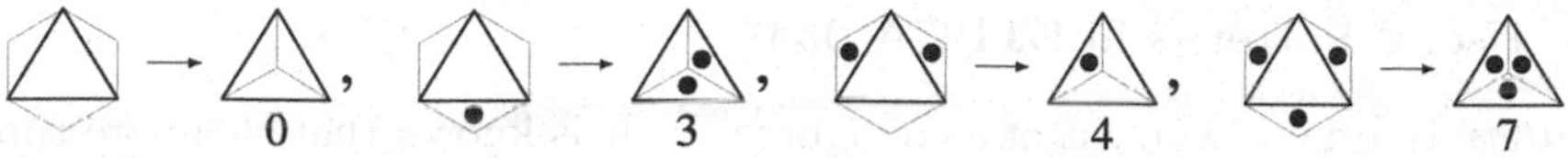

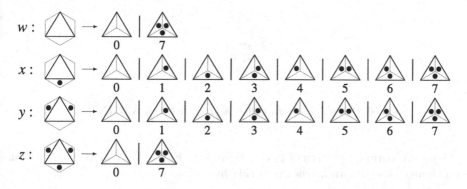

Fig. 4. Local function of ETPCA 0347 defined by the four local transition rules [9]. States 0 and 1 are indicated by a blank and ●

determined by these four rules. Hereafter, we use ETPCA 0347 as our model of a reversible world.

Generally, each ETPCA has an ID number of the form $wxyz$ ($w, z \in \{0, 7\}$, $x, y \in \{0, 1, ..., 7\}$), and is denoted by ETPCA $wxyz$. Figure 5 shows how an ID number corresponds to the four local transition rules. Note that w and z must be 0 or 7, since an ETPCA is isotropic. Thus, there are 256 ETPCAs in total.

Fig. 5. Correspondence between the ID number $wxyz$ and the four local transition rules of ETPCA $wxyz$ ($w, z \in \{0, 7\}$, $x, y \in \{0, 1, ..., 7\}$). Vertical bars indicate alternatives of a right-hand side of each local transition rule

We can verify that the local function of ETPCA 0347 is injective, since there is no pair of local transition rules that have the same right-hand side (see Fig. 4). Therefore, its global function is injective, and thus ETPCA 0347 is *reversible*. We can see every configuration of ETPCA 0347 has exactly one predecessor.

3 Useful Patterns and Phenomena in the Reversible Cellular Space of ETPCA 0347

Here, we make various experiments in the cellular space of ETPCA 0347, and look for useful patterns and phenomena. It corresponds to the level 2 in Fig. 1. Note that most experiments described below were firstly done in [6,9].

3.1 Useful Patterns in ETPCA 0347

A *pattern* is a finite segment of a configuration. It is known that there are three kinds of patterns in ETPCA 0347 since it is reversible [9]. They are a periodic pattern, a space-moving pattern, and an (eventually) expanding pattern. Here, a periodic pattern and a space-moving pattern are important. As we shall see below two periodic patterns called a *block* and a *fin*, and one space-moving pattern called a *glider* are particularly useful.

A *periodic pattern* is one such that the same pattern appears at the same position after p steps of time $(p > 0)$. The minimum of such p's is the *period* of the pattern. The pattern that appears at time t $(0 \leq t \leq p - 1)$ is called the pattern of *phase t*. A periodic pattern of period 1 is called a *stable pattern*.

A *block* is a stable pattern shown in Fig. 6. We can verify that a block does not change its pattern by the application of the local function given in Fig. 4.

Fig. 6. A stable pattern called a *block* in ETPCA 0347 [9]

A *fin* is a periodic pattern of period 6 given in Fig. 7. We can also verify that a fin changes its pattern as shown in this figure.

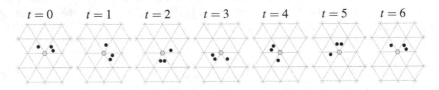

Fig. 7. A periodic pattern of period 6 called a *fin* in ETPCA 0347 [9]. It rotates around the point indicated by ○. The pattern at t $(0 \leq t \leq 5)$ is called a fin of phase t

A *space-moving pattern* is one such that the same pattern appears at a different position after p steps of time. The minimum of such p's is the period. The pattern that appears at time t $(0 \leq t \leq p - 1)$ is called the pattern of *phase t*.

A *glider* is a space-moving pattern shown in Fig. 8. It is the most useful pattern. If we start with the pattern given at $t = 0$ in Fig. 8, the same pattern appears at $t = 6$, and its position is shifted rightward. Thus, it swims like a fish or an eel in the reversible cellular space. It will be used as a *signal* when we implement a logic element in ETPCA 0347.

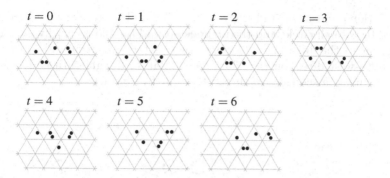

Fig. 8. A space-moving pattern of period 6 called a *glider* in ETPCA 0347 [9]. It moves rightward. The pattern at t ($0 \leq t \leq 5$) is called a glider of phase t

3.2 Interacting Patterns in ETPCA 0347 to Find Useful Phenomena

Next, we make various experiments of interacting a glider with blocks or a fin. By this, we can find several phenomena that can be used as "gadgets" for composing a logic element in Sect. 4.4.

It should be noted that despite the simplicity of the local function (Fig. 4) time evolutions of configurations in ETPCA 0347 are generally very complex. Therefore, it is very hard to follow evolution processes by paper and pencil. We developed an emulator for ETPCA 0347 that works on a general-purpose high-speed CA simulator *Golly* [15]. The emulator file and many pattern files are available in [7] (though its new version has not yet been uploaded).

First, we create several gadgets for controlling the move direction of a glider. Figure 9 shows a 60°-*right-turn gadget* composed of two blocks. It is newly introduced in this paper. Using several (rotated and unrotated) copies of this gadget, the move direction of a glider is changed freely.

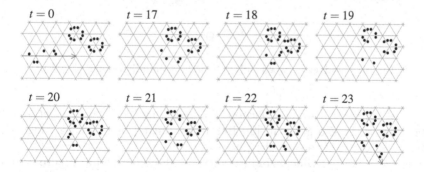

Fig. 9. 60°-right-turn gadget for a glider composed of two blocks

We can make a 120°-right-turn gadget as in Fig. 10. If we collide a glider with a sequence of two blocks as shown in Fig. 10 ($t = 0$), it is first decomposed into a "body" (left) and a fin (right) ($t = 56$). The body rotates around the point indicated by a small circle, and the fin goes around the blocks clockwise. Finally, the body meets the fin, and a glider is reconstructed. The resulting glider moves to the south-west direction ($t = 334$). A similar 120°-right-turn gadget is also possible by using a sequence of three blocks or five blocks.

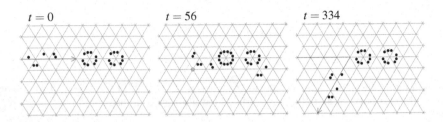

Fig. 10. 120°-right-turn gadget for a glider composed of two blocks [9]

It should be noted that 120°-right-turn is also realized by using two (rotated and unrotated) copies of a 60°-right-turn gadget. Furthermore, in the latter implementation, right-turn is performed more quickly. Hence a 60°-right-turn gadget is more useful in this respect. However, a 120°-right-turn gadget can be used as an interface between a bidirectional signal path and unidirectional signal paths as shown in Fig. 11. Such a gadget is necessary for constructing a logic element in Sect. 4.4, since a fin-shifting (Fig. 14) uses a bidirectional path.

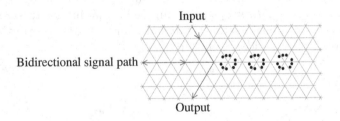

Fig. 11. Interface gadget between bidirectional and unidirectional signal paths [9]

Figures 12 and 13 show a *backward-turn gadget* and a *U-turn gadget*. A 120°-*left-turn gadget* is also given in [9], but it is omitted here. These gadgets are needed when we want to shift the phase of a glider (see [9]).

Next, we make experiments of interacting a glider with a fin. Figure 14 shows that shifting the position of a fin is possible if we collide a glider with the right phase to it [6]. Thus, a fin can be used as a kind of memory, where memory states (say 0 and 1) are distinguished by the positions of the fin. In this case, change of the memory state can be done by shifting the fin appropriately.

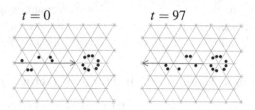

Fig. 12. Backward-turn gadget for a glider [9]

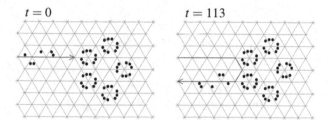

Fig. 13. U-turn gadget for a glider [9]

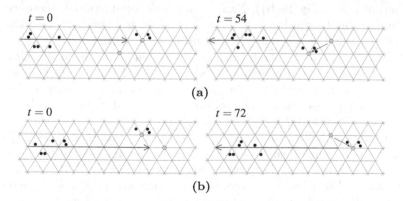

(a)

(b)

Fig. 14. Shifting a fin by a glider [6]. (a) Pulling, and (b) pushing

4 Composing Reversible Logic Element with Memory

Using useful phenomena found in Sect. 3, a logic element is composed. It corresponds to the level 3 in Fig. 1. Here, a reversible logic element with memory, rather than a reversible logic gate, is implemented in ETPCA 0347.

4.1 Reversible Logic Element with Memory (RLEM)

A *reversible logic element with memory* (RLEM) [8,12] is a kind of a reversible finite automaton having both input and output ports, which is sometimes called a reversible sequential machine of Mealy type. A *sequential machine M* is defined by $M = (Q, \Sigma, \Gamma, \delta)$, where Q is a finite set of states, Σ and Γ are finite sets of input and output symbols, and $\delta : Q \times \Sigma \to Q \times \Gamma$ is a move function (Fig. 15(a)). If δ is injective, it is called a *reversible sequential machine* (RSM).

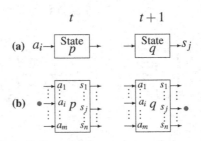

Fig. 15. (a) A sequential machine, and (b) an interpretation of it as a module having decoded input ports and output ports for utilizing it as a circuit module

To use an SM as a circuit module, we interpret it as the one with decoded input/output ports (Fig. 15(b)). Namely, for each input symbol, there exists a unique input port to which a signal (or a particle) is given. It is also the case for the output symbols. Therefore, we assume signals should not be given to two or more input ports at the same time. Its operation is undefined if such a case occurs. Of course, it could be extended so that an SM can receive two or more signals simultaneously. However, we do not do so, because we want to keep its operation as simple as possible. Moreover, as described in Sect. 4.3, RSMs are sufficiently powerful without such an extension.

An RLEM is an RSM that satisfies $|\Sigma| = |\Gamma|$. A 2-state RLEM (i.e., $|Q| = 2$) is particularly important, since it is simple yet powerful (see Sect. 4.3). In the following we shall use a specific 2-state 4-symbol RLEM No. 4-31.

Advantages of RLEMs over reversible logic gates are as follows. As described above, an RLEM receives only one signal at the same time, while a logic gate generally receives two or more signals simultaneously. Therefore, in the case of a logic gate, some synchronization mechanism is necessary so that signals arrive at exactly the same time at each gate. On the other hand, in the case of an

RLEM, a signal can arrive at any time, since a signal interacts with a state of the RLEM, not with another signal. An RLEM is thus completely different from a logic gate in this respect. By this, realization of an RLEM and its circuit becomes much simpler than that of a logic gate at least in an RCA. This problem will be discussed again in Sect. 4.5.

4.2   RLEM 4-31

Here, we consider a specific 2-state 4-symbol RLEM 4-31 such that $Q = \{0, 1\}$, $\Sigma = \{a, b, c, d\}$, $\Gamma = \{w, x, y, z\}$, and δ is defined as follows:

$$\delta(0, a) = (0, w), \ \delta(0, b) = (0, x), \ \delta(0, c) = (0, y), \ \delta(0, d) = (1, w),$$
$$\delta(1, a) = (1, x), \ \delta(1, b) = (0, z), \ \delta(1, c) = (1, z), \ \delta(1, d) = (1, y).$$

In RLEM 4-31, "4" stands for "4-symbol," and "31" is its serial number in the class of 2-state 4-symbol RLEMs [8].

The move function δ of RLEM 4-31 is represented in a graphical form as shown in Fig. 16(a). Two rectangles in the figure correspond to the two states 0 and 1. Solid and dotted lines show the input-output relation in each state. If an input signal goes through a dotted line, then the state does not change (Fig. 16(b)). On the other hand, if a signal goes through a solid line, then the state changes (Fig. 16(c)).

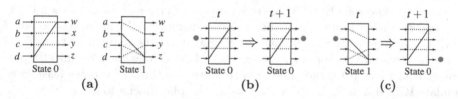

Fig. 16. RLEM 4-31, and its operation examples. (a) Two states of RLEM 4-31. (b) The case that the state does not change, and (c) the case that the state changes

4.3   Universality of RLEMs

There are infinitely many 2-state RLEMs if we do not restrict the number of input/output symbols. Hence, it is an important problem which RLEMs are sufficiently powerful, and which are not. Remarkably, it is known almost all 2-state RLEMs are universal.

An RLEM E is called *universal* if any RSM is composed only of E. The following results on the universality are known. First, every non-degenerate 2-state k-symbol RLEM is universal if $k > 2$ [12]. Second, among four non-degenerate 2-state 2-symbol RLEMs, three RLEMs 2-2, 2-3 and 2-4 have been proved to be non-universal [14] (but the set {2-3, 2-4} is universal [5]). Figure 17 summarizes these results. Note that the definition of *degeneracy* is given in [8,12].

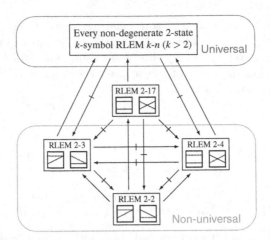

Fig. 17. Universality/non-universality of 2-state RLEMs [8,14]. Here, $A \to B$ ($A \not\to B$, respectively) indicates that A can (cannot) be simulated by B

4.4   Composing RLEM 4-31 in the Reversible ETPCA 0347

As we shall see in Sect. 5.2, a finite state control, and a memory cell, which corresponds to one tape square, of a reversible Turing machine (RTM) can be formalized as RSMs. Hence, any universal RLEM can be used to compose RTMs.

Here, we choose RLEM 4-31 for this purpose. The reason is as follows. First, it is known that a finite state control and a memory cell can be composed of RLEM 4-31 compactly [13]. Second, in RLEM 4-31, the number of transitions from one state to another (i.e., the number of solid lines in a graphical representation like Fig. 16) is only one in each state. By this, it becomes feasible to simulate RLEM 4-31 in ETPCA 0347 using the phenomena found in Sect. 3.

Figure 18 shows the complete pattern realized in ETPCA 0347 that simulates RLEM 4-31. Two circles in the middle of the pattern show possible positions of a fin. In this figure, the fin is at the lower position, which indicates the state of the RLEM 4-31 is 0. Many blocks are placed to form various turn gadgets shown in Figs. 9, 10, 11, 12 and 13. They are for controlling the direction and the phase of a glider.

In Fig. 18, a glider is given to the input port d. The path from d to the output port w shows the trajectory of the glider. The glider first goes to the north-east position. From there the glider moves to the south-west direction, and collides with the fin. By this, the fin is pulled upward by the operation shown in Fig. 14(a). Then the glider goes to the south-east position. From there, it pushes the fin (Fig. 14(b)). By this, the fin moves to the position of the upper circle, which means the state changes from 0 to 1. The glider finally goes out from the port w. The whole process above simulates the one step move $\delta(0, d) = (1, w)$ of RLEM 4-31. Other cases are also simulated similarly. Note that the pattern in Fig. 18 is an improved version of the one given in [6] using the 60°-right-turn gadget in Fig. 9.

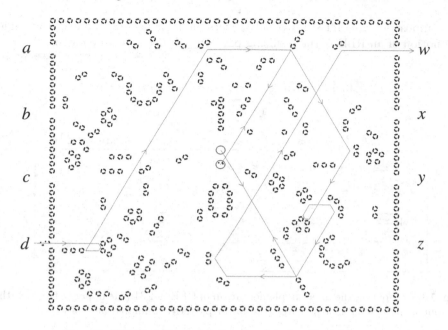

Fig. 18. RLEM 4-31 module implemented in ETPCA 0347

4.5 Comparing with the Method that Uses Reversible Logic Gates

In [9] it is shown that a Fredkin gate [2], a universal reversible logic gate, can
be implemented in ETPCA 0347. There, a Fredkin gate is constructed out of
two switch gates and two inverse switch gates. Therefore, it is in principle possible to implement a reversible Turing machine in ETPCA 0347 using a Fredkin
gate. However, as stated in Sect. 4.1, it will become very complex since adjust-
ment of signal timings at each gate is necessary. Here, we realize RLEM 4-31
in ETPCA 0347 using reversible logic gates, and compare it with the "direct
implementation" given in Fig. 18.

Figure 19 shows two implementations of RLEM 4-31 simulated on Golly.
The upper pattern is the direct implementation of RLEM 4-31 (the same as
in Fig. 18), while the lower is constructed using four switch gates, two Fredkin
gates, and four inverse switch gates. The size and the period of the former pattern are 82×163 and 6, and those of the latter are 462×1505 and 24216. Note
that the period of the former is 6, since it contains a fin to memorize the state
of RLEM 4-31. In the latter pattern, we need a circulating signal in the module
to memorize the state since it is composed only of logic gates that are memory-
less elements. This circulating signal determines the period 24216. Therefore, an
input signal must be given at time t that satisfies $(t \bmod 24216) = 0$.

These values, of course, give only upper-bounds of the complexities of these
two implementations. Hence they cannot be a proof for showing the advantage
of the direct implementation. However, empirically, they suggest that it is much
better *not* to use reversible logic gates in an RCA to make RTMs. Actually, if

we compose a whole RTM using only reversible logic gates without introducing the notion of an RLEM, the resulting pattern will become quite complex.

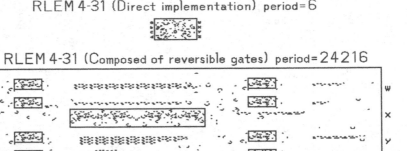

RLEM 4-31 (Direct implementation) period=6

RLEM 4-31 (Composed of reversible gates) period=24216

Fig. 19. Comparing the direct implementation of RLEM 4-31 (the upper pattern) with the one using reversible logic gates (the lower pattern) simulated on Golly

5   Making Reversible Turing Machines in ETPCA 0347

Here we realize reversible Turing machines in the cellular space of ETPCA 0347. To do it systematically, functional modules for RTMs are composed out of RLEM 4-31, and then they are assembled to make circuits that simulate RTMs. Finally the circuits are embedded in the space of ETPCA 0347. These steps correspond to the levels 4 and 5 in Fig. 1.

5.1   Reversible Turing Machine

A one-tape *Turing machine* (TM) in the quintuple form is defined by a system $T = (Q, S, q_0, F, s_0, \delta)$, where Q is a non-empty finite set of states, S is a non-empty finite set of tape symbols, q_0 is an initial state ($q_0 \in Q$), F is a set of final states ($F \subseteq Q$), and s_0 is a blank symbol ($s_0 \in S$). The item δ is a *move relation*, which is a subset of $(Q \times S \times S \times \{L, R\} \times Q)$, where L and R stand for left-shift and right-shift of the head. An element of δ is a *quintuple* of the form $[p, s, t, d, q]$. It means that if T is in the state p and reads the symbol s, then it writes the symbol t, shifts the head to the direction d and goes to the state q.

A TM T is called *deterministic*, if the following holds for any pair of distinct quintuples $[p_1, s_1, t_1, d_1, q_1]$ and $[p_2, s_2, t_2, d_2, q_2]$ in δ.

$$(p_1 = p_2) \Rightarrow (s_1 \neq s_2)$$

A TM T is called *reversible*, if the following holds for any pair of distinct quin-tuples $[p_1, s_1, t_1, d_1, q_1]$ and $[p_2, s_2, t_2, d_2, q_2]$ in δ.

$$(q_1 = q_2) \Rightarrow (d_1 = d_2 \wedge t_1 \neq t_2)$$

In the following we consider only deterministic TMs, and thus the word "deter-ministic" will be omitted. A TM that is reversible and deterministic is now called a *reversible Turing machine* (RTM). In an RTM, every computational configura-tion of it has at most one predecessor. See, e.g., [8] for a more detailed definition on RTMs.

Example 1. Consider the RTM $T_{\text{parity}} = (\{q_0, q_1, q_2, q_{\text{acc}}, q_{\text{rej}}\}, \{0, 1\}, q_0, \{q_{\text{acc}}\},$ $0, \delta_{\text{parity}})$. The set δ_{parity} consists of the following five quintuples.

$$[q_0, 0, 1, R, q_1], [q_1, 0, 1, L, q_{\text{acc}}], [q_1, 1, 0, R, q_2], [q_2, 0, 1, L, q_{\text{rej}}], [q_2, 1, 0, R, q_1]$$

It is a very simple example of an RTM. In Sect. 5.3 a configuration that simulates it in ETPCA 0347 will be shown. It is easy to see that T_{parity} is deterministic and reversible. Assume a symbol string $0\,1^n\,0$ $(n = 0, 1, \ldots)$ is given as an input. Then, T_{parity} halts in the accepting state q_{acc} if and only if n is even, and all the read symbols are complemented. The computing process for the input string 0110 is as follows: $q_0 0110 \vdash 1 q_1 110 \vdash 10 q_2 10 \vdash 100 q_1 0 \vdash 10 q_{\text{acc}} 01$. □

It is known that any (irreversible) TM can be simulated by an RTM without generating garbage information [1]. Hence, RTMs are computationally universal. In the following, we consider only 2-symbol RTMs with a rightward-infinite tape, since any RTM can be converted into such an RTM (see, e.g., [8]).

5.2   Functional Modules Composed of RLEM 4-31 for RTMs

We compose two kinds of functional modules out of RLEM 4-31. They are a memory cell and a q_i-module (or state module) for 2-symbol RTMs [13].

A *memory cell* simulates one tape square and the movements of the head. It is formulated as a 4-state RSM, since it keeps a tape symbol 0 or 1, and the information whether the head is on this tape square or not (its precise formulation as a 4-state RSM is found in [13]). It has ten input symbols listed in Table 1, and ten output symbols corresponding to the input symbols (for example, for the input symbol W0, there is an output symbol W0′).

A memory cell is composed of nine RLEM 4-31's as shown in Fig. 20(a). Its top RLEM keeps a tape symbol. Namely, if the tape symbol is 0 (1, respectively), then the top RLEM is in the state 0 (1). The position of the head is kept by the remaining eight RLEMs. If all the eight RLEMs are in the state 1, then the head is on this square. If they are in the state 0, the head is not on this square. Figure 20(a) shows that the tape symbol is 1 and the head is not on this square. The eight RLEMs also process the instruction/response signals in Table 1 properly.

Table 1. Ten kinds of input symbols of the memory cell [13]

Symbol	Instruction/Response	Meaning
W0	Write 0	Instruction of writing the tape symbol 0 at the head position. By this instruction, read operation is also performed
W1	Write 1	Instruction of writing the tape symbol 1 at the head position. By this instruction, read operation is also performed
R0	Read 0	Response signal telling the read symbol at the head is 0
R1	Read 1	Response signal telling the read symbol at the head is 1
SL	Shift-left	Instruction of shift-left operation
SLI	Shift-left immediate	Instruction of placing the head on this cell by shifting left
SLc	Shift-left completed	Response (completion) signal of shift-left operation
SR	Shift-right	Instruction of shift-right operation
SRI	Shift-right immediate	Instruction of placing the head on this cell by shifting right
SRc	Shift-right completed	Response (completion) signal of shift-right operation

Connecting an infinite number of memory cells in a row, we obtain a tape unit. The read, write and head-shift operations are executed by giving an instruction signal to an input port of the leftmost memory cell. Its response signal comes out from an output port of the leftmost one. Note that a read operation is performed by the Write 0 (W0) instruction. Thus it is a destructive read. The details of how these operations are performed in this circuit is found in [13].

A q_i-*module* corresponds to the state q_i of an RTM. It has five RLEM 4-31's as shown in Fig. 20(b), which is for a shift-right state. Since a module for a shift-left state is similar, we explain only the case of shift-right below. It is further decomposed into a *pre-q_i-submodule* (left half), and a *post-q_i-submodule* (right-half). Note that only the post-q_i-submodule is used for the initial state, while only the pre-q_i-submodule is used for a halting state.

The pre-q_i-submodule is activated by giving a signal from the port $0Rq_i$ or $1Rq_i$ in the figure. Then, a write operation and a shift-right operation that should be done before going to q_i are performed. Namely, it first sends an instruction W0 or W1 to write a tape symbol 0 or 1. Here we assume the previous tape symbol under scan is 0. Then it receives a response signal R0 (i.e., the read symbol is 0). Next, it sends a shift-right instruction SR, and receives a completion signal SRc. After that, it goes to the state q_i, and activates the post-q_i-submodule. The red particle in the figure shows that it has become the state q_i.

In the post-q_i-submodule, a read operation is performed, which should be executed just after becoming the state q_i. By giving an instruction W0, a destructive read operation of a tape symbol is executed. Thus it receives a response signal R0 or R1, and finally a signal goes out from the port q_i0 or q_i1.

Let Q be the set of states of an RTM. For each $q_i \in Q$ prepare a q_i-module and place them in a row. If there is a quintuple $[q_i, s, t, d, q_j]$, then connect the port q_is of the post-q_i-submodule to the port tdq_j of the pre-q_j-submodule. By this, the operation of the quintuple $[q_i, s, t, d, q_j]$ is correctly simulated. Note that such a connection is done in a one-to-one manner (i.e., connection lines neither branch nor merge) since the TM is deterministic and reversible. In this way, a circuit module for the finite state control of the RTM is composed.

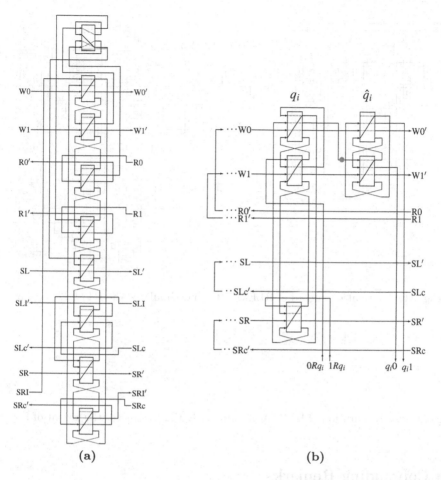

Fig. 20. (a) A memory cell, and (b) a q_i-module composed of RLEM 4-31 for 2-symbol RTMs [13]. The q_i-module consists of a *pre-q_i-submodule* (left half), and a *post-q_i-submodule* (right-half)

5.3 Constructing RTMs in ETPCA 0347

Assembling memory cells and q_i-modules by the method described in Sect. 5.2, we can compose any 2-symbol RTM. Figure 21 shows the whole circuit that simulates T_{parity} given in Example 1. If a signal is given to the "Begin" port, it starts to compute. Its answer will be obtained at "Accept" or "Reject" port.

Putting copies of the pattern of RLEM 4-31 given in Fig. 18 at the positions corresponding to the RLEMs in Fig. 21, and connecting them appropriately, we have a complete configuration of ETPCA 0347 that simulates T_{parity} in Example 1. Figure 22 shows the configuration simulated on Golly. Giving a glider to "Begin" port, its computation starts. Whole computing processes of RTMs embedded in ETPCA 0347 can be seen on Golly using its emulator [7].

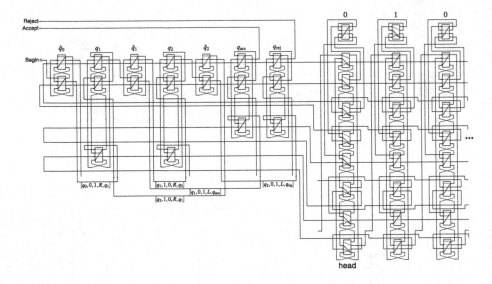

Fig. 21. A circuit composed of RLEM 4-31 that simulates the RTM T_{parity} [13]

Fig. 22. A configuration of ETPCA 0347 in Golly that simulates the circuit of Fig. 21

6   Concluding Remarks

We studied the problem of how we can find a method of constructing reversible computers from a simple reversible microscopic law. We put several conceptual levels properly on the construction pathway as in Fig. 1. By this, the problem was decomposed into several subproblems, and it became feasible to solve it. Here we saw that it is possible to compose RTMs even from the extremely simple local function of reversible ETPCA 0347 using RLEM 4-31 in the intermediate step of the pathway.

Only the specific ETPCA 0347 is considered here, but there are many other ETPCAs. In [10], this problem is studied using reversible ETPCA 0137. There, observed phenomena in the level 2 and composing technics of RLEM 4-31 in the level 3 are very different. However, also in this case, the systematic and hierarchical method shown in Fig. 1 can be applied, and works effectively.

References

1. Bennett, C.H.: Logical reversibility of computation. IBM J. Res. Dev. **17**, 525–532 (1973). https://doi.org/10.1147/rd.176.0525
2. Fredkin, E., Toffoli, T.: Conservative logic. Int. J. Theoret. Phys. **21**, 219–253 (1982). https://doi.org/10.1007/BF01857727
3. Imai, K., Morita, K.: A computation-universal two-dimensional 8-state triangular reversible cellular automaton. Theoret. Comput. Sci. **231**, 181–191 (2000). https://doi.org/10.1016/S0304-3975(99)00099--7
4. Kari, J.: Reversibility and surjectivity problems of cellular automata. J. Comput. Syst. Sci. **48**, 149–182 (1994). https://doi.org/10.1016/S0022-0000(05)80025-X
5. Lee, J., Peper, F., Adachi, S., Morita, K.: An asynchronous cellular automaton implementing 2-state 2-input 2-output reversed-twin reversible elements. In: Umeo, H., Morishita, S., Nishinari, K., Komatsuzaki, T., Bandini, S. (eds.) ACRI 2008. LNCS, vol. 5191, pp. 67–76. Springer, Heidelberg (2008). https://doi.org/10.1007/978-3-540-79992-4_9
6. Morita, K.: Finding a pathway from reversible microscopic laws to reversible computers. Int. J. Unconventional Comput. **13**, 203–213 (2017)
7. Morita, K.: Reversible world : Data set for simulating a reversible elementary triangular partitioned cellular automaton on Golly. Hiroshima University Institutional Repository. http://ir.lib.hiroshima-u.ac.jp/00042655 (2017)
8. Morita, K.: Theory of Reversible Computing. Springer, Tokyo (2017). https://doi.org/10.1007/978-4-431-56606-9
9. Morita, K.: A universal non-conservative reversible elementary triangular partitioned cellular automaton that shows complex behavior. Nat. Comput. **18**(3), 413–428 (2017). https://doi.org/10.1007/s11047-017-9655-9
10. Morita, K.: Constructing reversible Turing machines in a reversible and conservative elementary triangular cellular automaton. J. Automata, Lang. Combinatorics (to appear)
11. Morita, K., Harao, M.: Computation universality of one-dimensional reversible (injective) cellular automata. Trans. IEICE **E72**, 758–762 (1989). http://ir.lib.hiroshima-u.ac.jp/00048449
12. Morita, K., Ogiro, T., Alhazov, A., Tanizawa, T.: Non-degenerate 2-state reversible logic elements with three or more symbols are all universal. J. Multiple-Valued Logic Soft Comput. **18**, 37–54 (2012)
13. Morita, Kenichi, Suyama, Rei: Compact realization of reversible turing machines by 2-state reversible logic elements. In: Ibarra, Oscar H.., Kari, Lila, Kopecki, Steffen (eds.) UCNC 2014. LNCS, vol. 8553, pp. 280–292. Springer, Cham (2014). https://doi.org/10.1007/978-3-319-08123-6_23
14. Mukai, Y., Ogiro, T., Morita, K.: Universality problems on reversible logic elements with 1-bit memory. Int. J. Unconventional Comput. **10**, 353–373 (2014)
15. Trevorrow, A., Rokicki, T., Hutton, T., et al.: Golly: an open source, cross-platform application for exploring Conway's Game of Life and other cellular automata (2005). http://golly.sourceforge.net/

Variational Quantum Eigensolver and Its Applications

Atsushi Matsuo[1,2](✉)

[1] IBM Quantum, IBM Research - Tokyo, Tokyo 103-8510, Japan
MATSUOA@jp.ibm.com
[2] Graduate School of Information Science and Engineering, Ritsumeikan University,
Shiga 525-8577, Japan

Abstract. The Variational Quantum Eigensolver (VQE) algorithm is attracting much attention to utilize current limited quantum devices. The VQE algorithm requires a quantum circuit with parameters, called a parameterized quantum circuit (PQC), to prepare a quantum state, and the quantum state is used to calculate the expectation value of a given Hamiltonian. Creating sophisticated PQCs is important from the perspective of the convergence speed. Thus, we propose problem-specific PQCs of the VQE algorithm for optimization problems. Our idea is to dynamically create a PQC that reflects the constraints of an optimization problem. With a problem-specific PQC, it is possible to reduce a search space by restricting unitary transformations in favor of the VQE algorithm. As a result, we can speed up the convergence of the VQE algorithm. Experimental results show that the convergence speed of the proposed PQCs is significantly faster than that of the state-of-the-art PQC.

Keywords: VQE algorithm · Optimization problem · Problem-specific parameterized quantum circuit

1 Introduction

Many companies have been competing to develop quantum computers recently. Quantum computing promises advantages in solving certain tasks, e.g., integer factorization [30] and database search [6]. However, the number of errors in current quantum devices cannot be ignored, and they do not yet have the capability of the error correction. Thus, they have the limitation of the size of quantum circuits that can be executed [26]. Due to this limitation, we cannot yet execute quantum circuits for such complicated tasks.

To utilize such limited quantum devices, variational quantum algorithms have emerged and have attracted the attention [3,16]. Variational quantum algorithms use both quantum and classical computers. By effectively combining quantum and classical computers, it is expected that variational quantum algorithms can achieve quantum advantage with even current limited quantum devices. Many kinds of variational quantum algorithms are proposed for problems in various

© Springer Nature Switzerland AG 2021
S. Yamashita and T. Yokoyama (Eds.): RC 2021, LNCS 12805, pp. 22–41, 2021.
https://doi.org/10.1007/978-3-030-79837-6_2

fields so far such as chemistry [1,11,23], optimization [2,5,7,18,33], machine learning [8,17,29], quantum gate synthesis [10,13], and so on.

The Variational Quantum Eigensolver (VQE) algorithm is a kind of variational quantum algorithms and it has been studied intensively [12,16,22,23,32] among them. The VQE algorithm is an algorithm to find the minimal eigenvalue and its eigenvector of a given Hamiltonian. It consists of two parts like other variational quantum algorithms. One is executed on quantum computers, and the other on classical computers. The part executed on quantum computers has a shallow quantum circuit with parameters called a *parameterized quantum circuit (PQC)*. A PQC prepare a quantum state from an initial state, and it can also prepare various quantum states by changing the parameters. With the created quantum state, the expectation value of a given Hamiltonian is calculated by sampling outcomes. Since the VQE algorithm uses the variational method based on the results of sampling, making sophisticated PQCs is important from the perspective of the convergence speed.

The VQE algorithm can also be used to solve optimization problems by creating the corresponding Hamiltonian for an optimization problem [2,18]. Formulations of the Hamiltonian for many NP-complete and NP-hard problems have been discussed in [14]. A converged expectation value corresponds to a solution to the optimization problem. Also, a quantum state for the converged expectation value corresponds to an assignment of variables for the optimization problem.

Although the VQE algorithm is being studied intensively and PQCs of the VQE algorithm are important, there are a few researches considering PQCs of the VQE algorithm for optimization problems. Hence, we would like to point out two problems in known PQCs. (1) Only a few types of PQCs are known. Even the state-of-the-art library for quantum computers [27] has only four types of PQCs such as *Ry, RyRz, SwapRz* and *UCCSD*. They are all general PQCs with static structures and can be used for any problems. (2) Existing PQCs do not take into account the feasibility of output solutions, and they often output infeasible solutions. We need to ensure that results are feasible solutions to corresponding optimization problems when using the VQE algorithm for optimization problems.

In this paper, we propose novel PQCs for the traveling salesman problem that is a well-know optimization problem. In the proposed PQCs, we pay attention to the constraints of an optimization problem, and we dynamically create a PQC that reflects those constraints of the optimization problem. We call such a PQC for the specific problem as a *problem-specific PQC* [15]. Since problem-specific PQCs reflect the constraints of optimization problems, they naturally take into account the feasibility of output solutions. With problem-specific PQCs, it is possible to reduce search spaces significantly. Thus, we can speed up the convergence of the VQE algorithms.

The rest of the paper is organized as follows. Section 2 covers the background on quantum circuits and the VQE algorithm. In Sect. 3, we explain the proposed problem-specific PQCs for the optimization problems. Section 4 summarizes the experimental results of the proposed PQCs. Finally, Sect. 5 concludes the paper.

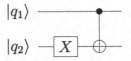

Fig. 1. An example of a quantum circuit

2   Background

In this section, we introduce the basics of quantum circuits and the VQE algorithm.

2.1   Quantum Circuits

A quantum circuit is a model of quantum computation [21] and contains qubits and a sequence of quantum gates. It represents a sequence of operations applied to qubits graphically. Figure 1 shows an example of a quantum circuit. The horizontal wires in Fig. 1 represent qubits q_1 and q_2. Each diagram in the quantum circuit represents quantum gates.

In quantum computation, we use qubits instead of bits. A bit in classical computers has to be either zero or one. However, a qubit can be $|0\rangle$, $|1\rangle$, or the superposition state. The superposition state is a linear combination of $|0\rangle$ and $|1\rangle$ such as $\alpha|0\rangle + \beta|1\rangle$, where $\alpha, \beta \in \mathbb{C}$ and $|\alpha|^2 + |\beta|^2 = 1$. These α and β are called amplitudes of the corresponding bases. We also represent an n-qubit state as $|\psi\rangle = \sum_{k \in \{0,1\}^n} \alpha_k |k\rangle$, where $\alpha_k \in \mathbb{C}$ and $\sum_{k \in \{0,1\}^n} |\alpha_k|^2 = 1$. It is represented with a 2^n-dimensional state vector such as $(\alpha_0, \alpha_1, ..., \alpha_{2^n-1})^T$.

We apply quantum operators to state vectors and change state vectors to calculate tasks in quantum computation. Each quantum gate has the functionality corresponding to the particular unitary operator. With qubits, a quantum gate represents what unitary operator is applied to which qubits. A quantum gate is represented with a $2^n \times 2^n$ unitary matrix. Thus, we repeatedly multiply between a $2^n \times 2^n$ unitary matrix and a 2^n-dimensional state vector in a quantum circuit. We explain the details of quantum gates used in the proposed PQCs in Sect. 3.

2.2   The VQE Algorithm

The VQE algorithm is an algorithm to find the minimal eigenvalue and its eigenvector of a given Hamiltonian. To do this, the VQE algorithm uses the Rayleigh-Ritz variational principle as shown in Eq. (1). H and $|\psi\rangle$ represent a given Hamiltonian and a quantum state, respectively in Eq. (1). λ_{min} represents the minimal eigenvalue of H.

$$\lambda_{min} \leq \langle\psi|H|\psi\rangle \tag{1}$$

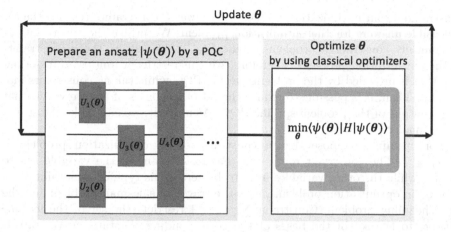

Fig. 2. An overview of the VQE algorithm

The variational principle holds for an arbitrary quantum state. Thus, for an arbitrary quantum state, $|\psi\rangle$, the expectation value, $\langle\psi|H|\psi\rangle$, is greater than or equal to the minimal eigenvalue of H.

Figure 2 shows an overview of the VQE algorithm. The VQE algorithm consists of two parts. One is executed on quantum computers, and the other one is on classical computers. As we mentioned, the part executed on quantum computers has a shallow quantum circuit with parameters called a PQC. A PQC prepare a quantum state (often called an *ansatz*), $|\psi(\theta)\rangle$, from an initial state. It can prepare various quantum state by changing the parameters, θ. With the created quantum state, the expectation values of each term in a given Hamiltonian are obtained by sampling outcomes. Then, classical computers calculate the total of the expectation values by summing those of each term. After that, classical computers determine the next parameters for the PQC by using classical optimization algorithms such as the Nelder–Mead algorithm [20], the Powell algorithm [24], and many more [9,19,25,31]. The PQC creates a new quantum state with new parameters, and the expectation values of each term in the given Hamiltonian are obtained by sampling outcomes again with the new quantum state. Note that expectation value $\langle\psi(\theta)|H|\psi(\theta)\rangle$ is always greater than or equal to minimal eigenvalue of H for any θ based on the Rayleigh-Ritz variational principle. This process is repeated until the expectation value of the given Hamiltonian converges.

3 The Proposed Problem-Specific PQCs

3.1 Overview of the Problem-Specific PQC

In this subsection, first, we introduce the general idea of the problem-specific PQC. After mapping binary variables x_i to qubits q_i, we pay attention to the constraints of an optimization problem. As always, constraints restrict the set of feasible answers for the optimization problem. We utilize the constraints to dynamically construct a problem-specific PQC that reflects those constraints of the optimization problem. Therefore, we can restrict a unitary transformation that is provided by the problem-specific PQC while taking constraints into account. Then, it is possible to reduce the set of the bases of a state vector that is the output of the problem-specific PQC. As a result, we can make the search space smaller.

For example, suppose that a constraint of an optimization problem is $\sum_i x_i = 1$. The constraint represents that exactly one of the variable has to be one, while the other variables have to be zero. This type of constraint often appears in optimization problems, e.g., the traveling salesman problem and the job scheduling problem. Constraint $\sum_i x_i = 1$ restricts the set of the feasible answers to the set of the bases of the corresponding W state. A W state is a superposition of states that exactly one of the qubits is $|1\rangle$ while the other qubits are $|0\rangle$ with equal amplitudes. A W state of n qubits is represented as $|W\rangle = \frac{1}{\sqrt{2^n}}(|10...0\rangle + |01...0\rangle + |00...1\rangle)$. Each base of $|W\rangle$ exactly corresponds to an assignment of variables that satisfies $\sum_i x_i = 1$. We do not need to consider other bases since all of them are obviously infeasible due to the constraint $\sum_i x_i = 1$.

The basic concept of the problem-specific PQC is as follows. Let $\mathbb{S}_{all}$ be the set of all the bases of n qubits, so $|\mathbb{S}_{all}|$ is 2^n. Then, let $\mathbb{S}_{feasible}$ the a set of bases corresponding the feasible answers of an optimization problem after mapping variables to qubits. $\mathbb{S}_{all}$ includes $\mathbb{S}_{feasible}$ from the definition. For example, when one of the feasible answers is $x_0 = 1, x_1 = 0$ and $x_2 = 0$, the corresponding base is $|q_0 q_1 q_2\rangle = |100\rangle$. Thus, $|100\rangle$ is in $\mathbb{S}_{feasible}$. With the problem-specific PQC, we consider set $\mathbb{S}_{proposed}$ that includes $\mathbb{S}_{feasible}$, but the size of the set is smaller than $|\mathbb{S}_{all}|$. The relation between each set is described as $\mathbb{S}_{feasible} \subseteq \mathbb{S}_{proposed} \subseteq \mathbb{S}_{all}$. By using such $\mathbb{S}_{proposed}$, the basic concept of the problem-specific PQC is written as Eq. (2). $U_{proposed}$ represents a unitary transformation that is provided by a problem-specific PQC. $|0\rangle$ represents a base whose index is all zeros. We use $|0\rangle$ as an initial state for the problem-specific PQC. α_i represents an amplitude of $|\psi_i\rangle$. These amplitudes are controlled by parameters of the problem-specific PQC. With a proper problem-specific PQC, we can change only α_i while keeping the amplitudes of the other states not included in $\mathbb{S}_{proposed}$ 0. We explain how the problem-specific PQC works with examples later.

$$U_{proposed}|0\rangle = \sum_i \alpha_i |\psi_i\rangle, \quad |\psi_i\rangle \in \mathbb{S}_{proposed} \tag{2}$$

Usually, an optimization problem has more than one constraint. For such cases, we create multiple problem-specific parameterized quantum sub-circuits each of which reflects the corresponding constraint. Then, by combining those sub-circuit properly, even though the optimization problem has more than one constraint, it is still possible to create a problem-specific PQC and reduce the search space.

3.2   Problem-Specific PQCs for the TSP

In this subsection, we introduce problem-specific PQCs for the traveling salesman problem (TSP). The TSP is a well-known NP-hard problem in combinatorial optimization problems. The traveling salesman goes from city to city to sell products, and the objective is to find the shortest path that the salesman can visit all the cities once and return to his starting point. With an undirected graph $G = (V, E)$, we can formulate the TSP as follows. Each edge $(u, v) \in E$ in the graph has weight $W_{u,v}$, then find the Hamiltonian cycle such that the sum of the weights of each edge in the cycle is minimized. Let $N = |V|$ and let us label the vertices $1, ..., N$. For a linear program, we use N^2 variables $x_{v,p}$ where v represents the vertex and p represents its order in a prospective cycle. Then, the linear program of the TSP is formulated as Eq. (3). Note that $N + 1$ should be read as 1 in Eq. (3).

$$
\begin{aligned}
Minimize \quad & \sum_{(u,v) \in E} W_{u,v} \sum_{p=1}^{N} x_{u,p} x_{v,p+1} \\
Subject\ to \quad & \sum_{v=1}^{N} x_{v,p} = 1, \quad p = 1...N \\
& \sum_{p=1}^{N} x_{v,p} = 1, \quad v = 1...N \\
& x_{v,p} \in \{0, 1\}
\end{aligned}
\tag{3}
$$

In this paper, we propose four PQCs for the TSP. Each of them has different characteristics such as the types of the constraints considered, the number of quantum gates, and the number of parameters. Their details will be explained in Sect. 3.2, Sect. 3.2, Sect. 3.2, and Sect. 3.2, respectively.

PQCs Satisfying only the Constraints on the First Line. For the first proposed PQC, we take into account only the constraints on the first line. In each constraint of Eq. (3), exactly one variable has to be one while the other variables have to be zero. As we have already explained in this paper, this type of constraint restricts the set of the feasible answers to the set of the bases of the corresponding W state. The total number of the constraints represented by the first line in the constraints, $\sum_{v=1}^{N} x_{v,p} = 1$, is N since we have a constraint for each $p = 1, ..., N$. Thus, after mapping binary variables to qubits, with the tensor product of the corresponding N W states, we can restrict a search space to $\bigotimes_{p=1}^{N} |W_p\rangle$. We do not need to consider other bases, not in $\bigotimes_{p=1}^{N} |W_p\rangle$, since they do not satisfy $\sum_{v=1}^{N} x_{v,p} = 1$, $p = 1...N$. Note that we do not consider constraints represented by the second line in the constraints. Thus, some bases in $\mathbb{S}_{proposed}$ may not satisfy these constraints in the second line of constraints. However, the relation between each set, $\mathbb{S}_{feasible} \subseteq \mathbb{S}_{proposed} \subseteq \mathbb{S}_{all}$, still holds, and we can reduce the search space.

Therefore, we need to create quantum circuits that create W states. The deterministic methods for creating W states of arbitrary sizes are discussed in previous studies [4,28]. However, a conventional W state has equal amplitudes for each base. For the VQE algorithm, we need to control the amplitudes of each base with parameters as shown in Eq. (4), and optimize them with a classical optimizer to find the minimum eigenvalue.

$$|W(\phi)\rangle = \sum_i \alpha_{i(\phi)} |\psi_i\rangle,$$

$$\sum_i |\alpha_{i(\phi)}|^2 = 1, \quad |\psi_i\rangle \in \{|10...0\rangle, |01...0\rangle, |00...1\rangle\} \tag{4}$$

In Eq. (4), $|\psi_i\rangle$ represents one of the bases in the corresponding W state where the i-th qubit is $|1\rangle$ while other qubits are $|0\rangle$. An amplitude α_i has the set of parameters, ϕ, to change its value. Note that ϕ can have multiple parameters such as $\{\theta_1, \theta_2, ...\} \in \phi$. We call this $|W(\phi)\rangle$ in Eq. (4) as a parameterized W state.

Let us introduce quantum gates before explaining how to create a quantum circuit for a parameterized W state. An X gate and a $R_y(\theta)$ gate act on a single qubit while a *Controlled Z* (*CZ*) gate and a *Controlled NOT* (*CNOT*) gate act on two qubits. A two-qubit gate has the control bit and the target bit. If the control bit of a two-qubit gate is $|1\rangle$, the two-qubit gate applies a particular operation to its target bit. If the control bit of a two-qubit gate is $|0\rangle$, the two-qubit gate does not apply any operations to its target bit. For example, in the case of a *CNOT* gate, if the control bit of the *CNOT* gate is $|1\rangle$, it applies an X gate to its target bit. If its control bit is $|0\rangle$, it does not apply any operations to its target bit. A *Controlled SWAP* (*CSWAP*) gate is a three-qubit gate, which acts on the control qubit and the two target qubits. If the control qubit is $|1\rangle$, then the two target qubits are swapped.

The unitary matrices of each gate are as follows.

$$X \equiv \begin{bmatrix} 0 & 1 \\ 1 & 0 \end{bmatrix}, \tag{5}$$

$$R_y(\theta) \equiv \begin{bmatrix} \cos\frac{\theta}{2} & -\sin\frac{\theta}{2} \\ \sin\frac{\theta}{2} & \cos\frac{\theta}{2} \end{bmatrix}, \tag{6}$$

$$CZ \equiv \begin{bmatrix} 1 & 0 & 0 & 0 \\ 0 & 1 & 0 & 0 \\ 0 & 0 & 1 & 0 \\ 0 & 0 & 0 & -1 \end{bmatrix}, \tag{7}$$

$$CNOT \equiv \begin{bmatrix} 1 & 0 & 0 & 0 \\ 0 & 1 & 0 & 0 \\ 0 & 0 & 0 & 1 \\ 0 & 0 & 1 & 0 \end{bmatrix}, \tag{8}$$

$$
CSWAP \equiv
\begin{bmatrix}
1 & 0 & 0 & 0 & 0 & 0 & 0 & 0 \\
0 & 1 & 0 & 0 & 0 & 0 & 0 & 0 \\
0 & 0 & 1 & 0 & 0 & 0 & 0 & 0 \\
0 & 0 & 0 & 1 & 0 & 0 & 0 & 0 \\
0 & 0 & 0 & 0 & 1 & 0 & 0 & 0 \\
0 & 0 & 0 & 0 & 0 & 0 & 1 & 0 \\
0 & 0 & 0 & 0 & 0 & 1 & 0 & 0 \\
0 & 0 & 0 & 0 & 0 & 0 & 0 & 1
\end{bmatrix}.
\tag{9}
$$

Note that a $R_y(\theta)$ gate has a parameter θ and its matrix elements can be changed dynamically by θ. On the other hand, the matrix elements of an X gate, a CZ gate, and a $CNOT$ gate do not change. We sometimes use an index for a gate to represent which qubit the gate was applied. For example, an X_i gate means an X gate for q_i. For a $R_y(\theta)$ gate, we also use an index for its parameter. A $R_{y_i}(\theta_p)$ gate means a $R_y(\theta)$ gate for q_i where its parameter is θ_p Since two-qubit gates have control bits and target bits, we use two numbers for their index. The left number in an index represents the control bit of a two-qubit gate, and the right number represents its target bit. For example, a $CNOT_{i,j}$ gate means a $CNOT$ gate whose control bit is q_i and target bit is q_j. Note that which qubit is the control bit or the target bit of a CZ gate is not important since $CZ_{i,j} = CZ_{j,i}$. $CSWAP_{i,j,k}$ represents a $CSWAP$ gate whose control bit is q_i and target bits are q_j and q_k. Note that the target qubits in a $CSWAP$ gate is permutation invariant, i.e. $CSWAP_{i,j,k} = CSWAP_{i,k,j}$

We use the above gates to create such parameterized W states and use existing methods [28] as the base. However, we do not determine the parameters of $R_y(\theta)$ gates yet for parameterized W states. For ease of explanation, we consider a case with three qubits, q_1, q_2, and q_3. We explain an algorithm for arbitrary sizes of qubits later. The initial state is $|q_1 q_2 q_3\rangle = |000\rangle$. Firstly, we apply an X gate to q_1. Then, the state will change as $X_1 |000\rangle = |100\rangle$. Then we apply two $R_y(\theta)$ gates and a CZ gate in the following order.

1. Apply a $R_{y_2}(\theta_1)$ gate.
2. Apply a $CZ_{1,2}$ gate.
3. Apply a $R_{y_2}(-\theta_1)$ gate. Note that the same parameter θ_1 is used in 1) and 3), but with a different sign.

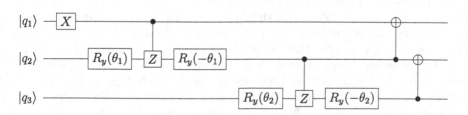

Fig. 3. A quantum circuit for a parameterized W state of three qubits

After that, we apply two $R_y(\theta)$ gates and a CZ gate in the same order. However, at this time, we apply a $R_{y_3}(\theta_2)$ gate, a $CZ_{2,3}$ gate, and a $R_{y_3}(-\theta_2)$ gate. The state will be as Eq. (10).

$$\alpha_{1(\phi)}|100\rangle + \alpha_{2(\phi)}|110\rangle + \alpha_{3(\phi)}|111\rangle,$$

$$\sum_{i=1}^{3} |\alpha_{i(\phi)}|^2 = 1, \tag{10}$$

$$\alpha_{1(\phi)} = \cos\theta_1, \ \alpha_{2(\phi)} = -\sin\theta_1\cos\theta_2, \ \alpha_{3(\phi)} = \sin\theta_1\sin\theta_2$$

Amplitude $\alpha_{i(\phi)}$ depends on the values of θ_1 and θ_2. Then, we apply a $CNOT_{2,1}$ gate and a $CNOT_{3,2}$ gate. After applying $CNOT$ gates, the final state will be as Eq. (11).

$$\alpha_{1(\phi)}|100\rangle + \alpha_{2(\phi)}|010\rangle + \alpha_{3(\phi)}|001\rangle,$$

$$\sum_{i=1}^{3} |\alpha_{i(\phi)}|^2 = 1, \tag{11}$$

$$\alpha_{1(\phi)} = \cos\theta_1, \ \alpha_{2(\phi)} = -\sin\theta_1\cos\theta_2, \ \alpha_{3(\phi)} = \sin\theta_1\sin\theta_2$$

This state is the same as a parameterized W state of three qubits. Figure 3 shows a quantum circuit for a parameterized W state of three qubits. The text in the boxes of each quantum gate represents its unitary matrix. The leftmost gate in Fig. 3 represents that an X gate is applied to q_1. The second gate from the left in Fig. 3 represents that a $R_y(\theta)$ gate is applied to q_2 with parameter θ_1. The third gate from the left in Fig. 3 represents that a CZ gate is applied to q_1 and q_2, and its control bit is q_1 and its target bit is q_2. The rightmost gate in Fig. 3 represents a $CNOT$ gate is applied to q_2 and q_3, and its control bit is q_3 and its target bit is q_2.

By combining quantum circuits to create parameterized W states, we can create a problem-specific PQC of the VQE algorithm for the TSP. As mentioned above, a linear program of the TSP is represented as Eq. (3). For the VQE algorithm, we need to map these variables to qubits. To do this, we prepare N^2 qubits $q_{v,p}$ and map each variable $x_{v,p}$ to the corresponding qubit $q_{v,p}$. Note that N is the number of vertices. We use N independent quantum circuits to create parameterized W states of N qubits. For qubits $q_{1,1}, q_{1,2}, ..., q_{1,N}$, we insert the first quantum circuit to create a parameterized W state of N qubits. Then, for qubits $q_{2,1}, q_{2,2}, ..., q_{2,N}$, We insert the second one. In the same manner, we keep inserting quantum circuits to create parameterized W states. The last one will be for $q_{N,1}, q_{N,2}, ..., q_{N,N}$. After that, we obtain a quantum circuit as shown in Fig. 4. Each box represents a quantum circuit to create a parameterized W state with the set of parameters ϕ_i for the corresponding qubits. Each $|W_i(\phi_i)\rangle$ $(i = 1, ..., N)$ on the right in Fig. 4 represents the output of the corresponding circuit. Note that each $|W_i(\phi_i)\rangle$ $(i = 1, ..., N)$ has the different set of parameters. With the circuit in Fig. 4, we can create a tensor product of the parameterized W states $\bigotimes_{p=1}^{N} |W_p(\phi_p)\rangle$.

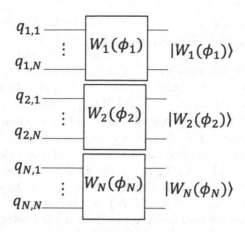

$q_{1,1}$
$\vdots$ $W_1(\phi_1)$ $|W_1(\phi_1)\rangle$
$q_{1,N}$

$q_{2,1}$
$\vdots$ $W_2(\phi_2)$ $|W_2(\phi_2)\rangle$
$q_{2,N}$

$q_{N,1}$
$\vdots$ $W_N(\phi_N)$ $|W_N(\phi_N)\rangle$
$q_{N,N}$

Fig. 4. A problem-specific PQC of the VQE algorithm for the TSP

PQCs Satisfying an L-Shaped Constraint with CNOT Operations. For the second PQC, we take into account not only the first line but also taking into account constraint $\sum_{p=1}^{N} x_{1,p} = 1$ in the second line of the constraints of Eq. 3 to further reduce the search space, as is shown in Fig. 5(b). Unlike the first PQC, the situation requires more "correlations" among qubits being mapped from variables, since variables $x_{1,p}$, $p = 1 \ldots N$ appear in both the first and the second line; it is no longer possible to realize the constraints by a tensor product of N quantum states. Hence, we utilize CNOT gates together with the parameterized W state gates to create such a quantum circuit.

The protocol of creating the PQC follows two steps. First, we construct a quantum circuit satisfying both two constraints, $\sum_{p=1}^{N} x_{1,p} = 1$ and $\sum_{v=1}^{N} x_{v,1} = 1$, which we call "an L-shaped constraint" because the involved variables form L-shape in Fig. 5(b). In the L-shaped constraint, one variable in each set of

(a) The first case   (b) The second / third case   (c) The fourth case

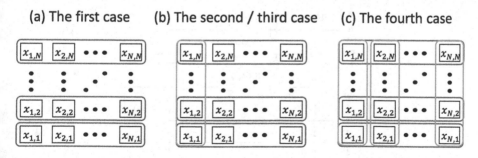

Fig. 5. Schematic of the constraints considered for each case; (a) only the first line, (b) a constraint in the second line as well as the first line and (c) all constraints. The blue box represents a constraint in the first line, while the red box indicates a constraint in the second line of constraints of Eq. 3. (Color figure online)

$\{x_{1,p'}|p'=2\ldots N\}$ and $\{x_{v',1}|v'=2\ldots N\}$ has to be one if $x_{1,1}$ is zero, while all variables in $\{x_{1,p'}|p'=2\ldots N\}$ and $\{x_{v',1}|v'=2\ldots N\}$ are zeros if $x_{1,1}$ is one. According to this, one can easily understand that the corresponding unitary operations on the initialized qubits $q_{i,j}$ being mapped from variables $x_{i,j}$ is realized by applying parameterized W state gates to each set of qubits $\{q_{1,p'}|p'=2\ldots N\}$ and $\{q_{v',1}|v'=2\ldots N\}$ if $|0\rangle_{q_{1,1}}$, and applying identity gates if $|1\rangle_{q_{1,1}}$. Thus, the PQC can be created with CNOT gates and parameterized W state gates, as depicted in Fig. 6(a). In a quantum circuit of Fig. 6(a), the leftmost R_y gate with the trainable parameter ϕ_0 and the following two CNOT gates, $CNOT_{q_{1,1},q_{1,2}}$ and $CNOT_{q_{1,1},q_{2,1}}$, determine whether $|0\rangle_{q_{1,1}}$ or $|1\rangle_{q_{1,1}}$, and whether W state gates or identity gates are applied to each set of qubits $\{q_{1,p'}|p'=2\ldots N\}$ and $\{q_{v',1}|v'=2\ldots N\}$ depending on the condition of $q_{1,1}$, respectively. Note that we here use the fact that a parameterized W state gate is exactly an identity gate if an X gate is applied to the first qubits beforehand, which can be checked readily by looking into Fig. 3. As a result, the quantum circuit can create the desired quantum state expressed as

$$\cos\frac{\phi_0}{2}\,|0\rangle_{q_{1,1}}\,|W(\phi_{p'})\rangle_{\{q_{1,p'}|p'=2\ldots N\}}\,|W(\phi_{v'})\rangle_{\{q_{v',1}|v'=2\ldots N\}}$$
$$+\sin\frac{\phi_0}{2}\,|1\rangle_{q_{1,1}}\,|0\rangle_{\{q_{1,p'}|p'=2\ldots N\}}^{\otimes n-1}\,|0\rangle_{\{q_{v',1}|v'=2\ldots N\}}^{\otimes n-1}\,,\tag{12}$$

where ϕs are all trainable parameters.

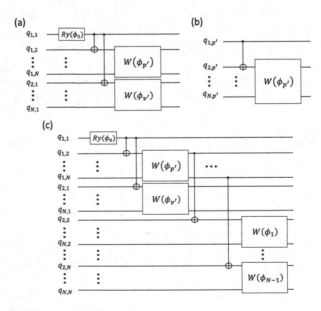

Fig. 6. A PQC for the second case; (a) a quantum circuit for an L-shaped constraint, (b) a quantum circuit corresponding to the constraint, $\sum_{v=1}^{N} x_{v,p'} = 1$ and (c) a whole picture of the PQC for the second case.

Second, we apply unitary operations for the remaining constraints, $\sum_{v=1}^{N} x_{v,p'} = 1$, $p' = 2 \ldots N$, to a resultant quantum state in Eq. 12. Here, since the qubits corresponding to the variables $\{x_{1,p'} | p' = 2 \ldots N\}$ in the constraints have already been determined, the constraints can be read in the similar way to the first step as follows; if $x_{1,p'}$ is one, all variables $\{x_{v',p'} | v' = 2 \ldots N\}$ are zeros, while if $x_{1,p'}$ is zero one variable in $\{x_{v',p'} | v' = 2 \ldots N\}$ has to be one. As we have seen in the first step, the corresponding unitary operation can be realized by a $CNOT_{q_{1,p'},q_{2,p'}}$ gate followed by parameterized W state gates on the set of qubits $\{q_{v,p'} | v = 2 \ldots N\}$ as represented in Fig. 6(b). Thus, using $N - 1$ $CNOT$ gates and $N - 1$ circuits for parameterized W sates, we can create the unitary operators that create a quantum state satisfying the remaining constraints.

Following the above two steps, we can create the problem-specific PQC in Fig. 6(c).

PQCs Satisfying an L-Shaped Constraint with Parameter Sharing. For the third PQC, we modify the second PQC to reduce the cost of the implementation for the current quantum processors [26]. Since current noisy devices suffer from an exponential decay of quantum coherence, deep circuits would be problematic. In the second case, the circuit becomes deep due to the dependence in its own structure; firstly, a quantum circuit for an L-shaped constraint is constructed, and then other gates are applied for the remaining constraints.

To remedy this issue, we introduce the technique, *parameter sharing*, which makes the circuit shallower with fewer CNOT gates. The main point of this technique is as follows; CNOT gates (and also X gates in parameterized W state gates) used in Fig. 5 are replaced with R_y gates with the shared parameters such

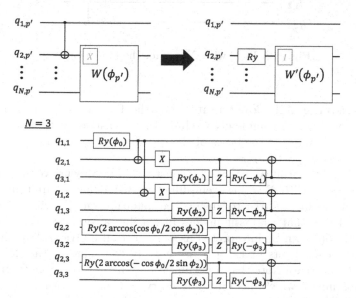

Fig. 7. A PQC with $N = 3$ for the third case. To create the PQC, the top-left circuit appearing in the quantum circuit of the second case is replaced with the top-right circuit.

that the probability of obtaining $|1\rangle_{q_{1,p'}}$ is equal to that of $|0\rangle^{\otimes N-1}_{\{q_{v',p'}|v'=2...N\}}$. To demonstrate the parameter sharing in detail, we provide a simple example of the quantum circuit with $N = 3$ in Fig. 7. In this scenario, parameters ϕ_0 and ϕ_2 are used for not only $q_{1,1}$ and $q_{1,2}$, but also $q_{2,2}$ and $q_{3,2}$ in unique ways such as $2\arccos(\cos\phi_0/2\cos\phi_2)$. Indeed, the trigonometric functions inside the inverse trigonometric function, $\cos\phi_0/2\cos\phi_2$ and $-\cos\phi_0/2\sin\phi_2$ are the amplitudes of $|1\rangle_{q_{1,2}}$ and $|1\rangle_{q_{1,3}}$, respectively. Therefore, the amplitude of $|00\rangle_{\{q_{v,2}|v=2,3\}}$ is always the same as that of $|1\rangle_{q_{1,2}}$ by the parameter sharing (similarly, this is true to $q_{1,3}$, $q_{2,3}$, and $q_{3,3}$). Note that this technique can be easily extended for PQCs with arbitrary N since the probability of obtaining $|1\rangle_{q_{1,p'}}$ for all $p' = 2\ldots N$ is analytically calculated in the similar way as shown in Eq. (11).

By utilizing such "classical correlation", we can create a shallower PQC satisfying the constraints in Fig. 5(b), which is expected to be more suitable for current noisy devices. However, the technique has a limitation on the ability to restrict the set of bases compared to the second case. As we can see in Fig. 7, the quantum state created by the PQC is not fully entangled, i.e. it can be written as the tensor product of small quantum states. Consequently, the set of the bases of the quantum state includes the bases that are not in the second case. However, the probability to obtain such extra bases is at most a half. This characteristic contributes to interesting results which we will discuss in Sect. 4

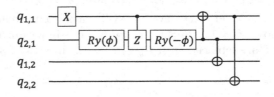

Fig. 8. A PQC with $N = 2$ for the fourth case.

PQCs Satisfying All Constraints. For the fourth PQC, we consider all constraints of Eq. 3 to completely exclude the infeasible answers as shown in Fig. 5(c). Thus, the set of the bases of the quantum states includes only feasible answers , i.e. $\mathbb{S}_{case\ 4} = \mathbb{S}_{feasible}$.

Such a PQC for arbitrary N can be constructed in a recursive manner. After a quantum circuit with $N = 2$ is exemplified, we will demonstrate that the PQC with $N = k$ can be constructed using the quantum circuit with $N = k - 1$. The basic idea is that the assignments of feasible answers on the 2D grid as shown in Fig. 5(c) can be interpreted as permutation matrices. It is due to the fact that the constraints of Eq. (3) are exactly the same as the definition of permutation matrices. Note that a permutation matrix is a square matrix, every row and column of which has only one entry, 1 while the other entries are 0. Hence, with the equivalence of permutation matrices and the assignment of the feasible answers on the 2D grid, we construct the quantum circuit.

Firstly, we show the PQC with $N = 2$. For the number of city $N = 2$, two feasible answers exist, as there are two 2×2 permutation matrices, $\begin{bmatrix} 1 & 0 \\ 0 & 1 \end{bmatrix}$ and $\begin{bmatrix} 0 & 1 \\ 1 & 0 \end{bmatrix}$. Thus, a quantum state we want to create can be described by the superposition of two bases, $|0110\rangle$ and $|1001\rangle$ with the order of qubits $|q_{1,1}q_{2,1}q_{1,2}q_{2,2}\rangle$. A quantum circuit for $N = 2$ can be created as shown in Fig. 8, where the quantum state is represented as $\cos\phi |1001\rangle - \sin\phi |0110\rangle$.

Secondly, we show that the PQCs with $N = k$ can be constructed by using the quantum circuit with $N = k - 1$. The conceptual overview to create PQCs for the forth case is as shown in Fig. 9.

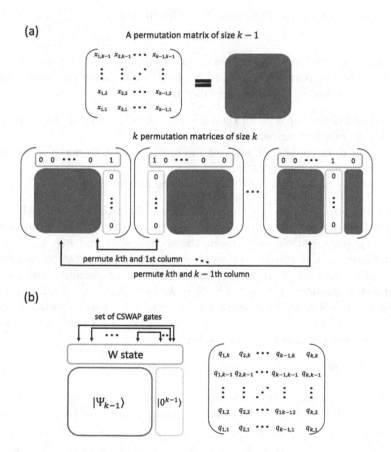

Fig. 9. The conceptual overview to create PQCs for the forth case. (a) illustrates the property of permutation matrices, which is used for constructing PQCs. (b) is a schematic view to create the desired quantum state for $N = k$ by using a quantum state for $N = k - 1$.

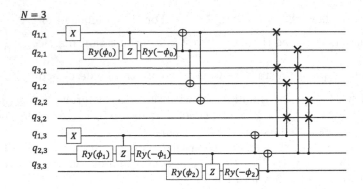

Fig. 10. A PQC with $N = 3$ for the fourth case.

Suppose that we have all the permutation matrices of size $k - 1$, so the total number of the permutation matrices is $(k - 1)!$. Then one can obtain $k!$ permutation matrices of size k in the following way.

1. Pad the additional zeros to all the $(k - 1) \times (k - 1)$ permutation matrices to form $k \times k$ square matrices.
2. Set the top right element in each of the matrices as 1 to make them permutation matrices.
3. Permute the k-th and the j-th column of the matrices for all $j = 1 \ldots k - 1$.

Note that we here use the fact that exchanging the i-th and the j-th column of a permutation matrix results in also a permutation matrix. Consequently, with $(k - 1)!$ permutation matrices in the second step and $k(k - 1)!$ permutation matrices in the third step, we can obtain $k!$ permutation matrices of size k by the above steps. In analogous to the case of permutation matrices, we construct a quantum circuit with $N = k$. Let $|\Psi_{k-1}\rangle$ be a quantum state whose bases are all feasible answers for $N = k - 1$ with the order of qubits $|q_{1,1} \ldots q_{1,k-1} q_{2,1} \cdots q_{2,k-1} \cdots q_{k-1,1} \cdots q_{k-1,k-1}\rangle$. Then, in a similar way, we can create the desired quantum states as follows;

1. Prepare the initialized $2k - 1$ qubits, labeled as $q_{k,p'}, p' = 2 \ldots k$ and $q_{v,k}, v = 1 \ldots k$.
2. Apply a parameterized W state gate to the set of qubits, $\{q_{v,k} | v = 1 \ldots k\}$.
3. Apply $CSWAP$ gates to the corresponding qubits in $|\Psi_{k-1}\rangle$, $|W_k(\psi)\rangle_{\{q_{v,k}|v=1\ldots k\}}$, and $|0\rangle^{\otimes k-1}_{\{q_{k,p'}|p'=1\ldots k-1\}}$; the set of $CSWAP$ operations, $\{CSWAP_{q_{v',k},q_{k,p'},q_{v',p'}} | p' = 1 \ldots k - 1\}$ are applied for all $v' = 1 \ldots k - 1$.

In this procedure, the parameterized W state gate is used to represent the additional k-th row of $k \times k$ matrix, which can be regarded as the permutation inside the k-th row. Then, $CSWAP$ gates are used to serve as the permutation of the remaining rows depending on the state of k-th row; the states of $\{q_{k,p'} | p' = 1 \ldots k - 1\}$ and $\{q_{v,p'} | p' = 1 \ldots k - 1\}$ are exchanged if $|1\rangle_{q_{v,k}}$, while

Table 1. The comparison of necessary parameters and gates among the proposed problem-specific PQCs and a Ry PCQ for the TSP with n qubits

Necessary resources	Ry	Proposed 1	Proposed 2	Proposed 3	Proposed 4
# of Parameters	$(D+1)n$	$n - \sqrt{n}$	$n - \sqrt{n} - 1$	$n - \sqrt{n} - 1$	$\frac{1}{2}n - \frac{1}{2}\sqrt{n}$
# of one-qubit gates	$(D+1)n$	$2n - \sqrt{n}$	$2n - \sqrt{n} - 4$	$2n - \sqrt{n} - 4$	$n - 1$
# of two-qubit gates	$D(n-1)$	$2n - 2\sqrt{n}$	$2n - \sqrt{n} - 3$	$2n - 2\sqrt{n} - 2$	$n - \sqrt{n} + 2$
# of CSWAP gates	—	—	—	—	$\frac{1}{3}n\sqrt{n} - \frac{1}{2}n + \frac{1}{6}\sqrt{n} - 1$

the states of $\{q_{k,p'} | p' = 1 \dots k - 1\}$ and $\{q_{v,p'} | p' = 1 \dots k - 1\}$ remain unchanged if $|0\rangle_{q_{p,k}}$. As a demonstration, we give a simple example of the PQC with $N = 3$ for the forth case as shown in Fig. 10.

Then the corresponding quantum state is represented as Eq. (13), with the order of qubits $|q_{1,1}q_{2,1}q_{3,1}q_{1,2}q_{2,2}q_{3,2}q_{1,3}q_{2,3}q_{3,3}\rangle$, which is exactly the superposition of bases of six feasible answers.

$$
\begin{aligned}
|\Psi_{k-1}\rangle = &- \cos\phi_0 \sin\phi_1 \cos\phi_2 \,|100001010\rangle \\
&+ \cos\phi_0 \sin\phi_1 \sin\phi_2 \,|001100010\rangle \\
&+ \cos\phi_0 \sin\phi_1 \sin\phi_2 \,|100010001\rangle \\
&- \sin\phi_0 \sin\phi_1 \cos\phi_2 \,|010100001\rangle \\
&+ \cos\phi_0 \cos\phi_1 \,|001010100\rangle \\
&- \sin\phi_0 \cos\phi_1 \,|010001100\rangle
\end{aligned}
\tag{13}
$$

Therefore, we can construct the PQC for arbitrary N by recursively performing the procedure explained in the above starting from the quantum circuit with $N = 2$.

4   Experimental Results

We conducted simulation experiments to compare the convergence speed of each proposed PQCs and the Ry PQCs using Python. Qiskit Aqua 0.7.5 was used to convert optimization problems to the corresponding Ising Hamiltonians. We run the VQE algorithm in Qiskit with the QASM simulator for the TSP. The number of the shots of the QASM simulator used in each experiments was 1024. We conduct 10 trials with different initial parameters for each PQC except the Ry PQCs. The COBYLA algorithm [25] was used as the classical optimizing algorithm of the VQE algorithm for the TSP. For the experiments of the TSP, we used a complete graph with four nodes as the graph of the TSP. The experiments were conducted on a MacBook Pro with 2.9 GHz Intel Core i5 and DDR3 8 GB memory running macOS 10.14.6.

Figure 11 shows the comparison between each proposed problem-specific PQC and Ry PQCs with depth one, two, and three. Proposed 1, Proposed 2, Proposed 3, and Proposed 4 correspond to the PQCs in Sect. 3.2, Sect. 3.2, Sect. 3.2, and Sect. 3.2, respectively. As we can see, the convergence of the

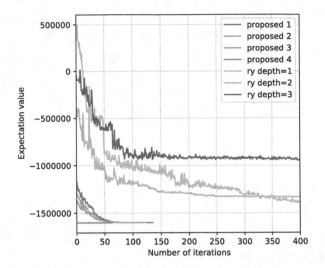

Fig. 11. The comparison between each proposed problem-specific PQC and the Ry PQCs with depth one, two, and three for the TSP with four cities.

proposed PQCs is significantly faster than that of the Ry PQCs. The average execution time of Proposed 1, Proposed 2, Proposed 3, and Proposed 4 was 98 sec, 78 sec, 101 sec, and 22 sec. The execution time of Ry PQCs with depth 1, 2, and 3 was 3606 sec, 4941 sec, and 8732 sec. The expectation values of the proposed PQCs are rapidly decreased in the first 60 iterations compared to the Ry PQCs. Also, the initial expectation values of the proposed PQCs are remarkably lower than that of the Ry PQCs. A graph in Fig. 12 is extracted from the graph in Fig. 11 to focus the experimental results of the proposed PQCs more. The order of the convergence speed was Proposed 4 < Proposed 2 < Proposed 3 < Proposed 1 < Ry. This is closely related to the set of the bases $|\mathbb{S}|$, i.e. $\mathbb{S}_{feasible} = \mathbb{S}_{Proposed\ 4} \subseteq \mathbb{S}_{Proposed\ 2} \subseteq \mathbb{S}_{Proposed\ 1} \subseteq \mathbb{S}_{Proposed\ 3} \subseteq \mathbb{S}_{all}$. Note that the convergence speed of Proposed 3 was faster than Proposed 1 despite the fact the Proposed 3 has more bases than Proposed 1. It is because that the probability to obtain extra infeasible answers (bases) is at most a half due to the parameter sharing as we explained in Sect. 3.2. By utilizing such "classical correlation", the convergence speed of Proposed 3 is faster than Proposed 1 even though Proposed 3 has more bases than Proposed 1.

We also analyzed whether each PQC can reach to the global minimum. The result is as follows; For proposed 4, every trial reached to the global minimum while others did not. Proposed 1, 2, and 3 could find the feasible answers and they could sometime reach to the global minimum. More specifically, More specifically, Proposed 1, 2, and 3 reached to the global minimum forth, four times, four times, and two times, respectively. Ry PQCs didn't converge well and they produced infeasible answers even after 400 iterations. Of course, whether we can reach the global minimum depends on not only the PQCs, but also different factors such as problem configurations, the types of classical optimizers, and initial parameters.

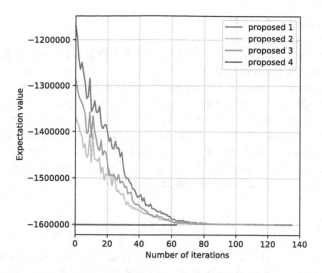

Fig. 12. A graph extracted from the graph in Fig. 11 for the comparison between each proposed problem-specific PQC.

We will continue to study the convergence to the global minimum as our future work.

Table 1 shows the number of necessary gates and parameters for each PQC. In Table 1, the # of Parameters row, the # of one-qubit gates row, the # of two-qubit gates columns, and the # of $CSWAP$ gates row correspond to the number of independent parameters used in $R_y(\theta)$ gates, the total number of X gates and $R_y(\theta)$ gates, the total number of CZ gates and $CNOT$ gates, and the total number of $CSWAP$ gates, respectively. D in the Ry column corresponds to the depth of Ry PQCs. From the experimental results, we observed that the Proposed 4 is the best in terms of the convergence speed and the convergence to the global minimum. However, it requires a lot of $CSWAP$ gates that realizing a $CSWAP$ gate is expected to be difficult on current noisy devices. More specifically, a $CSWAP$ gate requires 9 one-qubit gates and 8 two-qubit gates to be realized. Thus, the total number of the required one-qubit gates and two-qubit gates will be larger than other proposed PQCs. This will lead to challenges in the implementation on current noisy devices. To tacke this issue, we are considering to combine the parameter sharing and excitation preserving gates to replace high-cost $CSWAP$ gates.

Each amplitude is not completely independent in the proposed problem-specific PQCs. They have slight correlation between each other. However, it ensures that amplitudes of the bases that correspond to the answer of optimization problems can be 1. We need to carefully examine the relationship between the proposed method for the VQE algorithm and existing methods for classical computers.

5 Conclusions

In this paper, we proposed the problem-specific PQCs of the VQE algorithm for the TSP. In the proposed PQCs, we pay attention to the constraints of an optimization problem, and we dynamically create a PQC that reflects those constraints of the optimization problem. By doing this, it is possible to significantly reduce search spaces. As a result, we can speed up the convergence of the VQE algorithms. We conducted the simulation experiments to compare the proposed PQCs and the state-of-the-art PQC. In experiments, the proposed PQCs could reduce the search spaces, and the convergence of the proposed PQCs was significantly faster than that of the state-of-the-art PQC.

References

1. Aspuru-Guzik, A., Dutoi, A.D., Love, P.J., Head-Gordon, M.: Simulated quantum computation of molecular energies. Science **309**(5741), 1704–1707 (2005). https://doi.org/10.1126/science.1113479, https://science.sciencemag.org/content/309/5741/1704
2. Barkoutsos, P.K., Nannicini, G., Robert, A., Tavernelli, I., Woerner, S.: Improving variational quantum optimization using CVaR. Quantum **4**, 256 (2020). https://doi.org/10.22331/q-2020-04-20-256
3. Cerezo, M., et al.: Variational quantum algorithms. arXiv preprint arXiv:2012.09265 (2020)
4. Diker, F.: Deterministic construction of arbitrary w states with quadratically increasing number of two-qubit gates. arXiv preprint arXiv:1606.09290 (2016)
5. Farhi, E., Goldstone, J., Gutmann, S.: A quantum approximate optimization algorithm. arXiv preprint arXiv:1411.4028 (2014)
6. Grover, L.K.: A fast quantum mechanical algorithm for database search. In: STOC 1996: Proceedings of the Twenty-Eighth Annual ACM Symposium on Theory of Computing, pp. 212–219, July 1996
7. Hadfield, S., Wang, Z., O'Gorman, B., Rieffel, E.G., Venturelli, D., Biswas, R.: From the quantum approximate optimization algorithm to a quantum alternating operator Ansatz. Algorithms **12**(2) (2019). https://doi.org/10.3390/a12020034, https://www.mdpi.com/1999-4893/12/2/34
8. Havlíček, V., et al.: Supervised learning with quantum-enhanced feature spaces. Nature **567**(7747), 209–212 (2019)
9. Hestenes, M.R., Stiefel, E., et al.: Methods of conjugate gradients for solving linear systems, vol. 49. NBS Washington, DC (1952)
10. Heya, K., Suzuki, Y., Nakamura, Y., Fujii, K.: Variational quantum gate optimization. arXiv preprint arXiv:1810.12745 (2018)
11. Higgott, O., Wang, D., Brierley, S.: Variational quantum computation of excited states. Quantum **3**, 156 (2019). https://doi.org/10.22331/q-2019-07-01-156
12. Kandala, A., et al.: Hardware-efficient variational quantum Eigensolver for small molecules and quantum magnets. Nature **549**(7671), 242–246 (2017)
13. Khatri, S., LaRose, R., Poremba, A., Cincio, L., Sornborger, A.T., Coles, P.J.: Quantum-assisted quantum compiling. Quantum **3**, 140 (2019). https://doi.org/10.22331/q-2019-05-13-140, https://doi.org/10.22331/q-2019-05-13-140
14. Lucas, A.: Ising formulations of many NP problems. Front. Phys. **2**, 5 (2014)

15. Matsuo, A., Suzuki, Y., Yamashita, S.: Problem-specific parameterized quantum circuits of the VQE algorithm for optimization problems. arXiv preprint arXiv:2006.05643 (2020)
16. McClean, J.R., Romero, J., Babbush, R., Aspuru-Guzik, A.: The theory of variational hybrid quantum-classical algorithms. New J. Phys. 18(2), 023023 (2016)
17. Mitarai, K., Negoro, M., Kitagawa, M., Fujii, K.: Quantum circuit learning. Phys. Rev. A 98, (2018). https://doi.org/10.1103/PhysRevA.98.032309, https://link. aps.org/doi/10.1103/PhysRevA.98.032309
18. Moll, N., et al.: Quantum optimization using variational algorithms on near-term quantum devices. Quantum Sci. Technol. 3(3), 030503 (2018). https://doi.org/10. 1088/2058-9565/aab822, https://doi.org/10.1088/2058-9565/aab822
19. Nakanishi, K.M., Fujii, K., Todo, S.: Sequential minimal optimization for quantum-classical hybrid algorithms. Phys. Rev. Res. 2(4), 043158 (2020)
20. Nelder, J.A., Mead, R.: A simplex method for function minimization. Comput. J. 7(4), 308–313 (1965). https://doi.org/10.1093/comjnl/7.4.308
21. Nielsen, M.A., Chuang, I.L.: Quantum Computation and Quantum Information: 10th, Anniversary edn. Cambridge University Press, Cambridge (2010)
22. Parrish, R.M., Hohenstein, E.G., McMahon, P.L., Martínez, T.J.: Quantum computation of electronic transitions using a variational quantum eigensolver. Phys. Rev. Lett. 122(23), 230401 (2019)
23. Peruzzo, A., et al.: A variational eigenvalue solver on a photonic quantum processor. Nat. Commun. 5(1), 4213 (2014). https://doi.org/10.1038/ncomms5213
24. Powell, M.J.D.: An efficient method for finding the minimum of a function of several variables without calculating derivatives. Comput. J. 7(2), 155–162 (1964). https://doi.org/10.1093/comjnl/7.2.155
25. Powell, M.J.D.: A Direct Search Optimization Method That Models the Objective and Constraint Functions by Linear Interpolation, pp. 51–67. Springer, Netherlands, Dordrecht (1994). https://doi.org/10.1007/978-94-015-8330-5_4
26. Preskill, J.: Quantum computing in the NISQ era and beyond. Quantum 2, 79 (2018)
27. Qiskit: Qiskit: An open-source framework for quantum computing. https://www. qiskit.org/
28. Qiskit-Community: W state 1 multi-qubit systems. https://github.com/Qiskit/ qiskit-community-tutorials/blob/master/awards/teach_me_qiskit_2018/w_state/ W%20State%201%20-%20Multi-Qubit%20Systems.ipynb. Accessed 30 Apr 2020
29. Schuld, M., Killoran, N.: Quantum machine learning in feature Hilbert spaces. Phys. Rev. Lett. 122 (2019). https://doi.org/10.1103/PhysRevLett.122.040504, https://link.aps.org/doi/10.1103/PhysRevLett.122.040504
30. Shor, P.W.: Polynomial-time algorithms for prime factorization and discrete logarithms on a quantum computer. SIAM J. Comput. 26(5), 1484–1509 (1997). https://doi.org/10.1137/S0097539795293172
31. Spall, J.C.: Multivariate stochastic approximation using a simultaneous perturbation gradient approximation. IEEE Trans. Autom. Control 37(3), 332–341 (1992)
32. Wang, D., Higgott, O., Brierley, S.: Accelerated variational quantum Eigensolver. Phys. Rev. Lett. 122 (2019). https://doi.org/10.1103/PhysRevLett.122.140504, https://link.aps.org/doi/10.1103/PhysRevLett.122.140504
33. Wang, Z., Hadfield, S., Jiang, Z., Rieffel, E.G.: Quantum approximate optimization algorithm for maxcut: a fermionic view (2017). https://doi.org/10.1103/ PhysRevA.97.022304

Programming and Programming Languages

Reversible Functional Array Programming

Torben Ægidius Mogensen[✉]

DIKU, University of Copenhagen, Universitetsparken 5,
2100 Copenhagen O, Denmark
torbenm@di.ku.dk

Abstract. Functional array programming is a style of programming that enables massive parallelism through use of combinators (such as map and reduce) that apply functions to whole arrays. These can be readily parallelised when the functions these combinators are applied to are pure and, in some cases, also associative.

We introduce reversible variants of well-known array combinators and show how these can be implemented in parallel using only reversible operations and without accumulating garbage.

We introduce a simple reversible functional array programming language, Agni, and show some examples of use.

1 Introduction

The world of computing is becoming more and more parallel. This is seen in the exploding number of cores in general-purpose processors but even more clearly in the increasing use of highly parallel vector processors such as graphics processors. Graphics processors are known to be power hungry, so the potentially much lower energy requirements of reversible logic could be a way of reducing power use of highly parallel programming. Reversibility adds extra constraints to programming, but graphics processors already have significant constraints to their programming, so users may be more willing to accept the constraints of reversible programming in this setting than for general-purpose programming. Languages, such as Futhark [2], are being developed to provide a machine-independent high-level abstraction on top of graphics processors without significantly impacting performance, often through functional array programming.

Functional array programming typically uses a predefined set of parallelisable combinators such as map and reduce. A typical set includes combinators like those shown in Fig. 1. You can combine these to make more complex parallel functions, and a compiler can use fusion to optimise nested combinators to reduce the overhead and exploit parallelism better than if the combinators are applied one at a time.

The combinators shown in Fig. 1 are not all reversible, nor are the functions that are passed to map, filter, scan, or reduce typically reversible, so we need to modify these to a reversible setting, and we need to create a reversible language

© Springer Nature Switzerland AG 2021
S. Yamashita and T. Yokoyama (Eds.): RC 2021, LNCS 12805, pp. 45–63, 2021.
https://doi.org/10.1007/978-3-030-79837-6_3

`map` : $\forall('a, 'b).('a \to 'b) \to ['a] \to ['b]$ If $ys = \text{map}\, f\, xs$, then $ys[i] = f(xs[i])$.
`filter` : $\forall'a.('a \to \text{bool}) \to ['a] \to ['a]$ If $ys = \text{filter}\, f\, xs$, then ys contains exactly the elements $xs[i]$ where $f(xs[i]) = \text{true}$ in the same order that these elements appear in xs.
`reduce` : $\forall'a.('a \times 'a \to 'a) \to ['a] \to 'a$ `reduce` $f\,[]$ is undefined,   `reduce` $f\,[x] = x$ `reduce` $f\,[x_0, x_1, \ldots, x_n] = f(x_0, f(x_1, f(\ldots, x_n)))$, if $n > 0$.   If f is associative, `reduce` can be parallelised. If f has a neutral element i, `reduce` $f\,[]$ can be defined to be equal to i.
`scanl` : $\forall'a.('a \times 'a \to 'a) \to ['a] \to ['a]$ If $ys = \text{scanl}\, f\, xs$, then $ys[0] = xs[0]$ and $ys[i+1] = f(ys[i], xs[i+1])$.   If f is associative, `scanl` can be parallelised.
`zip` : $\forall('a, 'b, m).['a]^m \times ['b]^m \to ['a \times 'b]^m$ If $zs = \text{zip}\,(xs\,ys)$, then $zs[i] = (xs[i], ys[i])$.
`unzip` : $\forall('a, 'b).['a \times 'b] \to ['a] \times ['b]$ If $(ys, zs) = \text{unzip}\, xs$, then $(ys[i], zs[i]) = xs[i]$.
`iota` : $\text{int} \to [int]$ If $ys = \text{iota}\, m$, then $ys[i] = i$ for $0 \le i < m$.

Fig. 1. Typical array combinators

that can use the modified combinators. We also need to argue that this language can realistically be implemented on future reversible computers that combine reversible general-purpose processors and reversible vector processors.

2 Modifying for Reversibility

We will indicate reversible functions by using an alternative function-space arrow: $\rightleftharpoons$. Combinators like `map` are not fully reversible – you can't get both a function and a list back by applying `map` in reverse, but a partial application of `map` to a reversible function is reversible. So we will use the following type signature for `map`:

$$\text{map} : \forall('a, 'b).('a \rightleftharpoons 'b) \to ['a] \rightleftharpoons ['b]$$

The "normal" function arrow $\to$ indicates an irreversible function space where $\rightleftharpoons$ indicates a reversible function space. $['a]$ indicates an array with elements of type $'a$, which is a type variable. To run `map` backwards, we need to supply both a function of type $a \rightleftharpoons b$ and an array of type $[b]$ for some types a and b.

That reversible languages contain irreversible elements should not be surprising: Janus [4] allows arbitrary irreversible expressions in reversible updates, for example `x += y mod 2` is allowed in Janus, even though the expression `y mod 2` is not reversible: There is no way to get from the result (0 or 1) to the value of `y`. This is allowed in Janus because, after the update to `x` (which is reversible), the expression can be "uncomputed". Generally, if we retain the values of all variables in an expression, we can reversibly compute the value of the expression, use the value in a reversible operation, and then uncompute the expression, leaving no net garbage. We will exploit this to a larger degree than in Janus: We will allow local variables and functions to be defined using irreversible expressions, as long as these can be uncomputed at the end of their scope.

Other array combinators are clearly reversible: zip and unzip are inverses of each other, and iota is inverted by a function that takes an array $[0, 1, \ldots, m-1]$ and returns m (and is undefined on inputs that do not have this form). Equally obviously, filter and reduce are not reversible: filter discards any number of elements, and reduce can, for example, reduce an array of numbers to their sum or their maximum, which throws away a lot of information about the original array. Also, reduce and scanl use functions of type $'a \times 'a \to 'a$, which are not usually reversible.

We first take a stab at scanl, modifying its type to $('a \times 'a \rightleftharpoons 'a \times 'a) \to ['a] \rightleftharpoons ['a]$, so it takes a reversible function as argument. We then define

$$
\begin{aligned}
&\text{scanl } f \; [] &&= [] \\
&\text{scanl } f \; [x] &&= [x] \\
&\text{scanl } f \; ([x_1, x_2]@xs) &&= [y_1]@(\text{scanl } f \; ([y_2]@xs)) \quad \textbf{where} \; (y_1, y_2) = f \, (x_1, x_2)
\end{aligned}
$$

where @ is concatenation of arrays. Note that this sequential definition does not imply that the work has to be sequential – a traditional scan can be parallelised if the operator is associative, and with suitable restrictions on the function argument, the reversible version can too. We will explore parallelising the reversible scanl and other reversible combinators in Sect. 3.

If we define reversible addition by $++(x, y) = (x, x + y)$ (with the inverse $--$ defined by $--(x, y) = (x, y - x)$), we see that scanl $++$ $[1, 2, 3, 4] = [1, 3, 6, 10]$, so this works as we would expect a traditional scan using addition to do.

A reversible reduce will have to return an array as well as the reduced value, as it would rarely be possible to restore the original array from the reduced value alone. Letting reduce return its argument alongside the reduced value seems the most natural choice. We can define a reversible reduce by

$$
\begin{aligned}
&\textbf{reduce } f \; [x] &&= (x, [x]) \\
&\textbf{reduce } f \; ([x]@xs) &&= (z_1, [z_2]@ys) \\
&&&\textbf{where} \; (y, ys) = \textbf{reduce } f \; xs \; \textbf{and} \; (z_1, z_2) = f \, (x, y)
\end{aligned}
$$

Note that this is undefined on empty lists, as we would otherwise need a default value. reduce $++$ xs will return $(sum \; xs, xs)$. Note that, since we use x twice in the first rule, the inverse of reduce is only defined if these are equal.

We, additionally, need combinators to combine and split arrays: concat : $\forall 'a.['a] \times ['a] \rightleftharpoons \text{int} \times ['a]$ concatenates two arrays and returns both the size of the first array and the concatenated array. The inverse splitAt : $\forall 'a.\text{int} \times ['a] \rightleftharpoons ['a] \times ['a]$ splits an array into two such that the first has the size given by a parameter. If the array is smaller than this size, the result is undefined.

copy : $\forall'a.['a] \rightleftharpoons ['a] \times ['a]$ **copy** $x = (x, x)$
uncopy : $\forall'a.['a] \times ['a] \rightleftharpoons ['a]$ **uncopy** $(x, x) = x$. If $x[i] \neq y[i]$ for any i, then **uncopy** (x, y) is undefined.
map : $\forall'a, 'b.('a \rightleftharpoons 'b) \rightarrow ['a] \rightleftharpoons ['b]$ If $ys = $ **map** $f\, xs$, then $ys[i] = f(xs[i])$.
zip : $\forall('a, 'b).['a] \times ['b] \rightleftharpoons ['a \times 'b]$ If $zs = $ **zip** $(xs\, ys)$, then $zs[i] = (xs[i], ys[i])$. If xs and ys have different sizes, the result is undefined.
unzip : $\forall'a, 'b.['a \times 'b] \rightleftharpoons ['a] \times ['b]$ If $(ys, zs) = $ **unzip** xs, then $(ys[i], zs[i]) = xs[i]$.
iota : $\texttt{int} \rightleftharpoons [\texttt{int}]$ **iota** $m = [0, 1, \ldots, m-1]$
atoi : $[\texttt{int}] \rightleftharpoons \texttt{int}$ **atoi** $[0, 1, \ldots, m-1] = m$. It is undefined on inputs not having this form.
scanl : $\forall'a.('a \times 'a \rightleftharpoons 'a \times 'a) \rightarrow ['a] \rightleftharpoons ['a]$ See definition in Section 2.
reduce : $\forall'a.('a \times 'a \rightleftharpoons 'a \times 'a) \rightarrow ['a] \rightleftharpoons 'a \times ['a]$ See definition in Section 2.
concat : $\forall'a.['a] \times ['a] \rightleftharpoons \texttt{int} \times ['a]$ If $(m, zs) = $ **concat** (xs, ys), then $m = |xs|$, $|zs| = m + |ys|$, and $xs[i] = zs[i]$ if $i < m$, and $zs[i] = xs[i]$ if $i < m$, and $zs[i] = ys[i - m]$ otherwise.
splitAt : $\forall'a.\texttt{int} \times ['a] \rightleftharpoons ['a] \times ['a]$ If $(xs, ys) = $ **splitAt** (m, zs), then $m = |xs|$, $|zs| = m + |ys|$, and $xs[i] = zs[i]$ if $i < m$, and $ys[i] = zs[i + m]$ otherwise. If m is greater than the size of zs, the result is indefined.
reorder : $\forall'a.[\texttt{int} \times 'a] \rightleftharpoons [\texttt{int} \times 'a]$ If $ys = $ **reorder** xs and $xs[i] = (j, v)$, then $ys[j] = (i, v)$.

Fig. 2. Reversible array combinators

Lastly, we might want to reorder the elements of an array. **reorder** : $\forall'a.[\texttt{int} \times 'a] \rightleftharpoons [\texttt{int} \times 'a]$ takes a list of pairs of indices and values, and creates a new array where each element is at the given index, and the elements are paired with their old indices. It is its own inverse. If there are duplicated indices or any index is outside the array, the result is undefined. For example, **reorder** [(2,17), (1,21), (0,13)] = [(2,13), (1,21), (0,17)]. **reorder** is similar to the gather operation in normal array programming.

We will omit an explicit filter combinator, as this can not be made reversible. We will in the examples later show how you can code something similar to a filter using the other combinators.

The set of reversible array combinators and their types is shown in Fig. 2.

3   Parallel Implementation

We choose a simple model of vector-parallel reversible computers. We use Janus-like reversible updates [4], procedures with call-by-reference parameters (as in Janus), and add a parallel loop `parloop` that when given a variable i, a number n, and some reversible code that uses i, in parallel executes the code for i being equal to all numbers from 0 to $n-1$. It is assumed that the loop "iterations" are independent: No two iterations write to the same location, and if one iteration writes to a location, no other iteration may read from this location.

A function $f : a \rightleftharpoons b$ is implemented as a procedure f' that takes references to argument and result locations, and as a net effect clears the argument location, and puts the result in the result location (not necessarily in this order). A cleared array variable is a null pointer, a cleared number has the value 0, and a cleared pair has two cleared components. Some functions $g : a \rightleftharpoons a$ can be implemented in-place: g' returns its result in the location in which the argument was given. We do not allow aliasing of the parameters. A function $h : c \rightarrow a \rightleftharpoons b$ is implemented by a procedure h' that takes three arguments, where the first is a read-only pointer (typically to a procedure) and the other two are handled as above. We assume access to a reversible memory allocation procedure `alloc` that allocates a zero-initialised array of a given size, and its inverse that frees an array that is assumed to be all zeroes. Such an allocator is described in earlier literature [1]. We subscript `malloc` with the element type, as that affects the size of the allocation.

3.1   The Simple Cases

$y = \mathsf{map}\ f\ x$; where $f : a \rightleftharpoons b$ can be implemented in parallel using `parloop`.

```
procedure map'(f : a ⇌ b,  x : [a],  y : [b])
    local t : int;    t += size(x);    call alloc_b(y,t);
    parloop i t {    call f'(x[i], y[i]);  }
    uncall alloc_a(x,t);    t -= size(y);
end
```

If $a = b$, we can reuse the space for x instead of allocating new space:

```
procedure mapInPlace'(f' : a ⇌ a,  x : [a])
    local t : int;    t += size(x);
    parloop i t { local u : a;   u <-> x[i];    call f'(u, x[i]); }
    t -= size(x);
end
```

Note that we need a local variable u to avoid aliasing in the call to f' and to obey the invariant that the second parameter to f' is initially clear and that the first will be cleared as a result of applying f'. If f'' is an in-place procedure implementing f, we can simplify even further:

```
procedure mapInPlace2'(f" : a ⇌ a,  x : [a])
   local t : int;    t += size(x);
   parloop i t {  call f"(x[i]); }
   t -= size(x);
end
```

$(y, z) =$ copy x, where $x : [a]$ is similarly implemented:

```
procedure copy'(x : [a],  yz : [a] × [a])
   local t : int, z : [a];    t += size(x);
   call alloc_a(z,t);
   parloop i t {  z[i] += x[i];  }
   t -= size(x);    call makePair(x,z,yz)
end
```

Note that we reuse x for y. makePair(x, z, yz) is procedure that creates in yz a pair of x and z and resets x and z to zero.

$z =$ zip (x, y); where $x : [a]$ and $y : [b]$ can be implemented by

```
procedure zip'(x : [a],  y : [b],  z : [a × b])
   local t : int;    t += size(x);    call alloc_{a×b}(z,t);
   parloop i t {  z[i].0 <-> x[i];    z[i].1 <-> y[i];  }
   uncall alloc_a(x,t);    uncall alloc_b(y,t);    t -= size(z);
end
```

where z[i].0 and z[i].1 are the first and second components of the pair z[i]. Note that we assume the sizes of the arrays x and y to be the same.

$x =$ iota n can be implemented as

```
procedure iota'(n : int,  x : [int])
   call alloc_int(x,n);
   parloop i n {  x[i] += i;  }
   n -= size(x)
end
```

$(n, z) =$ concat (x, y), where $x : a$ can be implemented as

```
procedure concat'(x : [a],  y : [a],  nz : int × [a])
   local t : int, u : int;    t += size(x);    u += size(y);
   call alloc_a(nz.1,t+u);
   parloop i t {   nz.1[i] <-> x[i];  }
   parloop i u {   nz.1[i+t] <-> y[i];  }
   uncall alloc_a(x,t);    uncall alloc_a(y,u);
   u -= size(nz.1) - t;    nz.0 <-> t; end
```

$y =$ reorder x, where $x : [int × a]$ can be implemented as

```
procedure reorder'(x : [int × a], y : [int × a])
   local t : int;     t += size(x)     alloc_{int×a}(y,t);
   parloop i t {
   local j : int;
      j += x[i].0;    y[j].0 += i;
      y[j].1 <-> x[i].1;    j -= x[i].0;
   }
   parloop i t {
   local j : int;
      j += y[i].0;    x[j].0 -= i;    j -= y[i].0;
   }
   free_{int×a}(x,t);    t -= size(y)
end
```

The first parloop gives y its correct values and clears the second component of each pair in the x array. We need a second parloop to clear the first components of the pairs in the x array. Note that if j takes on the same value in different iterations of the parallel loop, there may be race conditions that makes the result undefined.

3.2   reduce

In the irreversible case, reduce can be parallelised if the reduction operator $\oplus : a \times a \rightarrow a$ is associative. In the reversible case, we work with functions of the type $f : a \times a \rightleftharpoons a \times a$, so we need to find conditions on such functions that allow parallel implementation. The method below works if f is the identity in its first parameter and associative in its second parameter, i.e., $f(m, n) = (m, m \oplus n)$, where $\oplus$ is an associative operator. An example is ++, as $++(m, n) = (m, m+n)$.

(v, x) = reduce $f\, x$ (note that we reuse x in the output) is implemented by the procedure reduce' in Fig. 3. It takes as arguments f', which is an implementation of f, v which is a location for the result, and x, which is the array to be reduced.

If the size of x is 1, we just copy the sole element of x into v. This is the base case of our induction. Otherwise, we allocate space for an intermediate array y of half the size of x. In the first parloop, we compute f' on pairs of consecutive elements of x, putting the identity part of the result back into x (leaving every other element as 0) and the sum part into y, so $x[2i] = x^0[2i]$, $x[2i+1] = 0$, and $y[i] = x^0[2i] \oplus x^0[2i+1]$, where x^0 is the original x array before the updates. We then call reduce' recursively on y, which (by induction) leaves y unchanged and stores the result of the reduction in v. We now need to uncompute y and restore x to its original values. We do that in the second parloop which is the reverse of the first. The conditional after the second parloop handles odd-sized arrays: The last element of x is "added" to v. Finally, we free the y array.

We illustrate this by an example: applying reduce ++ to an array $x = [x_0, x_1, x_2, x_3, x_4, x_5]$. After the parloop and before the first recursive call, we have $x = [x_0, 0, x_2, 0, x_4, 0]$ and $y = [x_0 + x_1, x_2 + x_3, x_4 + x_5]$. In the recursive

```
procedure reduce'(f' : a × a ⇌ a × a, v : a, x : [a])
    local t : int, y : [a];
    t += size(x);
    if t == 1 then
        v += x[0];
    else {
        call alloc_a(y, ⌊(t/2)⌋;
        parloop i ⌊(t/2)⌋ {
            local u : a × a, w : a × a;
            u.0 <-> x[2*i];   u.1 <-> x[2*i+1];
            call f'(u, w);
            w.0 <-> x[2*i];   w.1 <-> y[i];
        }
        call reduce'(f', v, y);
        parloop i ⌊(t/2)⌋ {
            local u : a × a, w : a × a;
            w.1 <-> y[i];   w.0 <-> x[2*i];
            uncall f'(u, w);
            u.1 <-> x[2*i+1];   u.0 <-> x[2*i];
        }
        if t%2 != 0 then {
            local u : a × a, w : a × a;
            u.0 <-> x[t-1];   u.1 <-> v;
            call f'(u, w);
            w.0 <-> x[t-1];   w.1 <-> v;
        }
        fi t%2 != 0
        uncall alloc_a(y, ⌊(t/2)⌋);
    }
    fi t == 1;
    t -= size(x);
end
```

Fig. 3. Parallel implementation of reduce

invocation, we have $x = [x_0 + x_1, x_2 + x_3, x_4 + x_5]$. After the parloop, we have $x = [x_0 + x_1, 0, x_4 + x_5]$ and $y = [x_0 + x_1 + x_2 + x_3]$. In the next recursive call, the array size is 1, so it will return $v = x_0 + x_1 + x_2 + x_3$ and y unchanged. The second parloop is the inverse of the first, so it returns x to $[x_0 + x_1, x_2 + x_3, x_4 + x_5]$ and clear y. Since t is odd, we enter the conditional and modify v to $x_0 + x_1 + x_2 + x_3 + x_4 + x_5$. When we return, we have $x = [x_0, 0, x_2, 0, x_4, 0]$, $y = [x_0 + x_1, x_2 + x_3, x_4 + x_5]$, and $v = x_0 + x_1 + x_2 + x_3 + x_4 + x_5$. The second parloop restores x to $[x_0, x_1, x_2, x_3, x_4, x_5]$ and clears y. Since t is even, we skip the conditional and return $v = x_0 + x_1 + x_2 + x_3 + x_4 + x_5$ along with the original x.

3.3   scanl

In the irreversible setting, scans of associative operators can be parallelised using a method called *parallel scan* or *prefix sum*. We use a variant of this that shares some structure with the implementation of reduce above and also requires that the reversible function used in the scan is identity in its first parameter and

```
procedure scanl'(f' : a × a ⇌ a × a,  x : [a])
    local t : int, y : [a];
    t += size(x),
    if t < 2 then
        skip;
    else
        call alloc_a(y, ⌊(t/2)⌋;
        parloop i ⌊(t/2)⌋ {
            local u : a × a, w : a × a
            u.0 <-> x[2*i];   u.1 <-> x[2*i+1];
            call f'(u, w);
            w.0 <-> x[2*i];   w.1 <-> y[i];
        }
        call scanl'(f', y);
        parloop i ⌊((t-1)/2)⌋ {
            local u : a × a, w : a × a
            u.0 <-> y[i];   u.1 <-> x[2*i+2];
            call f'(u, w);
            w.0 <-> x[2*i+1];   w.1 <-> x[2*i+2];
        }
        if t%2 == 0 then
            x[t-1] <-> y[t/2-1];        fi t%2 == 0;
        uncall alloc_a(y, ⌊(t/2)⌋);
    fi t < 2;
    t -= size(x);
end
```

Fig. 4. Parallel implementation of scanl

associative in its second parameter. We output the result in the same array as the input. A procedure scanl' that implements $x := \text{scanl}(f, x)$ can be seen in Fig. 4. It takes as arguments f', which is an implementation of f and the array x, which is updated in place.

The base case is an array x of size less than two, which is left unchanged. In the general case, we allocate an array y of half the size of x. The first parloop is as in reduce', and computes f' on pairs of consecutive elements of x, putting the identity part of the result back into x (leaving every other element as 0) and the sum part into y, so $x[2i] = x^0[2i]$, $x[2i+1] = 0$, and $y[i] = x^0[2i] \oplus x^0[2i+1]$, where x^0 is the original x array before the updates. We then call scanl' recursively on y, which by induction makes y the scan of the original y. The elements of this y are the odd-indexed elements of the reduced x^0. The odd elements of x are currently 0, so we can just swap the elements of y with the odd-indexed elements of x. The even-indexed elements of x contain the original values of the even-indexed elements of x^0. The first of these is correct, but the subsequent ones needs to be added to the preceding element of x. We do this in the second parloop with calls to f' and suitable swaps. Again, we need to do some fix-up to handle odd-sized arrays, where the last element of x (which is currently 0) is swapped with the last element of y (which contains the "sum" of all elements of x^0). Finally, y, which is now cleared, is freed.

We use scanl ++ x, where $x = [x_0, x_1, x_2, x_3, x_4, x_5]$ as an example. After the parloop and before the first recursive call, we have $x = [x_0, 0, x_2, 0, x_4, 0]$

and $y = [x_0 + x_1, x_2 + x_3, x_4 + x_5]$. In the recursive invocation, we have $x = [x_0 + x_1, x_2 + x_3, x_4 + x_5]$. After the parloop, we have $x = [x_0 + x_1, 0, x_4 + x_5]$ and $y = [x_0 + x_1 + x_2 + x_3]$. The next recursive call will return y unchanged, as its size is 1. $t = 3$, so we do one iteration of the second parloop, getting $x = [x_0 + x_1, x_0 + x_1 + x_2 + x_3, x_0 + x_1 + x_2 + x_3 + x_4 + x_5]$ and $y = [0]$. Since t is odd, we skip the conditional, free y, and return. At the return, we get $x = [x_0, 0, x_2, 0, x_4, 0]$ and $y = [x_0 + x_1, x_0 + x_1 + x_2 + x_3, x_0 + x_1 + x_2 + x_3 + x_4 + x_5]$. $t = 6$, so we do two iterations of the second parloop and get $x = [x_0, x_0 + x_1, x_0 + x_1 + x_2, x_0 + x_1 + x_2 + x_3, x_0 + x_1 + x_2 + x_3 + x_4, 0]$ and $y = [0, 0, x_0 + x_1 + x_2 + x_3 + x_4 + x_5]$. t is now even, so we enter the conditional and get $x = [x_0, x_0 + x_1, x_0 + x_1 + x_2, x_0 + x_1 + x_2 + x_3, x_0 + x_1 + x_2 + x_3 + x_4, x_0 + x_1 + x_2 + x_3 + x_4 + x_5]$ and $y = [0, 0, 0]$, so we can free y and return.

The scan is not entirely in-place, as we use local arrays y, the total size of which is almost that of the original. We could make it entirely in-place by doubling the stride in each recursive call instead of copying to a new array of half the size.

4   A Reversible Array Programming Language

We are now ready to define a reversible array programming language, which we will call "Agni", named after the two-faced Hindu god of fire. The syntax is shown in Fig. 5. Note that <=> is an easier-to-type alternative notation for ⇌. → is easily accessible on an international keyboard, so we have not replaced this with the pure-ASCII alternative ->.

We work with both heap-allocated and stack-allocated variables Heap-allocated variables are denoted *HVar* in the grammar, and contain values that are consumed nad produced by reversible operations. Stack-allocated variables are denoted *SVar*, and contain values or functions that are locally defined using irreversible expressions and then uncomputed at the end of their scope. To distinguish these, heap-allocated variable names start with upper-case letters, while stack-allocated variable and function names start with lower-case letters. Heap-allocated variables have heap types (denoted *HType*) and stack-allocated variables have stack types (denoted *SType*).

A stack-allocated variable is introduced using a let-expression that initialises it, allows multiple uses of the variable inside its body, and uncomputes its value at the end. In reverse, the uncomputation and initialisation swap roles. The expressions used by initialisation and uncomputation need not be reversible. This is analogous to how reversible updates in Janus can use irreversible expressions. A stack-allocated variable can not hold an array, but array elements and sizes can be used in its initialisation and uncomputation expressions. An irreversible expression is denoted *Exp* in the grammar.

Variables holding heap-allocated values are explicitly initialised using a reversible initialisation. The heap-allocated variables on the right-hand side of this initialisation are consumed and can no longer be used. In reverse, the variables on the left-hand side are consumed and those on the right are initialised.

$SType$	$\rightarrow$ **int**
$SType$	$\rightarrow TypeVar$
$SType$	$\rightarrow SType \times SType$
$SType$	$\rightarrow SType \rightarrow SType$
$SType$	$\rightarrow HType$ **<=>** $HType$

$HType$	$\rightarrow$ **int**
$HType$	$\rightarrow TypeVar$
$HType$	$\rightarrow HType \times HType$
$HType$	$\rightarrow [HType]$

$Rinit$	$\rightarrow$
$Rinit$	$\rightarrow HPattern := Rexp;$
$Rinit$	$\rightarrow Rinit\ Rinit$
$Rinit$	$\rightarrow$ **let** $SPattern = Exp$ **in** $Rinit$ **end** $SPattern = Exp;$
$Rinit$	$\rightarrow$ **def** $FunDef$ **in** $Rinit$ **end**;

$Rexp$	$\rightarrow HVar$
$Rexp$	$\rightarrow SVar$
$Rexp$	$\rightarrow (Rexp, Rexp)$
$Rexp$	$\rightarrow Fname\ Rexp$
$Rexp$	$\rightarrow$ **uncall** $Fname\ Rexp$
$Rexp$	$\rightarrow Fname\ Svar\ Rexp$
$Rexp$	$\rightarrow$ **uncall** $Fname\ Svar\ Rexp$

Exp	$\rightarrow IntConst$
Exp	$\rightarrow SVar$
Exp	$\rightarrow HVar[Exp]$
Exp	$\rightarrow$ **size** $HVar$
Exp	$\rightarrow (Exp, Exp)$
Exp	$\rightarrow Fname\ Exp$
Exp	$\rightarrow$ **let** $SPattern = Exp$ **in** Exp
Exp	$\rightarrow$ **def** $FunDef$ **in** Exp

$FunDef$	$\rightarrow Fname\ SPattern = Exp$
$FunDef$	$\rightarrow Fname\ HPattern = Rinit\ Rexp$
$FunDef$	$\rightarrow Fname\ SPattern\ HPattern = Rinit\ Rexp$

$HPattern$	$\rightarrow SVar$
$HPattern$	$\rightarrow HVar : HType$
$HPattern$	$\rightarrow (HPattern, HPattern)$

$SPattern$	$\rightarrow SVar : SType$
$SPattern$	$\rightarrow (SPattern, SPattern)$

$Program$	$\rightarrow FunDef$

Fig. 5. Syntax of Agni

A heap-allocated variable is in scope from its initialisation to its consumption, and can in this scope be used in expressions that define stack-allocated variables. Reversible initialisations are denoted $Rinit$ in the grammar, and can in addition to a simple initialisation be a (possible empty) sequence of initialisations or a local definition of a function or stack-allocated variable that is locally used for an initialisation.

Function definitions are defined using def-expressions, and have scope until the end of the def-expression. A function definition can not consume heap-allocated variables that are not given as parameters or initialised locally, and all parameters or locally initialised variables that are heap-allocated must be either consumed in the function body or returned as part of the result. In a function type, parameters that appear in the function type before a $\rightleftharpoons$ arrow are heap allocated, whereas parameters (including function parameters) that appear before a $\rightarrow$ arrow are stack-allocated. All stack-allocated parameters must occur before heap-allocated parameters. The body of a reversible function is an optional reversible initialisation followed by a reversible expression. The body of an irreversible function is an irreversible expression. Note that function definitions can occur in both reversible initialisations and in irreversible expressions with slightly different syntax.

A program is a single function definition that defines a reversible function, so it must have type $t_1 \rightleftharpoons t_2$ for some types t_1 and t_2. Its body is a reversible initialisation followed by a reversible expression.

A reversible expression is a variable, a pair of two reversible expressions, or a (possibly inverse) reversible function application.

A reversible expression can be a stack-allocated variable. This will not be consumed by the expression. Likewise, a reversible pattern can be a stack-allocated variable ($SVar$). This is not a defining instance (so no type needs to be given), but when a heap-allocated value is matched against a stack-allocated variable, it must have the same value as the variable, and is consumed by this. If the variable does not match the value, the behaviour is undefined. When a heap-allocated variable ($HVar$) occurs in a pattern for heap-allocated values, it defines a new variable, so a type is given.

The program is evaluated in a context that defines both a number of irreversible functions for use in initialisation and uncomputation of stack-allocated variables and a number of reversible functions for defining heap-allocated variables. The latter includes the array combinators shown in Fig. 2. Note that "normal" addition $+ : \text{int} \times \text{int} \rightarrow \text{int}$ and similar operators are part of the set of irreversible functions that can be used.

For simplicity, we do not have an explicit boolean type, so truth values are represented as integers. Non-zero integers are considered true and 0 is considered false. We have also omitted reals, as garbage-free reversible arithmetic on floating point numbers is still an open issue.

$$\overline{\rho,\gamma \vdash k : \texttt{int}}$$

$$\frac{\gamma\, X = [t]}{\rho,\gamma \vdash \texttt{size } X : \texttt{int}}$$

$$\frac{\gamma\, X = [t] \quad \rho,\gamma \vdash e : \texttt{int}}{\rho,\gamma \vdash X[e] : t}$$

$$\frac{\rho\, x = t}{\rho,\gamma \vdash x : t}$$

$$\frac{\rho,\gamma \vdash e_1 : t_1 \quad \rho,\gamma \vdash e_2 : t_2}{\rho,\gamma \vdash (e_1, e_2) : t_1 \times t_2}$$

$$\frac{\rho\, f = \tau \quad t_1 \rightarrow t_2 = instantiate\, \tau \quad \rho,\gamma \vdash e : t_1}{\rho,\gamma \vdash f\, e : t_2}$$

$$\frac{\rho,\gamma \vdash e_1 : t_1 \quad \rho \vdash_s s_1 \rhd \rho_1/t_3 \quad t_1 = t_3 \quad \rho_1,\gamma \vdash e_2 : t_2}{\rho,\gamma \vdash \texttt{let } s_1 = e_1 \texttt{ in } e_2 : t_2}$$

$$\frac{\rho \vdash_s s \rhd \rho_1/t_1 \quad \rho_1[f : t_1 \rightarrow t_2],\gamma \vdash e_1 : t_2}{\tau = generalize(t_1 \rightarrow t_2, \rho) \quad \rho[f : \tau],\gamma \vdash e_2 : t_3}{\rho,\gamma \vdash \texttt{def } f\, s = e_1 \texttt{ in } e_2 : t_3}$$

$$\overline{\rho \vdash_s x : t \rhd \rho[x : t]/t}$$

$$\frac{\rho \vdash_s s_1 \rhd \rho_1/t_1 \quad \rho_1 \vdash_s s_2 \rhd \rho_2/t_1}{\rho \vdash_s (s_1, s_2) \rhd \rho_2/(t_1 \times t_2)}$$

Fig. 6. Type rules for irreversible expressions and patterns

5   A Type System for Reversible Array Programming

We use different environments for stack-allocated variables and functions and for heap-allocated variables. Evaluating an expression has no net effect on the environment of stack-allocated variables and functions, but it may affect the environment of heap-allocated variables, as some of these are consumed and others initialised in a way that does not follow block structure. We use (possibly subscripted) ρ for environments of stack-allocated variables and functions, and γ for environments heap-allocated variables. When we evaluate an irreversible expression, we can use variables (and functions) from both environments, but modify none of them. When we evaluate a reversible expression, we can also use both, but we may remove variables from γ, as these are used. When evaluating a reversible initialisation, we can use variables from ρ and both remove and add variables in γ.

We start by defining type rules for irreversible expressions and patterns in Fig. 6. We use t to denote an $SType$, x to denote an $SVar$, X to denote an $HVar$, and s to denote an $SPattern$. The rules are straightforward except the function rule which uses implicit unification to allow recursive definitions, and use generalisation and instantiation to implement parametric polymorphism. τ denotes a polymorphic type. We omit descriptions of generalisation and instantiation, but note that these are as in Hindley-Milner type inference. The two last rules are for patterns, which both extend an environment with new bindings and build a type for the pattern. We assume no variable occurs twice in a pattern.

Figure 7 shows rules for reversible expressions. T denotes an $HType$, and r denotes an $RExp$. $\uparrow(t)$ transforms an $Stype$ (excluding function types) to the equivalent $HType$. Note how γ is threaded around in the rules.

$$\overline{\rho, \gamma[X : T] \vdash_R X : T/\gamma} \qquad \overline{\rho[x : t], \gamma \vdash_R x : \uparrow(t)/\gamma}$$

$$\frac{\rho, \gamma \vdash_R r_1 : T_1/\gamma_1 \quad \rho, \gamma_1 \vdash_R r_2 : T_2/\gamma_2}{\rho, \gamma \vdash_R (r_1, r_2) : (T_1 \times T_2)/\gamma_2}$$

$$\frac{\rho f = \tau \quad (T_1 \rightleftharpoons T_2) = instantiate\, \tau \quad \rho, \gamma \vdash_R r : T_1/\gamma_1}{\rho, \gamma \vdash_R f\, r : T_2/\gamma_1}$$

$$\frac{\rho f = \tau \quad (T_1 \rightleftharpoons T_2) = instantiate\, \tau \quad \rho, \gamma \vdash_R r : T_2/\gamma_1}{\rho, \gamma \vdash_R \mathtt{uncall}\, f\, r : T_1/\gamma_1}$$

$$\frac{\rho f = \tau \quad (t \to T_1 \rightleftharpoons T_2) = instantiate\, \tau \quad \rho\, x = t \quad \rho, \gamma \vdash_R r : T_1/\gamma_1}{\rho, \gamma \vdash_R f\, x\, r : T_2/\gamma_1}$$

$$\frac{\rho f = \tau \quad (t \to T_1 \rightleftharpoons T_2) = instantiate\, \tau \quad \rho\, x = t \quad \rho, \gamma \vdash_R r : T_2/\gamma_1}{\rho, \gamma \vdash_R \mathtt{uncall}\, f\, x\, r : T_1/\gamma_1}$$

Fig. 7. Type rules for reversible expressions

Figure 8 shows rules for reversible initialisations and patterns. Like reversible expressions, reversible initialisations thread γ around, but they do not return values. The most complicated rule is for $\mathtt{let}\, s_1 = e_1\, \mathtt{in}\, I\, \mathtt{end}\, s_2 = e_2$, where s_1 and s_2 are required to contain the same variables so the variables that are introduced in s_1 are eliminated in s_2. The rules for function definitions are similar to those for irreversible expressions, except that they also include reversible function definitions. Note that a reversible function definition starts and ends with empty γs, as they can only consume their arguments and produce their results with no remaining unconsumed $RVars$.

Reversible patterns produce both a $Htype$ and a new γ. The first rule states that when using an $SVar$ in a pattern, its $SType$ is converted to the equivalent $HType$ using the $\uparrow$ operator. Only non-functional $STypes$ can be converted.

6 Examples

Since the reversible functional array programming language is limited compared to irreversible array programming languages, we need to justify that it can be used to solve real problems. We do so by showing some example programs.

6.1 Inner Product

An inner product of two vectors reduces these vectors to a single number, so we need to return these vectors along with the result. The code is

$$\frac{}{\rho,\gamma\vdash_I\leadsto\gamma}\qquad\frac{\rho,\gamma\vdash_I I_1\leadsto\gamma_1\quad\rho,\gamma_1\vdash_I I_2\leadsto\gamma_2}{\rho,\gamma\vdash_I I_1\ I_2\leadsto\gamma_2}$$

$$\frac{\rho,\gamma\vdash_R r:T/\gamma_1\quad\rho,\gamma_1\vdash_P p\triangleright\gamma_2/T}{\rho,\gamma\vdash_I p:=r;\leadsto\gamma_2}$$

$$\frac{\rho,\gamma\vdash e_1:t_1\quad\rho\vdash_S s_1\triangleright\rho_1/t_3\quad t_1=t_3\quad\rho,\gamma\vdash_I I\leadsto\gamma_1}{\rho,\gamma_1\vdash e_2:t_2\quad\rho\vdash_S s_2\triangleright\rho_1/t_4\quad t_2=t_4}{\rho,\gamma\vdash\mathbf{let}\ s_1=e_1\ \mathbf{in}\ I\ \mathbf{end}\ s_2=e_2;\leadsto\gamma_1}$$

$$\frac{\rho\vdash_S s\triangleright\rho_1/t_1\quad\rho_1[f:t_1\to t_2],\gamma\vdash e_1:t_2}{\tau=generalize(t_1\to t_2,\rho)\quad\rho[f:\tau],\gamma\vdash_I I\leadsto\gamma_1}{\rho,\gamma\vdash\mathbf{def}\ f\ s=e\ \mathbf{in}\ I;\leadsto\gamma_1}$$

$$\frac{\rho,[]\vdash_P p\triangleright\gamma_1/T_1\quad\rho_1[f:T_1\rightleftharpoons T_2],\gamma_1\vdash_I I_1\leadsto\gamma_2}{\rho_1,\gamma_2\vdash_R r:T_2/[]\quad\tau=generalize(f:T_1\rightleftharpoons T_2,\rho)\quad\rho[f:\tau],\gamma\vdash_I I_2\leadsto\gamma_3}{\rho,\gamma\vdash\mathbf{def}\ f\ p=I_1\ r\ \mathbf{in}\ I_2;\leadsto\gamma_3}$$

$$\frac{\rho\vdash_S s\triangleright\rho_1/t\quad\rho,[]\vdash_P p\triangleright\gamma_1/T_1\quad\rho_1[f:t\to T_1\rightleftharpoons T_2],\gamma_1\vdash_I I_1\leadsto\gamma_2}{\rho_1,\gamma_2\vdash_R r:T_2/[]\quad\tau=generalize(f:t\to T_1\rightleftharpoons T_2,\rho)\quad\rho[f:\tau],\gamma\vdash_I I_2\leadsto\gamma_3}{\rho,\gamma\vdash\mathbf{def}\ f\ s\ p=I_1\ r\ \mathbf{in}\ I_2;\leadsto\gamma_3}$$

$$\frac{T=\uparrow(\rho\,x)}{\rho,\gamma\vdash_P x\triangleright\gamma/T}\qquad\frac{}{\rho,\gamma\vdash_P X:T\triangleright\gamma[X:T]}$$

$$\frac{\rho,\gamma\vdash_P p_1\triangleright\gamma_1/T_1\quad\rho,\gamma_1\vdash_P p_2\triangleright\gamma_2/T_1}{\rho,\gamma\vdash_P (p_1,p_2)\triangleright\gamma_2/(T_1\times T_2)}$$

Fig. 8. Type rules for reversible initialisations and patterns

```
fun inner (Xs: [int], Ys: [int]) =
  (Xs: [int], Prods: [int]) := unzip (map ** (zip (Xs, Ys)));
  (Ip: int, Prods: [int]) := reduce ++ Prods;
  (Ip, unzip (map // (zip (Xs, Prods))))
```

We note that $**(x,y)=(x,x*y)$ and $//(\texttt{x},\texttt{y})=(x,y/x)$, so they are inverses and both undefined if $x=0$.

We first zip the two vectors, map ** to get the product of each pair (while retaining one operand), unzip to get separate arrays for the product and the copies, reduce with ++ to get the inner product, and undo the multiplications to get the original vectors back. Note that we redefine xs, but since the original xs has already been consumed at this point, it leads to no ambiguity.

This is, admittedly, more cumbersome than doing inner product in a normal irreversible language. We could shorten it somewhat by adding a zipWith combinator that combines map and zip.

6.2   Counting the Number of Elements that Satisfy a Predicate

We don't have a separate boolean type, so we use zero/nonzero instead. A reversible predicate has the type $'a \rightleftharpoons 'a \times \text{int}$ for some type $'a$ and will pair a value with the result of the predicate, which is 1 for true and 0 for false. We can map this on an array, extract the numbers, add them using **reduce**, zip the numbers back to the array, and map the inverse of the predicate (which is done by uncalling map) to eliminate the numbers. The result is a pair of the count and the original list.

```
count (p: 'a <=> '{a}\times{int}) (Xs: ['a]) =
  (Xs: ['a], Ps: [int]) := unzip (map p Xs);
  (Count: int, Ps: [int]) := reduce ++ Ps;
  Xs: ['a] := uncall map p (zip (Xs,Ps));
  (Count, Xs)
```

Note that the third line is the inverse of the first line.

6.3   Separation by Predicate

As noted in Sect. 2, we don't include a filter operator, but sometimes, we will need to separate the elements where the predicate is true from the elements where it is false. This can be used, e.g., for quicksort or radix sort. Such a separation is not reversible, so we should expect some garbage output as well. In this example, this garbage is two arrays of integers, each the size of the original array:

$$\text{separate} : ('a \rightleftharpoons 'a \times \text{int}) \rightarrow ['a] \rightleftharpoons ['a] \times ['a] \times [\text{int}] \times [\text{int}]$$

The garbage can be reduced to a copy of the original array by calling **separate**, copying the separated arrays, uncalling **separate**, and combining the separated arrays with the original, as shown in the function **separateClean** below. The **separate** function works in the following steps:

1. Map the predicate over the array, pairing each element with (1,0) if the predicate is true and (0,1) if the predicate is false.
2. Use **scanl** twice to compute the number of true and false values before each array element.
3. Extract the total number of true booleans **tmax** from the last element of the new array.
4. Use **map findLoc** to compute the new location of each element, where **findLoc** chooses between the number of previous true elements and the number of false elements + **tmax** depending on the predicate.
5. Use **reorder** to place elements in their new locations.
6. Split into true and false arrays.
7. Returns these array and the garbage arrays.

The code is shown in Fig. 9

```
separate (p: 'a <=> 'a×int) (Xs: ['a]) =
  let one: int = 1 in
    def tf N: int = --(N,one) in
      (Xs: ['a], Ps: [int]) := unzip (map p Xs);
      (Ts: [int], Fs: [int]) := unzip (map tf Ps);
      Tsbefore: [int] := scanl ++ Ts;
      Fsbefore: [int] := scanl ++ Fs;
      let tmax: int = Tsbefore[size Tsbefore - 1]) in
        Bsbefore: [int×int] := zip (Tsbefore, Fsbefore);
        Bsxs: [(int×int)×'a] := zip (Bsbefore, Xs);
        def findLoc ((Tsb: int, Fsb: int), X: 'a) =
          (X: 'a, P: int) := p X;
          (tmax, Fsb1: int) := ++(tmax, Fsb);
          (P: int, Loc: int, G: int) := cswap(P, Fsb1, Tsb);
          Loc: int := dec Loc;
          X: 'a := uncall p (X, P);
          ((Loc, X), G)
        in
          (Lsxs: [int×'a], G0: [int]) := unzip (map findLoc Bsxs);
        end;
        (G1: [int], Newxs: ['a]) := unzip (reorder Lsxs);
        (Txs: ['a], Fxs: ['a]) := splitAt (tmax, Newxs);
      end tmax = size Txs
    end
  end one: int = 1;
  (Txs, Fxs, G0, G1)

separateClean (p: 'a <=> 'a×int) (Xs: ['a]) =
  (Txs: ['a], Fxs: ['a], G0: [int], G1: [int]) := separate p Xs;
  (Txs: ['a], Txs1: ['a]) := copy Txs;
  (Fxs: ['a], Fxs1: ['a]) := copy Fxs;
  Xs: ['a] := uncall separate p (Txs, Fxs, G0, G1);
  (Txs1, Fxs1, Xs)
```

Fig. 9. Implementation of separate

Note that the uncomputation expression for the local variable tmax is different from its initialisation expression. cswap is a predefined function that does a
conditional swap: It returns the first argument unchanged, and if this is nonzero,
returns the two other arguments swapped, otherwise unchanged. It can likely be
implemented by a single instruction on a reversible processor. dec is a predefined reversible function that decrements its argument. We need to locally define
a variable to be equal to 1, because we can not use constants in patterns and
reversible expressions.

7 Conclusion and Future Work

We have presented reversible implementations of a number of reversible array combinators, including `reduce` and `scanl`, and we have presented a reversible functional array language, Agni, that uses these combinators. The reversible implementations of the combinators are interesting in their own right, and can be used for other languages.

Agni is, in its current form, somewhat limited, and it can be challenging to code non-trivial functions in Agni, as witnessed by the complexity of the `separate` function. We believe that the potential of getting highly parallel reversible code will make it worthwhile. Adding extra combinators, for example `zipWith` that combines `zip` and `map`, and `map2` that combines `zip`, `map`, and `unzip`, would also make coding easier and would also reduce the number of intermediate values produced. A general fusion transformation that combines several sequentially applied combinators to a single combinator would be an useful optimisation. We have avoided conditionals (except conditional swap), as conditional execution does not fit well with vector parallelisation.

We do not at the time of writing have an implementation of Agni, but we have tested the reversible implementations of the array combinators using the imperative reversible language Hermes [3], albeit with sequential loops rather than parallel loops. If and when reversible vector processors become available, we will certainly attempt to implement Agni on these. Until then, we will have to do with implementations on classical hardware, where Agni has no obvious advantage over existing functional array programming languages, such as Futhark [2]. Nevertheless, we plan in the future to make sequential and parallel implementations of Agni on classical hardware. Experiences with this may spark modifications to the language.

Speaking of Futhark, this language has an interesting type system where arrays can be constrained by size (so you can, e.g., specify that a scan preserves array size). It would be interesting to adapt this idea to Agni. It would also be useful to add type inference, so many of the type declarations can be avoided.

References

1. Cservenka, M.H., Glück, R., Haulund, T., Mogensen, T.Æ.: Data structures and dynamic memory management in reversible languages. In: Kari, J., Ulidowski, I. (eds.) RC 2018. LNCS, vol. 11106, pp. 269–285. Springer, Cham (2018). https://doi.org/10.1007/978-3-319-99498-7_19
2. Henriksen, T., Serup, N.G.W., Elsman, M., Henglein, F., Oancea, C.E.: Futhark: purely functional GPU-programming with nested parallelism and in-place array updates. In: Proceedings of the 38th ACM SIGPLAN Conference on Programming Language Design and Implementation, PLDI 2017, pp. 556–571. ACM, New York (2017)

3. Mogensen, T.Æ.: Hermes: a language for light-weight encryption. In: Lanese, I., Rawski, M. (eds.) RC 2020. LNCS, vol. 12227, pp. 93–110. Springer, Cham (2020). https://doi.org/10.1007/978-3-030-52482-1_5

4. Yokoyama, T., Axelsen, H.B., Glück, R.: Principles of a reversible programming language. In: Proceedings of the 5th Conference on Computing Frontiers, CF 2008, pp. 43–54. ACM, New York (2008)

Compiling Janus to RSSA

Martin Kutrib[2] , Uwe Meyer[1(✉)] , Niklas Deworetzki[1], and Marc Schuster[1]

[1] Technische Hochschule Mittelhessen, Wiesenstr. 14, 35390 Giessen, Germany
uwe.meyer@mni.thm.de
[2] Institut für Informatik, Universität Giessen, Arndtstr. 2, 35392 Giessen, Germany
kutrib@informatik.uni-giessen.de

Abstract. Reversible programming languages have been a focus of research for more than the last decade mostly due to the work of Glück, Yokoyama, Mogensen, and many others. In this paper, we report about our recent activities to compile code written in the reversible language Janus to reversible static-single-assignment form RSSA and to three-address-code, both of which can thereafter be compiled to C. In particular, this is – to our knowledge – the first compiler from Janus to RSSA. In addition, we have implemented a novel technique for a reversible compiler by executing the code generator itself in reverse. Our compiler provides the basis for optimizations and further analysis of reversible programs.

Keywords: Reverse computing · Reversible programming languages · Janus · Reversible static-single-assignment

1 Introduction

Reverse computing, although the initial ideas can be traced back to the 1960s [10], has been a major research area over the last decade. With the growing importance of sustainability and reduced energy consumption, reverse computing promises contributions by avoiding the waste of energy through deletion of information [5].

More than twenty years after the first creation of a reversible language called Janus [11], the papers of the Copenhagen group [17] brought new life into the area of reversible languages by formally defining and extending Janus. Interpretation and partial evaluation [12] as well self-interpretation [18] were studied and in [4] Axelsen published his results on the compilation of Janus. In [19] a reversible flowchart language as a foundation for imperative languages is described and its r-Turing-completeness, i.e. their ability to compute exactly all injective computable functions, is proved.

Whilst it was now possible to execute programs forwards and backwards, there seem to be no results about the optimization of Janus programs. Optimization in this regard refers to improving the execution time of programs or their memory consumption [14].

It is well known from the discipline of compiler construction that optimization can most effectively be performed on some intermediate representation of

S. Yamashita and T. Yokoyama (Eds.): RC 2021, LNCS 12805, pp. 64–78, 2021.
https://doi.org/10.1007/978-3-030-79837-6_4

the source rather than the source code itself or its abstract syntax tree. Such intermediate representations include three-address-code [1] and static-single-assignment [16].

In 2015, Mogensen published his work on RSSA, which is a special form of static-single-assignment that can be executed forwards and backwards [13]. We are going to describe the major concepts of RSSA in Sect. 2.2. However, we are not aware of any work to connect the dots between Janus and RSSA.

In this paper, we report on a new Janus compiler, called *rc3* (*reversible computing compiler collection*) with multiple backends including RSSA. The compiler is available at https://git.thm.de/thm-rc3/release. and has been written with two intentions:

- Provide the ability to execute Janus programs forwards and backwards.
- Establish the basis for further research on the optimization of reversible languages.

Based on the Janus definition in [17], we developed a compiler front-end focusing on the semantic analysis required for a reversible language. The compiler allows for pluggable back-ends with currently three of them in place (see Fig. 1 for an overview):

1. Interpreter: Instead of generating code, the interpreter back-end directly allows the execution of Janus programs forwards or backwards.
2. Three-Address Code: This backend will generate intermediate code in form of non-reversible three-address code that can be translated to a "forwards" as well as a "backwards" C-program including all necessary declarations and function definitions to be able to compile the code on any platform.
3. RSSA: This backend will firstly generate RSSA-code, and at the same time also construct building blocks and a program graph (in order to be able to use these for further analysis of control and data flow). To be able to verify the RSSA code, the RSSA code can be translated into C-code, as well. In addition, we have created a virtual machine for RSSA that allows direct execution of RSSA code.

In summary, this paper describes two important new aspects for the compilation of reversible languages:

- Whilst optimization techniques such as dead code elimination, common subexpression elimination, and many more are very well understood for "traditional" languages, no results are known for reversible languages. These optimizations are typically implemented on some low-level intermediate code. Our compiler is – to our knowledge – the first compiler from Janus to reversible static-single-assignment intermediate code and work to implement optimizations is already underway.
- In addition, we have implemented a novel technique to let the code generator itself operate "in reverse". For instance, the Janus language provides stack primitives such as push and pop. We have implemented only the former, whereas the code for pop is automatically created by inverting the code for push.

We will start by briefly explaining Janus as well as RSSA in order to provide a basis for the description of our compiler in Sect. 3. This chapter forms the main part of the paper and contains detailed descriptions and examples of our code generation schemes. Lastly, we will provide insights into the "reverse code generator", followed by an outlook on current achievements on optimization of RSSA.

2   Preliminaries – Janus and RSSA

2.1   Janus

The procedural and reversible programming language *Janus* has originally been proposed in 1982 [11]. Since then, Yokoyama and Glück have formalized the language [18], and together with Axelsen, have considerably extended Janus and shown that it is Turing-complete [17]. We specifically use the extended version as defined in [17].

In this version, a Janus program consists of a `main`-procedure followed by a sequence of additional procedure declarations. Procedures represent a parameterized list of statements, which are the smallest reversible building blocks of a Janus program. Statements can change the state or control flow of the execution by inspecting and manipulating variables. All variables are defined locally, either as an integer, an array of integers, or a stack of integers. While the size of an array must be known at compile-time, stacks can grow arbitrarily at runtime.

A statement is either a reversible assignment, one of the reversible control flow operators (conditional, loop), a procedure invocation, one of the stack operations (push, pop), a local variable block, or an empty skip statement. Each of those statements has a well-defined inverse, which is used during backwards execution. To change the execution direction, procedure invocations are used. In addition to the destination of a procedure invocation, the call direction must be specified using either the `call` or `uncall` keyword. If the `uncall` keyword is used, the invoked procedure is executed in reverse execution direction. Since the keywords `call` and `uncall` interchange their meanings in reverse execution direction, it is possible to restore the original execution direction.

For a program to be reversible, all information must be preserved during runtime. To ensure that no information is lost when exiting the scope of a variable, all local variables are restricted to the body of a local variable block. In these blocks, variables are allocated and deallocated in a structured way that preserves information. For the same reason, parameters for procedures are passed by reference so that the information stored in the parameters is preserved when the procedure ends.

2.2   The Reversible Intermediate Code RSSA

Reversible static-single-assignment (RSSA) was firstly introduced by Mogensen [13] as a reversible variant of SSA (Static-Single-Assignment), which in turn is an intermediate language to facilitate data-flow analysis and was proposed by Alpern, Wegman, and Zadek in 1988 [2]. SSA forms an intermediate representation in which each variable has only one definition and new "versions" of the variables are used for each assignment to it. This is often accomplished by inserting Φ-functions to merge potentially different versions occurring due to branches in the control flow.

RSSA uses variables and constants defined as atoms. A memory location can be accessed in the form $M[a]$ where $M[a]$ represents the location to which an atom a points. Atoms and memory accesses can be used in conditions. If a variable is used on both sides of an assignment, a new version of the variable, a so-called fresh variable, must be created on the right side of the expression so that it can not be defined and used simultaneously [13].

In RSSA, a program is a set of basic blocks, each consisting of a sequence of assignments or a call. Each block is enclosed by an entry and an exit point. Entry and exit points use labels, which must be utilized at exactly one entry and exit point. Valid RSSA programs need to entail one entry point *begin main* and a corresponding exit point *end main* [13]. Entry and exit points may occur in a conditional or unconditional form. Conditional entry points are used in the following manner, $L_1(x,\dots)L_2 \leftarrow C$. Depending on whether it is entered through a jump to L_1 or L_2, the condition C will be evaluated to either true or false. Conditional exit points are used in a similar manner using the form $C \rightarrow L_1(y,\dots)L_2$. The condition C is evaluated and depending on the evaluation, a jump to either L_1 or L_2 is performed [13]. These conditional entry and exit points are an alternative means to implement the Φ-functions in RSSA [13], and are used because $\Phi - functions$ use two inputs to compute one output, and would thus prohibit reversibility. RSSA defines a set of reversible instructions, that can be used to compose reversible programs. The most important ones – as shown in Table 1 – are assignments, call, and uncall instructions, as well as entry and exit points. Operands for these instructions are separated into *atoms* or *memory locations*.

Table 1. Important RSSA instructions

Assignment:	`x := y ⊕ (a ⊙ b)`
Call:	`(x₁, ...) := call p (y₁, ...)`
Uncall:	`(x₁, ...) := uncall p (y₁, ...)`
Uncond. Entry:	`L(x₁, ...) <-`
Cond. Entry:	`L1(x₁, ...)L2 <- c`
Uncond. Exit:	`-> L(x₁, ...)`
Cond. Exit:	`c -> L1(y₁, ...)L2`

Similar to statements in the programming language Janus, every instruction has a well-defined inverse. Therefore a whole program can be inverted by inverting every single instruction in it and the order in which those instructions appear in. Since RSSA is reversible, every subroutine should be runnable in a forwards and backwards manner. Running a subroutine backwards is performed by calling the inverted form of the subroutine [13].

3 Our Compiler

This section briefly explains the structure and implementation of our compiler's front-end and back-ends. Our approach to implement the compiler in Java largely resembles the approach for a classical multi-pass compiler [3]. The backends are pluggable, such that adding new backends is easy. The next version of the compiler includes an additional layer to optimize the RSSA code.

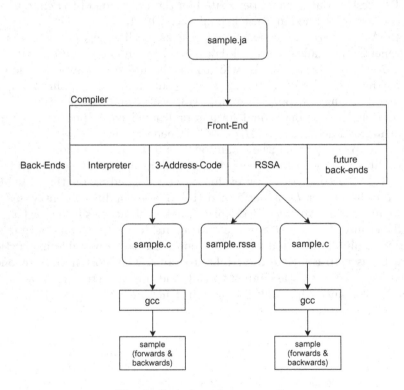

Fig. 1. Overview of our compiler

3.1 Compiler Front-End

The front-end consists of a dedicated scanner and parser, which are generated using the scanner generator *JFlex* [9] and the parser generator *CUP* [7] respectively. The scanner performs the lexical analysis, converting the input characters into a sequence of tokens. These tokens are then passed to the parser, which performs the syntactic analysis and constructs an abstract syntax tree. After the construction of an abstract syntax tree, it is passed to the semantic analysis.

With the implementation of the semantic analysis, the particularities arising from the properties of a reversible language become clear: As in a conventional language, Janus defines rules for the visibility of identifiers and restrictions on types of variables and expressions. In addition to classical analysis passes, that enter declarations into a symbol table and check the visibility and types of used variables and expressions, another pass has to be defined, the aim of which is to check the reversibility of individual instructions.

Even though Janus specifically defines reversible variants of classical statements, it is possible to construct a statement that cannot be reversed. In total, there are four different variants of assignments, that may not be reversible at runtime, but can be recognized at compile time. In [17] these are mentioned as a "syntactic rule". We have chosen to split them into four cases which are checked during the semantic analysis.

$$x \quad \odot= \quad x + k \tag{1}$$
$$M[e_1] \quad \odot= \quad M[e_2] + k \tag{2}$$
$$x \quad \odot= \quad M[x] + k \tag{3}$$
$$M[M[e_1] + k] \quad \odot= \quad e_2 \tag{4}$$

Fig. 2. Four variants of non-reversible assignments

Figure 2 shows these different variants, where x is an integer variable, M is an array variable, and e_i as well as k are expressions. Variants (1) and (2) are not reversible, since both sides of the assignment can point to the same memory location. In this case, the result of the assignment is the result of modifying a value with itself, which potentially leads to a constant result, causing information to be destroyed. Variants (3) and (4) are not reversible, since the assignment may modify the index, that is used to access an array as part of the assignment. After the index has been modified, it is no longer possible to deterministically identify the values needed to reverse the assignment.

Since we need to compare the identifiers of variables to identify the variants above, it is crucial that two identifiers cannot refer to the same memory location at runtime to guarantee reversibility of assignments at runtime. This so-called *aliasing* can occur when the same variable is passed more than once as an argument to a procedure. Because parameters are passed by reference, the names of the parameters would then refer to the same memory location. This check is part of the semantic analysis, too.

3.2   Compiler Back-End

In this chapter, we are going to explain the translation for the most important Janus elements to RSSA, followed by some remarks on the translation from RSSA to C. To our knowledge, this is the first compiler not only handling reversible languages but also itself using reverse code.

Since Janus' semantics requires the reversal of code for some language features – for instance, to destroy all local variables with the inverse function used for the construction of these – we have chosen to build our compiler in a way that allows for the code generator to also emit inverse code in reverse order. Thus, for the language constructs requiring reversal, we have only implemented the forwards translation and let the code generator itself create the inverse code. A good example is the translation of the Janus' stack operations *push* and *pop*, where we only have implemented *push* and let the compiler work backwards when a *pop* operation occurs. In [18] a similar idea is described, but for an interpreter for Janus written in Janus itself.

More details will be provided below after the explanation of the basics of code generation.

3.3   Assignments and Expressions

Janus assignments to simple variables are of the form $V \oplus = E$, where $\oplus$ is a reversible operator. We will come to assignments to arrays in Subsect. 3.7. Mogensen defines assignments in RSSA in a similar fashion and allows $\oplus =$ to be either $+ =$, $- =$, $\hat{} =$. Hence, such assignments are reversible: $+ =$ and $- =$ are the inverse of each other, and $\hat{} =$ is inverse to itself.

While the translation of simple expressions such as constants and simple variables is straightforward, composite expressions with multiple operators require a split into multiple assignments to temporary variables as shown in Fig. 3. This is due to the fact that temporary variables will need to be destroyed again with a finalizer (see the fourth line in the example) to avoid producing garbage. As explained in the section about RSSA, we need to ensure that we use "fresh" versions of the variables to ensure that there is always at most one assignment to a variable. Hence, we append version numbers to the names of the variables – see the example depicted in Fig. 3 with the Janus code on the left- and the RSSA code on the right-hand side.

procedure main()	begin main(n0, m0)
int n	T0 := 0 ^ (2 * 3)
int m	n1 := n0 + (1 + T0)
	0 := T0 ^ (2 * 3)
n += 1+2*3	m1 := m0 + (n1 + 1)
m += n+1	end main(n1, m1)

Fig. 3. Example for translation of simple expressions

Note: While RSSA uses only a limited set of arithmetic operators, we have chosen to add the remaining Janus operators, too.

Janus also provides primitives to manipulate stacks and their translation will be shown in Subsect. 3.7.

3.4   If-Then-Else

The only means in RSSA for expressing conditions is via entry points and exit points: An exit point $C \to L_1(Y,\dots)L_2$ firstly evaluates the condition C, and if true, jumps to L_1, or to L_2 otherwise. Similarly, a conditional entry point $L_1(Y,\dots)L_2 \leftarrow C$ consists of two labels L_1 and L_2. Via the Ys parameters can be passed from an exit to an entry point. As previously explained, Φ-functions can thus easily be implemented in RSSA.

The parameters in the entry point will always have a higher version number than the corresponding parameters in the exit points to ensure proper SSA form.

Hence, for a Janus if-then-else statement *if C then S_1 else S_2 fi E*, we first evaluate the Boolean expression C and use it in a conditional exit point to label L_1 (if the condition was evaluated to true) or L_2 otherwise.

We then create the label $L_1(\dots)$ as an unconditional entry point, followed by the translation of S_1 and a jump to L_3. Now comes the else-part starting with label L_2 and ending in a jump to L_4. Lastly, we join both branches with the conditional entry point $L_3(\dots)L_4 \leftarrow E$ – see Fig. 4.

	n0 == 0 -> L1(n0)L2
	L1(n1) <-
if (n=0)	n2 := n1 + (1 ^ 0)
then n+=1	-> L3(n2)
else n-=1	L2(n3) <-
fi (n=1)	n4 := n3 - (1 ^ 0)
	-> L4(n4)
	L3(n5)L4 <- n5 == 1

Fig. 4. Example for translation of if-then-else statements

3.5   Loops

The translation of a loop *from C do S_1 loop S_2 until E* into RSSA basically follows the same rules as for the conditional statement. Firstly, we will unconditionally jump to L_1, which is used to mark the entry point of the loop. The condition is evaluated and used in a conditional entry point $L_1(\dots)L_3$ followed by the translation of the body S_1. Now, according to the semantics of Janus, we have to evaluate the end-condition E and conditionally jump to L_4, respectively L_2.

Label L_2 marks the body S_2 and thereafter, we jump back to the start of the loop at L_3. Lastly, we emit label L_4, which will be reached should the end-condition E evaluate to true.

Figure 5 shows a procedure that sums up all numbers from 0 to n and returns the result in r.

procedure sum(int n, int r)	begin sum(n0, r0)
local int k = 0	k0 := 0 ^ (0 ^ 0)
	-> L1(n0, k0, r0)
	L1(n1, k1, r1)L3 <- k1 == 0
from k = 0 do	r2 := r1 + (k1 ^ 0)
r += k	k1 == n1 -> L4(k1, n1, r2)L2
loop	L2(k2, n2, r3) <-
k += 1	k3 := k2 + (1 ^ 0)
until k = n	-> L3(n2, k3, r3)
	L4(k4, n3, r4) <-
delocal int k=n	0 := k4 ^ (n3 ^ 0)
	end sum(n3, r4)

Fig. 5. Example for translation of loops

3.6   Procedure Calls

Procedure calls can easily be translated to RSSA, since RSSA provides a call mechanism, too. Janus' procedure calls have already been designed in a careful way that avoids problems with reversibility. That is, call-by-reference is the only parameter-passing mode, there are no global variables, and it is not possible to use a variable multiple times in the same procedure call to prohibit aliasing. Hence, we can use the RSSA call statement $(y, \dots):=call\ l(x, \dots)$ where l will be the name of the called procedure, the x's are the parameters, which will be destroyed after the call in case they are variables. The final values of the parameters after the call will be copied into the y's. An example is shown in Fig. 6.

3.7   Arrays and Stacks

Arrays and stacks are the only type constructors available in Janus. Arrays provide, as one would expect, random access to a defined number of integers only in one dimension.

Since access to memory locations using $M[A]$ is restricted to specific operands and instructions in RSSA, code has to be generated to manage the memory used for arrays and stacks, as well as code to implement array access and operations on the stack. Suppose a has been declared as an array of 10 integer values, the RSSA code to access an array element $a[index]$ will contain the evaluation of

```
procedure inc(int n, int res)      begin inc(n0, res0)
    res += n                           res1 := res0 + (n0 ^ 0)
    res += 1                           res2 := res1 + (1 ^ 0)
                                   end inc(n0, res1)
procedure main()
    int i                          begin main(i0, x0)
    int x                              i1 := i0 + (10 ^ 0)
    i += 10                            (i2,x1) := call inc(i1,x0)
    call inc(i, x)                 end main(i2, x1)
```

Fig. 6. Example for translation of a procedure call

the index expression, add the result to the base address, e.g. $a_{ref} + index$ and assign it to a temporary variable T. After accessing the memory at address T, we need to destroy T with a finalizer. Lastly, we compute the reverse of the index expression (see Sect. 3.3).

In addition to arrays, Janus provides the feature to declare stacks as data structures. As usual, stacks can be manipulated using *empty*, *top*, *push*, and *pop* operations.

We have to add a remark here: The language definition of Janus [17] is – to our minds – not entirely clear about whether stacks can be assigned to each other, and what the semantics are (deep copy vs. shallow copy), e.g. *local stack s1=s2*. We have chosen to allow these kinds of assignments and apply deep copies. The implementation of this behaviour is encapsulated in a separate class and could easily be adapted to different semantics.

Please note that in RSSA M is not an identifier denoting the name of an array, rather M is fixed and stands for "memory", but can be addressed "like" an array.

Hence, the generated code for a stack s contains two variables s_{ref} and s_{top} with s_{ref} being the base address of the stack in memory and s_{top} pointing to the next free element of the stack.

A *push(n,s)* operation (n being a variable and s being a stack) will be translated into multiple RSSA commands: Firstly, we have to compute the address of the memory location where the value to be pushed will be stored, i.e. $s_{ref} + s_{top}$. Due to the limitations of RSSA, this address needs to be stored in a temporary variable $T0$. Now, $M[T0]$ needs to be updated with the current value of n. Moreover, the semantics of Janus is that the variable n will be "zero-cleared" thereafter. Hence, we use the special assignment $n1 := M[T0] := n$ as defined in RSSA, which will set the top-most element of the stack to n, destroy n, and store the former value into $n1$, i.e. the next version of n. In the subsequent RSSA instruction, it will be verified that $n1$ is zero. Lastly, we have to undo the computation of the temporary variable $T0$ with the inverse of its computation, and increment s_top.

As mentioned before, we have not defined the translation scheme for *pop*, rather we instruct the code generator to work backwards, i.e., the RSSA commands will be emitted in reverse order and each command will be inverted, that is, in an assignment left- and right-hand side are switched, plus becomes minus, etc.

The Java code for the implementation of the reverse code generator is remarkably small and itself uses a stack to intermediately store "forward" RSSA commands. Figure 7 shows an example.

procedure main()
  stack s
  int n
  int m
 	
  push(n, s)
  pop(m, s)
	begin main(s_ref0, s_top0, n0, m0)
	  // push(n,s)
	  T0 := 0 + (s_ref0 + s_top0)
	  n1 := M[T0] := n0
	  0 := 0 ^ (n1 ^ 0)
	  0 := T0 − (s_ref0 + s_top0)
	  s_top1 := s_top0 + (1 ^ 0)
	  // pop(m, s)
	  s_top2 := s_top1 − (1 ^ 0)
	  T1 := 0 + (s_ref1 + s_top2)
	  0 := 0 ^ (m0 ^ 0)
	  m1 := M[T1] := m0
	  0 := T1 − (s_ref1 + s_top2)
	end main(s_ref1, s_top2, n1, m1)

Fig. 7. Example for translation of stacks

3.8   Implementation

The translations, which are part of the RSSA backend, have been implemented as a syntax-directed translation, using the well-known visitor pattern [6].

For each of Janus' constructs, we have defined a translation scheme as explained above. When given the abstract syntax-tree of an input program, our backend traverses this tree and generates instructions according to the scheme. Statements are translated into a series of instructions, while expressions are mainly translated as operands. If it is not possible to translate an expression directly into a single operand, we need to emit instructions, which bind the value of the expression to a temporary variable and destroy this variable afterwards.

The output of our code generator is a list of the generated instructions. When an instruction is emitted during code generation, it is appended to the list.

As mentioned earlier, our code generator is capable of reverse code generation. This behavior is provided by a single method, that accepts an unparameterized lambda expression, whose body may contain arbitrary Java statements. Before these Java statements are executed, the internal state of the code generator is changed so that emitted instructions are no longer appended to the output list but rather to a temporary data structure. The Java statements passed to this method are then executed, which are able to emit instructions without being aware of the inverted generation direction. After the Java statements have been executed, the temporary data structure holds all instructions emitted by these statements. These instructions are then retrieved in reverse order and are inverted according to the rules described in [13] before they are emitted by the code generator.

Using this technique we were able to considerably reduce the amount of Java code in the code generator as opposed to the former code generator with "hand-crafted" reverse code.

4   Results

We have described rc3, consisting of a frontend for Janus as well a set of backends with RSSA being the most important of them.

Since the compiler developed by Axelsen [4] was not available to us, we used the online Janus interpreter ("Janus playground") [15] by Copenhagen University to compare the results of the execution of Janus test programs against our interpreter, RSSA, and Three-Address-Code back-ends.

Some results for sample Janus programs are shown in Table 2.

Table 2. Experiments

Sample Program		original	optimized
feistelcipher.ja	Janus loc	211	
	rssa instructions (loc)	598	531
	executed rssa instructions	61355	59152
C Exec	average c execution time in clocks	159	156
Janus-to-RSSA	average compile time in ms	189	228
Janus-to-RSSA-to-C	average compile time in ms	271	244
teax.ja	Janus loc	88	
	rssa instructions (loc)	632	418
	executed rssa instructions	30957	20513
C Exec	average c execution time in clocks	101	92
Janus-to-RSSA	average compile time in ms	163	191
Janus-to-RSSA-to-C	average compile time in ms	191	189
njvm-v4.ja + simple.bin	Janus loc	544	
	rssa instructions (loc)	2369	2109
	executed rssa instructions	24203	22440
C Exec	average c execution time in clocks	105	91
Janus-to-RSSA	average compile time in ms	573	671
Janus-to-RSSA-to-C	average compile time in ms	680	661

Feistelcipher and Teax are both programs implementing encryption schemes; NJVM is a virtual machine for a small imperative language. Lines of code are excluding empty lines as well as lines with comments only. As you can see, the time required for compilation even for the largest program is well below one second. For instance, the Feistelcipher Janus program is compiled to a program of 598 RSSA instructions. Running this program executes 61335 instructions in the version further compiled to C, requiring 159 microseconds. In case of the Teax program, the speedup through optimization (see Table 2) is 33%, measured in the number of RSSA instructions executed. All tests were executed on a Linux computer with an AMD Ryzen 5 processor with a clock speed of 3600 Mhz using GCC 10.2.0 to create executables from the generated C-code.

Due to the "classic" implementation of the compiler in multiple phases, it is easy to add more language features to Janus, as well as to add further backends.

The ability to translate Janus and RSSA each to two non-reversible C-programs has also been proven to be extremely helpful as it facilitates quick regression testing of the compiler.

The compiler including all three backends comprises roughly 12.500 lines of Java code (excluding the generated lexer and parser). As you can see, the generated RSSA code is typically 3–7 times longer than the original Janus code, mostly due to the split of complex expressions into SSA's and the insertion of finalizers.

The C-Code generated from the RSSA code is considerably longer, mainly due to the insertion of C-functions for memory management, and of course because C-code is generated twice (forwards and backwards).

5   Conclusions and Outlook

We have shown a scheme for compiling reversible Janus programs into reversible RSSA code including the novel method for reverse code generation. The compiler has been implemented and is being extended to be able to optimize the generated RSSA code. In addition, a virtual machine for RSSA has been created that includes a debugger with a GDB-like CLI, allowing to step through the program forwards and backwards.

Mogensen [13] provides some suggestions on potential optimizations, further work or implementations of these are currently not known to us.

As per the time of writing of this paper, we have implemented local common subexpression elimination and constant propagation/folding (i.e., within a building block) using a directed acyclic multigraph. Work is underway to explore data-flow analysis of RSSA – however, the inherent requirements of reversible computing seem to require extensions of "traditional" algorithms to be able to apply them to reversible languages: Traditional data flow analysis determines IN and OUT sets either in a forwards manner, i.e. stepping from one basic block to its successors or vice versa. But, in a reversible world, "forwards" and "backwards" in terms of the direction of execution are not distinguishable, making the application of these well-known algorithms by Kildall [8] and others quite difficult.

A report on first optimizations (local common-subexpression elimination and constant propagation/folding) on the generated RSSA code will be presented at

ACM SOAP 2021. Future work will also include the formalization of the code generation scheme from Janus to RSSA, as well as a more detailed description of the compiler techniques applied for the reverse code generator.

The current state of the work looks very promising and should be helpful to gain further insights into reversible programming languages and compilers.

Acknowledgements. We would like to thank the reviewers who had provided valuable feedback and suggestions for improvement.

References

1. Aho, A.V., Sethi, R., Ullman, J.D.: Compilers: Principles, Techniques, and Tools. Addison-Wesley, Reading (1986)
2. Alpern, B., Wegman, M.N., Zadeck, F.K.: Detecting equality of variables in programs. In: Ferrante, J., Mager, P. (eds.) Principles of Programming Languages (POPL 1988), pp. 1–11. ACM Press (1988). https://doi.org/10.1145/73560.73561
3. Appel, A.W.: Modern Compiler Implementation in Java. Cambridge University Press, Cambridge (1998)
4. Axelsen, H.B.: Clean translation of an imperative reversible programming language. In: Knoop, J. (ed.) CC 2011. LNCS, vol. 6601, pp. 144–163. Springer, Heidelberg (2011). https://doi.org/10.1007/978-3-642-19861-8_9
5. Frank, M.P.: The future of computing depends on making it reversible. IEEE Spectrum, September 2017
6. Gamma, E., Helm, R., Johnson, R., Vlissides, J.: Design Patterns: Elements of Reusable Object-Oriented Software. Addison-Wesley, Boston (1995)
7. Hudson, S., Flannery, F., Scott Ananian, C., Petter, M.: CUP User's Manual. Technische Universität München, v0.11b edn. (2014) http://www2.in.tum.de/projects/cup/docs.php
8. Kildall, G.A.: A unified approach to global program optimization. In: Fischer, P.C., Ullman, J.D. (eds.) Principles of Programming Languages (POPL 1973), pp. 194–206. ACM Press (1973)
9. Klein, G., Rowe, S., Décamps, R.: JFlex User's Manual, version 1.8.2 edn. (2020). https://www.jflex.de/manual.html
10. Landauer, R.: Irreversibility and heat generation in the computing process. IBM J. Res. Dev. **5**(3), 183–191 (1961)
11. Lutz, C.: Janus - A Time-Reversible Language (1986), http://tetsuo.jp/ref/janus.pdf, Letter to R. Landauer
12. Mogensen, T.Æ.: Partial evaluation of the reversible language Janus. In: Khoo, S., Siek, J.G. (eds.) SIGPLAN Workshop on Partial Evaluation and Program Manipulation (PEPM 2011), pp. 23–32. ACM Press (2011). https://doi.org/10.1145/1929501.1929506
13. Mogensen, T.Æ.: RSSA: a reversible SSA form. In: Mazzara, M., Voronkov, A. (eds.) PSI 2015. LNCS, vol. 9609, pp. 203–217. Springer, Cham (2016). https://doi.org/10.1007/978-3-319-41579-6_16
14. Muchnick, S.S.: Advanced Compiler Design and Implementation. Morgan Kaufmann (1997)
15. Nielsen, C.S., Budde, M., Thomsen, M.K.: Program Inversion and Reversible Computation - Janus Extended Playground http://topps.diku.dk/pirc/?id=janusP

16. Rosen, B.K., Wegman, M.N., Zadeck, F.K.: Global value numbers and redundant computations. In: Ferrante, J., Mager, P. (eds.) Principles of Programming Languages (POPL 1988), pp. 12–27. ACM Press (1988). https://doi.org/10.1145/73560.73562
17. Yokoyama, T., Axelsen, H.B., Glück, R.: Principles of a reversible programming language. In: Ramírez, A., Bilardi, G., Gschwind, M. (eds.) Computing Frontiers, pp. 43–54. ACM Press (2008). https://doi.org/10.1145/1366230.1366239
18. Yokoyama, T., Glück, R.: A reversible programming language and its invertible self-interpreter. In: Ramalingam, G., Visser, E. (eds.) SIGPLAN Workshop on Partial Evaluation and Semantics-based Program Manipulation (PEPM 2007), pp. 144–153. ACM Press (2007). https://doi.org/10.1145/1244381.1244404
19. Yokoyama, T., Axelsen, H.B., Glück, R.: Fundamentals of reversible flowchart languages. Theoret. Comput. Sci. **611**, 87–115 (2016). https://doi.org/10.1016/j.tcs.2015.07.046

Causal-Consistent Debugging
of Distributed Erlang Programs

Giovanni Fabbretti[1]($\boxtimes$)(iD), Ivan Lanese[2]($\boxtimes$)(iD), and Jean-Bernard Stefani[1]($\boxtimes$)(iD)

[1] Université Grenoble Alpes, INRIA, CNRS, Grenoble INP, LIG,
38000 Grenoble, France
{giovanni.fabbretti,jean-bernard.stefani}@inria.fr
[2] Focus Team, University of Bologna, INRIA, 40137 Bologna, Italy

Abstract. Debugging concurrent programs is an interesting application of reversibility. It has been renewed with the recent proposal by
Giachino et al. to base the operations of a concurrent debugger on a
causal-consistent reversible semantics, and subsequent work on CauDEr,
a causal-consistent debugger for the Erlang programming language. This
paper extends CauDEr and the related theory with the support for distributed programs. Our extension allows one to debug programs in which
processes can run on different nodes, and new nodes can be created at
runtime. From the theoretical point of view, the primitives for distributed
programming give rise to more complex causal structures than those arising from the concurrent fragment of Erlang handled in CauDEr, yet we
show that the main results proved for CauDEr still hold. From the practical point of view, we show how to use our extension of CauDEr to find
a non trivial bug in a simple way.

Keywords: Debugging · Actor model · Distributed computation ·
Reversible computing

1 Introduction

Debugging concurrent programs is an interesting application of reversibility. A
reversible debugger allows one to explore a program execution by going forward –
letting the program execute normally –, or backward – rolling back the program
execution by undoing the effect of previously executed instructions. Several works
have explored this idea in the past, see, e.g., the survey in [6], and reversible
debugging is used in mainstream tools as well [21]. It is only recently, however,
that the idea of a causal-consistent debugger has been proposed by Giachino et
al. in [10]. The key idea in [10] was to base the debugger primitives on a causal-
consistent reversible semantics for the target programming language. Causal

The work has been partially supported by French ANR project DCore ANR-18-CE25-
0007.
I. Lanese—partially supported by INdAM – GNCS 2020 project *Sistemi Reversibili
Concorrenti: dai Modelli ai Linguaggi*.

S. Yamashita and T. Yokoyama (Eds.): RC 2021, LNCS 12805, pp. 79–95, 2021.
https://doi.org/10.1007/978-3-030-79837-6_5

consistency, introduced by Danos and Krivine in their seminal work on reversible CCS [5], allows one, in reversing a concurrent execution, to undo any event provided that its consequences, if any, are undone first. On top of a causal-consistent semantics one can define a rollback operator [15] to undo an arbitrary past action. It provides a minimality guarantee, useful to explore concurrent programs which are prone to state explosion, in that only events in the causal future of a target one are undone, and not events that are causally independent but which may have been interleaved in the execution.

The CauDEr debugger [11,17,18] builds on these ideas and provides a reversible debugger for a core subset of the Erlang programming language [3]. Erlang is interesting for it mixes functional programming with a concurrency model inspired by actors [1], and has been largely applied since its initial uses by Ericsson[1], to build distributed infrastructures.

This paper presents an extension of CauDEr to take into account distribution primitives which are not part of the core subset of Erlang handled by CauDEr. Specifically, we additionally consider the three Erlang primitives called start, to create a new node for executing Erlang processes, node, to retrieve the identifier of the current node, and nodes, which allows the current process to obtain a list of all the currently active nodes in an Erlang system. We also extend the spawn primitive handled by CauDEr to take as additional parameter the node on which to create a new Erlang process.

Adding support for these primitives is non trivial for they introduce causal dependencies in Erlang programs that are different than those originating from the functional and concurrent fragment considered in CauDEr, which covers, beyond sequential constructs, only message passing and process creation on the current node. Indeed, the set of nodes acts as a shared set variable that can be read, checked for membership, and extended with new elements. Interestingly, the causal dependencies induced by this shared set cannot be faithfully represented in the general model for reversing languages introduced in [14], which allows for resources that can only be produced and consumed.

The contributions of the current work are therefore as follows: (i) we extend the reversible semantics for the core subset of the Erlang language used by CauDEr with the above distribution primitives; (ii) we present a rollback semantics that underlies primitives in our extended CauDEr debugger; (iii) we have implemented an extension of the CauDEr debugger that handles Erlang programs written in our distributed fragment of the language; (iv) we illustrate on an example how our CauDEr extension can be used in capturing subtle bugs in distributed Erlang programs. Due to space constraints, we do not detail in this paper our extended CauDEr implementation, but the code is publicly available in the dedicated GitHub repository [8].

The rest of this paper is organized as follows. Section 2 briefly recalls the reversible semantics on which CauDER is based [19]. Section 3 presents the Erlang distributed language fragment we consider in our CauDEr extension, its

---

[1] erlang-solutions.com/blog/which-companies-are-using-erlang-and-why-mytopdogstatus.html.

$$module ::= fun_1 \ldots fun_n$$
$$fun ::= fname = \text{fun } (X_1, \ldots, X_n) \rightarrow expr$$
$$fname ::= Atom/Integer$$
$$lit ::= Atom \mid Integer \mid Float \mid [\,]$$
$$expr ::= Var \mid lit \mid fname \mid [expr_1|expr_2] \mid \{expr_1, \ldots, expr_n\}$$
$$\mid \text{ call } expr \ (expr_1, \ldots, expr_n) \mid \text{apply } expr \ (expr_1, \ldots, expr_n)$$
$$\mid \text{ case } expr \text{ of } clause_1; \ldots; clause_m \text{ end}$$
$$\mid \text{ let } Var = expr_1 \text{ in } expr_2 \mid \text{receive } clause_1; \ldots; clause_n \text{ end}$$
$$\mid \text{ spawn}(expr, [expr_1, \ldots, expr_n]) \mid expr_1 \,!\, expr_2 \mid \text{self}()$$
$$clause ::= pat \text{ when } expr_1 \rightarrow expr_2$$
$$pat ::= Var \mid lit \mid [pat_1|pat_2] \mid \{pat_1, \ldots, pat_n\}$$

Fig. 1. Language syntax

reversible semantics and the corresponding rollback semantics. Section 4 briefly describes our extension to CauDEr, and presents an example that illustrates bug finding in distributed Erlang programs with our extended CauDEr. Section 5 discusses related work and concludes the paper with hints for future work. Due to space constraints we omit some technicalities, for further details we refer the interested read to the companion technical report [9] or to the master thesis of the first author [7].

2 Background

We recall here the main aspects of the language in [19], as needed to understand our extension. We refer the interested reader to [19] for further details.

2.1 The Language Syntax

Figure 1 shows the language syntax. The language depicted is a fragment of Core Erlang [2], an intermediate step in Erlang compilation. A module is a collection of function definitions, a function is a mapping between the function name and the function expression. An expression can be a variable, a literal, a function name, a list, a tuple, a call to a built-in function, a function application, a case expression, or a let binding. An expression can also be a spawn, a send, a receive, or a self, which are built-in functions. Finally, we distinguish expressions, patterns and variables. Here, patterns are built from variables, tuples, lists and literals, while values are built from literals, tuples and lists, i.e., they are ground patterns. When we have a case e of ... expression we first evaluate e to a value, say v, then we search for a clause that matches v. When one is found, if the guard when $expr$ is satisfied then the case construct evaluates to the clause expression, otherwise the search continues with the next clause. The let $X = expr_1$ in $expr_2$ expression binds inside $expr_2$ the fresh variable X to the value to which $expr_1$ reduces.

As for the concurrent features, since Erlang implements the actor model, there is no shared memory. An Erlang system is a pool of processes that interact by exchanging messages. Each process is uniquely identified by its pid and has its own queue of incoming messages. Function spawn $(expr, [expr_1, \ldots, expr_n])$ evaluates to a fresh process pid p. As a side-effect, it creates a new process with pid p. Process p will apply the function to which $expr$ evaluates to the arguments to which the expressions $expr_1, \ldots, expr_n$ evaluate. As in [19], we assume that the only way to introduce a new pid is through the evaluation of a spawn. Then, $expr_1 \,!\, expr_2$ allows a process to send a message to another one. Expression $expr_1$ must evaluate to a pid (identifying the receiver process) and $expr_2$ evaluates to the content of the message, say v. The whole function evaluates to v and, as a side-effect, the message will eventually be stored in the receiver queue. The counterpart of message sending is receive $clause_1, \ldots, clause_n$ end. This construct traverses the queue of messages searching for the first message v that matches one of the n clauses. If no message is found then the process suspends. Finally, self evaluates to the current process pid.

2.2   The Language Semantics

This subsection provides key elements to understand the CauDEr semantics. We start with the definition of process.

Definition 1 (Process). *A process is denoted by a tuple* $\langle p, \theta, e, q \rangle$, *where* p *is the process' pid,* θ *is an environment, i.e. a map from variables to their actual value,* e *is the current expression to evaluate, and* q *is the queue of messages received by the process.*

Two operations are allowed on queues: $v : q$ *denotes the addition of a new message on top of the queue and* $q \backslash\!\backslash v$ *denotes the queue* q *after removing* v *(note that* v *may not be the first message).*

A (running) system can be seen as a pool of running processes.

Definition 2 (System). *A system is denoted by the tuple* $\Gamma; \Pi$. *The global mailbox* Γ *is a multiset of pairs of the form* $(target\_process\_pid, \ message)$, *where a message is stored after being sent and before being scheduled to its receiver.* Π *is the pool of processes, denoted by an expression of the form*

$$\langle p_1, \theta_1, e_1, q_1 \rangle \mid \ldots \mid \langle p_n, \theta_n, e_n, q_n \rangle$$

where "$\mid$*" is an associative and commutative operator.* $\Gamma \cup \{(p, v)\}$, *where* $\cup$ *is multiset union, is the global mailbox obtained by adding the pair* (p, v) *to* Γ. *We write* $p \in \Gamma; \Pi$ *when* Π *contains a process with pid* p.

We highlight a process p in a system by writing $\Gamma; \langle p, \theta, e, q \rangle \mid \Pi$. The presence of the global mailbox Γ, which is similar to the "ether" in [24], allows one to simulate all the possible interleavings of messages. Indeed, in this semantics the order of the messages exchanged between two processes belonging to the same runtime may not be respected, differently from what happens in current Erlang implementations. See [24] for a discussion on this design choice.

The semantics in [19] is defined in a modular way, similarly to the one presented in [4], i.e., there is a semantics for the expression level and one for the system level. This approach simplifies the design of the reversible semantics since only the system one needs to be updated. The expression semantics is defined as a labelled transition relation of the form:

$$\{Env, Expr\} \times Label \times \{Env, Expr\}$$

where Env represents the environment, i.e., a substitution, and $Expr$ denotes the expression, while $Label$ is an element of the following set:

$$\{\tau, \mathsf{send}(v_1, v_2), \mathsf{rec}(\kappa, \overline{cl_n}), \mathsf{spawn}(\kappa, a/n, [\overline{v_n}]), \mathsf{self}(\kappa)\}$$

The semantics is a classical call-by-value semantics for a first order language. Label τ denotes the evaluation of a (sequential) expression without side-effects, like the evaluation of a case expression or a let binding. The remaining labels denote a side-effect associated to the rule execution or the request of some needed information. The system semantics will use the label to execute the associated side-effect or to provide the necessary information. More precisely, in label $\mathsf{send}(v_1, v_2)$, v_1 and v_2 represent the pid of the sender and the value of a message. In label $\mathsf{rec}(\kappa, \overline{cl_n})$, $\overline{cl_n}$ denotes the n clauses of a receive expression. Inside label $\mathsf{spawn}(\kappa, a/n, [\overline{v_n}])$, a/n represents the function name, while $[\overline{v_n}]$ is the (possibly empty) list of arguments of the function. Where used, κ acts as a future: the expression evaluates to κ, then the corresponding system rule replaces it with its actual value.

For space reasons, we do not show here the system rules, which are available in [19]. We will however show in the next section how sample rules are extended to support reversibility.

2.3 A Reversible Semantics

The reversible semantics is composed by two relations: a *forward* relation $\rightharpoonup$ and a *backward* relation $\leftharpoondown$. The forward reversible semantics is a natural extension of the system semantics by using a typical *Landauer embedding* [13]. The idea underlying Landauer's work is that any formalism or programming language can be made reversible by adding the *history* of the computation at each state. Hence, this semantics at each step saves in an external device, called history, the previous state of the computation so that later on such a state can be restored. The backward semantics allows us to undo a step while ensuring causal consistency [5, 16], indeed before undoing an action we must ensure that all its consequences have been undone.

In the reversible semantics each message exchanged must be uniquely identified in order to allow one to undo the sending of the "right" message, hence we denote messages with the tuple $\{\lambda, v\}$, where λ is the unique identifier and v the message body. See [19] for a discussion on this design choice.

Due to the Landauer embedding the notion of process is extended as follows.

$(Spawn)$ $\dfrac{\theta, e \xrightarrow{\text{spawn}(\kappa, a/n, [\overline{v_n}])} \theta', e' \quad p' \text{ is a fresh identifier}}{\Gamma; \langle p, h, \theta, e, q \rangle \mid \Pi \rightarrow \Gamma; \langle p, \text{spawn}(\theta, e, p') : h, \theta', e'\{\kappa \mapsto p'\}, q \rangle}$
$\qquad\qquad\qquad\qquad\qquad\qquad\qquad\qquad\quad \mid \langle p', [\,], id, \text{apply } a/n(\overline{v_n}), [\,] \rangle \mid \Pi$

$(\overline{Spawn})$ $\Gamma; \langle p, \text{spawn}(\theta, e, p') : h, \theta', e', q \rangle \mid \langle p', [\,], id, e'', [\,] \rangle \mid \Pi \leftarrow \Gamma; \langle p, h, \theta, e, q \rangle \mid \Pi$

Fig. 2. An example of a rule belonging to the forward semantics and its counterpart.

Definition 3 (Process). *A process is denoted by a tuple* $\langle p, h, \theta, e, q \rangle$, *where* h *is the* history *of the process. The other elements are as in Definition 1. The expression* $\text{op}(\ldots) : h$ *denotes the history* h *with a new history item added on top. The generic history item* $\text{op}(\ldots)$ *can span over the following set.*

$$\{\tau(\theta, e), \text{send}(\theta, e, \{\lambda, v\}), \text{rec}(\theta, e, \{\lambda, v\}, q), \text{spawn}(\theta, e, p), \text{self}(\theta, e)\}$$

Here, each history item carries the information needed to restore the previous state of the computation. For rules that do not cause causal dependencies (i.e., τ and self) it is enough to save θ and e. For the other rules we must carry additional information to check that every consequence has been undone before restoring the previous state. We refer to [19] for further details.

Figure 2 shows a sample rule from the forward semantics (additions w.r.t. the standard system rule are highlighted in red) and its counterpart from the backward semantics. In the premises of the rule *Spawn* we can see the expression-level semantics in action, transitioning from the configuration (θ, e) to (θ', e') and the corresponding label that the forward semantics uses to determine the associated side-effect. When rule *Spawn* is applied the system transits in a new state where process p' is added to the pool of processes and the history of process p is enriched with the corresponding history item. Finally, the forward semantics takes care of updating the value of the future κ by substituting it with the pid p' of the new process.

The reverse rule, $\overline{Spawn}$, can be applied only when all the consequences of the spawn, namely every action performed by the spawned process p', have been undone. Such constraint is enforced by requiring the history of the spawned process to be empty. Since the last history item of p is the spawn, and thanks to the assumption that every new pid, except for the first process, is introduced by evaluating a spawn, we are sure that there are no pending messages for p'. Then, if the history is empty, we can remove the process p' from Π and we can restore p to the previous state.

3 Distributed Reversible Semantics for Erlang

In this section we discuss how the syntax and the reversible semantics introduced in the previous section have been updated to tackle the three distribution primitives start, node and nodes. Lastly, we extend the rollback operator introduced in [19,20], which allows one to undo an arbitrary past action together with all and only its consequences, to support distribution.

3.1 Distributed System Semantics

The updated syntax is like the one in Fig. 1, with the only difference that now *expr* can also be start(e), node() and nodes(), and spawn takes an extra argument that represents the node where the new process must be spawned.

Let us now briefly discuss the semantics of the new primitives. First, in function start, e must evaluate to a node identifier (also called a nid), which is an atom of the form 'name@host'. Then, the function, as a side-effect, starts a new node, provided that no node with the same identifier exists in the network, and evaluates to the node identifier in case of success or to an error in case of failure. Node identifiers, contrarily to pids which are always generated fresh, can be hardcoded, as it usually happens in Erlang. Also, function node evaluates to the local node identifier. Finally, function nodes evaluates to the list (possibly empty) of nodes to which the executing node is connected. A formalization of the intuition above can be found in [7]. Here, we assume that each node has an atomic view of the network, therefore we do not consider network partitioning.

Notions of process and system are updated to cope with the extension above.

Definition 4 (Process). *A process is denoted by a tuple $\langle nid, p, \theta, e, q \rangle$, where nid is an atom of the form name@host, called a node identifier (nid), pointing to the node on which the process is running. For the other elements of the tuple the reader can refer to Definition 1.*

The updated definitions of node and network follow.

Definition 5 (Node and network). *A node is a pool of processes, identified by a nid. A network, denoted by Ω, is a set of nids. Hence, nids in a network should all be distinct.*

Now, we can proceed to give the formal definition of a distributed system.

Definition 6 (Distributed system). *A distributed system is a tuple $\Gamma; \Pi; \Omega$. The global mailbox Γ and the pool of running processes Π are as before (but processes now include a nid). Instead, Ω represents the set of nodes connected to the network. We will use $\cup$ to denote set union.*

3.2 Causality

To understand the following development, one needs not only the operational semantics informally discussed above, but also a notion of causality. Indeed, backward rules can undo an action only if all its causal consequences have been undone, and forward rules should store enough information to both decide whether this is the case and, if so, to restore the previous state.

Thus, to guide the reader, we discuss below the possible causal links among the distribution primitives (including spawn). About the functional and concurrent primitives, the only dependencies are that a message receive is a consequence of the scheduling of the same message to the target process, which is a consequence of its send[2].

---

[2] For technical reasons the formalization provides an approximation of this notion.

$(SpawnS)$
$$\dfrac{\theta, e \xrightarrow{\mathsf{spawn}(\kappa, nid', a/n, [\overline{v_n}])} \theta', e' \quad p' \text{ is a fresh pid} \quad nid' \in \Omega}{\begin{aligned}\Gamma; \langle nid, p, h, \theta, e, q\rangle \mid \Pi; \Omega \rightharpoonup \Gamma; \langle nid, p, \mathsf{spawn}(\theta, e, nid', p') : h, \theta', e'\{\kappa \mapsto p'\}, q\rangle \\ \mid \langle nid', p', [\,], id, \mathsf{apply}\ a/n(\overline{v_n}), [\,]\rangle \mid \Pi; \Omega\end{aligned}}$$

$(SpawnF)$
$$\dfrac{\theta, e \xrightarrow{\mathsf{spawn}(\kappa, nid', a/n, [\overline{v_n}])} \theta', e' \quad p' \text{ is a fresh pid} \quad nid' \notin \Omega}{\Gamma; \langle nid, p, h, \theta, e, q\rangle \mid \Pi; \Omega \rightharpoonup \Gamma; \langle nid, p, \mathsf{spawn}(\theta, e, nid', p') : h, \theta', e'\{\kappa \mapsto p'\}, q\rangle \mid \Pi; \Omega}$$

$(StartS)$
$$\dfrac{\theta, e \xrightarrow{\mathsf{start}(\kappa, nid')} \theta', e' \quad nid' \notin \Omega}{\begin{aligned}\Gamma; \langle nid, p, h, \theta, e, q\rangle \mid \Pi; \Omega \rightharpoonup \\ \Gamma; \langle nid, p, \mathsf{start}(\theta, e, \mathsf{succ}, nid') : h, \theta', e'\{\kappa \mapsto nid'\}, q\rangle \mid \Pi; \{nid'\} \cup \Omega\end{aligned}}$$

$(StartF)$
$$\dfrac{\theta, e \xrightarrow{\mathsf{start}(\kappa, nid')} \theta', e' \quad nid' \in \Omega \quad err \text{ represents the error}}{\Gamma; \langle nid, p, h, \theta, e, q\rangle \mid \Pi; \Omega \rightharpoonup \Gamma; \langle nid, p, \mathsf{start}(\theta, e, \mathsf{fail}, nid') : h, \theta', e'\{\kappa \mapsto err\}, q\rangle \mid \Pi; \Omega}$$

$(Node)$
$$\dfrac{\theta, e \xrightarrow{\mathsf{node}(\kappa)} \theta', e'}{\Gamma; \langle nid, p, h, \theta, e, q\rangle \mid \Pi; \Omega \rightharpoonup \Gamma; \langle nid, p, \mathsf{node}(\theta, e) : h, \theta', e'\{\kappa \mapsto nid\}, q\rangle \mid \Pi; \Omega}$$

$(Nodes)$
$$\dfrac{\theta, e \xrightarrow{\mathsf{nodes}(\kappa)} \theta', e'}{\begin{aligned}\Gamma; \langle nid, p, h, \theta, e, q\rangle \mid \Pi; \Omega \rightharpoonup \\ \Gamma; \langle nid, p, \mathsf{nodes}(\theta, e, \Omega) : h, \theta', e'\{\kappa \mapsto list(\Omega \setminus \{nid\})\}, q\rangle \mid \Pi; \Omega\end{aligned}}$$

Fig. 3. Distributed forward reversible semantics

Intuitively, there is a dependency between two consecutive actions if either they cannot be executed in the opposite order (e.g., a message cannot be scheduled before having been sent), or by executing them in the opposite order the result would change (e.g., by swapping a successful start and a nodes the result of the nodes would change).

Beyond the fact that later actions in the same process are a consequence of earlier actions, we have the following dependencies:

1. every action of process p depends on the (successful) spawn of p;
2. a (successful) spawn on node nid depends on the start of nid;
3. a (successful) start of node nid depends on previous failed spawns on the same node, if any (if we swap the order, the spawn will succeed);
4. a failed start of node nid depends on its (successful) start;
5. a nodes reading a set Ω depends on the start of all nids in Ω, if any (as discussed above).

3.3 Distributed Forward Reversible Semantics

Figure 3 shows the forward semantics of distribution primitives, which are described below. The other rules are as in the original work [19] but for the introduction of Ω.

$$(\overline{SpawnS})\quad \begin{array}{l}\Gamma; \langle nid, p, \mathsf{spawn}(\theta, e, nid', p') : h, \theta', e', q\rangle \mid \langle nid', p', [\,], id, e'', [\,]\rangle \mid \Pi; \Omega \\ \quad \leftharpoondown_{p,\mathsf{spawn}(p'),\{s,sp_{p'}\}} \Gamma; \langle nid, p, h, \theta, e, q\rangle \mid \Pi; \Omega\end{array}$$

$$(\overline{SpawnF})\quad \begin{array}{l}\Gamma; \langle nid, p, \mathsf{spawn}(\theta, e, nid', p') : h, \theta', e', q\rangle \mid \Pi; \Omega \\ \quad \leftharpoondown_{p,\mathsf{spawn}(p'),\{s,sp_{p'}\}} \Gamma; \langle nid, p, h, \theta, e, q\rangle \mid \Pi; \Omega \\ \quad \text{if } nid' \notin \Omega\end{array}$$

$$(\overline{StartS})\quad \begin{array}{l}\Gamma; \langle nid, p, \mathsf{start}(\theta, e, \mathsf{succ}, nid') : h, \theta', e', q\rangle \mid \Pi; \Omega \cup \{nid'\} \\ \quad \leftharpoondown_{p,\mathsf{start}(nid'),\{s,st_{nid'}\}} \Gamma; \langle nid, p, h, \theta, e, q\rangle \mid \Pi; \Omega \\ \text{if } spawns(nid', \Pi) = [\,] \wedge reads(nid', \Pi) = [\,] \wedge failed_starts(nid', \Pi) = [\,]\end{array}$$

$$(\overline{StartF})\quad \begin{array}{l}\Gamma; \langle nid, p, \mathsf{start}(\theta, e, \mathsf{fail}, nid') : h, \theta', e', q\rangle \mid \Pi; \Omega \\ \quad \leftharpoondown_{p,\mathsf{start}(nid'),\{s\}} \Gamma; \langle nid, p, h, \theta, e, q\rangle \mid \Pi; \Omega\end{array}$$

$$(\overline{Node})\quad \Gamma; \langle nid, p, \mathsf{node}(\theta, e) : h, \theta', e', q\rangle \mid \Pi; \Omega \leftharpoondown_{p,\mathsf{node},\{s\}} \Gamma; \langle nid, p, h, \theta, e, q\rangle \mid \Pi; \Omega$$

$$(\overline{Nodes})\quad \begin{array}{l}\Gamma; \langle nid, p, \mathsf{nodes}(\theta, e, \Omega') : h, \theta', e', q\rangle \mid \Pi; \Omega \leftharpoondown_{p,\mathsf{nodes},\{s\}} \Gamma; \langle nid, p, h, \theta, e, q\rangle \mid \Pi; \Omega \\ \quad \text{if } \Omega = \Omega'\end{array}$$

Fig. 4. Extended backward reversible semantics

The forward semantics in [19] has just one rule for spawn, since it can never fail. Here, instead, a spawn can fail if the node fed as first argument is not part of Ω. Nonetheless, following the approach of Erlang, we always return a fresh pid, independently on whether the spawn has failed or not. Also, the history item created in both cases is the same. Indeed, thanks to uniqueness of pids, one can ascertain whether the spawn of p' has been successful or not just by checking whether there is a process with pid p' in the system: if there is, the spawn succeeded, otherwise it failed. Hence, the unique difference between rules *SpawnS* and *SpawnF* is that a new process is created only in rule *SpawnS*.

Similarly, two rules describe the start function: rule *StartS* for a successful start, which updates Ω by adding the new nid nid', and rule *StartF* for a start which fails because a node with the same nid already exists. Here, contrarily to the spawn case, the two rules create different history items. Indeed, if two or more processes had a same history item $\mathsf{start}(\theta, e, nid)$, then it would not be possible to decide which one performed the start first (and, hence, succeeded).

Lastly, the *Nodes* rule aves, together with θ and e, the current value of Ω. This is needed to check dependencies on the start executions, as discussed in Sect. 3.2. The *Node* rule, since node is a sequential operation, just saves the environment and the current expression.

3.4 Distributed Backward Reversible Semantics

Figure 4 depicts the backward semantics of the distribution primitives.

The semantics is defined in terms of the relation $\leftharpoondown_{p,r,\Psi}$, where:

- p represents the pid of the process performing the backward transition
- r describes which action has been undone
- Ψ lists the requests satisfied by the backward transition (the supported requests are listed in Sect. 3.5)

These labels will come into play later on, while defining the rollback semantics. We may drop them when not relevant.

As already discussed, to undo an action, we need to ensure that its consequences, if any, have been undone before. When consequences in other processes may exist, side conditions are used to check that they have already been undone.

Rule $\overline{SpawnS}$ is analogous to rule $\overline{Spawn}$ in Fig. 2. Rule $\overline{SpawnF}$ undoes a failed spawn. As discussed in Sect. 3.2, we first need to undo, if any, a start of a node with the target nid, otherwise the spawn will now succeed. To this end, we check that $nid' \notin \Omega$.

Then, we have rule $\overline{StartS}$ to undo the (successful) creation of node nid'. Before applying it we need to ensure three conditions: (i) that no process is running on node nid'; (ii) that no nodes has read nid'; and (iii) that no other start of a node with identifier nid' failed. The conditions, discussed in Sect. 3.2, are checked by ensuring that the lists of pids computed by auxiliary functions $spawns$, $reads$ and $failed\_starts$ are empty. Indeed, they compute the list of pids of processes in Π that have performed, respectively, a spawn on nid', a nodes returning a set containing nid', and a failed start of a node with identifier nid. Condition (i) needs to be checked since nids are hardcoded, hence any process could perform a spawn on nid'. The check would be redundant if nids would be created fresh by the start function.

Rule $\overline{StartF}$ instead requires no side condition: start fails only if the node already exists, but this condition remains true afterwards, since we do not have primitives to stop a node. Rule $\overline{Node}$ has no dependency either.

To execute rule $\overline{Nodes}$ we must ensure that the value of Ω' in the history item and of Ω in the system are the same, as discussed in Sect. 3.2.

We now report a fundamental result of the reversible semantics. As most of our results, it holds for *reachable* systems, that is systems that can be obtained using the rules of the semantics from a single process with empty history.

Lemma 1 (Loop Lemma). *For every pair of reachable systems, s_1 and s_2, we have $s_1 \rightharpoonup s_2$ iff $s_2 \leftharpoonup s_1$.*

Proof. The proof that a forward transition can be undone follows by rule inspection. The other direction relies on the restriction to reachable systems: consider the process undoing the action. Since the system is reachable, restoring the memory item would put us back in a state where the undone action can be performed again (if the system would not be reachable the memory item would be arbitrary, hence there would not be such a guarantee), as desired. Again, this can be proved by rule inspection.   □

Note that, as exemplified above, this result would fail if we allow one to undo an action before its consequences.

3.5   Distributed Rollback Semantics

Since undoing steps one by one may be tedious and unproductive for the developer, CauDEr provides a rollback operator, that allows the developer to undo several steps in an automatic manner, while maintaining causal consistency. We extend it to cope with distribution. Our definition takes inspiration from the formalization style used in [20], but it improves it and applies it to a system with explicit local queues for messages. Dealing with explicit local queues is not trivial. Indeed, without local queues, the receive primitive takes messages directly from Γ. With local queues we use a rule called *Sched* to move a message from Γ to the local queue of the target process, and the receive takes the message from the local queue. A main point is that the *Sched* action does not create an item in the history of the process receiving the message, and as a result it is concurrent to all other actions of the same process but receive. We refer to [19] for a formalization of rule *Sched* and of its inverse. When during a rollback both a $\overline{Sched}$ and another backward transition are enabled at the same time one has to choose which one to undo, and selecting the wrong one may violate the property that only consequences of the target action are undone.

We denote a system in rollback mode by $[\![\mathcal{S}]\!]_{\{p,\psi\}}$, where the subscript means that we wish to undo the action ψ performed by process p and every action which depends on it. More generally, the subscript of $[\![\ ]\!]$, often depicted with Ψ or Ψ' (where Ψ can be empty while Ψ' cannot), can be seen as a stack (with : as cons operator) of undo requests that need to be satisfied. Once the stack is empty, the system has reached the state desired by the user. We consider requests $\{p, \psi\}$, asking process p to undo a specific action, namely:

- $\{p, s\}$: a single step back;
- $\{p, \lambda^{\Downarrow}\}$: the receive of the message uniquely identified by λ;
- $\{p, \lambda^{\Uparrow}\}$: the send of the message uniquely identified by λ;
- $\{p, \lambda^{sched}\}$: the scheduling of the message uniquely identified by λ;
- $\{p, st_{nid}\}$: the successful start of node nid';
- $\{p, sp_{p'}\}$: the spawn of process p'.

The rollback semantics is defined in Fig. 5 in terms of the relation $\rightsquigarrow$, selecting which backward rule to apply and when. There are two categories of rules: (i) U-rules that perform a step back using the backward semantics; (ii) rule *Request* that pushes a new request on top of Ψ whenever it is not possible to undo an action since its consequences need to be undone before.

Let us analyse the U-rules. During rollback, more than one backward rule could be applicable to the same process. In our setting, the only possibility is that one of the rules is a $\overline{Sched}$ and the other one is not. It is important to select which rule to apply, to ensure that only consequences of the target action are undone.

First, if an enabled transition satisfies our target, then it is executed and the corresponding request is removed (rule $U - Satisfy$). Intuitively, since two applications of rule *Sched* to the same process are always causally dependent, if the target action is an application of *Sched*, an enabled *Sched* is for sure one of

$$(U - Satisfy) \ \frac{S \twoheadleftarrow_{p,r,\Psi'} S' \ \wedge \ \psi \in \Psi'}{[\![S]\!]_{\{p,\psi\}:\Psi} \rightsquigarrow [\![S']\!]_\Psi} \qquad (U - Sched) \ \frac{S \twoheadleftarrow_{p,r,\{s,\lambda'^{sched}\}} S' \ \wedge \ \lambda'^{sched} \neq \lambda^{sched}}{[\![S]\!]_{\{p,\lambda^{sched}\}:\Psi} \rightsquigarrow [\![S']\!]_{\{p,\lambda^{sched}\}:\Psi}}$$

$$(U - Unique) \ \frac{S \twoheadleftarrow_{p,r,\Psi'} S' \ \wedge \ \psi \notin \Psi' \ \wedge \ \forall r'', \Psi'' \ S \twoheadleftarrow_{p,r'',\Psi''} S'' \Rightarrow S' = S''}{[\![S]\!]_{\{p,\psi\}:\Psi} \rightsquigarrow [\![S']\!]_{\{p,\psi\}:\Psi}}$$

$$(U - Act) \ \frac{S \twoheadleftarrow_{p,r,\Psi'} S' \ \wedge \ \psi \notin \Psi' \ \wedge \ \lambda^{sched} \notin \Psi' \ \wedge \ \psi \neq \lambda^{sched} \ \forall \lambda \in \mathbb{N}}{[\![S]\!]_{\{p,\psi\}:\Psi} \rightsquigarrow [\![S']\!]_{\{p,\psi\}:\Psi}}$$

$$(Request) \ \frac{S = \Gamma; \langle nid, p, h, \theta, e, q \rangle \mid \Pi; \Omega \ \wedge \ S \nleftarrow_{p,r,\Psi'} \ \wedge \ \{p', \psi'\} = dep(\langle nid, p, h, \theta, e, q \rangle, S)}{[\![S]\!]_{\{p,\psi\}:\Psi} \rightsquigarrow [\![S']\!]_{\{p',\psi'\}:\{p,\psi\}:\Psi}}$$

Fig. 5. Rollback semantics

$$
\begin{aligned}
&dep(< \_, \_, \mathsf{send}(\_, \_, p', \{\lambda, v\}) : h, \_, \_, \_ >, \_; \_; \_) &&= \{p', \lambda^{sched}\} \\
&dep(< \_, \_, \mathsf{nodes}(\_, \_, \Omega) : h, \_, \_, \_ >, \_; \Pi; \{nid\} \cup \Omega') &&= \{parent(nid, \Pi), st_{nid}\} && \text{if } nid \notin \Omega \\
&dep(< \_, \_, \mathsf{spawn}(\_, \_, \_, p') : h, \_, \_, \_ >, \_; \Pi; \_) &&= \{p', s\} && \text{if } p' \in \Pi \\
&dep(< \_, \_, \mathsf{spawn}(\_, \_, nid', \_) : h, \_, \_, \_ >, \_; \Pi; \_) &&= \{parent(nid', \Pi), st_{nid'}\} && \text{if } p' \notin \Pi \\
&dep(< \_, \_, \mathsf{start}(\_, \_, \mathsf{succ}, nid') : h, \_, \_, \_ >, \_; \Pi; \_) &&= \{fst(reads(nid', \Pi)), s\} && \text{if } reads(nid', \Pi) \neq [] \\
&dep(< \_, \_, \mathsf{start}(\_, \_, \mathsf{succ}, nid') : h, \_, \_, \_ >, \_; \Pi; \_) &&= \{fst(spawns(nid', \Pi)), s\} && \text{if } spawns(nid', \Pi) \neq [] \\
&dep(< \_, \_, \mathsf{start}(\_, \_, \mathsf{succ}, nid') : h, \_, \_, \_ >, \_; \Pi; \_) &&= \{fst(failed\_start(nid', \Pi)), s\}
\end{aligned}
$$

Fig. 6. Dependencies operator

its consequences, hence it needs to be undone (rule $U - Sched$). Dually, if the target is not a *Sched* and a non *Sched* is enabled, we do it (rule $U - Act$). If a unique rule is applicable, then it is selected (rule $U - Unique$).

Rule *Request* considers the case where no backward transition in the target process is enabled. This depends on some consequence on another process of the action on top of the history. Such a consequence needs to be undone before, hence the rule finds out using operator dep in Fig. 6 both the dependency and the target process and adds on top of Ψ the corresponding request.

Let us discuss operator dep. In the first case, a send cannot be undone since the sent message is not in the global mailbox, hence a request has to be made to the receiver p' of undoing the *Sched* of the message λ.

In case of multiple dependencies, we add them one by one. This happens, e.g., in case nodes, where we need to undo the start of all the nodes which are in $\{nid'\} \cup \Omega'$ but not in Ω. Adding all the dependencies at once would make the treatment more complex, since by solving one of them we may solve others as well, and thus we would need an additional check to avoid starting a computation to undo a dependency which is no more there. Adding the dependencies one by one solves the problem, hence operator dep nondeterministically selects one of them. Notice also that the order in which dependencies are solved is not relevant.

In some cases (e.g., send) we find a precise target event, in others we use just s, that is a single step. In the latter case, a backward step is performed (and its consequences are undone), then the condition is re-checked and another backward step is required, until the correct step is undone. We could have computed more precise targets, but this would have required additional technicalities.

Function $parent(nid', \Pi)$, used in the definition of dep, returns the pid of the process that started nid' while function $fst(\cdot)$ returns the first element of a list.

An execution of the rollback operator corresponds to a backward derivation, while the opposite is generally false.

Theorem 1 (Soundness of rollback). *If* $\llbracket S \rrbracket_{\Psi'} \rightsquigarrow^* \llbracket S' \rrbracket_\Psi$ *then* $S \leftarrow^* S'$ *where* $*$ *denotes reflexive and transitive closure.*

Proof. The rollback semantics is either executing backward steps using the backward semantics or executing administrative steps (i.e., pushing new requests on top of Ψ), which do not alter the state of the system. The thesis follow. $\square$

In addition, the rollback semantics generates the shortest computation satisfying the desired rollback request.

Theorem 2 (Minimality of rollback). *If* $\llbracket S \rrbracket_\Psi \rightsquigarrow^* \llbracket S' \rrbracket_\emptyset$ *then the backward steps occurring as first premises in the derivation of* $\llbracket S \rrbracket_\Psi \rightsquigarrow^* \llbracket S' \rrbracket_\emptyset$ *form the shortest computation from* S *satisfying* Ψ *derivable in the reversible semantics.*

A precise formalization and proof of this result is quite long, hence for space reasons we refer to [7, Theorem 3.2].

4   Distributed CauDEr

CauDEr [11,17,18] is the proof-of-concept debugger that we extended to support distribution following the semantics above. Notably, CauDEr works on Erlang, but primitives for distribution are the same in Core Erlang and in Erlang, hence our approach can be directly applied. CauDEr is written completely in Erlang and bundled up with a convenient graphical user interface to facilitate the interaction. The usual CauDEr workflow is the following. The user selects the Erlang source file, then CauDEr loads the program and shows the source code to the user. Then, the user can select the function that will act as entry point, specify its arguments, and the node identifier where the first process is running. The user can either perform single steps on some process (both forward and backward), or perform n steps in the chosen direction in an automatic manner (a scheduler decides which process will perform each step), or use the rollback operator.

The interface (see Fig. 7) is organized as follow: CauDEr shows the source code on the top left, the selected process' state and history (log is not considered in this paper) on the bottom left, and information on system structure and execution on the bottom right. Execution controls are on the top right.

We illustrate below how to use CauDEr to find a non-trivial bug.

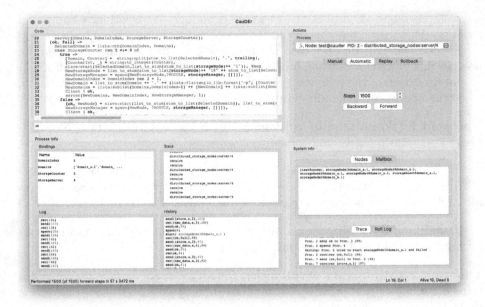

Fig. 7. A screenshot of CauDEr.

Finding Distributed Bugs with CauDEr. Let us consider the following scenario. A client produces a stream of data and wants to store them in a distributed storage system. A server acts as a hub: it receives data from the client, forwards them to a storage node, receives a confirmation that the storage node has saved the data, and finally sends an acknowledgement to the client. Each storage node hosts one process only, acting as node manager, and has an id as part of its name, ranging from one to five. Each node manager is able to store at most m packets. Once the manager reaches the limit, it informs the server that its capacity has been reached. The server holds a list of domains and an index referring to one of them. Each domain is coupled with a counter, i.e., an integer, and each domain can host at most five storage nodes. Each time the server receives a notification from a node manager stating that the node maximum capacity has been reached, it proceeds as follows. If the id of the current storage manager is five it means that such domain has reached its capacity. Then, the server selects the next domain in the list, resets its counter and starts a new node (and a corresponding storage manager) on the new domain. If the id of the node is less than five then the server increases its counter and then starts a new node (and storage manager) on the same domain, using the value of the counter as new id. Each node should host at most one process.

Let us now consider the program distributed_storage_node.erl, available in the GitHub repository [8], which shows a wrong implementation of the program described above. In order to debug the program one has to load it and start the system. Then, it is sufficient to execute about 1500 steps forward to notice that something went wrong. Indeed, by checking the Trace box (Fig. 7) one can see a warning: a start has failed since a node with the same identifier already existed. Then, since no check is performed on the result of the start, the program spawns a new storage manager on a node with the same identifier as the one that failed to start. Hence, now two storage managers run on the same node.

To investigate why this happened one can roll back to the reception of the message {store, full} right before the failed start. Note that it would not be easy to obtain the same result without reversibility: one would need to re-run the program, and, at least in principle, a different scheduling may lead to a different state where the error may not occur. After rolling back one can perform forward steps on the server in manual mode since the misbehavior happened there. After receiving the message, the server enters the case where the index of the storage manager is 5, which is correct because so far we have 5 storage nodes on the domain. Now, the server performs the start of the node (and of the storage manager) on the selected domain and only afterwards it selects the new domain, whereas it should have first selected a new domain and then proceeded to start a new storage node (and a new storage manager) there. This misbehavior has occurred because a few lines of code have been swapped.

5 Related Work and Conclusion

In this work we have presented an extension of CauDEr, a causal-consistent reversible debugger for Erlang, and the related theory. CauDEr has been first introduced in [17] (building on the theory in [19]) and then improved in [11] with a refined graphic interface and to work directly on Erlang instead of Core Erlang. We built our extension on top of this last version. CauDEr was able to deal with concurrent aspects of Erlang: our extension supports also some distribution primitives (start, node and nodes). We built the extension on top of the modular semantics for Erlang described in [11,19]. Monolithic approaches to the semantics of Erlang also exist [22], but the two-layer approach is more convenient for us since the reversible extension only affects the system layer.

Another work defining a formal semantics for distributed Erlang is [4]. There the emphasis is on ensuring the order of messages is respected in intra-node communications but not in inter-node communications (an aspect we do not consider). Similarly to us, they have rules to start new nodes and to perform remote spawns, although they do not consider the case where these rules fail.

In the context of CauDEr also replay has been studied [20]. In particular CauDEr supports causal-consistent replay, which allows one to replay the execution of the system up to a selected action, including *all and only* its *causes*. This can be seen as dual to rollback. Our extension currently does not support replay, we leave it for future work.

To the best of our knowledge causal-consistent debugging has been explored in a few settings only. The seminal paper [10] introduced causal-consistent debugging in the context of the toy language μOz. Closer to our work is Actoverse [23], a reversible debugger for the Akka actor model. Actoverse provides message-oriented breakpoints, which allow the user to stop when some conditions on messages are satisfied, rollback, state inspection, message timeline and session replay, which allows one to replay the execution of a program given the log of a computation, as well as the capacity to go back in the execution. While many of these features will be interesting for CauDEr, they currently do not support distribution.

Reversible debugging of concurrent programs has also been studied for imperative languages [12]. However, differently from us, they force undoing of actions in reverse order of execution, and they do not support distribution.

As future work it would be interesting to refine the semantics to deal with failures (node crashes, network partitions). Indeed, failures are unavoidable in practice, and we think reverse debugging in a faulty context could be of great help to the final user. Also, it would be good to extend CauDEr and the related theory to support additional features of the Erlang language, such as error handling, failure notification, and code hot-swapping. Finally, it would be good to experiment with more case studies to understand the practical impact of our tool.

References

1. Agha, G.A.: Actors: A Model of Concurrent Computation in Distributed Systems. The MIT Press (1986)
2. Carlsson, R., et al.: Core erlang 1.0.3. language specification (2004). https://www.it.uu.se/research/group/hipe/cerl/doc/core_erlang-1.0.3.pdf
3. Cesarini, F., Thompson, S.: ERLANG Programming. O'Reilly Media, Inc. (2009)
4. Claessen, K., Svensson, H.: A semantics for distributed Erlang. In: Proceedings of the 2005 ACM SIGPLAN Workshop on Erlang, pp. 78–87. ACM (2005)
5. Danos, V., Krivine, J.: Reversible communicating systems. In: Gardner, P., Yoshida, N. (eds.) CONCUR 2004. LNCS, vol. 3170, pp. 292–307. Springer, Heidelberg (2004). https://doi.org/10.1007/978-3-540-28644-8_19
6. Engblom, J.: A review of reverse debugging. In: Proceedings of the 2012 System, Software, SoC and Silicon Debug Conference, pp. 1–6 (2012)
7. Fabbretti, G.: Causal-Consistent Debugging of Distributed Erlang. Master's thesis. University of Bologna (2020). https://amslaurea.unibo.it/22195/
8. Fabbretti, G., Lanese, I.: Distributed CauDEr Website. https://github.com/gfabbretti8/cauder-v2.git (2021)
9. Fabbretti, G., Lanese, I., Stefani, J.B.: Causal-consistent debugging of distributed Erlang - Technical report (2021). https://team.inria.fr/spades/RC2021-TR
10. Giachino, E., Lanese, I., Mezzina, C.A.: Causal-consistent reversible debugging. In: Gnesi, S., Rensink, A. (eds.) FASE 2014. LNCS, vol. 8411, pp. 370–384. Springer, Heidelberg (2014). https://doi.org/10.1007/978-3-642-54804-8_26
11. González-Abril, J.J., Vidal, G.: Causal-consistent reversible debugging: improving CauDEr. In: Morales, J.F., Orchard, D. (eds.) PADL 2021. LNCS, vol. 12548, pp. 145–160. Springer, Cham (2021). https://doi.org/10.1007/978-3-030-67438-0_9
12. Hoey, J., Ulidowski, I.: Reversible imperative parallel programs and debugging. In: Thomsen, M.K., Soeken, M. (eds.) RC 2019. LNCS, vol. 11497, pp. 108–127. Springer, Cham (2019). https://doi.org/10.1007/978-3-030-21500-2_7
13. Landauer, R.: Irreversibility and heat generation in the computing process. IBM J. Res. Dev. 5(3), 183–191 (1961)

14. Lanese, I., Medic, D.: A general approach to derive uncontrolled reversible semantics. In: CONCUR. LIPIcs, vol. 171, pp. 33:1–33:24. Schloss Dagstuhl - Leibniz-Zentrum für Informatik (2020)
15. Lanese, I., Mezzina, C.A., Schmitt, A., Stefani, J.-B.: Controlling reversibility in higher-order Pi. In: Katoen, J.-P., König, B. (eds.) CONCUR 2011. LNCS, vol. 6901, pp. 297–311. Springer, Heidelberg (2011). https://doi.org/10.1007/978-3-642-23217-6_20
16. Lanese, I., Mezzina, C.A., Tiezzi, F.: Causal-consistent reversibility. Bull. EATCS 114 (2014)
17. Lanese, I., Nishida, N., Palacios, A., Vidal, G.: CauDEr: a causal-consistent reversible debugger for Erlang. In: Gallagher, J.P., Sulzmann, M. (eds.) FLOPS 2018. LNCS, vol. 10818, pp. 247–263. Springer, Cham (2018). https://doi.org/10.1007/978-3-319-90686-7_16
18. Lanese, I., Nishida, N., Palacios, A., Vidal, G.: CauDEr website (2018). https://github.com/mistupv/cauder-v2
19. Lanese, I., Nishida, N., Palacios, A., Vidal, G.: A theory of reversibility for Erlang. J. Log. Algebraic Meth. Program. 100, 71–97 (2018)
20. Lanese, I., Palacios, A., Vidal, G.: Causal-consistent replay reversible semantics for message passing concurrent programs. Fundam. Informaticae 178, 229–266 (2021)
21. McNellis, J., Mola, J., Sykes, K.: Time travel debugging: root causing bugs in commercial scale software. CppCon talk (2017). https://www.youtube.com/watch?v=l1YJTg_A914
22. Caballero, R., Martin-Martin, E., Riesco, A., Tamarit, S.: Declarative debugging of concurrent Erlang programs. J. Log. Algebraic Meth. Program. 101, 22–41 (2018)
23. Shibanai, K., Watanabe, T.: Actoverse: a reversible debugger for actors. In: ACM SIGPLAN, pp. 50–57 (2017)
24. Svensson, H., Fredlund, L., Benac Earle, C.: A unified semantics for future Erlang. In: Proceedings of the 9th ACM SIGPLAN Workshop on Erlang, pp. 23–32 (2010)

Towards a Unified Language Architecture for Reversible Object-Oriented Programming

Lasse Hay-Schmidt[1]([✉]), Robert Glück[1], Martin Holm Cservenka[1],
and Tue Haulund[2]

[1] DIKU, University of Copenhagen, Copenhagen, Denmark
{lvf228,djp595}@alumni.ku.dk, glueck@acm.org
[2] Siteimprove ApS, Copenhagen, Denmark
tha@siteimprove.com

Abstract. A unified language architecture for an advanced reversible object-oriented language is described. The design and implementation choices made for a tree-walking interpreter and source-language inverter are discussed, as well as the integration with an existing monadic parser, type checker and PISA compiler backend. A demonstration of the web interface and the interactions required to interpret, compile and invert reversible object-oriented programs is given. Our aim is that this platform will make reversible programming approachable to a wider community.

1 Introduction

In this tool paper, we report on an integrated language architecture for the reversible object-oriented language (ROOPL) [2,6], which aims to provide a platform for the development and testing of reversible object-oriented programs. The architecture provides a common framework including a parser and type-checker, an interpreter, a compiler to reversible machine code (PISA), and a program inverter. The Haskell implementation is designed as an open system for experimental research and educational purposes that can be extended with further components such as static analyzers and code-generators for reversible and irreversible target machines. In particular, we describe the components of the architecture and demonstrate the system. The complete system can be downloaded[1] or used via the web interface[2].

Reversible programming and algorithms are still a largely uncharted territory. This tool integrates a reversible interpreter and compiler for the first time. These combined tools allows a development cycle consisting of interpreting programs for quicker development, testing, debugging and finally compiling programs to machine instructions to be executed on target machines or simulators. It is our aim that a unified architecture can help enable advances in several directions

---

[1] Source code host: https://github.com/haysch/ROOPLPP.
[2] Web interface: https://topps.di.ku.dk/pirc/roopl-playground.

© Springer Nature Switzerland AG 2021
S. Yamashita and T. Yokoyama (Eds.): RC 2021, LNCS 12805, pp. 96–106, 2021.
https://doi.org/10.1007/978-3-030-79837-6_6

within the field of reversible computing including novel reversible algorithms on complex data structures, a more advanced programming methodology, compilation and optimization for reversible and irreversible machines, as well as language development for advanced reversible object-oriented languages. This tool paper complements our previous papers [2, 6]. The reversible object-oriented languages Joule [8] and ROOPL were recently described [7, Sect. 4].

Overview After a brief review of ROOPL (Sect. 2), we present the unified language architecture (Sect. 3) and demonstrate the system (Sect. 4). Finally, we discuss future work in the conclusion (Sect. 5). A complete program example is provided for the interested reviewer (Appendix A).

2   ROOPL

The *Reversible Object-Oriented Programming Language* (ROOPL) is a reversible programming language with built-in support for object-oriented programming and user-defined types. ROOPL is statically typed and supports inheritance, encapsulation, dynamic memory management with reference counting and subtype-polymorphism via dynamic dispatch. ROOPL is cleanly reversible, in the sense that no computational history is required for backward execution. Rather, each component of a program is locally invertible at no extra cost to program size.

Object-orientation enables rich reversible data structures (e.g., queues, trees, graphs) through reversible dynamic memory management as well as subtype-polymorphism. Existing reversible languages with simpler type systems such as Janus (static integer arrays) [12], RWhile (Lisp-like lists and symbols) [4], and RFun (tree-structured constructor terms) [11] have the same computational power (r-Turing complete) but are not as expressive.

3   Design, Structure and Implementation

The present section gives an overview of the system architecture. We begin by describing the phases of the compiler frontend followed by the compilation to reversible machine code, the program inverters and finally providing the relevant details about the JIT-inverting interpreter and the JSON encoded output.

3.1   System Architecture

An overview of the system architecture can be seen in Fig. 1. The figure shows the four phases of the frontend as well as the compiler and interpreter backends. The web interface provides an easy way to access the system and also includes several program examples and direct access to the program inverter. Together these components provide compilation, interpretation and source-level inversion of the ROOPL language. The entire system is implemented in Haskell. The components of the system are summarized in the follow subsections.

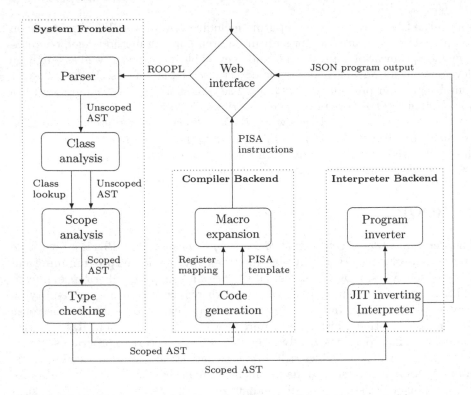

Fig. 1. Unified language architecture for the reversible object-oriented language.

3.2   Frontend Structure

The frontend provides the infrastructure for syntactic and semantic analysis that is shared by the compiler and interpreter backends. The frontend consists of four separate phases:

1. **Syntax Analysis.** The parser transforms the input program from textual representation to an abstract syntax tree using parser combinators.
2. **Class Analysis.** The class analysis phase verifies a number of properties of the classes in the program: Detection of inheritance cycles, duplication of method and field names and unknown base classes.
3. **Scope Analysis.** The scope analysis phase maps every occurrence of every identifier to a unique variable or method declaration. The scope analysis phase is also responsible for constructing the class virtual tables and the symbol table.
4. **Type Checking.** The type checker uses the symbol table and the abstract syntax tree to verify that the program satisfies the ROOPL type system.

3.3 Compiler Structure

The ROOPL compiler (described in detail in [1,5]), targets the Pendulum reversible machine architecture and its instruction set PISA [3,10]. The compiler backend consists of two separate phases:

1. **Code Generation.** The code generation phase translates the abstract syntax tree to a series of PISA instructions.
2. **Macro Expansion.** The macro expansion phase is responsible for expanding macros left in the translated PISA program after code generation and for final processing of the output.

The resulting PISA code can be executed using the Pendulum virtual machine[3].

3.4 Program Inverters

The ROOPL compiler includes a PISA inverter which operates on one instruction at a time. This inverter is needed to generate semantically symmetric load/unload sequences and reversible function preludes in the target programs.

Since the compiler targets a reversible machine, it has *no need* for a source-language inverter. Because the Pendulum reversible machine architecture supports inverted execution natively, the compiler can simply reverse the flow of execution in the PISA output to invert whatever method was being uncalled.

For interpreters running on irreversible machines this is not the case. In order to uncall a method, first the method must be inverted. Therefore a ROOPL inverter is a required component of our interpreter. A method is inverted by the interpreter on-demand whenever an uncall statement is executed (JIT inversion). As each ROOPL statement has a unique inverse there is no need for a global program analysis and the inversion can be done locally in time linear to the size of the program text.

The inverter also serves a purpose as a standalone component in our system. It is useful to be able to display the inverse of a given sequence of ROOPL statements while developing reversible programs - thus the inverter is exposed through our web interface. The inverter would also be an integral component in any future optimization steps added to the compiler, of which there are currently none. Static analyses like data-flow analysis or liveness analysis would also need inversion of methods to work out the propagation of data and the bidirectional nature of the reversible control flow. Figure. 2 illustrates how whole-program inversion of ROOPL proceeds class-by-class and method-by-method and by extension how ROOPL is well-suited to just-in-time inversion of class methods during interpretation.

---

[3] Source code [3,10] rehosted at: https://github.com/TueHaulund/PendVM.

$$\mathcal{I}_{class} \left[\!\!\left[\begin{array}{l} \textbf{class } c \; \cdots \\ \qquad \textbf{method } q_1 \; (\dots) \; s_1 \\ \qquad \vdots \\ \qquad \textbf{method } q_n \; (\dots) \; s_n \end{array} \right]\!\!\right] = \begin{array}{l} \textbf{class } c \; \cdots \\ \qquad \textbf{method } q_1 \; (\dots) \; \mathcal{I}_{stmt}[\![s_1]\!] \\ \qquad \vdots \\ \qquad \textbf{method } q_n \; (\dots) \; \mathcal{I}_{stmt}[\![s_n]\!] \end{array}$$

$$\mathcal{I}_{prog} [\![c_1 \; \cdots \; c_n]\!] = \mathcal{I}_{class}[\![c_1]\!] \; \cdots \; \mathcal{I}_{class}[\![c_n]\!]$$

Fig. 2. Program inverter $\mathcal{I}_{prog}$ and class inverter $\mathcal{I}_{class}$ for ROOPL. See [1] for the definition of the statement inverter $\mathcal{I}_{stmt}$.

3.5   Interpreter Design

Like the compiler, the ROOPL interpreter operates on the AST produced by the language frontend. At this point the program has been statically verified to be syntactically correct as well as being well typed. The interpreter then walks the AST and maintains the program state as it executes each statement.

The interpreter does not invert methods up front. Inverting an entire program ahead-of-time produces unnecessary overhead in case none of the methods is uncalled during the execution of the program. Inverting methods *just-in-time* (JIT), the interpreter ensures that only the necessary methods are inverted. The interpreter defines a cache for inverted methods, i.e. whenever a method has been inverted, it is saved to the cache for later use, that is JIT inversion. Only methods that are eventually uncalled will thus be inverted, avoiding the overhead of inverting all methods up front.

Inverting all methods *ahead-of-time* allows methods to run in any direction without performing inversions during execution. Each of the inversion techniques is better suited to different scenarios. Providing inverted methods ahead-of-time reduces compute runtime, whereas inverting just-in-time reduces pre-compute runtime. Both inversion techniques produce inverted methods. Alternatively, the AST can be organized in a way such that it can be efficiently walked backward thereby allowing to inverse interpret the statements *on the fly* during an uncall.

Program State. Before describing the object layout in memory, it is important to define the terms, *environment* and *store*. The store is a mapping from an identifier to a value or an object. An environment is a mapping from a class variable to a store. Every class defined in a ROOPL program is translated to a scoped representation with unique incremental identifiers by the scope analyzer, e.g. a class Node defines variables value, left and right, which

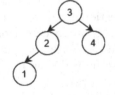

Fig. 3. Binary tree

are given identifiers 0, 1 and 2, respectively, and a class Tree defines a variable root, which is given identifier 3. A global environment would assign duplicate identifiers to objects instantiated from the same class. For this reason, environments are defined for each instantiated object instead.

To illustrate the behavior of the interpreter store, a binary search tree example is showcased to highlight these important aspects of mapping member variable values to class instances references. Figure 4 shows the example store after construction of the binary search tree show in Fig. 3 using the program from Appendix A.

	0	1	2	3	4	5	6	7	8
Store	Tree { 3: 2 }	Constant 3	Node { 0: 1, 1: 4, 2: 6 }	Constant 2	Node { 0: 3, 1: 8, 2: nil }	Constant 4	Node { 0: 5, 1: nil, 2: nil }	Constant 1	Node { 0: 7, 1: nil, 2: nil }

Fig. 4. Store after constructing binary search tree show in Fig. 3 using the program from Appendix A

Error Handling. The PISA programs produced by the ROOPL compiler will jump to an error state in case an error occurs. They are not however able to provide any context about the erroneous circumstance or the memory state.

As the interpreter has access to the full AST of the program and the entire program state, it is able to produce rich information about the cause of any given error during runtime. For example, entry and exit conditions for a conditional or a loop might not align due to programmer error or an object could have been deleted before being called (a so-called *use-after-free* situation).

Being able to give detailed error reports eases development by providing insight into the unexpected program state with a detailed stack trace. The stack trace contains information about the statement that caused the error and the program state at the given moment. As the environment values depend on the object, the stack trace shows the statement trace and the current variables in the object environment.

Program Output. The interpreter will serialize the final state of the program to JSON. This format is both human and machine-readable and so the ROOPL interpreter can be integrated with other systems for automated processing.

This is a significant improvement over the output produced by compiled ROOPL programs, which needs to be extracted from the PendVM memory store manually. Since JSON is an industry standard, there are a wealth of libraries and tools available to process and display the output.

4   Web Interface

The ROOPL compiler, inverter and interpreter are accessible through a web interface which also provides an editor with syntax highlighting and detailed error reporting.

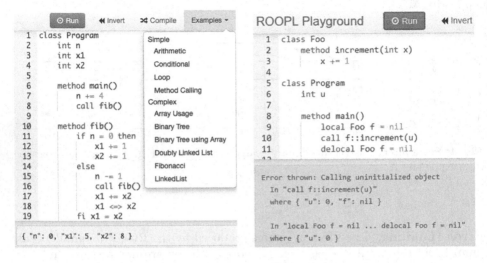

Fig. 5. ROOPL interface computing the fourth Fibonacci number

Fig. 6. ROOPL interface showing an error and its stack trace

The web interface allows programmers to access the system from anywhere via a browser[2]. The interface makes it possible to develop and test ROOPL programs without having the system installed locally. The goal is to lower the entry barrier for newcomers and to encourage the development of reversible software. To provide some aesthetic familiarity, the interface is based on the Janus interface[4].

When interpreting or inverting a program, the output state is shown in a separate pane, and when compiling a program the interface will download a file containing compiled PISA instructions. Figure 5 shows a reversible Fibonacci program. The output state in the bottom of the figure shows the result of finding the fourth Fibonacci number. Furthermore, the interface also contains numerous example programs. The *Simple* section showcases ROOPL syntax and the *Complex* section contains implementations of several reversible algorithms.

As described in Sect. 3, the interpreter is capable of detailed error reporting. Errors are displayed in the web interface alongside information about the root cause, a stack trace and the corresponding state for each trace. Figure 6 shows an error state due to calling a method on an uninitialized object.

---

[4] https://topps.di.ku.dk/pirc/janus-playground
  https://github.com/mbudde/jana.

5   Conclusion

Reversible computation is still an unfamiliar and emerging computing paradigm. Reversible algorithms, programming techniques, and practical experiences with the design and implementation of reversible systems are still not well established. The aim of the work reported here is to provide a productive integrated platform for the development and evaluation of reversible programs and algorithms, and for educational purposes with a reversible object-oriented language.

We hope that this will also lower the barrier to entry for non-experts to learn, experience and explore programming in an advanced reversible language and make reversible computation more accessible to a wider community. It will be interesting to investigate the design of dynamic reversible data structures, practical programming techniques, and the development of the ROOPL language design and debugging support.

Considering future work, our unified ROOPL architecture is open and other backends can be added, targeting other reversible instruction set architectures like Bob ISA [9] or irreversible mainstream architectures. One could consider adding optimization steps to the compilation pipeline and static analyses to improve reversible program quality. Additionally, providing access to an interface for developing ROOPL programs, adding breakpoints and advanced debugging techniques such as live debugging would provide a better development platform. They can also take advantage of the trace-free reversibility when stepping through a program. Finally, we propose exposing the Pendulum VM in the web interface to allow for end-to-end compilation and execution of ROOPL programs.

A   Binary Search Tree Example

The ROOPL example program in this appendix is provided for the interested reader. It is based on a binary search tree example [2] and accessible in the **Examples** tab of the web interface as *Binary Tree using Array*. A binary search tree allows fast look up of data items given a node value (the key). The example constructs a binary search tree by inserting new nodes while preserving the invariant that all node values in a node's left subtree are smaller and those in the node's right subtree are not smaller than the node's value. In our example, the node values are stored in an array and then iteratively inserted into the tree. Given the node values 3, 4, 2, 1, the resulting tree can be seen in Fig. 3.

A.1   Example Program

Appendix A.2 contains the complete source code for the example program. The class **Program** defines the main method of our program (lines 40–63). The method **main** is the program's entry point and creates a new binary search tree. A new object of class **Tree** is created by statement **new Tree tree**, which sets variable **tree** to the new object's reference (line 46). Similarly, a new array **nodeVals** is created and initialized with our four example values (lines 47–52).

The iteration over the example array is performed by a reversible loop (lines 54–62). It asserts that the initial value of index variable x is 0 and its final value is nodeCount. The control-flow operators in ROOPL are those of Janus; e.g. see [12]. The paired statements local and delocal open and close the scope of a variable by specifying its initial and final value, e.g. x has the initial value 0 (line 53). All method calls and uncalls refer to an object, e.g. call node::setValue(nodeVals[x]) sends method setValue to object node with a parameter being the value of an element in array nodeVals (line 58).

Class Node defines a labeled node as containing an integer value and links to the roots of its left and right subtree (lines 2–4). Usually, this class also defines the variables for the data items stored in a node. If there is no subtree then the corresponding link is nil. The class defines two methods: setValue reversibly updates the label of a node and insertNode recursively inserts a new node with a value newValue. The latter performs a recursive descent over the left or right subtree depending on the node value to be inserted.

A reversible conditional has two predicates that are evaluated at run time: an entry test at if (e.g., nodeValue < value at line 10) and an exit assertion at fi (e.g., left != nil at line 17). After executing the then-branch, the assertion must evaluate to true, and after executing the else-branch, it must evaluate to false; otherwise, an error occurs and an exception is raised.

Finally, class Tree defines the root of a binary search tree and provides a method for inserting nodes into the search tree. More variables can be added to this class, e.g. the number of nodes in a tree. Which of the two insert methods defined in the classes Node and Tree is invoked depends on the class of the object to which it is sent (e.g. root::insertNode(...) vs. tree::insertNode(...)).

A.2   Source Code

```
1   class Node                        // Class: node of binary search tree
2       int value                     // Value of node
3       Node left                     // Root of left subtree
4       Node right                    // Root of right subtree
5
6       method setValue(int newValue)
7           value += newValue
8
9       method insertNode(Node node, int nodeValue)
10          if nodeValue < value then // Determine if we insert left or right
11              if left = nil & node != nil then left <=> node // put in left
12              else skip
13              fi left != nil & node = nil
14              // If current node has left, continue
15              if left != nil then call left::insertNode(node, nodeValue)
16              else skip
17              fi left != nil
18          else
19              if right = nil & node != nil then right <=> node // put in right
20              else skip
21              fi right != nil & node = nil
22              // If current node has right, continue
23              if right != nil then call right::insertNode(node, nodeValue)
24              else skip
25              fi right != nil
26          fi nodeValue < value
```

```
27
28  class Tree                          // Class: binary search tree
29    Node root                         // Root of binary search tree
30
31    method insertNode(Node node, int value)
32      if root = nil & node != nil then root <=> node // set root
33      else skip
34      fi root != nil & node = nil
35      if root != nil then             // If root exists, insert node
36        call root::insertNode(node, value)
37      else skip
38      fi root != nil
39
40  class Program                       // Class: main program
41    Tree tree                         // Binary search tree
42    int nodeCount                     // Number of example nodes
43    int[] nodeVals                    // Array for example values
44
45    method main()
46      new Tree tree                   // Create new tree object
47      nodeCount += 4                  // Set number of example nodes
48      new int[nodeCount] nodeVals     // Create array for example values
49      nodeVals[0] += 3                // Set array values
50      nodeVals[1] += 2
51      nodeVals[2] += 4
52      nodeVals[3] += 1
53      local int x = 0                 // Open scope
54      from x = 0 do skip              // Loop creates binary search tree
55      loop
56        local Node node = nil                   // Open scope
57        new Node node                           // Create new node
58        call node::setValue(nodeVals[x])        // Set node value
59        call tree::insertNode(node, nodeVals[x])// Insert node in tree
60        delocal Node node = nil                 // Close scope
61        x += 1                                  // Increment index
62      until x = nodeCount
63      delocal int x = nodeCount                 // Close scope
```

References

1. Cservenka, M.H.: Design and implementation of dynamic memory management in a reversible OO programming lang. Master's thesis, University of Copenhagen (2018)

2. Cservenka, M.H., Glück, R., Haulund, T., Mogensen, T.Æ.: Data structures and dynamic memory management in reversible languages. In: Kari, J., Ulidowski, I. (eds.) RC 2018. LNCS, vol. 11106, pp. 269–285. Springer, Cham (2018). https://doi.org/10.1007/978-3-319-99498-7_19

3. Frank, M.P.: Reversibility for efficient computing. Ph.D. thesis, MIT (1999)

4. Glück, R., Yokoyama, T.: A linear-time self-interpreter of a reversible imperative language. Comput. Softw. **33**(3), 108–128 (2016)

5. Haulund, T.: Design and implementation of a reversible object-oriented programming language. Master's thesis, University of Copenhagen (2016)

6. Haulund, T., Mogensen, T.Æ., Glück, R.: Implementing reversible object-oriented language features on reversible machines. In: Phillips, I., Rahaman, H. (eds.) RC 2017. LNCS, vol. 10301, pp. 66–73. Springer, Cham (2017). https://doi.org/10.1007/978-3-319-59936-6_5

7. Mezzina, C.A., et al.: Software and reversible systems: a survey of recent activities. In: Ulidowski, I., Lanese, I., Schultz, U.P., Ferreira, C. (eds.) RC 2020. LNCS, vol. 12070, pp. 41–59. Springer, Cham (2020). https://doi.org/10.1007/978-3-030-47361-7_2

8. Schultz, U.P., Axelsen, H.B.: Elements of a reversible object-oriented language. In: Devitt, S., Lanese, I. (eds.) RC 2016. LNCS, vol. 9720, pp. 153–159. Springer, Cham (2016). https://doi.org/10.1007/978-3-319-40578-0_10

9. Thomsen, M.K., Axelsen, H.B., Glück, R.: A reversible processor architecture and its reversible logic design. In: De. Vos, A., Wille, R. (eds.) RC 2011. LNCS, vol. 7165, pp. 30–42. Springer, Heidelberg (2012). https://doi.org/10.1007/978-3-642-29517-1_3

10. Vieri, C.J.: Rev. computer engineering and architecture. Ph.D. thesis, MIT (1999)

11. Yokoyama, T., Axelsen, H.B., Glück, R.: Towards a reversible functional language. In: De. Vos, A., Wille, R. (eds.) RC 2011. LNCS, vol. 7165, pp. 14–29. Springer, Heidelberg (2012). https://doi.org/10.1007/978-3-642-29517-1_2

12. Yokoyama, T., Glück, R.: A reversible programming language and its invertible self-interpreter. In: PEPM Proceedings, pp. 144–153. ACM (2007)

Reversible Concurrent Computation

Towards a Truly Concurrent Semantics
for Reversible CCS

Hernán Melgratti[1], Claudio Antares Mezzina[2(✉)], and G. Michele Pinna[3]

[1] ICC - Universidad de Buenos Aires - Conicet, Buenos Aires, Argentina
[2] Dipartimento di Scienze Pure e Applicate, Università di Urbino, Urbino, Italy
claudio.mezzina@uniurb.it
[3] Università di Cagliari, Cagliari, Italy

Abstract. Reversible CCS (RCCS) is a well-established, formal model for reversible communicating systems, which has been built on top of the classical Calculus of Communicating Systems (CCS). In its original formulation, each CCS process is equipped with a memory that records its performed actions, which is then used to reverse computations. More recently, abstract models for RCCS have been proposed in the literature, basically, by directly associating RCCS processes with (reversible versions of) event structures. In this paper we propose a detour: starting from one of the well-known encoding of CCS into Petri nets we apply a recently proposed approach to incorporate causally-consistent reversibility to Petri nets, obtaining as result the (reversible) net counterpart of every RCCS term.

Keywords: Petri nets · Reversible CCS · Concurrency

1 Introduction

CCS [17] is a foundational calculus for concurrent systems. Typically, systems are described as the parallel composition of *processes* (i.e., components) that communicate by sending and receiving messages over named channels. Processes are then defined in terms of communication actions performed over specific channels: we write a and $\bar{a}$ to respectively represent a receive and a send over the channel a. Basic actions can be composed through prefixing (i.e., sequencing) (_._), choice (_+_) and parallel (_ || _) operators. The original formulation of the semantics of CCS adheres to the so called *interleaved* approach, which only accounts for the executions that arise from a single processor; hence, parallelism can be reduced to non-deterministic choices and prefixing. For instance, the CCS processes $a \parallel b$ and $a.b + b.a$ are deemed *equivalent*, i.e., it does not distinguish a process that

Partially supported by the EU H2020 RISE programme under the Marie Skłodowska-Curie grant agreement 778233, by the French ANR project DCore ANR-18-CE25-0007 and by the Italian INdAM – GNCS 2020 project Sistemi Reversibili Concorrenti: dai Modelli ai Linguaggi, and by the UBACyT projects 20020170100544BA and 20020170100086BA.

© Springer Nature Switzerland AG 2021
S. Yamashita and T. Yokoyama (Eds.): RC 2021, LNCS 12805, pp. 109–125, 2021.
https://doi.org/10.1007/978-3-030-79837-6_7

can perform a and b concurrently from one that sequentialises their execution in any possible order (interleaving/schedule). Successive works have addressed the problem of equipping CCS with *true concurrent* semantics in the style of Petri nets and Event Structures. It has been shown that every CCS process can be associated with a Petri net that can mimic its computations. Different flavours of Petri nets have been used in the literature; for instance, *occurrence* nets [6], a variant of *Conditions/Events* nets [5], and *flow* nets [3]. The works in [20] and [3] have additionally shown that the computation of a CCS process can be represented by using event structures.

Many efforts were made in the last decades to endow computation models with reversible semantics [1,16] and, in particular, two different models have been proposed for CCS: RCCS [4,9] and CCSK [19]. Both of them incorporate a logging mechanism in the operational semantics of CCS that enables the undoing of computation steps. Moreover, it has been shown that they are isomorphic [10] since they only differ on the information that they log: while RCCS relies on some form of *memory/monitor*, CCSK uses *keys*. Previous approaches have also developed true concurrent semantics for reversible versions of CCS. For instance, it has been shown that CCSK can be associated with reversible bundle event structures [7,8]. However, we still lack a Petri net model for RCCS processes. We may exploit some recent results that connect reversible occurrence nets with reversible event structures [13–15] to indirectly recover a Petri net model from the reversible bundle event structures defined in [7]. However, we follow a different approach, which is somehow more *direct*:

1. we encode (finite) CCS processes into a generalization of occurrence nets, namely *unravel* nets, in the vein of Boudol and Castellani [3];
2. we show that *unravel* nets can be made *causally-consistent* reversible by applying the approach in [13];
3. we finally shows that the reversible unravel nets derived by our encoding are an interpratation of RCCS terms.

An interesting aspect of the proposed encoding is that it highlights that all the information needed for reversing an RCCS process is already *encoded* in the structure of the net corresponding to the original CCS process, i.e., RCCS memories are represented by the structure of the net. Concretely, if an RCCS process R is a derivative of some CCS process P, then the encoding of R is retrieved from the encoding of P, what changes is the position of the markings. Consider the CCS process $P = a.0$ that executes a and then terminates. It can be encoded as the Petri net on the left in Fig. 1 (the usage of the apparently redundant places in the postset of a will be made clearer in Fig. 3).

The reversible version of P is $R = \langle\rangle \triangleright a.0$, where $\langle\rangle$ denotes an initially empty memory. According to RCCS semantics, R evolves to $R' = \langle *, a, 0 \rangle \cdot \langle\rangle \triangleright 0$ by executing a. The memory $\langle *, a, 0 \rangle \cdot \langle\rangle$ in R' indicates that it can go back to the initial process R by undoing a. Note that the net corresponding to P (on the left) has already all the information needed to reverse the action a; morally, a can be undone by firing it in the opposite direction (i.e., by consuming tokens from the postset and producing them in its preset), or equivalently, by performing a

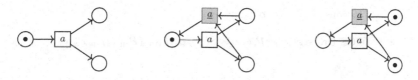

Fig. 1. Encoding of $R = \langle\rangle \triangleright a.0$

reversing transition $\underline{a}$ that does the job, as shown in the net drawn in the middle of Fig. 1. It should be noted that the net on the right of Fig. 1 corresponds to the derivative R'. Consequently, the encoding of a CCS term as a net already bears all the information needed for reversing it; which contrasts with the required memories of RCCS. This observation gives an almost straightforward true concurrent representation of RCCS processes.

Organization of the Paper. After setting up some notation, we recall CCS and RCCS (Sect. 2). In Sect. 3 we summarise the basics of Petri nets, *unravel* nets and present their reversible counterpart. In Sect. 4, describe the encoding of CCS into unravel nets and introduce the mapping from RCCS terms into reversible unravel nets. In the final section we draw some conclusions and discuss future developments.

Preliminaries. We denote with $\mathbb{N}$ the set of natural numbers. Let A be a set, a *multiset* of A is a function $m : A \to \mathbb{N}$. The set of multisets of A is denoted by ∂A. We assume the usual operations on multisets such as union $+$ and difference $-$. We write $m \subseteq m'$ if $m(a) \leq m'(a)$ for all $a \in A$. For $m \in \partial A$, we denote with $[m]$ the multiset defined as $[m](a) = 1$ if $m(a) > 0$ and $[m](a) = 0$ otherwise. When a multiset m of A is a set, *i.e.* $m = [m]$, we write $a \in m$ to denote that $m(a) \neq 0$, and often confuse the multiset m with the set $\{a \in A \mid m(a) \neq 0\}$ or a subset $X \subseteq A$ with the multiset $X(a) = 1$ if $a \in A$ and $X(a) = 0$ otherwise. Furthermore we use the standard set operations like $\cap$, $\cup$ or $\setminus$. The multiset m such that $[m] = \emptyset$ is denoted with abuse of notation as $\emptyset$.

2   CCS and Reversible CCS

Let $\mathcal{A}$ be a set of actions $a, b, c, \ldots$, and $\overline{\mathcal{A}} = \{\overline{a} \mid a \in \mathcal{A}\}$ the set of their co-actions. We denote the set of all possible actions with $\mathsf{Act} = \mathcal{A} \cup \overline{\mathcal{A}}$. We write α, β for the elements of $\mathsf{Act}_\tau = \mathsf{Act} \cup \{\tau\}$, where $\tau \notin \mathsf{Act}$ stands for a *silent* action. The syntax of (finite) CCS is reported in Fig. 2. A prefix (or action) is either an input a, an output $\overline{a}$ or the silent action τ. A term of the form $\sum_{i \in I} \alpha_i.P_i$ represents a process that (non-deterministically) starts by selecting and performing some action α_i and then continues as P_i. We write $\mathbf{0}$, the idle process, in lieu of $\sum_{i \in I} \alpha_i.P_i$ when $I = \emptyset$; similarly, $\alpha_i.P$ for a unitary sum in which I is the singleton $\{i\}$. The term $P||Q$ represents the parallel composition of the processes P and Q. An action a can be restricted so to be visible only

(Actions) α $::= a \mid \bar{a} \mid \tau$

(CCS Processes) $P, Q ::= \sum_{i \in I} \alpha_i.P_i \mid (P \parallel Q) \mid P \backslash a$

Fig. 2. CCS Syntax

$$\sum_{i \in I} \alpha_i.P \xrightarrow{\alpha_z} P_z \ \text{(ACT)} \qquad \frac{P \xrightarrow{\alpha} P'}{P \parallel Q \xrightarrow{\alpha} P' \parallel Q} \ \text{(PAR-L)} \qquad \frac{Q \xrightarrow{\alpha} Q'}{P \parallel Q \xrightarrow{\alpha} P \parallel Q'} \ \text{(PAR-R)}$$

$$\frac{P \xrightarrow{\alpha} P' \quad Q \xrightarrow{\bar{\alpha}} Q'}{P \parallel Q \xrightarrow{\tau} P' \parallel Q'} \ \text{(SYN)} \qquad \frac{P \xrightarrow{\alpha} P' \quad \alpha \notin \{a, \bar{a}\}}{P \backslash a \xrightarrow{\alpha} P' \backslash a} \ \text{(R-RES)}$$

Fig. 3. CCS semantics

inside process P, written $P \backslash a$. Restriction is the only binder in CCS: a occurs bound in $P \backslash a$.

We write $\mathbf{n}(P)$ for the set of names of a process P, and, respectively, $\mathbf{fn}(P)$ and $\mathbf{bn}(P)$ for the sets of free and bound names. The set $\mathcal{P}$ denotes the set of all CCS processes.

Definition 1 (CCS Semantics). *The operational semantics of CCS is defined as the LTS $(\mathcal{P}, \mathsf{Act}_\tau, \rightarrow)$ where the transition relation $\rightarrow$ is the smallest relation induced by the rules in Fig. 3.*

Let us comment on rules of Fig. 3. Rule ACT transforms an action α into a label. Rules PAR-L and PAR-R permit respectively the left and the right process of a parallel composition to propagate an action. Rule SYN regulates the synchronization allowing two process in parallel to handshake. Rule HIDE forbids a restricted action to be further propagated.

Reversible CCS. Reversible CCS (RCCS) [4,9] is a reversible variant of CCS. Processes in RCCS are equipped with a *memory*, in which a process keeps information about its past actions. The syntax of RCCS is in Fig. 4, where CCS processes are defined as in the original formulation. A reversible process is either a *monitored* process $m \triangleright P$ with m a memory and P a CCS process, the parallel composition $R \parallel S$ of the reversible processes R and S, and the restriction $R \backslash a$ in which a is restricted to R. A *memory* is a (possible empty) stack of events that encodes the history of actions previously performed by a process; whose top-most element corresponds to the very last action performed by the monitored process. Memories can contain three different kinds of events[1]: *partial* synchronisations

---

[1] In this paper we use the original *RCCS* semantics with partial synchronisation. Later versions, e.g. [9], use communication keys to univocally identify actions.

(CCS Processes)	$P, Q ::= \sum_{i \in I} \alpha_i.P_i \mid (P \parallel Q) \mid P \backslash a$
(RCCS Processes)	$R, S ::= m \triangleright P \mid (R \parallel S) \mid R \backslash a$
(Memories)	$m \quad ::= \langle *, \alpha, Q \rangle \cdot m \mid \langle m, \alpha, Q \rangle \cdot m' \mid \langle 1 \rangle \cdot m \mid \langle 2 \rangle \cdot m \mid \langle \rangle$

Fig. 4. RCCS syntax

$\langle *, \alpha, Q \rangle$, *full* synchronisations $\langle m, \alpha, Q \rangle$, and memory *splits* $\langle 1 \rangle$ and $\langle 2 \rangle$. The action α and the process Q in a synchronisation (either partial or full) record the selected action α of a choice and the discarded branches Q. The (technical) distinction between partial and full synchronisation will be made clear when describing the semantics or RCCS. Events $\langle 1 \rangle$ and $\langle 2 \rangle$ represent the split of a process in two parallel ones. The empty memory is represented by $\langle \rangle$. Let us note that in RCCS memories serves also as unique process identifiers.

As for CCS, the only binder in RCCS is restriction (at the level of both CCS and RCCS processes). We extend functions **n**, **fn** and **bn** to RCCS processes and memories accordingly. We define $\mathcal{M}$ the set of all the possible memories and $\mathcal{P}_R$ the set of all RCCS processes.

Definition 2 (RCCS Semantics). *The operational semantics of RCCS is defined as a pair of LTSs on the same set of states and set of labels: a forward LTS $(\mathcal{P}_R, \mathcal{M} \times \text{Act}_\tau, \rightarrow)$ and a backward LTS $(\mathcal{P}_R, \mathcal{M} \times \text{Act}_\tau, \rightsquigarrow)$. Transition relations $\rightarrow$ and $\rightsquigarrow$ are the smallest relations induced by the rules in Fig. 5 (left and right columns, respectively). Both relations exploit the structural congruence relation $\equiv$, which is the smallest congruence on RCCS processes containing the rules in Fig. 6. We define $\rightleftharpoons \; = \; \rightarrow \cup \rightsquigarrow$.*

Let us comment on the forward rules (Fig. 5, left column). Rule R-ACT allows a monitored process to perform a forward action. The action goes along with the memory m of the process. Since at this point we do not know whether the process will synchronise or not with the context a partial synchronisation event of the form $\langle *, \alpha_z^z, \sum_{i \in I \backslash z} \alpha_i.P_i \rangle$ is put on top of the memory. The '*' will be replaced by a memory, say, m_1 if the process will eventually synchronise with a process monitored by m_1. Let us note that the discarded process Q is recorded in the memory. Moreover, along with the prefix we also store its position 'z' within the sum. This piece of information is redundant for RCCS, and indeed was not present in the original semantics. However, it will be of help when encoding a RCCS process into a net, and when proving the operational correspondence. We remark that this simple modification does not intact the original semantics of RCCS. Rules R-PAR-L and R-PAR-R propagate an action through a parallel composition. Rule R-SYN allows two parallel processes to synchronize. To do so, they have to match both the action α and then the two partial synchronisation of the two processes are updated to two full synchronisation through the operator '@'. Let R be a monitored process and m_1 and m_2 two memories,

$$m \rhd \sum_{i \in I} \alpha_i.P_i \xrightarrow{m:\alpha_z} \langle *, \alpha_z^z, \sum_{i \in I \setminus \{z\}} \alpha_i.P_i \rangle \cdot m \rhd P_z \text{ (R-ACT)}$$

$$\langle *, \alpha_z^z, \sum_{i \in I \setminus \{z\}} \alpha_i.P_i \rangle \cdot m \rhd P_z \xrightsquigarrow{m:\alpha_z} m \rhd \sum_{i \in I} \alpha_i.P_i \text{ (R-ACT}^\bullet)$$

$$\text{(R-PAR-L)} \quad \frac{R \xrightarrow{m:\alpha} R'}{R \parallel S \xrightarrow{m:\alpha} R' \parallel S} \qquad\qquad \frac{R \xrightsquigarrow{m:\alpha} R'}{R \parallel S \xrightsquigarrow{m:\alpha} R' \parallel S} \text{ (R-PAR-L}^\bullet)$$

$$\text{(R-PAR-R)} \quad \frac{S \xrightarrow{m:\alpha} S'}{R \parallel S \xrightarrow{m:\alpha} R \parallel S'} \qquad\qquad \frac{S \xrightsquigarrow{m:\alpha} S'}{R \parallel S \xrightsquigarrow{m:\alpha} R \parallel S'} \text{ (R-PAR-R}^\bullet)$$

$$\text{(R-SYN)} \quad \frac{R \xrightarrow{m_1:\alpha} R' \quad S \xrightarrow{m_2:\bar{\alpha}} S'}{R \parallel S \xrightarrow{m1,m2:\tau} R'_{m_2 @ m_1} \parallel S'_{m_1 @ m_2}} \qquad \frac{R \xrightsquigarrow{m_1:\alpha} R' \quad S \xrightsquigarrow{m_2:\bar{\alpha}} S'}{R \parallel S \xrightsquigarrow{m1,m2:\tau} R' \parallel S'} \text{ (R-SYN}^\bullet)$$

$$\text{(R-RES)} \quad \frac{R \xrightarrow{m:\alpha} R' \quad \alpha \notin \{a, \bar{a}\}}{R \backslash a \xrightarrow{m:\alpha} R' \backslash a} \qquad\qquad \frac{R \xrightsquigarrow{m:\alpha} R' \quad \alpha \notin \{a, \bar{a}\}}{R \backslash a \xrightsquigarrow{m:\alpha} R' \backslash a} \text{ (R-RES}^\bullet)$$

$$\text{(R-EQUIV)} \quad \frac{R \equiv R' \quad R' \xrightarrow{m:\alpha} S' \quad S' \equiv S}{R \xrightarrow{m:\alpha} S} \qquad \frac{R \equiv R' \quad R' \xrightsquigarrow{m:\alpha} S' \quad S' \equiv S}{R \xrightsquigarrow{m:\alpha} S} \text{ (R-EQUIV}^\bullet)$$

Fig. 5. RCCS semantics

then $R_{m_2 @ m_1}$ stands for the process obtained from R by substituting all occurrences of $\langle *, \alpha, Q \rangle \cdot m_1$ by $\langle m_2, \alpha, Q \rangle \cdot m_1$. Rule R-RES propagates actions through restriction provided that the action is not on the restricted name. Rule R-EQUIV allows one to exploit structural congruence of Fig. 6. Structural rule SPLIT allows a monitored process with a top-level parallel composition to split into a left and right branch, duplicating the memory. Structural rule RES allows one to push restriction outside monitored processes. Structural rule α allows one to exploit α-conversion, denoted by $=_\alpha$.

Definition 3 (Initial Process and Coherent process). *A RCCS process of the form $\langle \rangle \rhd P$ is called initial. Every process R derived from an initial process is called coherent process.*

3 Petri Nets, Unravel Nets and Reversible Unravel Nets

A *Petri net* is a tuple $N = \langle S, T, F, m \rangle$, where S is a set of *places* and T is a set of *transitions* (with $S \cap T = \emptyset$), $F \subseteq (S \times T) \cup (T \times S)$ is the *flow* relation, and $m \in \partial S$ is called the *initial marking*.

Petri nets are depicted as usual: transitions are boxes, places are circles and the flow relation is depicted using directed arcs. The presence of tokens in places

(SPLIT) $m \triangleright (P \parallel Q) \equiv \langle 2 \rangle \cdot m \triangleright P \parallel \langle 1 \rangle \cdot m \triangleright Q$

(RES) $m \triangleright P \backslash a \equiv (m \triangleright P) \backslash a$ if $a \notin \mathfrak{fn}(m)$

(α) $R \equiv S$ if $R =_\alpha S$

Fig. 6. RCCS Structural laws

is signaled by a number of '•' in it. The marking represents the *state* of the distributed and concurrent system modeled by the net, and it is distributed.

Given a net $N = \langle S, T, F, \mathsf{m} \rangle$ and $x \in S \cup T$, we define the following multisets: $^\bullet x = \{y \mid (y, x) \in F\}$ and $x^\bullet = \{y \mid (x, y) \in F\}$. If x is a place then $^\bullet x$ and $x^\bullet$ are (multisets) of transitions; analogously, if $x \in T$ then $^\bullet x \in \partial S$ and $x^\bullet \in \partial S$. A transition $t \in T$ is enabled at a marking $m \in \partial S$, denoted by $m \left[t\right\rangle$, whenever $^\bullet t \subseteq m$. A transition t enabled at a marking m can *fire* and its firing produces the marking $m' = m - {}^\bullet t + t^\bullet$. The firing of t at a marking m is denoted by $m \left[t\right\rangle m'$. We assume that each transition t of a net N is such that $^\bullet t \neq \emptyset$, meaning that no transition may fire *spontaneously*. Given a generic marking m (not necessarily the initial one), the *firing sequence* (shortened as fs) of $N = \langle S, T, F, \mathsf{m}, \ell \rangle$ starting at m is defined as: (i) m is a firing sequence (of length 0), and (ii) if $m \left[t_1\right\rangle m_1 \cdots m_{n-1} \left[t_n\right\rangle m_n$ is a firing sequence and $m_n \left[t\right\rangle m'$, then also $m \left[t_1\right\rangle m_1 \cdots m_{n-1} \left[t_n\right\rangle m_n \left[t\right\rangle m'$ is a firing sequence. The set of firing sequences of a net N starting at a marking m is denoted by $\mathcal{R}_m^N$ and it is ranged over by σ. Given a fs $\sigma = m \left[t_1\right\rangle \sigma' \left[t_n\right\rangle m_n$, $start(\sigma)$ is the marking m, $lead(\sigma)$ is the marking m_n and $tail(\sigma)$ is the fs $\sigma' \left[t_n\right\rangle m_n$. Given a net $N = \langle S, T, F, \mathsf{m}, \ell \rangle$, a marking m is *reachable* iff there exists a fs $\sigma \in \mathcal{R}_m^N$ such that $lead(\sigma)$ is m. The set of reachable markings of N is $\mathcal{M}_N = \{lead(\sigma) \mid \sigma \in \mathcal{R}_m^N\}$. Given a fs $\sigma = m \left[t_1\right\rangle m_1 \cdots m_{n-1} \left[t_n\right\rangle m'$, we write $X_\sigma = \sum_{i=1}^n t_i$ for the multiset of transitions associated to fs, which we call an *execution* of the net and we write $\mathbb{E}(N) = \{X_\sigma \in \partial T \mid \sigma \in \mathcal{R}_m^N\}$ for the set of the executions of N. Observe that an execution simply says which transitions (and the relative number of occurrences of them) has been executed, not their (partial) ordering. Given a fs $\sigma = m \left[t_1\right\rangle m_1 \cdots m_{n-1} \left[t_n\right\rangle m_n \cdots$, with ρ_σ we denote the sequence $t_1 t_2 \cdots t_n \cdots$.

Definition 4. *A net* $N = \langle S, T, F, \mathsf{m} \rangle$ *is said to be* safe *if each marking* $m \in \mathcal{M}_N$ *is such that* $m = \llbracket m \rrbracket$.

The notion of subnet will be handy in the following. A subnet is obtained by restricting places and transitions, and correspondingly the flow relation and the initial marking.

Definition 5. *Let* $N = \langle S, T, F, \mathsf{m} \rangle$ *be a Petri net and let* $T' \subseteq T$ *be a subset of transitions and* $S' = {}^\bullet T' \cup T'^\bullet$. *Then, the subnet generated by* T' $N|_{T'} = \langle S', T', F', \mathsf{m}' \rangle$, *where* F' *is the restriction of* F *to* S' *and* T', *and* m' *is the multiset on* S' *obtained by* m *restricting to the places in* S'.

Unravel Nets. To define *unravel nets* we need the notion of *causal net*. A safe Petri net $N = \langle S, T, F, \mathsf{m} \rangle$ is a *causal net* (CA for short) when $\forall s \in S. \, |{}^\bullet s| \leq 1$ and $|s^\bullet| \leq 1$, F^* is acyclic, $T \in \mathbb{E}(N)$, and $\forall s \in S \, {}^\bullet s = \emptyset \Rightarrow \mathsf{m}(s) = 1$. Requiring that $T \in \mathbb{E}(N)$ implies that each transition can be executed and F^* acyclic means that dependencies among transitions are settled. A causal net has no isolated and unmarked places as $\forall s \in S \, {}^\bullet s = \emptyset \Rightarrow \mathsf{m}(s) = 1$.

Definition 6. *An* unravel net *(UN for short)* $N = \langle S, T, F, \mathsf{m} \rangle$ *is a safe net such that for each execution* $X \in \mathbb{E}(N)$ *the subnet* $N|_X$ *is a causal net.*

Unravel nets describe the dependencies among the transitions in the executions of a concurrent and distributed device and are similar to *flow nets* [2,3]. Flow nets are safe nets where, for each possible firing sequence, each place can be marked just once. This requirement implies that the subnet obtained by the transitions executed in the firing sequence is a causal net and also that all the transitions t are such that ${}^\bullet t \neq \emptyset$.

In an UN conflicting pair of transitions t and t' are those that are never together in an execution, *i.e.* $\forall X \in \mathbb{E}(N). \, \{t, t'\} \nsubseteq X$. Given a place s in an unravel net, if ${}^\bullet s$ contains more than one transition, then the transitions in ${}^\bullet s$ are in conflict.

It is worthwhile to observe that the classical notion of *occurrence net* [18,20] is indeed a particular kind of UN namely one where the conflict relation is *inherited* along the transitive closure of the flow relation and it can can be inferred from the structure of the net itself. A further evidence that unravel nets generalize occurrence nets is implied also by the fact that flow nets generalize occurrence nets as well [2].

An unravel net $N = \langle S, T, F, \mathsf{m} \rangle$ is *complete* whenever $\forall t \in T \, \exists s_t \in S.$ ${}^\bullet s_t = \{t\} \wedge s_t{}^\bullet = \emptyset$. Thus in a complete UN the execution of a transition t is signaled by the marked place s_t. Given an UN N, it can be turned easily into a complete one by adding for each transition the suitable place, without changing the executions of the net, thus we consider complete UNs only. Completeness comes handy when defining the reversible counterpart of an UN.

Reversible Unravel Nets. The definition of *reversible unravel net* follows the one of *reversible occurrence net* [13] and generalize reversible occurrence nets as unravel nets generalize occurrence nets.

Definition 7. *A* reversible unravel net *(rUN for short) is a quintuple* $N = \langle S, T, U, F, \mathsf{m} \rangle$ *such that*

1. $U \subseteq T$ *and* $\forall u \in U. \, \exists! \, t \in T \setminus U$ *such that* ${}^\bullet u = t^\bullet$ *and* $u^\bullet = {}^\bullet t$,
2. $\forall t, t' \in T. \, {}^\bullet t = {}^\bullet t' \wedge t^\bullet = t'^\bullet \Rightarrow t = t'$,
3. $\bigcup_{t \in T} ({}^\bullet t \cup t^\bullet) = S$, *and*
4. $N|_{T \setminus U}$ *is a complete unravel net and* $\langle S, T, F, \mathsf{m} \rangle$ *is safe one.*

The transitions in U are the reversing ones; hence, we often say that a reversible unravel net N is *reversible with respect to* U. A reversing transition u is associated with a unique non-reversing transition t (condition 1) and its effects are intended to *undo* t. The second condition ensures that there is an injective mapping $h : U \to T$ which in turn implies that each reversible transition has exactly one reversing transition. The third requirement guarantees that there are no isolated conditions and the final one states that the subnet obtained forgetting all the reversing transitions is indeed an unravel net.

Along the lines of [13], we can prove that the set of reachable markings of a reversible unravel net is not influenced by performing a reversing transition. Let $N = \langle S, T, U, F, \mathsf{m} \rangle$ be an rUN. Then $\mathcal{M}_N = \mathcal{M}_{N|_{T \setminus U}}$. A consequence of this fact is that each marking can be reached by using just *forward events*. Let $N = \langle S, T, U, F, \mathsf{m} \rangle$ be an rUN and σ be an fs. Then, there exists an fs σ' such that $X_{\sigma'} \subseteq T \setminus U$ and $lead(\sigma) = lead(\sigma')$.

Given an unravel net and a subset of transitions to be reversed, it is straightforward to obtain a reversible unravel net.

Proposition 1. *Let $N = \langle S, T, F, \mathsf{m} \rangle$ be a complete unravel net and $U \subseteq T$ the set of transitions to be reversed. Define $\overleftarrow{N}^U = \langle S', T', U', F', \mathsf{m}' \rangle$ where $S = S'$, $U' = U \times \{\mathtt{r}\}$, $T' = (T \times \{\mathtt{f}\}) \cup U'$,*

$$F' = \{(s, (t, \mathtt{f})) \mid (s, t) \in F\} \cup \{((t, \mathtt{f}), s) \mid (t, s) \in F\} \cup$$
$$\{(s, (t, \mathtt{r})) \mid (t, s) \in F\} \cup \{((t, \mathtt{r}), s) \mid (s, t) \in F\}$$

and $\mathsf{m}' = \mathsf{m}$. Then $\overleftarrow{N}^U$ is a reversible unravel net.

The construction above simply adds as many events (transitions) as transitions to be reversed in U. The preset of each added event is the postset of the corresponding event to be reversed, and its postset is the preset of the event to be reversed. We write $\overleftarrow{N}$ instead of $\overleftarrow{N}^T$ when $N = \langle S, T, F, \mathsf{m} \rangle$, i.e., when every transition is reversible.

In Fig. 7a we show a non-complete unravel net, whose complete version is in Fig. 7b. The reversible unravel net obtained by reversing every transition is depicted in Fig. 7c.

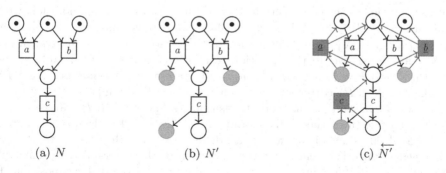

(a) N (b) N' (c) $\overleftarrow{N'}$

Fig. 7. An UN N, its complete version N' and the associated rUN $\overleftarrow{N'}$

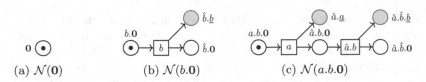

(a) $\mathcal{N}(\mathbf{0})$ (b) $\mathcal{N}(b.\mathbf{0})$ (c) $\mathcal{N}(a.b.\mathbf{0})$

Fig. 8. Example of nets corresponding to CCS processes

4 CCS Processes as Unravel Nets

We now recall the encoding of CCS terms into Petri nets due to Boudol and Castellani [3]. We just recall that originally the encoding was on proved terms instead of plain CCS. The difference between proved terms and CCS is that somehow in a proved term the labels carry the position of the process who did the action. Hence, we will use *decorated* version of labels. For instance, $\hat{a}.b$ denotes an event b which past was a. That is, if we want to indicate the event b of the term $a.b$ we will write $\hat{a}.b$. Analogously, labels carry also information about the syntactical structure of a term, actions corresponding to subterms of a choice and of a parallel composition are also decorated with an index i that indicates the subterm that performs the actions. An interesting aspect of this encoding is that these information is reflected in the name of the places and the transitions of the nets, which simplifies the formulation of the behavioural correspondence of a term and its associated net. We write $\ell(\_)$ for the function that removes decorations for a name, e.g., $\ell(\hat{a}.\hat{b}.c) = c$.

We now are in place to define and comment the encoding of a CCS term into a net. The encoding is inductively defined on the structure of the CCS process. For a CCS process P, its encoded net is $\mathcal{N}(P) = \langle S_P, T_P, F_P, \mathsf{m}_P \rangle$. The net corresponding to the inactive process $\mathbf{0}$, is just a net with just one marked place and with no transition, that is:

Definition 8. *The net* $\mathcal{N}(\mathbf{0}) = \langle \{\mathbf{0}\}, \emptyset, \emptyset, \{\mathbf{0}\} \rangle$ *is the net associated to* $\mathbf{0}$ *and it is called* zero.

To ease notation in the constructions we are going to present, we adopt following conventions: let $X \subseteq S \cup T$ be a set of places and transitions, we write $\hat{a}.X$ for the set $\{\hat{a}.x \mid x \in X\}$ containing the *decorated* versions of places and transitions in X. Analogously we lift this notation to relations: if R is a binary relation on $(S \cup T)$, then $\hat{a}.R = \{(\hat{a}.x, \hat{\alpha}.y) \mid (x, y) \in R\}$ is a binary relation on $(\alpha.S \cup \alpha.T)$.

The net $\mathcal{N}(\alpha.P)$ corresponding to a process $\alpha.P$ extends $\mathcal{N}(P)$ with two extra places $\alpha.P$ and $\hat{a}.\underline{\alpha}$ and one transition α. The place $\alpha.P$ stands for the process that executes the prefix α and follows by P. The place $\hat{a}.\underline{\alpha}$ is not in the original encoding of [3]; we have add it to ensure that the obtained net is *complete*, which is essential for the definition of the reversible net. This will become clearer when commenting the encoding of the parallel composition. It should be noted that this addition does not interfere with the behaviour of the net, since all added places are final. Also a new transition, named α is created and added to the net, and the flow relation is updated accordingly. Figures 8a, 8b and 8c report the respectively the encoding of the inactive process, of the process $b.0$ and $a.b.0$. Moreover the aforementioned figures systematically show how the prefixing operator is rendered into Petri nets. As a matter of fact, the net $a.b.0$ is built starting from the net corresponding to $b.0$ by adding the prefix a. We note that also the label of transitions is affected by appending the label of the new prefix at the beginning. This is rendered in Fig. 8c where the transition mimicking the action b is labeled as $\hat{a}.b$ indicating that an a was done before b. In what follows we will often omit such representation from figures.

Definition 9. *Let P a CCS process and $\mathcal{N}(P) = \langle S_P, T_P, F_P, \mathsf{m}_P \rangle$ be the associated net. Then $\mathcal{N}(\alpha.P)$ is the net $\langle S_{\alpha.P}, T_{\alpha.P}, F_{\alpha.P}, \mathsf{m}_{\alpha.P} \rangle$ where*

$$S_{\alpha.P} = \{\alpha.P, \hat{\alpha}.\underline{\alpha}\} \cup \hat{\alpha}.S_P$$
$$T_{\alpha.P} = \{\alpha\} \cup \hat{\alpha}.T_p$$
$$F_{\alpha.P} = \{(\alpha.P, \alpha), (\alpha, \hat{\alpha}.\underline{\alpha})\} \cup \{(\alpha, \hat{\alpha}.b) \mid b \in \mathsf{m}_{0P}\} \cup \hat{\alpha}.F_P$$
$$\mathsf{m}_{\alpha.P} = \{\alpha.P\}$$

For a set X of transitions we write $\|_i X$ for $\{\|_i x \mid x \in X\}$, which straightforwardly lifts to relations.

The encoding of the parallel goes along the line of the prefixing one. Also in this case we have to decorate the places (and transitions) with the position of the term in the syntax tree. To this end, each branch of the parallel is decorated with $\|_i$ with i being the i-th position. Regarding the transitions, we have to add all the possible synchronisations among the processes in parallel. This is why, along with the transitions of the branches (properly decorated with $\|_i$) we have to add extra transitions to indicate the possible synchronisation. Naturally a synchronisation is possible when one label is the co-label of the other transition. Figure 9a shows the net corresponding to the process $a.b \parallel \bar{a}.c$. As we can see, the encoding builds upon the encoding of $a.b$ and $\bar{a}.c$, by (i) adding to all the places and transitions whether the branch is the left one or the right one and (ii) adding an extra transition and place for the only possible synchronisation. We add an extra place (in line with the prefixes) to mark the fact that a synchronisation has taken place. Let us note that the extra places $\underline{a}$, $\underline{\bar{a}}$ and $\underline{\tau}$ are used to understand whether the two prefixes have been executed singularly (e.g., no synchronisation) or they contributed to do a synchronisation. Suppose, for example, that the net had not such places, and suppose that we have two tokens in the places $\|_0 \hat{a}.b$ and $\|_1 \hat{\bar{a}}.b$. Now, how can we understand whether these two tokens are the result of the firing sequence $a, \bar{a}$ or they are the result of the τ transition? It is impossible, but by using the aforementioned extra-places, which are instrumental to tell if a single prefix has executed, we can distinguish the τ from the firing sequence $a, \bar{a}$ and then reverse accordingly.

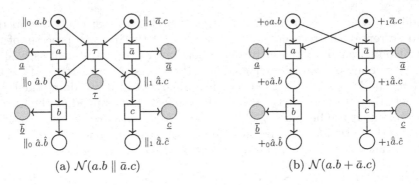

(a) $\mathcal{N}(a.b \parallel \bar{a}.c)$ (b) $\mathcal{N}(a.b + \bar{a}.c)$

Fig. 9. Example of nets corresponding to CCS parallel and choice operator. We omit the trailing **0**

Definition 10. *Let $\mathcal{N}(P_1)$ and $\mathcal{N}(P_2)$ be the net associated to the processes P_1 and P_2. Then $\mathcal{N}(P_1 \| P_2)$ is the net $\langle S_{P_1 \| P_2}, T_{P_1 \| P_2}, F_{P_1 \| P_2}, \mathsf{m}_{P_1 \| P_2} \rangle$ where*

$$S_{P_1 \| P_2} = \|_0 S_{P_1} \cup \|_1 S_{P_2} \cup \{s_{\{t,t'\}} \mid t \in T_{P_1} \wedge t' \in T_{P_2} \wedge \overline{\ell(t)} = \ell(t')\}$$

$$T_{P_1 \| P_2} = \|_0 T_{P_1} \cup \|_1 T_{P_2} \cup \{\{t,t'\} \mid t \in T_{P_1} \wedge t' \in T_{P_2} \wedge \overline{\ell(t)} = \ell(t')\}$$

$$F_{P_1 \| P_2} = \|_0 F_{P_1} \cup \|_1 F_{P_2} \cup \{(\{t,t'\}, s_{\{t,t'\}}) \mid t \in T_{P_1} \wedge t' \in T_{P_2} \wedge \overline{\ell(t)} = \ell(t')\}$$
$$\cup \{(\|_i s, (t_1, t_2)) \mid (s, t_i) \in F_{P_i}\} \cup \{(\|_i s, (t_1, t_2)) \mid (s, t_i) \in F_{P_i}\}$$

$$\mathsf{m}_{P_0 \| P2} = \|_0 \mathsf{m}_{P_0} \cup \|_1 \mathsf{m}_{P_1}$$

The encoding of choice operator is similar to the parallel one. The only difference is that we do not have to deal with possible synchronisations since the branches of a choice operator are mutually exclusive. Figure 9b reports the net corresponding to the process $a.b + \bar{a}.c$. As in the previous examples, the net is built upon the subnets representing $a.b$ and $\bar{a}.c$.

Definition 11. *Let $\mathcal{N}(P_i)$ be the net associated to the processes P_i for $i \in I$. Then $+_{i \in I} P_i$ is the net $\langle S_{+_{i \in I} P_i}, T_{+_{i \in I} P_i}, F_{+_{i \in I} P_i}, \mathsf{m}_{+_{i \in I} P_i} \rangle$ where:*

$$S_{+_{i \in I} P_i} = \cup_{i \in I} +_i S_{P_i}$$
$$T_{+_{i \in I} P_i} = \cup_{i \in I} +_i T_{P_i}$$
$$F_{+_{i \in I} P_i} = \{(+_i x, +_i y) \mid (x, y) \in F_{P_i}\} \cup \{(+_j s, +_i t) \mid s \in \mathsf{m}_{P_j} \wedge {}^\bullet t \in \mathsf{m}_{P_i} \wedge i \neq j\}$$
$$\mathsf{m}_{+_{i \in I} P_i} = \cup_{i \in I} +_i \mathsf{m}_{P_i}.$$

We write T^a for the set $\{t \in T \mid \mathsf{nm}(\ell(t)) = a\}$. The encoding of the hiding operator simply removes all transitions whose labels corresponds to actions over the restricted name.

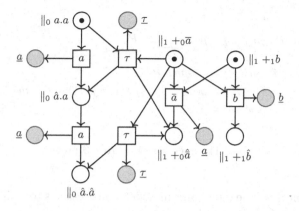

Fig. 10. A complex example: $\mathcal{N}(a.a \parallel \overline{a} + b)$

Definition 12. *Let P a CCS process and $\mathcal{N}(P) = \langle S_P, T_P, F_P, \mathsf{m}_P \rangle$ be the associated net. Then $\mathcal{N}(P \setminus a)$ is the net $\langle S_{P\setminus a}, T_{P\setminus a}, F_{P\setminus a}, \mathsf{m}_{P\setminus a} \rangle$ where*

$$S_{P\setminus a} = \backslash_a S_P$$
$$T_{P\setminus a} = \backslash_a (T_P \setminus T_a)$$
$$F_{P\setminus a} = \{(\backslash_a s, \backslash_a t) \mid (s,t) \in F_P, t \notin T_P^a\} \cup \{(\backslash_a t, \backslash_a s) \mid (t,s) \in F_P, t \notin T_P^a\}$$
$$\mathsf{m}_{P\setminus a} = \backslash_a \mathsf{m}_P.$$

Figure 10 shows a more complex example, the net corresponding to the process $a.a \parallel \overline{a} + b$. In this case, the process on the right of the parallel composition can synchronise with the one on the left one in two different occasions. This is why there are two different transitions representing the synchronisation. Also, since the right process of the parallel is a choice operator, it can happen that the right branch of it is executed, thus interdicting the synchronisation. Let us note that since the right branch of the parallel operator is a choice one, composed by two branches, the encoding labels these branches with '$\parallel_1 +_0$' and '$\parallel_1 +_1$' to indicate respectively the left and right branch of the choice operator, which is the right branch of a parallel operator. The following proposition is instrumental for our result.

Proposition 2. *The nets defined in Definition 8, Definition 9, Definition 10, Definition 11 and Definition 12 are complete unravel nets.*

We are now in place to define what is the net corresponding to a RCCS process. So far we have spoken about encoding CCS processes into nets. We remark that since RCCS is built upon CCS processes, also the encoding of RCCS is built upon the encoding of CCS. To do so, we first need the notion of ancestor, that is the initial process from which an RCCS process is derived. Let us note that since we are considering coherent RCCS processes (see Definition 3), an RCCS process has always an ancestor. The ancestor $\rho(R)$ of an RCCS process R can be calculated syntactically from R, since all the information about the past are

$$\rho(\langle\rangle \triangleright P) = P$$

$$\rho(\langle \_, \alpha_z^z, \sum_{i \in I \setminus \{z\}} \alpha_i.P_i \rangle \cdot m \triangleright P) = \rho(m \triangleright \sum_{i \in I} \alpha_i.P_i)$$

$$\rho(\langle i \rangle \cdot m \triangleright P) = \langle i \rangle \cdot m \triangleright P$$

$$\rho(P_1 \| P_2) = \rho(m \triangleright P_1' \| P_2') \text{ where } \rho(P_i) = \langle i \rangle \cdot m \triangleright P_i' \wedge i \in \{1, 2\}$$

$$\rho(P \setminus a) = \rho(P) \setminus a$$

Fig. 11. The ancestor of an RCCS process

stored into memories. The only point in which a process has to wait for its sibling is when a memory fork $\langle 1 \rangle$ or $\langle 2 \rangle$ is met.

Definition 13. *Given a coherent RCCS process R, its ancestor $\rho(R)$ is inductively defined as in Fig. 11.*

The idea behind the ancestor process is that the encoding of an RCCS process and of its ancestor should give the same net, what changes is the position where the markings are placed. And such position is derived by the information stored into memories. We then define the *marking* function $\mu(\cdot)$ defined inductively as follows:

$$\mu(\langle\rangle \triangleright P) = \{P\} \qquad \mu(P_0 \| P_1) = \|_0 \mu(P_0) \cup \|_1 \mu(P_1) \qquad \mu(P \setminus a) = \setminus_a \mu(P_1)$$

$$\mu(\langle m', \alpha^i, Q \rangle \cdot m \triangleright P) = \mu(m \triangleright +_i \hat{\alpha}.P) \cup \{s_{t,t'} \mid t = m \triangleright +_i \alpha \wedge t = m' \triangleright +_i' \overline{\alpha}\}$$

$$\mu(\langle *, \alpha^i, Q \rangle \cdot m \triangleright P) = \mu(m \triangleright +_i \hat{\alpha}.P) \cup \mu(m \triangleright +_i \underline{\alpha})$$

We are now in place to define what is the reversible net corresponding to an RCCS process:

Definition 14. *Let R be an RCCS term with $\rho(R) = P$. Then $\overleftarrow{\mathcal{N}(R)}$ is the net $\langle S, T, F, \mu(R) \rangle$ where $\mathcal{N}(P) = \langle S, T, F, \mathsf{m} \rangle$.*

Proposition 3. *Let R be an RCCS term with $\rho(R) = P$. Then $\overleftarrow{\mathcal{N}(R)}$ is a reversible unravel net.*

In a few words Proposition 3 tells us that the reversible net corresponding to a coherent RCCS R is that one of its ancestor. The contribution of R to the construction of its net relies in the markings, that is the computational history contained in R is what determines the markings. This is rendered in Figs. 12a and 12b where the two nets are the same since the two processes R_1 and R_2 shares the same origin. What changes is the where markings are placed, since R_1 and R_2 represents different computation from the origin process.

We can now state our main result in terms of bisimulation:

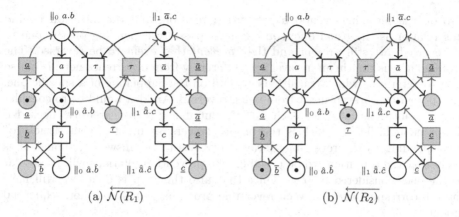

(a) $\overleftarrow{\mathcal{N}(R_1)}$ (b) $\overleftarrow{\mathcal{N}(R_2)}$

Fig. 12. Example of nets corresponding to RCCS process $R_1 = \langle *, a^1, \mathbf{0} \rangle \cdot \langle 1 \rangle \cdot \langle \rangle \triangleright b$
$\langle 2 \rangle \cdot \langle \rangle \triangleright \bar{a}.c$ and $R_2 = \langle *, b^1, \mathbf{0} \rangle \cdot \langle m_2, a_1, \mathbf{0} \rangle \cdot \langle 1 \rangle \cdot \langle \rangle \triangleright b$
$\langle m_1, \bar{a}^1, \mathbf{0} \rangle \cdot \langle 2 \rangle \cdot \langle \rangle \triangleright c$ with $m_i = \langle i \rangle \cdot \langle \rangle$

Theorem 1. *Let P be a finite CCS process, then $\langle \rangle \triangleright P \sim \overleftarrow{\mathcal{N}(P)}$.*

Proof sketch. It is sufficient to show that

$$\mathcal{R} = \{(R, \langle S, T, F, \mu(R) \rangle) \mid \rho(R) = P, \overleftarrow{\mathcal{N}(P)} = \langle S, T, F, m \rangle\}$$

is a bisimulation. Let us note that all the transitions in the generated net have a unique name, which is the path from the root to the term in the abstract syntax tree. There is a one to one correspondence between this path and the memory of a process which can mimic the same action/transition.

5   Conclusions and Future Works

On the line of previous research we have equipped a reversible process calculus with a non sequential semantics by using the classical encoding of process calculi into nets. What comes out from the encoding is that the machinery to reverse a process was already present in the encoding.

    Our result relies on unravel nets, that are able to represent *or*-causality. The consequence is that the same event may have different pasts. Unravel nets are naturally related to *bundle* event structures [11,12], where the dependencies are represented using *bundles*, namely finite subsets of conflicting events, and the bundle relation is usually written as $X \mapsto e$. Starting from an unravel net $\langle S, T, F, m \rangle$, and considering the transition $t \in T$, the bundles representing the dependencies are $^\bullet s \mapsto t$ for each $s \in {}^\bullet t$, and the conflict relation can be easily inferred by the semantic one definable on the unravel net. This result relies on the fact that in any unravel net, for each place s, the transitions in $^\bullet s$ are pairwise conflicting. The *reversible* bundle structures add to the bundle relation (defined also on the reversing events) a prevention relation, and the intuition behind this relation is the usual one: some events, possibly depending on the one to be reversed, are still present and they *prevent* that event to be reversed. The problem here is that in an unravel net, differently from occurrence nets, is not so easy to determine which transitions depend on the happening of a specific one, thus potentially preventing it from being reversed. An idea would be to consider all the transitions in $s^\bullet$ for each $s \in t^\bullet$, but it has to be carefully checked if this is enough. Thus, which is the proper "reversible bundle event structure" corresponding to the reversible unravel nets has to be answered, though it is likely that the conditions to be posed on the prevention relations will be similar to the ones considered in [7,8]. Once that also this step is done, we will have the full correspondence between reversible processes calculi and non sequential models.

References

1. Ulidowski, I., Lanese, I., Schultz, U.P., Ferreira, C. (eds.): RC 2020. LNCS, vol. 12070. Springer, Cham (2020). https://doi.org/10.1007/978-3-030-47361-7
2. Boudol, G.: Flow event structures and flow nets. In: Guessarian, I. (ed.) LITP 1990. LNCS, vol. 469, pp. 62–95. Springer, Heidelberg (1990). https://doi.org/10.1007/3-540-53479-2_4
3. Boudol, G., Castellani, I.: Flow models of distributed computations: three equivalent semantics for CCS. Inf. Comput. **114**(2), 247–314 (1994)
4. Danos, V., Krivine, J.: Reversible communicating systems. In: Gardner, P., Yoshida, N. (eds.) CONCUR 2004. LNCS, vol. 3170, pp. 292–307. Springer, Heidelberg (2004). https://doi.org/10.1007/978-3-540-28644-8_19
5. Degano, P., Nicola, R.D., Montanari, U.: A distributed operational semantics for CCS based on condition/event systems. Acta Informatica **26**(1/2), 59–91 (1988)
6. Goltz, U.: CCS and petri nets. In: Guessarian, I. (ed.) LITP 1990. LNCS, vol. 469, pp. 334–357. Springer, Heidelberg (1990). https://doi.org/10.1007/3-540-53479-2_14
7. Graversen, E., Phillips, I., Yoshida, N.: Event structure semantics of (controlled) reversible CCS. In: Kari, J., Ulidowski, I. (eds.) RC 2018. LNCS, vol. 11106, pp. 102–122. Springer, Cham (2018). https://doi.org/10.1007/978-3-319-99498-7_7
8. Graversen, E., Phillips, I., Yoshida, N.: Event structure semantics of (controlled) reversible CCS. J. Logic. Algebraic Methods Program. **121**, 100686 (2021)
9. Krivine, J.: A verification technique for reversible process algebra. In: Glück, R., Yokoyama, T. (eds.) RC 2012. LNCS, vol. 7581, pp. 204–217. Springer, Heidelberg (2013). https://doi.org/10.1007/978-3-642-36315-3_17
10. Lanese, I., Medic, D., Mezzina, C.A.: Static versus dynamic reversibility in CCS. Acta Informatica **58**(1), 1–34 (2021)
11. Langerak, R.: Bundle event structures: a non-interleaving semantics for LOTOS. In Formal Description Techniques, V. In: Proceedings of the IFIP TC6/WG6.1 FORTE 92, volume C-10 of IFIP Transactions, pp. 331–346. North-Holland (1992)
12. Langerak, R., Brinksma, E., Katoen, J.-P.: Causal ambiguity and partial orders in event structures. In: Mazurkiewicz, A., Winkowski, J. (eds.) CONCUR 1997. LNCS, vol. 1243, pp. 317–331. Springer, Heidelberg (1997). https://doi.org/10.1007/3-540-63141-0_22

13. Melgratti, H., Mezzina, C.A., Phillips, I., Pinna, G.M., Ulidowski, I.: Reversible occurrence nets and causal reversible prime event structures. In: Lanese, I., Rawski, M. (eds.) RC 2020. LNCS, vol. 12227, pp. 35–53. Springer, Cham (2020). https://doi.org/10.1007/978-3-030-52482-1_2

14. Melgratti, H.C., Mezzina, C.A., Pinna, G.M.: A distributed operational view of reversible prime event structures. In: Proceedings of the 36rd Annual ACM/IEEE Symposium on Logic in Computer Science, LICS 2021. ACM (2021). (to appear)

15. Melgratti, H.C., Mezzina, C.A., Ulidowski, I.: Reversing place transition nets. Log. Methods Comput. Sci. 16(4), (2020)

16. Mezzina, C.A., et al.: Software and reversible systems: a survey of recent activities. In: Ulidowski, I., Lanese, I., Schultz, U.P., Ferreira, C. (eds.) RC 2020. LNCS, vol. 12070, pp. 41–59. Springer, Cham (2020). https://doi.org/10.1007/978-3-030-47361-7_2

17. Milner, R.: A Calculus of Communicating Systems. LNCS 92, 1980 (1980)

18. Nielsen, M., Plotkin, G., Winskel, G.: Petri nets, event structures and domains, part 1. Theor. Comput. Sci. 13, 85–108 (1981)

19. Phillips, I.C.C., Ulidowski, I.: Reversing algebraic process calculi. J. Log. Algebraic Methods Program. 73(1–2), 70–96 (2007)

20. Winskel, G.: Event structures. In: Brauer, W., Reisig, W., Rozenberg, G. (eds.) ACPN 1986. LNCS, vol. 255, pp. 325–392. Springer, Heidelberg (1987). https://doi.org/10.1007/3-540-17906-2_31

Forward-Reverse Observational Equivalences in CCSK

Ivan Lanese[1]([⊠]) [ID] and Iain Phillips[2] [ID]

[1] Focus Team, University of Bologna/INRIA, Bologna, Italy
ivan.lanese@unibo.it
[2] Imperial College London, London, England

Abstract. In the context of CCSK, a reversible extension of CCS, we study observational equivalences that distinguish forward moves from backward ones. We present a refinement of the notion of forward-reverse bisimilarity and show that it coincides with a notion of forward-reverse barbed congruence. We also show a set of sound axioms allowing one to reason equationally on process equivalences.

Keywords: CCSK · Forward-reverse bisimilarity · Forward-reverse barbed congruence · Axiomatization

1 Introduction

Building concurrent systems is difficult and error-prone, since one has to reason on a large number of possible interleavings; yet concurrency is a must in current systems, such as the Internet, the Cloud, or parallel processors.

Reversible computing, allowing a system to execute both in the standard, forward direction, as well as backwards, recovering past states, has a number of interesting applications, including low-energy computing [18], simulation [6], biological modelling [5,33] and program debugging [11,21,24]. Many of these applications involve concurrent systems. Thus, a number of works have proposed reversible extensions of concurrent formalisms, including CCS [9,30], π-calculus [8], higher-order π [20], Petri nets [25], and the Erlang [22] programming language. Given the relevance of analysis techniques for concurrent systems, also a number of analysis techniques have been considered, e.g., following the session types approach [3,7,27]. Notions of observational equivalence have also been used in a few works, such as [1,2,26,30], yet the question of which notions of observational equivalence are suitable for reversible processes, and how they can be exploited to actually reason about them, has seldom been considered.

In this paper we tackle this issue. In particular, we consider a setting where reversibility is observable, that is forward actions are observationally distinguishable from their undo. This means that we are interested in systems where

---

The first author has also been partially supported by French ANR project DCore ANR-18-CE25-0007 and by INdAM – GNCS 2020 project *Sistemi Reversibili Concorrenti: dai Modelli ai Linguaggi*. We thank reviewers for their helpful comments.

S. Yamashita and T. Yokoyama (Eds.): RC 2021, LNCS 12805, pp. 126–143, 2021.
https://doi.org/10.1007/978-3-030-79837-6_8

reversibility is relevant, e.g., recovery protocols, reversible debuggers, and so on. If instead one considers reversibility as an implementation detail only, then also more abstract notions where forward moves can be matched by backward moves and vice versa could be of interest. We leave this analysis for future work. Also, we consider *causal-consistent reversibility* [9], which is currently the most used notion of reversibility for concurrent systems. It states that any action can be undone, provided that its consequences, if any, are undone beforehand. Among its properties, it ensures that every reachable state is also reachable by forward computation. This contrasts with other approaches, used, e.g., in biological modelling [33], where causes can be undone without undoing their consequences, thus leading to new states. This setting will be left for future work as well. Finally, we will focus on strong equivalences, where internal steps need to be matched by other internal steps. Weak equivalences, which abstract away from internal steps, are of course also relevant, but before tackling them the strong setting needs to be well understood, hence we leave also this analysis for future work.

In the setting of causal-consistent reversibility, we define and motivate a notion of (strong) revised forward-reverse bisimilarity, also comparing it with alternative formulations (Sect. 4). We support our proposal with two contributions: (i) we show that it admits an equivalent formulation in terms of forward-reverse barbed congruence (Sect. 5); (ii) we prove sound a number of axioms which can be used to reason equationally about reversible systems (Theorem 4.10).

From a technical point of view, we work on CCSK, which is the instance on CCS of a general approach to reverse process calculi presented in [30]. The reason for this design choice is that CCSK history representation as keys ensures, differently from alternative approaches such as the one of RCCS [9], no redundancy in process representation, and this is fundamental to have simple axioms. We will come back to this point in the related work (Sect. 6), where we will also contrast our proposal with other proposals in the literature.

For space reasons, most proofs are available only in the companion technical report [23].

2   CCSK

As anticipated in the Introduction, we base our work on CCSK as defined in [30], with a minor change that we will discuss in Remark 4.2. We recall below the syntax and semantics of CCSK, referring to [30] for more details. CCSK is built on top of CCS, adding a mechanism of keys to keep track of which part of the process has already been executed. Hence, during forward computation, executed actions are not discarded, but just labelled as already been executed.

We define the actions of CCS, representing communications over named channels, much as usual. Let $\mathcal{A}$ be a set of *names*, ranged over by $a, b, \ldots$. Let $\bar{a}$ be the *complement* of $a \in \mathcal{A}$, let $\overline{\mathcal{A}} = \{\bar{a} : a \in \mathcal{A}\}$, and let Act be the disjoint union of $\mathcal{A}$, $\overline{\mathcal{A}}$ and $\{\tau\}$. Also, let $\bar{\bar{a}} = a$ for $a \in \mathcal{A} \cup \overline{\mathcal{A}}$. Standard prefixes, ranged over by $\alpha, \beta, \ldots$, are drawn from Act. Intuitively, names represent input actions, co-names represent output actions, and τ is an internal synchronisation.

CCS processes, which we shall also call *standard* processes, are given by:

$$P, Q := 0 \mid \alpha.P \mid P + Q \mid P \mid Q \mid (\nu a)P$$

Intuitively, 0 is the inactive process, $\alpha.P$ is a process that performs action α and continues as P, $P + Q$ is nondeterministic choice, $P \mid Q$ is parallel composition and restriction $(\nu a)P$ binds channel a (both occurrences in input actions and in output actions) inside P. We do not consider renaming, adding it will not change the results of the paper. A channel is bound if inside the scope of a restriction operator, free otherwise. Function $\text{fn}(P)$ computes the set of free names in process P.

CCSK adds to CCS the possibility of going backwards. In order to remember which input interacted with which output while going forward, at each forward step fresh keys are created, and the same key is used to label an input and the corresponding output.

We denote the set of keys by Keys, ranged over by $m, n, k, \ldots$. Prefixes, ranged over by π, are of the form $\alpha[m]$ or α. The former denotes that α has already been executed, the latter that it has not.

CCSK processes are given by:

$$X, Y := 0 \mid \pi.X \mid X + Y \mid X \mid Y \mid (\nu a)X$$

hence they are like CCS processes but for the fact that some prefixes may be labelled with a key. In the following, we will drop trailing 0s.

We use predicate $\text{std}(X)$ to mean that X is standard, that is none of its actions has been executed, hence it has no keys. We assume function $\text{toStd}(X)$ that takes a CCSK process X and gives back the standard process obtained by removing from X all keys. Finally, we consider function $\text{keys}(X)$ which computes the set of keys in CCSK process X.

In a CCSK process we distinguish free from bound keys.

Definition 2.1 (Free and Bound Keys). *A key k is bound in a process X iff it occurs either twice, attached to complementary prefixes, or once, attached to a τ prefix. A key k is free if it occurs once, attached to a non-τ prefix.*

Intuitively, all the occurrences of a bound key are inside the process, while a free key has another occurrence in the environment.

Figure 1 shows the forward rules of CCSK. Backward rules in Fig. 2 are obtained from forward rules by reversing the direction of transitions.

Rule (TOP) allows a prefix to execute. The rule generates a key m. Freshness of m is guaranteed by the side conditions of the other rules. Rule (PRE-FIX) states that an executed prefix does not block execution. The two rules for (CHOICE) and the two for (PAR) allow processes to execute inside a choice or a parallel composition. The side condition of rule (CHOICE) ensures that at most one branch can execute. Rule (SYNCH) allows two complementary actions to synchronise producing a τ. The key of the two actions needs to be the same. Rule (RES) allows an action which does not involve the restricted channel to propagate through restriction.

$$(\text{TOP})\quad \frac{\text{std}(X)}{\alpha.X \xrightarrow{\alpha[m]}_f \alpha[m].X} \qquad (\text{PREFIX})\quad \frac{X \xrightarrow{\beta[n]}_f X'}{\alpha[m]..X \xrightarrow{\beta[n]}_f \alpha[m].X'}\ m \neq n$$

$$(\text{CHOICE})\quad \frac{X \xrightarrow{\alpha[m]}_f X' \quad \text{std}(Y)}{X + Y \xrightarrow{\alpha[m]}_f X' + Y} \qquad \frac{Y \xrightarrow{\alpha[m]}_f Y' \quad \text{std}(X)}{X + Y \xrightarrow{\alpha[m]}_f X + Y'}$$

$$(\text{PAR})\quad \frac{X \xrightarrow{\alpha[m]}_f X' \quad m \notin \text{keys}(Y)}{X \mid Y \xrightarrow{\alpha[m]}_f X' \mid Y} \qquad \frac{Y \xrightarrow{\alpha[m]}_f Y' \quad m \notin \text{keys}(X)}{X \mid Y \xrightarrow{\alpha[m]}_f X \mid Y'}$$

$$(\text{SYNCH})\quad \frac{X \xrightarrow{\alpha[m]}_f X' \quad Y \xrightarrow{\overline{\alpha}[m]}_f Y'}{X \mid Y \xrightarrow{\tau[m]}_f X' \mid Y'}\ (\alpha \neq \tau)$$

$$(\text{RES})\quad \frac{X \xrightarrow{\alpha[m]}_f X'}{(\nu a)X \xrightarrow{\alpha[m]}_f (\nu a)X'}\ \alpha \notin \{a, \overline{a}\}$$

Fig. 1. Forward SOS rules for CCSK

The forward semantics of a CCSK process is the smallest relation $\rightarrow_f$ closed under the rules in Fig. 1. The backward semantics of a CCSK process is the smallest relation $\rightarrow_r$ closed under the rules in Fig. 2. The semantics is the union of the two relations. We shall let μ range over transition labels $\alpha[m]$.

As standard in reversible computing (see, e.g., [30] or the notion of coherent process in [9]), all the developments consider only processes reachable from a standard process.

Definition 2.2 (Reachable Process). *A process X is* reachable *iff there exists a standard process P and a finite sequence of transitions from P to X.*

We recall here a main result of reversible computing, useful for our development: the Loop Lemma states that any action can be undone, and any undone action can be redone.

Lemma 2.3 (Loop Lemma [30, Prop. 5.1]). $X \xrightarrow{\alpha[m]}_f X'$ *iff* $X' \xrightarrow{\alpha[m]}_r X$.

3 Syntactic Characterisation of Reachable Processes

In this paper we discuss relevant notions of observational equivalence for CCSK. However, since, as described above, only reachable processes are of interest, we need to understand the structure of reachable processes. Hence, as a preliminary step, we propose in this section a sound and complete syntactic characterisation of reachable processes. This result is interesting in itself, since a similar preliminary step is needed for most of the reasonings on a calculus such as CCSK. Notably, many works in the literature study properties that reachable processes

$$(\text{BK-TOP}) \quad \frac{\text{std}(X)}{\alpha[m].X \xrightarrow{\alpha[m]}_r \alpha.X} \qquad (\text{BK-PREFIX}) \quad \frac{X \xrightarrow{\beta[n]}_r X'}{\alpha[m].X \xrightarrow{\beta[n]}_r \alpha[m].X'} \; m \neq n$$

$$(\text{BK-CHOICE}) \quad \frac{X \xrightarrow{\alpha[m]}_r X' \quad \text{std}(Y)}{X + Y \xrightarrow{\alpha[m]}_r X' + Y} \qquad \frac{Y \xrightarrow{\alpha[m]}_r Y' \quad \text{std}(X)}{X + Y \xrightarrow{\alpha[m]}_r X + Y'}$$

$$(\text{BK-PAR}) \quad \frac{X \xrightarrow{\alpha[m]}_r X' \quad m \notin \text{keys}(Y)}{X \mid Y \xrightarrow{\alpha[m]}_r X' \mid Y} \qquad \frac{Y \xrightarrow{\alpha[m]}_r Y' \quad m \notin \text{keys}(X)}{X \mid Y \xrightarrow{\alpha[m]}_r X \mid Y'}$$

$$(\text{BK-SYNCH}) \quad \frac{X \xrightarrow{\alpha[m]}_r X' \quad Y \xrightarrow{\bar{\alpha}[m]}_r Y'}{X \mid Y \xrightarrow{\tau[m]}_r X' \mid Y'} \; (\alpha \neq \tau)$$

$$(\text{BK-RES}) \quad \frac{X \xrightarrow{\alpha[m]}_r X'}{(\nu a)X \xrightarrow{\alpha[m]}_r (\nu a)X'} \; \alpha \notin \{a, \bar{a}\}$$

Fig. 2. Reverse SOS rules for CCSK

satisfy, but they do not provide a complete characterisation, see, e.g., [20, Lemma 3]. We are not aware of any such characterisation for reversible CCS.

A main item in the characterisation of reachability is that keys should define a partial order, thus given a process X we define a partial order $\leq_X$ on $\text{keys}(X)$ as follows.

Definition 3.1 (Partial Order on Keys). *We first define a function* $\text{ord}(\cdot)$ *that given a process computes a set of relations among its keys. The definition is by structural induction on X.*

$$\text{ord}(0) = \emptyset \qquad\qquad\qquad \text{ord}(\alpha.X) = \text{ord}(X)$$
$$\text{ord}(X + Y) = \text{ord}(X) \cup \text{ord}(Y) \qquad \text{ord}(X \mid Y) = \text{ord}(X) \cup \text{ord}(Y)$$
$$\text{ord}(\alpha[n].X) = \text{ord}(X) \cup \{n < k \mid k \in \text{keys}(X)\}$$
$$\text{ord}((\nu a)X) = \text{ord}(X)$$

The partial order $\leq_X$ on $\text{keys}(X)$ is the reflexive and transitive closure of $\text{ord}(X)$.

The definition above captures structural dependencies on keys. Combined with the property that prefixes that interact have the same key (see rule (SYNCH) in Fig. 1), it captures a form of Lamport's happened-before relation [17] adapted to synchronous communication.

In order to characterise reachable processes we need to define contexts.

Definition 3.2 (Context). *A CCSK context is a process with a hole, as generated by the grammar below:*

$$C := \bullet \mid \pi.C \mid C + Y \mid X + C \mid C \mid Y \mid X \mid C \mid (\nu a)C$$

We denote with $C[X]$ the process obtained by replacing $\bullet$ with X inside C.

We can now present our characterisation of reachable processes.

Definition 3.3 (Well-Formed Process). *A process* X *is* well-formed *if all the following conditions hold:*

1. *if* $X = C[\alpha.Y]$ *then* $\text{std}(Y)$, *that is standard prefixes have standard continuations;*
2. *if* $X = C[Y+Y']$ *then* $\text{std}(Y) \vee \text{std}(Y')$, *that is in choices at most one branch is non-standard;*
3. *each key occurs at most twice;*
4. *if a key occurs twice, then the two occurrences are attached to complementary prefixes;*
5. *if a key* n *occurs twice, then there are* C, Y, Y' *such that* $X = C[Y \mid Y']$, *and both* Y *and* Y' *contain exactly one occurrence of* n;
6. *if* $X = C[(\nu a)Y]$ *and a key* n *occurs in a prefix on channel* a *inside* Y, *then* n *occurs twice inside* Y;
7. $\leq_X$ *is acyclic.*

Thanks to conditions 3 and 4 each key is either free or bound.
Each well-formed process X is reachable from $\text{toStd}(X)$.

Lemma 3.4. *Let* X *be a well-formed process. Let* $k_1, \ldots, k_n$ *be a fixed total order on* $\text{keys}(X)$ *compatible with* $\leq_X$. *Then there is a computation* $\text{toStd}(X) \xrightarrow{\alpha[k_1]}_f \ldots \xrightarrow{\alpha[k_n]}_f X$.

The classes of reachable and well-formed processes coincide.

Proposition 3.5 (Reachable Coincides with Well-Formed). X *is reachable iff it is well-formed.*

The results above, enabled by the syntactic characterisation of reachable processes, are needed for our development, but can also help in general in the study of the theory of CCSK. Indeed, we can for instance derive as a corollary the Parabolic Lemma [30, Lemma 5.12], which can be rephrased as follows.

Corollary 3.6 (Parabolic Lemma [30, Lemma 5.12]). *Each reachable process is forward reachable.*

Proof. Thanks to Proposition 3.5 a reachable process is also well-formed. Hence, it is forward reachable thanks to Lemma 3.4.

4 Revised Forward-Reverse Bisimilarity

In this section we move to the main aim of this work, namely the definition of a strong observational equivalence for CCSK able to distinguish forward steps from backward ones. We consider as starting point for our analysis the notion of forward-reverse bisimulation introduced in the original CCSK paper [30, Definition 6.5], and rephrased below.

Definition 4.1 (Forward-Reverse Bisimulation). *A symmetric relation* $\mathcal{R}$ *is a* forward-reverse bisimulation *if whenever* $X \mathcal{R} Y$:

1. $\mathtt{keys}(X) = \mathtt{keys}(Y)$;
2. *if* $X \xrightarrow{\mu}_f X'$ *then there is* Y' *such that* $Y \xrightarrow{\mu}_f Y'$ *and* $X' \mathcal{R} Y'$;
3. *if* $X \xrightarrow{\mu}_r X'$ *then there is* Y' *such that* $Y \xrightarrow{\mu}_r Y'$ *and* $X' \mathcal{R} Y'$.

We first notice that clause 1 is redundant. Indeed, given a reachable process X we know that there is a computation $\mathtt{toStd}(X) \to_f^* X$. Thanks to the Loop Lemma, we also have a computation $X \to_r^* \mathtt{toStd}(X)$, whose labels exhibit all the keys in $\mathtt{keys}(X)$. Thus, any process Y related to X by the bisimulation should match these labels because of clause 3, hence it should have at least the same keys. By symmetry, it should actually have exactly the same keys.

However, we claim that requiring to match all keys in the labels, as done implicitly by clause 3, is too demanding. The intuition under this claim is that keys are only a technical means to:

1. distinguishing executed from non-executed prefixes, and the choice of the key is irrelevant for this purpose;
2. coupling together prefixes that synchronised (see rule (SYNCH) in Fig. 1): in this case the choice of the key is irrelevant as well, but it is important whether two occurrences refer to the same key (highlighting a performed synchronisation) or to different keys (denoting independent actions).

As for item 2, keys can be safely α-renamed provided that *all* the occurrences of a given key are renamed in the same way. Now, keys are linear in the sense of [15], that is each key can occur at most twice because of condition 3 in the characterisation of reachable processes (Definition 3.3, see also Proposition 3.5). One can think of an occurrence attached to a τ prefix as two occurrences attached to complementary actions. Now, a key k is bound (cfr. Definition 2.1) if both its occurrences are in the considered process, hence k can be safely α-renamed without affecting the context. For instance, we want to equate $\overline{a}[n] \mid a[n]$ and $\overline{a}[m] \mid a[m]$. If instead a key k is free in a process, then the other occurrence can appear in the context: here α-equivalence needs to be disallowed to ensure compositionality. Indeed, we cannot equate $\overline{a}[n]$ and $\overline{a}[m]$, since in a context such as $\cdot \mid a[n]$ the former needs to synchronise to go back, while the latter does not.

We decided to embed α-conversion of bound keys in the semantics. Given our choice of not observing bound keys, this is needed for compositionality reasons. Indeed, otherwise one could distinguish processes such as $\overline{a}[n] \mid a[n] \mid b$ and $\overline{a}[m] \mid a[m] \mid b$ since the former can take a forward transition with label $b[m]$, while the latter can not, due to the side condition of rule (PAR). Thanks to α-conversion, the two processes can both take a forward transition with label $b[m]$, provided that the latter first α-converts m to a different key.

We will come back to this issue in the discussion after Proposition 4.9, showing that dropping α-conversion of bound keys would break congruence of bisimilarity. Note that such an issue does not occur in [15], since they never create new linear prefixes, while we do create new keys.

In the light of the discussion above, we extend the semantics of CCSK with a structural equivalence, defined as the smallest equivalence relation (that is, reflexive, symmetric, and transitive relation) closed under the following rule:

$$X \equiv X[n/m] \qquad m \text{ bound in } X, n \notin \mathbf{keys}(X)$$

where $[n/m]$ denotes the substitution of all the occurrences of key m with key n. Notice that structural equivalence preserves well-formedness (this can be checked by inspection of the conditions in Definition 3.3), but it is not a congruence, since, e.g., $\tau[n] \equiv \tau[m]$ but $\tau[n].\tau[n] \not\equiv \tau[n].\tau[m]$. To avoid this issue we would need explicit binders for keys, but we prefer to avoid them to stay as close as possible to the original CCSK.

We also need to introduce rules enabling the use of structural equivalence in the derivation of transitions:

$$(\text{EQUIV}) \quad \frac{Y \equiv X \quad X \xrightarrow{\alpha[m]}_f X' \quad X' \equiv Y'}{Y \xrightarrow{\alpha[m]}_f Y'}$$

$$(\text{BK-EQUIV}) \quad \frac{Y \equiv X \quad X \xrightarrow{\alpha[m]}_r X' \quad X' \equiv Y'}{Y \xrightarrow{\alpha[m]}_r Y'}$$

Due to the problem above, these rules can only be used *as last rules in a derivation*.

Remark 4.2. The introduction of structural equivalence and of the related rules is the only difference between our semantics of CCSK and the one in [30]. Note that with a little abuse of notation from now on arrows $\xrightarrow{\mu}_f$, $\xrightarrow{\mu}_r$ and $\xrightarrow{\mu}$ refer to the semantics which includes structural equivalence.

Notice that the change to the semantics has no impact on well-formedness and on Proposition 3.5.

Thanks to structural equivalence we can show that keys attached to τ labels are irrelevant.

Proposition 4.3. *For each $X \xrightarrow{\tau[m]} X'$ and n not free in X we have $X \xrightarrow{\tau[n]} X''$ with $X'' \equiv X'$.*

Proof. The proof is by induction on the derivation of $X \xrightarrow{\tau[m]} X'$. The induction is trivial if $n \notin \mathbf{keys}(X)$. If n is bound then one can apply rule (EQUIV) or (BK-EQUIV) to first convert n to any fresh key.   □

Actually, by applying rule (EQUIV) or (BK-EQUIV) one can also obtain $X'' = X'$.

Given the result above, one could even use just label τ instead of $\tau[m]$. We prefer however not to do it so that all the labels feature a key. This is handy when writing rules such as (RES).

We can revise the notion of forward-reverse bisimulation (Definition 4.1) as follows:

Definition 4.4 (Revised Forward-Reverse Bisimulation). *A symmetric relation $\mathcal{R}$ is a* revised forward-reverse bisimulation *(revised FR bisimulation for short) if whenever $X\,\mathcal{R}\,Y$:*

1. *if $X \xrightarrow{\mu}_f X'$ then there is Y' such that $Y \xrightarrow{\mu}_f Y'$ and $X'\,\mathcal{R}\,Y'$;*
2. *if $X \xrightarrow{\mu}_r X'$ then there is Y' such that $Y \xrightarrow{\mu}_r Y'$ and $X'\,\mathcal{R}\,Y'$.*

The revised forward-reverse (FR) bisimilarity, *denoted as $\sim_b$, is the largest revised FR bisimulation.*

For uniformity, such a definition requires to match bound keys in labels, however thanks to structural equivalence and Proposition 4.3 this does not allow one to distinguish processes that only differ on bound keys. Indeed, structural equivalence is a bisimulation.

Proposition 4.5 (Structural Equivalence is a Bisimulation). $X \equiv Y$ *implies $X \sim_b Y$.*

Proof. The thesis follows by coinduction, using Proposition 4.3 to match labels whose keys have been α-converted (and, as such, are bound, and can only be attached to τ labels). $\qquad\square$

We now use revised FR bisimilarity to show on an example that, as expected, bound keys are not observable.

Example 4.6. We show that $\overline{a}[n]\,|\,a[n] \sim_b \overline{a}[m]\,|\,a[m]$. To this end we need to show that the relation:

$$R = \{(\overline{a}[n]\,|\,a[n], \overline{a}[m]\,|\,a[m])\} \cup \mathtt{Id}$$

where $\mathtt{Id}$ is the identity relation on reachable processes is a bisimulation.

This is trivial since the only possible transition is a backward $\tau[k]$ for any key k (using rule (BK-EQUIV)), leading to $\overline{a}\,|\,a$ on both the sides. Any further transition can be matched so to remain in the identity relation $\mathtt{Id}$. Notice that one can obtain the same result directly from Proposition 4.5.

We now show some properties of revised FR bisimilarity. They will also be useful in the next section, to prove a characterisation of revised FR bisimilarity as a barbed congruence.

First, two equivalent processes are either both standard or both non-standard.

Lemma 4.7. *If $X \sim_b Y$ then $\mathtt{std}(X)$ iff $\mathtt{std}(Y)$.*

Proof. A process is non-standard iff it can perform backward transitions. The thesis follows. $\qquad\square$

Also, equivalent processes have the same set of free keys.

Lemma 4.8. *If $X \sim_b Y$ and key n is free in X then key n is free in Y as well.*

$$X \,|\, Y = Y \,|\, X \qquad\qquad\qquad\qquad\qquad \text{(PAR-COMM)}$$
$$X \,|\, (Y \,|\, Z) = (X \,|\, Y) \,|\, Z \qquad\qquad\qquad\qquad \text{(PAR-ASS)}$$
$$X \,|\, 0 = X \qquad\qquad\qquad\qquad\qquad\qquad \text{(PAR-UNIT)}$$

$$X + Y = Y + X \qquad\qquad\qquad\qquad\qquad \text{(CH-COMM)}$$
$$X + (Y + Z) = (X + Y) + X \qquad\qquad\qquad \text{(CH-ASS)}$$
$$X + 0 = X \qquad\qquad\qquad\qquad\qquad\qquad \text{(CH-UNIT)}$$
$$X + P = X \qquad\qquad \text{iff } \mathtt{toStd}(X) = P \qquad \text{(CH-IDEM)}$$

$$(\nu a)(\nu b) X = (\nu b)(\nu a) X \qquad\qquad\qquad\qquad \text{(RES-COMM)}$$
$$(\nu a)(X \,|\, Y) = X \,|\, (\nu a) Y \qquad \text{iff } a \notin \mathtt{fn}(X) \qquad \text{(RES-PAR)}$$
$$(\nu a)(X + Y) = ((\nu a) X) + ((\nu a) Y) \qquad\qquad \text{(RES-CH)}$$
$$(\nu a) \pi . X = \pi . (\nu a) X \qquad \text{iff } a \notin \mathtt{fn}(\pi) \qquad \text{(RES-PREF)}$$
$$(\nu a) 0 = 0 \qquad\qquad\qquad\qquad\qquad\qquad \text{(RES-DROP)}$$
$$(\nu a) \alpha . P = 0 \qquad\qquad \text{iff } a \in \mathtt{fn}(\alpha) \qquad \text{(RES-LOCK)}$$
$$(\nu a) X = (\nu b) X [b/a] \qquad \text{iff } b \notin \mathtt{fn}(X) \qquad \text{(RES-ALPH)}$$

Fig. 3. CCSK axiomatisation

We now show that revised FR bisimilarity is a congruence.

Proposition 4.9 (Revised FR Bisimilarity is a Congruence). $X \sim_b Y$ *implies* $C[X] \sim_b C[Y]$ *for each* C *such that* $C[X]$ *and* $C[Y]$ *are both reachable.*

Note that α-conversion of bound keys is needed to prove congruence w.r.t. parallel composition. Otherwise, processes $\bar{a}[n] \,|\, a[n]$ and $\bar{a}[m] \,|\, a[m]$ would be distinguished by a parallel context performing a transition creating a new key m, since this would be allowed only in the first case. Thanks to α-conversion, this is possible in both the cases, by first α-converting m in $\bar{a}[m] \,|\, a[m]$ to a different key.

We now study the axiomatisation of revised FR bisimilarity. While we are not able to provide a sound and complete axiomatisation, we can prove sound a number of relevant axioms. These allow one to reason equationally on CCSK processes.

We consider the list of axioms in Fig. 3. Most axioms are standard CCS axioms [28], extended to deal with non-standard prefixes. There are however a few interesting differences. E.g., we notice the non-standard axiom (CH-IDEM). Indeed, the left-hand side of the standard axiom $X + X = X$ is not reachable if X is not standard, and $X + X = X$ is an instance of (CH-IDEM) if X is standard. We also note that in rule (RES-LOCK) replacing α with π would be useless since the resulting process would not be reachable.

Theorem 4.10. *The axioms in Fig. 3 are sound w.r.t. revised FR bisimilarity.*

$$(\nu a)(\overline{a}.P \mid a.Q) = \tau.(\nu a)(P \mid Q) \qquad \text{(RES-EXP)}$$
$$(\nu a)(\overline{a}[n].X \mid a[n].Y) = \tau[n].(\nu a)(X \mid Y) \qquad \text{(RES-EXP-BK)}$$
$$\tau \mid \tau = \tau.\tau \qquad \text{(TAU-EXP)}$$
$$\tau[n] \mid \tau = \tau[n].\tau \qquad \text{(TAU-EXP-BF)}$$
$$\tau[n] \mid \tau[m] = \tau[n].\tau[m] \qquad \text{(TAU-EXP-BK)}$$

Fig. 4. Sample instances of the Expansion Law

Proof. For each axiom, instances of the axiom form a bisimulation, hence the thesis follows.   □

Probably the most relevant axiom in CCS theory is the Expansion Law [28], which can be written as follows:

$$P_1 \mid P_2 = \sum\{\alpha.(P_1' \mid P_2) : P_1 \xrightarrow{\alpha} P_1'\} + \sum\{\alpha.(P_1 \mid P_2') : P_2 \xrightarrow{\alpha} P_2'\} +$$
$$\sum\{\tau.(P_1' \mid P_2') : P_1 \xrightarrow{\alpha} P_1', P_2 \xrightarrow{\overline{\alpha}} P_2'\}$$

where $\sum$ is n-ary choice.

It is well-known [30] that the Expansion Law does not hold for reversible calculi, and indeed we can falsify it on an example using revised FR bisimilarity.

Example 4.11. We show here that $a \mid b \not\sim_b a.b + b.a$. Indeed, $a \mid b$ can take forward actions $a[n]$, $b[m]$, and then undo $a[n]$, while $a.b + b.a$ cannot. Notably, also $a \mid a \not\sim_b a.a$, since $a \mid a$ can take forward actions $a[n]$, $a[m]$, and then undo $a[n]$, while $a.a$ cannot.

This shows that classical CCS bisimilarity [28] is not as distinguishing, on CCS processes, as revised FR bisimilarity. Indeed, as expected, revised FR bisimilarity is strictly finer.

Proposition 4.12. *$P \sim_b Q$ implies $P \sim Q$ where $\sim$ is classical CCS bisimilarity [28], while the opposite implication does not hold.*

Proof. Classical CCS bisimilarity corresponds to clause 1 in the definition of revised FR bisimilarity. The failure of the other inclusion follows from Example 4.11.   □

We show below that even if the full Expansion Law does not hold, a few instances indeed hold.

Proposition 4.13. *The instances of the Expansion Law in Fig. 4 are sound w.r.t. revised FR bisimilarity.*

Proof. Instances of axioms (RES-EXP) and (RES-EXP-BK) form a revised FR bisimulation. The last three axioms form a revised FR bisimulation as well.   □

5   Forward-Reverse Barbed Congruence

In order to further justify the definition of revised FR bisimilarity, we show it to be equivalent to a form of forward-reverse barbed congruence.

As classically [14,34], an (open) barbed congruence is obtained by defining a set of basic observables, called *barbs*, and then taking the smallest equivalence on processes closed under contexts and under reduction requiring equivalent processes to have the same barbs. In our setting of course reductions can be both forwards and backwards. We start by defining barbs.

Definition 5.1 (Barbs). *A process X has a* forward output barb *at a, written $\downarrow_{\overline{a}}$, iff $X \xrightarrow{\overline{a}[n]}_f X'$ for some n and X'. A process X has a* backward *(input or output) barb* at $\alpha[n]$ ($\alpha \neq \tau$), written $\uparrow_{\alpha[n]}$, iff $X \xrightarrow{\alpha[n]}_r X'$ for some X'.*

We notice some asymmetry in the definition. The issue here is that we want to distinguish processes such as $a[n]$ and $b[n]$ (or $\overline{a}[n]$ and $\overline{b}[n]$), but there is no context undoing any of the prefixes such that both the compositions are reachable. Hence, we need (backward) barbs distinguishing them. This issue does not occur in forward transitions. Indeed, allowing one to observe also forward input barbs or keys in forward barbs would not change the observational power.

We can now formalise the notion of forward-reverse barbed congruence.

Definition 5.2 (Forward-Reverse Barbed Congruence). *A symmetric relation $\mathcal{R}$ is a* forward-reverse (FR) barbed bisimulation *if whenever $X \mathcal{R} Y$:*

- *$X \downarrow_{\overline{a}}$ implies $Y \downarrow_{\overline{a}}$;*
- *$X \uparrow_{\alpha[n]}$ implies $Y \uparrow_{\alpha[n]}$;*
- *if $X \xrightarrow{\tau[n]}_f X'$ then there is Y' such that $Y \xrightarrow{\tau[n]}_f Y'$ and $X' \mathcal{R} Y'$;*
- *if $X \xrightarrow{\tau[n]}_r X'$ then there is Y' such that $Y \xrightarrow{\tau[n]}_r Y'$ and $X' \mathcal{R} Y'$.*

Forward-reverse (FR) barbed bisimilarity, *denoted as $\sim_{bb}$, is the largest FR barbed bisimulation. A* forward-reverse (FR) barbed congruence *is a FR barbed bisimulation such that $X \mathcal{R} Y$ implies $C[X] \mathcal{R} C[Y]$ for each C such that $C[X]$ and $C[Y]$ are both reachable. We denote as $\sim_c$ the largest FR barbed congruence.*

As discussed above, we sometimes need barbs to require to match free keys, e.g., to distinguish $a[n]$ from $b[n]$. Indeed, in this case there exists no context able to force the match such that both the compositions are reachable. Such a context would need to include occurrences of both $\overline{a}[n]$ and $\overline{b}[n]$, but then any composition involving such a context would not be reachable.

However, when such a context exists, processes which differ for free keys only can be distinguished without the need for barbs, as shown by the example below.

Example 5.3. We show that $\overline{a}[n] \not\sim_c \overline{a}[m]$ without relying on barbs. Indeed, if we put the two processes in the context $\bullet \mid a[n]$ they behave differently:

$$\overline{a}[n] \mid a[n] \xrightarrow{\tau[n]}_r \overline{a} \mid a \qquad \text{while} \qquad \overline{a}[m] \mid a[n]$$

cannot perform any backward τ move. We remark that both the processes above are reachable.

However, bound keys are not observable, as shown in Example 4.6 for revised FR bisimilarity. We will show that this holds as well for FR barbed congruence, since actually revised FR bisimilarity coincides with FR barbed congruence (Corollary 5.12). This can be seen as a justification of our choice of revised FR bisimilarity. Revised FR bisimilarity, as usual for bisimilarities, is easier to work with since it has no universal quantification over contexts. For instance, it allowed us to easily prove the equivalence in Example 4.6.

First, revised FR barbed bisimilarity implies FR barbed congruence.

Theorem 5.4. $X \sim_b Y$ implies $X \sim_c Y$.

Proof. It is trivial to show that $\sim_b$ is a FR barbed bisimulation. Congruence follows from Proposition 4.9. $\qquad\qquad\qquad\qquad\qquad\qquad\qquad\qquad\qquad\qquad\square$

We now move towards the proof of the other inclusion in the equivalence between revised FR bisimilarity and FR barbed congruence.

To this end, we introduce below the notion of fresh process.

Definition 5.5 (Fresh Process). *Given a process X, the corresponding* fresh *process* $\mathtt{toFresh}(X)$ *is inductively defined as follows:*

$$
\begin{aligned}
\mathtt{toFresh}(0) &= 0 \\
\mathtt{toFresh}(\pi.X) &= f_i^p.0 + \pi.(f_i^s.0 + X) \\
\mathtt{toFresh}(X + Y) &= \mathtt{toFresh}(X) + \mathtt{toFresh}(Y) \\
\mathtt{toFresh}(X \mid Y) &= \mathtt{toFresh}(X) \mid \mathtt{toFresh}(Y) \\
\mathtt{toFresh}((\nu a)X) &= (\nu a)\mathtt{toFresh}(X)
\end{aligned}
$$

where, in the clause for prefix, i is the number of prefixes before π in a pre-visit of the syntax tree of X. We call f_i^p (where p stands for previous) and f_i^s (where s stands for subsequent) fresh names and the corresponding prefixes fresh prefixes.

A process is fresh if it is obtained by applying function $\mathtt{toFresh}(\cdot)$ to some reachable process X.

Note that all fresh names are pairwise different. Indeed the use of a pre-visit of the syntax tree is just a way to generate fixed, pairwise different fresh names for each prefix; any other algorithm with the same property would be fine as well.

Example 5.6 (Function $\mathtt{toFresh}(\cdot)$). Consider the process $X = a.b.0 \mid \overline{a}.b.0$. We have $\mathtt{toFresh}(X) = f_0^p.0 + a.(f_0^s.0 + f_1^p.0 + b.(f_1^s.0 + 0)) \mid f_2^p.0 + \overline{a}.(f_2^s.0 + f_3^p.0 + b.(f_3^s.0 + 0))$. Note that, e.g., executing a will disable the forward barb at f_0^p and enable the one at f_0^s.

Fresh processes are closed under reductions not involving fresh names.

Lemma 5.7. $X \xrightarrow{\mu} Y$ iff $\mathtt{toFresh}(X) \xrightarrow{\mu} \mathtt{toFresh}(Y)$ and μ does not contain a fresh name.

Fresh processes obtained from reachable processes are reachable.

Lemma 5.8. *Let X be a reachable process. Then* $\mathtt{toFresh}(X)$ *is reachable.*

Proof. By inspection of the conditions in Definition 3.3.   □

Intuitively, in a fresh process one is always able to distinguish which prefix of the original process has been done or undone by checking which barbs have been enabled or disabled. Indeed, using the names in the definition, performing the i-th prefix enables the barb at f_i^s and disables the one at f_i^p, while undoing π does the opposite.

This is formalised by the following lemma.

Lemma 5.9. *If W is fresh, $W \xrightarrow{\mu'} W'$ and $W \xrightarrow{\mu''} W''$, and W' and W'' have the same barbs then there exists a substitution σ on keys such that $\mu' = \mu''\sigma$ and $W' = W''\sigma$. The substitution is the identity if the transition is backwards.*

Next proposition shows that to check barbed congruence it is enough to consider contexts which are parallel compositions with fresh processes.

Proposition 5.10. *The relation*

$$\mathcal{R} = \{(C[X], C[Y]) \mid W \mid X \sim_{bb} W \mid Y \ \forall W \text{ fresh}, C \text{ context}$$
$$\text{such that } C[X], C[Y], W \mid X, W \mid Y \text{ are all reachable}\}$$

is a barbed congruence.

We can now show that FR barbed congruence implies revised FR bisimilarity, hence the two notions coincide.

Theorem 5.11. *The relation* $\mathcal{R} = \{(X, Y) \mid X \sim_c Y\}$ *is a revised FR bisimulation.*

Corollary 5.12. $\sim_c$ *and* $\sim_b$ *coincide.*

Proof. By composing Theorem 5.4 and Theorem 5.11.   □

6   Related Work

In [19], CCSK has been proved equivalent to RCCS [9], the first reversible process calculus, thus, in principle, our results apply to RCCS as well. However, the mechanism of memories used in RCCS introduces much more redundancy than the key mechanism used in CCSK, hence a direct application of our results to RCCS is not easy. Let us take as example [9, page 299] the process

$$R = \langle\langle 2 \rangle, a, 0\rangle \cdot \langle 1 \rangle \rhd 0 \mid \langle\langle 1 \rangle, \bar{a}, 0\rangle \cdot \langle 2 \rangle \rhd 0$$

obtained by performing the synchronisation from $\langle\rangle \rhd (a.0 \mid \bar{a}.0)$. To apply commutativity of parallel composition to R we need not only to swap the two subprocesses, but also to exchange all the occurrences of 1 with 2 in the memories, otherwise the obtained process would not be reachable. This particular issue has been solved in successive works on RCCS [16], yet similar issues remain since, e.g., the history of a thread is duplicated every time a process forks, hence the application of an axiom may impact many subprocesses which are possibly syntactically far away. In such a setting it is not clear how to write axioms.

We now discuss various works which focus on observational equivalences with backward transitions. The seminal paper [10] discusses bisimulations with reverse transitions much before causal-consistent reversibility and CCSK or RCCS were introduced, yet it briefly anticipates the notion of causal-consistent reversibility but discards it in favour of a total order of actions. In this case the bisimilarity coincides with CCS bisimilarity. A total order of actions is also considered in in [26]. They study testing equivalences in a CCS with rollback and focus on finding easier characterisations of testing semantics. As such, their results are not directly related to ours.

It is shown in [29] that the process graphs of CCSK processes are so-called prime graphs, which correspond to prime event structures. Due to the keys these structures are 'non-repeating', i.e. no two events in a configuration can have the same label. It is further shown [29, Theorem 5.4] that FR bisimilarity corresponds to hereditary history-preserving bisimilarity [4,12] on non-repeating prime event structures.

Equivalences for reversible CCS are also studied in [1,2] via encodings in configuration structures. Their main aim is to show that the induced equivalence on CCS coincides with hereditary history-preserving bisimilarity. Differently from us, they work on RCCS instead of CCSK, and, unsurprisingly given the discussion above, they do not consider axiomatisations. In [2] no notion of barbed congruence is considered, and their notions of bisimulations are triples instead of pairs as in our case, since they additionally need to keep track of a bijection among identifiers (which are close to our keys). Barbed congruence is considered in [1], but they only allow for contexts which are coherent on their own, thus disallowing interactions between the context and the process in the hole when going backwards. This has a relevant impact on the theory, as discussed in [1] itself (see [1, Example 3]). Also, they consider only processes without auto-concurrency and without auto-conflict [1, Remark 1].

A hierarchy of equivalences with backward transitions, including hereditary history-preserving bisimilarity, was studied in the context of stable configuration structures in [31]. A logic with reverse as well as forward modalities which characterises hereditary history-preserving bisimilarity was introduced in [32].

CCSK has been given a denotational semantics using reversible bundle event structures in [13]. Although equivalences are not discussed there, this opens the way to defining an equivalence on CCSK processes based on an equivalence between their denotations as reversible event structures.

7   Conclusion and Future Work

We have discussed strong observational equivalences able to distinguish forward and backward moves in CCSK. As shown on many occasions, a main difference w.r.t. the theory of CCS is that in CCSK not all processes are reachable, and this limits what contexts can observe. This motivates, e.g., the use of backward barbs which are more fine-grained than forward ones in the definition of FR barbed congruence. As anticipated in the Introduction, other forms of observational equivalences, such as weak equivalences, are also of interest.

Other interesting directions for future work include comparing the equivalence that our definitions induce on standard processes with known CCS equivalences. We have shown that revised FR bisimilarity is finer than standard CCS bisimilarity, and we conjecture it to be equivalent to hereditary history-preserving bisimilarity [12], in line with the results in [1,2,29].

Finally, we have discussed how axiomatisation is easier in calculi such as CCSK which have no redundancy in the history information. However, this approach right now does not scale to more complex languages such as the π-calculus or Erlang. Hence, it would be interesting to study alternative technical means to represent their reversible extensions with no redundancy (while current versions have high redundancy), so to allow for simple equational reasoning.

References

1. Aubert, C., Cristescu, I.: Contextual equivalences in configuration structures and reversibility. J. Log. Algebr. Meth. Program. **86**(1), 77–106 (2017)
2. Aubert, C., Cristescu, I.: How reversibility can solve traditional questions: the example of hereditary history-preserving bisimulation. In: CONCUR, vol.171 of LIPIcs, pp. 7:1–7:23. Schloss Dagstuhl - Leibniz-Zentrum für Informatik (2020)
3. Barbanera, F., Lanese, I., de'Liguoro, U.: A theory of retractable and speculative contracts. Sci. Comput. Program. **167**, 25–50 (2018)
4. Bednarczyk, M.: Hereditary history preserving bisimulations or what is the power of the future perfect in program logics. Technical report, Institute of Computer Science, Polish Academy of Sciences, Gdańsk (1991)
5. Cardelli, L., Laneve, C.: Reversibility in massive concurrent systems. Sci. Ann. Comput. Sci. **21**(2), 175–198 (2011)
6. Carothers, C.D., Perumalla, K.S., Fujimoto, R.: Efficient optimistic parallel simulations using reverse computation. ACM Trans. Model. Comput. Simul. **9**(3), 224–253 (1999)
7. Castellani, I., Dezani-Ciancaglini, M., Giannini, P.: Reversible sessions with flexible choices. Acta Informatica **56**(7–8), 553–583 (2019)
8. Cristescu, I., Krivine, J., Varacca, D.: A compositional semantics for the reversible π-calculus. In: LICS, pp. 388–397. IEEE Computer Society (2013)
9. Danos, V., Krivine, J.: Reversible communicating systems. In: Gardner, P., Yoshida, N. (eds.) CONCUR 2004. LNCS, vol. 3170, pp. 292–307. Springer, Heidelberg (2004). https://doi.org/10.1007/978-3-540-28644-8_19
10. De Nicola, R., Montanari, U., Vaandrager, F.: Back and forth bisimulations. In: Baeten, J.C.M., Klop, J.W. (eds.) CONCUR 1990. LNCS, vol. 458, pp. 152–165. Springer, Heidelberg (1990). https://doi.org/10.1007/BFb0039058
11. Engblom, J.: A review of reverse debugging. In: Proceedings of the 2012 System, Software, SoC and Silicon Debug Conference, pp. 1–6 (2012)

12. Fröschle, S.B., Hildebrandt, T.T.: On plain and hereditary history-preserving bisimulation. In: Kutyłowski, M., Pacholski, L., Wierzbicki, T. (eds.) Mathematical Foundations of Computer Science 1999. LNCS, vol. 1672, pp. 354–365. Springer, Heidelberg (1999). https://doi.org/10.1007/3-540-48340-3_32

13. Graversen, E., Phillips, I., Yoshida, N.: Event structure semantics of (controlled) reversible CCS. J. Log. Algebr. Meth. Program. **121**, 100686 (2021)

14. Honda, K., Yoshida, N.: On reduction-based process semantics. Theor. Comput. Sci. **151**(2), 437–486 (1995)

15. Kobayashi, N., Pierce, B.C., Turner, D.N.: Linearity and the Pi-calculus. ACM Trans. Program. Lang. Syst. **21**(5), 914–947 (1999)

16. Krivine, J.: A verification technique for reversible process algebra. In: Glück, R., Yokoyama, T. (eds.) RC 2012. LNCS, vol. 7581, pp. 204–217. Springer, Heidelberg (2013). https://doi.org/10.1007/978-3-642-36315-3_17

17. Lamport, L.: Time, clocks, and the ordering of events in a distributed system. Commun. ACM **21**(7), 558–565 (1978)

18. Landauer, R.: Irreversibility and heat generated in the computing process. IBM J. Res. Dev. **5**, 183–191 (1961)

19. Lanese, I., Medic, D., Mezzina, C.A.: Static versus dynamic reversibility in CCS. Acta Informatica. **58**, 1–34 (2021). https://doi.org/10.1007/s00236-019-00346-6

20. Lanese, I., Mezzina, C.A., Stefani, J.: Reversibility in the higher-order π-calculus. Theor. Comput. Sci. **625**, 25–84 (2016)

21. Lanese, I., Nishida, N., Palacios, A., Vidal, G.: CauDEr: a Causal-consistent reversible Debugger for Erlang. In: Gallagher, J.P., Sulzmann, M. (eds.) FLOPS 2018. LNCS, vol. 10818, pp. 247–263. Springer, Cham (2018). https://doi.org/10.1007/978-3-319-90686-7_16

22. Lanese, I., Nishida, N., Palacios, A., Vidal, G.: A theory of reversibility for Erlang. J. Log. Algebraic Methods Program. **100**, 71–97 (2018)

23. Lanese, I., Phillips, I.: Forward-reverse observational equivalences in CCSK (TR). http://www.cs.unibo.it/~lanese/work/CCSKequivTR.pdf

24. McNellis, J., Mola, J., Sykes, K.: Time travel debugging: Root causing bugs in commercial scale software. CppCon talk. https://www.youtube.com/watch?v=l1YJTg_A914 (2017)

25. Melgratti, H.C., Mezzina, C.A., Ulidowski, I.: Reversing place transition nets. Log. Methods Comput. Sci. **16**(4), 5:1–5:28 (2020)

26. Mezzina, C.A., Koutavas, V.: A safety and liveness theory for total reversibility. In: TASE, pp. 1–8. IEEE Computer Society (2017)

27. Mezzina, C.A., Pérez, J.A.: Causally consistent reversible choreographies: a monitors-as-memories approach. In: PPDP, pp. 127–138. ACM (2017)

28. Milner, R.: Communication and Concurrency. PHI Series in Computer Science. Prentice Hall, Hoboken (1989)

29. Phillips, I., Ulidowski, I.: Reversibility and models for concurrency. In: SOS, vol. 192(1) of ENTCS, pp. 93–108. Elsevier (2007)

30. Phillips, I., Ulidowski, I.: Reversing algebraic process calculi. J. Log. Algebr. Program. **73**(1–2), 70–96 (2007)

31. Phillips, I., Ulidowski, I.: A hierarchy of reverse bisimulations on stable configuration structures. Math. Struct. Comput. Sci. **22**, 333–372 (2012)

32. Phillips, I., Ulidowski, I.: Event identifier logic. Math. Struct. Comput. Sci. **24**(2), E240204 (2014)

33. Phillips, I., Ulidowski, I., Yuen, S.: A reversible process calculus and the modelling of the ERK Signalling pathway. In: Glück, R., Yokoyama, T. (eds.) RC 2012. LNCS, vol. 7581, pp. 218–232. Springer, Heidelberg (2013). https://doi.org/10.1007/978-3-642-36315-3_18

34. Sangiorgi, D., Walker, D.: On Barbed Equivalences in π-Calculus. In: Larsen, K.G., Nielsen, M. (eds.) CONCUR 2001. LNCS, vol. 2154, pp. 292–304. Springer, Heidelberg (2001). https://doi.org/10.1007/3-540-44685-0_20

Explicit Identifiers and Contexts in Reversible Concurrent Calculus

Clément Aubert[1]([✉]) [iD] and Doriana Medić[2] [iD]

[1] School of Computer and Cyber Sciences, Augusta University, Augusta, USA
caubert@augusta.edu
[2] Focus Team/University of Bologna, Inria, Sophia Antipolis, France

Abstract. Existing formalisms for the algebraic specification and representation of networks of reversible agents suffer some shortcomings. Despite multiple attempts, reversible declensions of the Calculus of Communicating Systems (CCS) do not offer satisfactory adaptation of notions usual in "forward-only" process algebras, such as replication or context. Existing formalisms disallow the "hot-plugging" of processes during their execution in contexts with their own past. They also assume the existence of "eternally fresh" keys or identifiers that, if implemented poorly, could result in unnecessary bottlenecks and look-ups involving all the threads. In this paper, we begin investigating those issues, by first designing a process algebra endowed with a mechanism to generate identifiers without the need to consult with the other threads. We use this calculus to recast the possible representations of non-determinism in CCS, and as a by-product establish a simple and straightforward definition of concurrency. Our reversible calculus is then proven to satisfy expected properties. We also observe that none of the reversible bisimulations defined thus far are congruences under our notion of "reversible" contexts.

Keywords: Formal semantics · Process algebras and calculi · Context for reversible calculi

1 Introduction: Filling the Blanks in Reversible Process Algebras

Reversibility's Future is intertwined with the development of formal models for analyzing and certifying concurrent behaviors. Even if the development of quantum computers [30], CMOS adiabatic circuits [18] and computing biochemical systems promise unprecedented efficiency or "energy-free" computers, it would be a mistake to believe that whenone of those technologies—each with their own connection to reversibility—reaches a mature stage, distribution of the computing capacities will become superfluous. On the opposite, the future probably resides in connecting together computers using different paradigms

This work has been supported by French ANR project DCore ANR-18-CE25-0007.

S. Yamashita and T. Yokoyama (Eds.): RC 2021, LNCS 12805, pp. 144–162, 2021.
https://doi.org/10.1007/978-3-030-79837-6_9

(i.e., "traditional", quantum, biological, etc.), and possibly themselves heterogeneous (for instance using the "classical control of quantum data" motto [37]). In this coming situation, "traditional" model-checking techniques will face an even worst state explosion problem in presence of reversibility, that e.g. the usual "back-tracking" methods will likely fail to circumvent. Due to the notorious difficulty of connecting heterogeneous systems correctly and the "volatile" nature of reversible computers—that can erase all trace of their actions—, it seems absolutely necessary to design languages for the specification and verification of reversible distributed systems.

Process Algebras offer an ideal touch of abstraction while maintaining implementable specification and verification languages. In the family of process calculi, the Calculus of Communicating Systems (CCS) [35] plays a particular role, both as seminal work and as direct root of numerous systems (e.g. π- [42], Ambient [33], applied [1] and distributed [23] calculi). Reversible CCS (RCCS) [15] and CCS with keys (CCSK) [38] are two extensions to CCS providing a better understanding of the mechanisms underlying reversible concurrent computation—and they actually turned out to be the two faces of the same coin [27]. Most [3,14,32,34]—if not all—of the later systems developed to enhance the expressiveness with some respect (rollback operator, name-passing abilities, probabilistic features) stem from one approach or the other. However, those two systems, as well as their extensions, both share the same drawbacks, in terms of missing features and missing opportunities.

An Incomplete Picture is offered by RCCS and CCSK, as they miss "expected" features despite repetitive attempts. For instance, no satisfactory notion of context was ever defined: the discussed notions [5] do not allow the "hot-plugging" of a process with a past into a context with a past as well. As a consequence, defining congruence is impossible, forbidding the study of bisimilarities—though they are at the core of process algebras [41]. Also, recursion and replication are different [36], but only recursion have been investigated [22,25] or mentioned [15,16], and only for "memory-less" processes. Stated differently, the study of the duplication of systems with a past has been left aside.

Opportunities Have Been Missed as previous process algebras are *conservative extensions of restricted versions of CCS*, instead of considering "a fresh start". For instance, reversible calculi inherited the sum operator in its guarded version: while this restriction certainly makes sense when studying (weak) bisimulations for forward-only models, we believe it would be profitable to suspend this restriction and consider *all* sums, to establish their specificities and interests in the reversible frame. Also, both RCCS and CCSK have impractical mechanisms for keys or identifiers: aside from supposing "eternal freshness"—which requires to "ping" all threads when performing a transition, creating a potential bottle-neck—, they also require to inspect, in the worst case scenario, *all the memories of all the threads* before performing a backward transition.

Our Proposal for "yet" another language is guided by the desire to "complete the picture", but starts from scratch instead of trying to "correct" existing systems[1]. We start by defining an "identified calculus" that sidesteps the previous limitations of the key and memory mechanisms and considers multiple declensions of the sum: 1. the summation [35, p. 68], that we call "non-deterministic choice" and write ⊗, [44], 2. the guarded sum, +, and 3. the internal choice, ⊓, inspired from the Communicating Sequential Processes (CSP) [24]—even if we are aware that this operator can be represented [2, p. 225] in forward systems, we would like to re-consider all the options in the reversible set-up, where "representation" can have a different meaning.Our formalism meets the usual criterion, and allows to sketch interesting definitions for contexts, that allows to prove that, even under a mild notion of context, the usual bisimulation for reversible calculi is not a congruence. As a by-product, we obtain a notion of concurrency, both for forward and forward-and-backward calculi, that rests solely on identifiers and can be checked locally.

Our Contribution tries to lay out a solid foundation to study reversible process algebras in all generality, and opens some questions that have been left out. Our detailed frame explicits aspects not often acknowledged, but does not yet answer questions such as "what is the right structural *congruence* for reversible calculi" [7]: while we can define a structural *relation* for our calculus, we would like to get a better take on what a congruence for reversible calculi is before committing. How our three sums differ and what benefits they could provide is also left for future work, possibly requiring a better understanding of non-determinism in the systems we model. Another direction for future work is to study new features stemming from reversibility, such as the capacity of distinguishing between multiple replications, based on how they replicate the memory mechanism allowing to reverse the computation.

All proofs and some ancillary definitions are in the extended version [8].

2   Forward-Only Identified Calculus with Multiple Sums

We enrich CCS's processes and labeled transition system (LTS) with identifiers needed to define reversible systems: indeed, in addition to the usual labels, the reversible LTS developed thus far all annotate the transition with an additional key or identifier that becomes part of the memory. This development can be carried out independently of the reversible aspect, and could be of independent interest. Our formal "identifier structures" allows to precisely define how such identifiers could be generated while guaranteeing eternal freshness of the identifiers used to annotate the transitions (Lemma 1) of our calculus that extends CCS conservatively (Lemma 2).

---

[1] Of course, due credit should be given for those previous calculi, that strongly inspired ours, and into which our system can be partially embedded, cf. Sect. 3.3.

2.1   Preamble: Identifier Structures, Patterns, Seeds and Splitters

Definition 1 (Identifier Structure and Pattern). *An* identifier structure $\mathsf{IS} = (\mathsf{I}, \gamma, \oplus)$ *is s.t.*

- I *is an infinite set of* identifiers, *with a partition between infinite sets of* atomic identifiers I_a *and* paired identifiers I_p, *i.e.* $\mathsf{I}_a \cup \mathsf{I}_p = \mathsf{I}$, $\mathsf{I}_a \cap \mathsf{I}_p = \emptyset$,
- $\gamma : \mathbb{N} \to \mathsf{I}_a$ *is a bijection called a* generator,
- $\oplus : \mathsf{I}_a \times \mathsf{I}_a \to \mathsf{I}_p$ *is a bijection called a* pairing function.

Given an identifier structure IS, *an* identifier pattern ip *is a tuple* (c, s) *of integers called* current *and* step *such that* $s > 0$. *The* stream *of atomic identifiers generated by* (c, s) *is* $\mathsf{IS}(c, s) = \gamma(c), \gamma(c + s), \gamma(c + s + s), \gamma(c + s + s + s), \ldots$.

Example 1. Traditionally, a pairing function is a bijection between $\mathbb{N} \times \mathbb{N}$ and $\mathbb{N}$, and the canonical examples are Cantor's bijection and $(m, n) \mapsto 2^m(2n + 1) - 1$ [40,43]. Let p be any of those pairing function, and let $\mathsf{p}^-(m, n) = -(\mathsf{p}(m, n))$.
Then, $\mathbb{IZ} = (\mathbb{Z}, \mathrm{id}_{\mathbb{N}}, \mathsf{p}^-)$ is an identifier structure, with $\mathsf{I}_a = \mathbb{N}$ and $\mathsf{I}_p = \mathbb{Z}^-$. The streams $\mathbb{IZ}(0, 2)$ and $\mathbb{IZ}(1, 2)$ are the series of even and odd numbers.

We now assume given an identifier structure IS and use $\mathbb{IZ}$ in our examples.

Definition 2 (Compatible Identifier Patterns). *Two identifier patterns* ip_1 *and* ip_2 *are* compatible, $\mathsf{ip}_1 \perp \mathsf{ip}_2$, *if the identifiers in the streams* $\mathsf{IS}(\mathsf{ip}_1)$ *and* $\mathsf{IS}(\mathsf{ip}_2)$ *are all different.*

Definition 3 (Splitter). *A* splitter *is a function* $\cap$ *from identifier pattern to pairs of compatible identifier patterns, and we let* $\cap_1(\mathsf{ip})$ *(resp.* $\cap_2(\mathsf{ip})$*) be its first (resp. second) projection.*

We now assume that every identifier structure IS is endowed with a splitter.

Example 2. For $\mathbb{IZ}$ the obvious splitter is $\cap(c, s) = ((c, 2 \times s), (c + s, 2 \times s))$. Note that $\cap(0, 1) = ((0, 2), (1, 2))$, and it is easy to check that the two streams $\mathbb{IZ}(0, 2)$ and $\mathbb{IZ}(1, 2)$ have no identifier in common. However, $(1, 7)$ and $(2, 13)$ are not compatible in $\mathbb{IZ}$, as their streams both contain 15.

Definition 4 (Seed (Splitter)). *A* seed s *is either an identifier pattern* ip, *or a pair of seeds* $(\mathsf{s}_1, \mathsf{s}_2)$ *such that all the identifier patterns occurring in* s_1 *and* s_2 *are pairwise compatible. Two seeds* s_1 *and* s_2 *are compatible,* $\mathsf{s}_1 \perp \mathsf{s}_2$, *if all the identifier patterns in* s_1 *and* s_2 *are compatible.*
We extend the splitter $\cap$ *and its projections* $\cap_j$ *(for* $j \in \{1, 2\}$*) to functions from seeds to seeds that we write* $[\cap]$ *and* $[\cap_j]$ *defined by*

$$[\cap](\mathsf{ip}) = \cap(\mathsf{ip}) \qquad\qquad [\cap_j](\mathsf{ip}) = \cap_j(\mathsf{ip})$$
$$[\cap](\mathsf{s}_1, \mathsf{s}_2) = ([\cap](\mathsf{s}_1), [\cap](\mathsf{s}_2)) \qquad [\cap_j](\mathsf{s}_1, \mathsf{s}_2) = ([\cap_j](\mathsf{s}_1), [\cap_j](\mathsf{s}_2))$$

Example 3. A seed over $\mathbb{IZ}$ is $(\mathrm{id} \times \cap)(\cap(0, 1)) = ((0, 2), ((1, 4), (3, 4)))$.

2.2   Identified CCS and Unicity Property

We will now discuss and detail how a general version of (forward-only) CCS can be equipped with identifiers structures so that every transition will be labeled not only by a (co-)name, τ or υ^2, but also by an identifier that is guaranteed to be unique in the trace.

Definition 5 (Names, Co-names and Labels). *Let* $\mathsf{N} = \{a, b, c, \dots\}$ *be a set of* names *and* $\overline{\mathsf{N}} = \{\overline{a}, \overline{b}, \overline{c}, \dots\}$ *its set of* co-names. *We define the set of labels* $\mathsf{L} = \mathsf{N} \cup \overline{\mathsf{N}} \cup \{\tau, \upsilon\}$, *and use* α *(resp.* μ, λ*) to range over* L *(resp.* $\mathsf{L}\backslash\{\tau\}$, $\mathsf{L}\backslash\{\tau, \upsilon\}$*). The* complement *of a name is given by a bijection* $\overline{\cdot} : \mathsf{N} \to \overline{\mathsf{N}}$, *whose inverse is also written* $\overline{\cdot}$.

Definition 6 (Operators).

$$P, Q := \lambda.P \qquad \text{(Prefix)} \qquad P \oslash Q \quad \text{(Non-deterministic choice)}$$
$$P \mid Q \quad \text{(Parallel Composition)} \qquad (\lambda_1.P_1) + (\lambda_2.P_2) \quad \text{(Guarded sum)}$$
$$P\backslash\lambda \qquad \text{(Restriction)} \qquad P \sqcap Q \qquad \text{(Internal choice)}$$

As usual, the inactive process 0 *is not written when preceded by a prefix, and we call* P *and* Q *the "threads" in a process* $P \mid Q$.

The labeled transition system (LTS) for this version of CCS, that we denote $\xrightarrow{\alpha}$, can be read from Fig. 1 by removing the seeds and the identifiers. Now, to define an identified declension of that calculus, we need to describe how each thread of a process can access its own identifier pattern to independently "pull" fresh identifiers when needed, without having to perform global look-ups. We start by defining how a seed can be "attached" to a CCS process.

Definition 7 (Identified Process). *Given an identifier structure* IS, *an identified process is a CCS process* P *endowed with a seed* s *that we denote* $\mathsf{s} \circ P$.

We assume fixed a particular identifier structure $\mathsf{IS} = (\mathsf{I}, \gamma, \oplus, \sqcap)$, and now need to introduce how we "split" identifier patterns, to formalize when a process evolves from e.g. $\mathsf{ip} \circ a.(P \mid Q)$ that requires only one identifier pattern to $(\mathsf{ip}_1, \mathsf{ip}_2) \circ P \mid Q$, that requires two—because we want P and Q to be able to pull identifiers from respectively ip_1 and ip_2 without the need for an agreement. To make sure that our processes are always "well-identified" (Definition 10), i.e. with a matching number of threads and identifier patterns, we introduce an helper function.

---

[2] We use this label to annotate the "internally non-deterministic" transitions introduced by the operator $\sqcap$. It can be identified with τ for simplicity if need be, and as τ, it does not have a complement.

Definition 8 (Splitter Helper). *Given a process P and an identifier pattern* ip, *we define*

$$\sqcap^?(\text{ip}, P) = \begin{cases} (\sqcap^?(\sqcap_1(\text{ip}), P_1), \sqcap^?(\sqcap_2(\text{ip}), P_2)) & \text{if } P = P_1 \mid P_2 \\ \text{ip} \circ P & \text{otherwise} \end{cases}$$

and write e.g. $\sqcap^?$ip $\circ a \mid b$ *for the "recomposition" of the pair* $\sqcap^?(\text{ip}, a \mid b) = (\sqcap_1(\text{ip}) \circ a, \sqcap_2(\text{ip}) \circ b)$ *into the identified process* $(\sqcap_1(\text{ip}), \sqcap_2(\text{ip})) \circ a \mid b$.

Note that in the definition below, only the rules act., $+$ and $\sqcap$ can "uncover" threads, and hence are the only place where $\sqcap^?$ is invoked.

Definition 9 (ILTS). *We let the* identified labeled transition system *between identified processes be the union of all the relations* $\xrightarrow{i:\alpha}$ *for $i \in$ I and $\alpha \in$ L of Fig. 1.* Structural relation *is as usual [8] but will not be used.*

Example 4. The result of $\sqcap^?(0,1) \circ (a \mid (b \mid (c+d)))$ is $((0,2), ((1,4), (3,4))) \circ (a \mid (b \mid (c+d))$, and a (resp. b, $c+d$) would get its next transition identified with 0 (resp. 1, 3).

Definition 10 (Well-Identified Process). *An identified process* s $\circ P$ *is* well-identified *iff* s $= (s_1, s_2)$, $P = P_1 \mid P_2$ *and* $s_1 \circ P_1$ *and* $s_2 \circ P_2$ *are both well-identified, or P is not of the form $P_1 \mid P_2$ and s is an identifier pattern.*

We now always assume that identified processes are well-identified.

Definition 11 (Traces). *In a transition $t :$ s $\circ P \xrightarrow{i:\alpha}$ s$' \circ P'$, process s $\circ P$ is* the source, *and s$' \circ P'$ is* the target *of transition t. Two transitions are* coinitial *(resp.* cofinal*) if they have the same source (resp. target). Transitions t_1 and t_2 are* composable, $t_1; t_2$, *if the target of t_1 is the source of t_2. A sequence of pairwise composable transitions is called a* trace, *written $t_1; \cdots ; t_n$.*

Lemma 1 (Unicity). *The trace of an identified process contains any identifier at most once, and if a transition has identifier $i_1 \oplus i_2 \in$ I$_p$, then neither i_1 nor i_2 occur in the trace.*

Lemma 2. *For all CCS process P, $\exists$s s.t. $P \xrightarrow{\alpha_1} \cdots \xrightarrow{\alpha_n} P' \Leftrightarrow ($s $\circ P \xrightarrow{i_1:\alpha_1} \cdots \xrightarrow{i_n:\alpha_n}$ s$' \circ P')$.*

Definition 12 (Concurrency and Compatible Identifiers). *Two coinitial transitions* s $\circ P \xrightarrow{i_1:\alpha_1}$ s$_1 \circ P_1$ *and* s $\circ P \xrightarrow{i_2:\alpha_2}$ s$_2 \circ P_2$ *are* concurrent *iff i_1 and i_2 are* compatible, $i_1 \perp i_2$, *i.e. iff*

$$\begin{cases} i_1 \neq i_2 & \text{if } i_1, i_2 \in \text{I}_a \\ \text{there is no } i \in \text{I}_a \text{ s.t. } i_1 \oplus i = i_2 & \text{if } i_1 \in \text{I}_a, i_2 \in \text{I}_p \\ \text{there is no } i \in \text{I}_a \text{ s.t. } i \oplus i_2 = i_1 & \text{if } i_1 \in \text{I}_p, i_2 \in \text{I}_a \\ \text{for } i_1^1, i_1^2, i_2^1 \text{ and } i_2^2 \text{ s.t. } i_1 = i_1^1 \oplus i_1^2 \text{ and } i_2 = i_2^1 \oplus i_2^2, \\ \qquad i_1^j \neq i_2^k \text{ for } j, k \in \{1, 2\} & \text{if } i_1, i_2 \in \text{I}_p \end{cases}$$

Action and Restriction

$$\frac{}{(c,s)\circ\lambda.P\xrightarrow{\gamma(c):\lambda}\cap^?(c+s,s)\circ P}\;\text{act.}\qquad a\notin\{\alpha,\bar\alpha\}\;\frac{s\circ P\xrightarrow{i:\alpha}s'\circ P'}{s\circ P\backslash a\xrightarrow{i:\alpha}s'\circ P'\backslash a}\;\text{res.}$$

Parallel Group

$$s_1\perp s_2\;\frac{s_1\circ P\xrightarrow{i_1:\lambda}s_1'\circ P'\quad s_2\circ Q\xrightarrow{i_2:\overline\lambda}s_2'\circ Q'}{(s_1,s_2)\circ P\mid Q\xrightarrow{i_1\oplus i_2:\tau}(s_1',s_2')\circ P'\mid Q'}\;\text{syn.}$$

$$s_1\perp s_2\;\frac{s_1\circ P\xrightarrow{i:\alpha}s_1'\circ P'}{(s_1,s_2)\circ P\mid Q\xrightarrow{i:\alpha}(s_1',s_2)\circ P'\mid Q}\;|_{\text{L}}$$

$$s_1\perp s_2\;\frac{s_2\circ Q\xrightarrow{i:\alpha}s_2'\circ Q'}{(s_1,s_2)\circ P\mid Q\xrightarrow{i:\alpha}(s_1,s_2')\circ P\mid Q'}\;|_{\text{R}}$$

Sum Group

$$\frac{s\circ P\xrightarrow{i:\alpha}s'\circ P'}{s\circ P\oslash Q\xrightarrow{i:\alpha}s'\circ P'}\;\oslash_{\text{L}}\qquad\qquad\frac{s\circ Q\xrightarrow{i:\alpha}s'\circ Q'}{s\circ P\oslash Q\xrightarrow{i:\alpha}s'\circ Q'}\;\oslash_{\text{R}}$$

$$\frac{}{(c,s)\circ(\lambda_1.P_1)+(\lambda_2.P_2)\xrightarrow{\gamma(c):\lambda_1}\cap^?(c+s,s)\circ P_1}\;+_{\text{L}}$$

$$\frac{}{(c,s)\circ(\lambda_1.P_1)+(\lambda_2.P_2)\xrightarrow{\gamma(c):\lambda_2}\cap^?(c+s,s)\circ P_2}\;+_{\text{R}}$$

$$\frac{}{(c,s)\circ P\sqcap Q\xrightarrow{\gamma(c):\upsilon}\cap^?(c+s,s)\circ P}\;\sqcap_{\text{L}}$$

$$\frac{}{(c,s)\circ P\sqcap Q\xrightarrow{\gamma(c):\upsilon}\cap^?(c+s,s)\circ Q}\;\sqcap_{\text{R}}$$

Fig. 1. Rules of the identified labeled transition system (ILTS)

Example 5. The identified process $s\circ P=((0,2),(1,2))\circ a+b\mid\bar a.c$ has four possible transitions:

$$t_1:s\circ P\xrightarrow{0:a}((2,2),(1,2))\circ 0\mid\bar a.c\quad t_3:s\circ P\xrightarrow{1:\bar a}((0,2),(3,2))\circ a+b\mid c$$

$$t_2:s\circ P\xrightarrow{0:b}((2,2),(1,2))\circ 0\mid\bar a.c\quad t_4:s\circ P\xrightarrow{0\oplus 1:\tau}((2,2),(3,2))\circ 0\mid c$$

Among them, only t_1 and t_3, and t_2 and t_3 are concurrent: transitions are concurrent when they do not use overlapping identifiers, not even as part of synchronizations.

Hence, concurrency becomes an "easily observable" feature that does not require inspection of the term, of its future transitions—as for "the diamond property" [29]—or of an intermediate relation on proof terms [11, p. 415]. We believe this contribution to be of independent interest, and it will help significantly the precision and efficiency of our forward-and-backward calculus in multiple respect.

3   Reversible and Identified CCS

A reversible calculus is always defined by a forward calculus and a backward calculus. Here, we define the forward part as an extension of the identified calculus of Definition 9, without copying the information about the seeds for conciseness, but using the identifiers they provide. The backward calculus will require to make the seed explicit again, and we made the choice of having backward transitions re-use the identifier from their corresponding forward transition, and to restore the seed in its previous state. Expected properties are detailed in Sect. 3.2.

3.1   Defining the Identified Reversible CCS

Definition 13 (Memories and Reversible Processes). *Let $o \in \{\oslash, +, \sqcap\}$, $d \in \{L, R\}$, we define memory events, memories and identified reversible processes as follows, for $n \geq 0$:*

$$e := \langle i, \mu, ((o_1, P_1, d_1), \ldots (o_n, P_n, d_n))\rangle \qquad \text{(Memory event)}$$
$$m_s := e.m_s \mid \emptyset \qquad \text{(Memory stack)}$$
$$m_p := [m, m] \qquad \text{(Memory pair)}$$
$$m := m_s \mid m_p \qquad \text{(Memory)}$$
$$R, S := s \circ m \triangleright P \qquad \text{(Identified reversible processes)}$$

In a memory event, if $n = 0$, then we will simply write _. We generally do not write the trailing empty memories in memory stacks, e.g. we will write e instead of $e.\emptyset$.

Stated differently, our memory are represented as a stack or tuples of stacks, on which we define the following two operations.

Definition 14 (Operations on Memories). *The identifier substitution in a memory event is written $e[i \leftarrow j]$ and is defined as substitutions usually are. The identified insertion is defined by*

$$\langle i, \mu, ((o_1, P_1, d_1), \ldots (o_n, P_n, d_n))\rangle +\!\!+_j (o, P, d) =$$
$$\begin{cases} \langle i, \mu, ((o_1, P_1, d_1), \ldots (o_n, P_n, d_n), (o, P, d))\rangle & \text{if } i = j \\ \langle i, \mu, ((o_1, P_1, d_1), \ldots (o_n, P_n, d_n))\rangle & \text{otherwise} \end{cases}$$

The operations are easily extended to memories by simply propagating them to all memory events.

When defining the forward LTS below, we omit the identifier patterns to help with readability, but the reader should assume that those rules are "on top" of the rules in Fig. 1. The rules for the backward LTS, in Fig. 3, includes both the seeds and memories, and is the exact symmetric of the forward identified LTS with memory, up to the condition in the parallel group that we discuss later. A bit similarly to the splitter helper (Definition 8), we need an operation that duplicates a memory if needed, that we define on processes with memory but without seeds for clarity.

Definition 15 (Memory Duplication). *Given a process P and a memory m, we define*

$$\delta^?(m, P) = \begin{cases} (\delta^?(m, P_1), \delta^?(m, P_2)) & \text{if } P = P_1 \mid P_2 \\ m \rhd P & \text{otherwise} \end{cases}$$

and write e.g. $\delta^?(m) \rhd a \mid b$ for the "recomposition" of the pair of identified processes $\delta^?(m, a \mid b) = (\delta^?(m, a), \delta^?(m, b)) = (m \rhd a, m \rhd b)$ into the process $[m, m] \rhd a \mid b$.

Definition 16 (IRLTS). *We let the* identified reversible labeled transition system *between identified reversible processes be the union of all the relations $\xrightarrow{i:\alpha}$ and $\stackrel{i:\alpha}{\rightsquigarrow}$ for $i \in I$ and $\alpha \in L$ of Figs. 2 and 3, and let $\twoheadrightarrow = \rightarrow \cup \rightsquigarrow$. Structural relation is as usual [8] but will not be used.*

In its first version, RCCS was using the whole memory as an identifier [15], but then it moved to use specific identifiers [4,31], closer in inspiration to CCSK's keys [38]. This strategy, however, forces the act. rules (forward and backward) to check that the identifier picked (or present in the memory event that is being reversed) is not occurring in the memory, while our system can simply pick identifiers from the seed without having to inspect the memory, and can go backward simply by looking if the memory event has identifier in I_a—something enforced by requiring the identifier to be of the form $\gamma^{-1}(c)$. Furthermore, memory events and annotated prefixes, as used in RCCS and CCSK, do not carry information on whenever they synchronized with other threads: retrieving this information require to inspect all the memories, or keys, of all the other threads, while our system simply observes if the identifier is in I_p, hence enforcing a "locality" property. However, when backtracking, the memories of the threads need to be checked for "compatibility", otherwise i.e. $((1, 2), (2, 2)) \circ [\langle 0, a, \_\rangle, \langle 0, a, \_\rangle] \rhd P \mid Q$ could backtrack to $((1, 2), (0, 2)) \circ [\langle 0, a, \_\rangle, \emptyset] \rhd P \mid a.Q$ and then be stuck instead of $(0, 1) \circ \emptyset \rhd a.(P \mid Q)$.

3.2 Properties: From Concurrency to Causal Consistency and Unicity

We now prove that our calculus satisfies typical properties for reversible process calculi [13,15,26,38]. Notice that showing that the forward-only part of our

Action and Restriction

$$\frac{}{m \triangleright \lambda.P \xrightarrow{i:\lambda} \delta^?(\langle i, \lambda, \_\rangle.m) \triangleright P} \text{ act.}$$

$$a \notin \{\alpha, \bar{\alpha}\} \quad \frac{m \triangleright P \xrightarrow{i:\alpha} m' \triangleright P'}{m \triangleright P\backslash a \xrightarrow{i:\alpha} m' \triangleright P'\backslash a} \text{ res.}$$

Parallel Group

$$\frac{m_1 \triangleright P \xrightarrow{i_1:\lambda} m_1' \triangleright P' \quad m_2 \triangleright Q \xrightarrow{i_2:\bar{\lambda}} m_2' \triangleright Q'}{[m_1, m_2] \triangleright P \mid Q \xrightarrow{i_1 \oplus i_2 : \tau} [m_1'[i_1 \leftarrow i_1 \oplus i_2], m_2'[i_2 \leftarrow i_2 \oplus i_1]] \triangleright P' \mid Q'} \text{ syn.}$$

$$\frac{m_1 \triangleright P \xrightarrow{i:\alpha} m_1' \triangleright P'}{[m_1, m_2] \triangleright P \mid Q \xrightarrow{i:\alpha} [m_1', m_2] \triangleright P' \mid Q} \mid_L$$

Sum Group

$$\frac{m \triangleright P \xrightarrow{i:\alpha} m' \triangleright P'}{m \triangleright (P \oslash Q) \xrightarrow{i:\alpha} m' \mathbin{+\!\!+}_i (\oslash, Q, R) \circ P'} \oslash_L$$

$$\frac{}{m \triangleright ((\lambda_1.P_1) + (\lambda_2.P_2)) \xrightarrow{i:\lambda_1} \delta^?(\langle i, \lambda_1, (+, \lambda_2.P_2, R)\rangle.m) \triangleright P_1} +_L$$

$$\frac{}{m \triangleright (P \sqcap Q) \xrightarrow{i:\upsilon} \delta^?(\langle i, \upsilon, (\sqcap, Q, R)\rangle.m) \triangleright P} \sqcap_L$$

The rules $\mid_R$, $\oslash_R$, $+_R$ and $\sqcap_R$ can easily be inferred.

Fig. 2. Forward rules of the identified reversible labeled transition system (IRLTS)

calculus is a conservative extension of CCS is done by extending Lemma 2 to accommodate memories and it is immediate. We give a notion of concurrency, and prove that our calculus enjoys the required axioms to obtain causal consistency "for free" [28]. All our properties, as commonly done, are limited to the reachable processes.

Definition 17 (Initial, Reachable and Origin Process). *A process* $\mathsf{s}\circ m \triangleright P$ *is initial if* $\mathsf{s} \circ P$ *is well-identified and if* $m = \emptyset$ *if* P *is not of the form* $P_1 \mid P_2$, *or if* $m = [m_1, m_2]$, $P = P_1 \mid P_2$ *and* $[\sqcap_j](\mathsf{s}) \circ m_j \triangleright P_j$ *for* $j \in \{1, 2\}$ *are initial. A process* R *is* reachable *if it can be derived from an initial process, its* origin, *written* O_R, *by applying the rules in Figs. 2 and 3.*

Action and Restriction

$$\frac{}{\cap^?(\gamma^{-1}(i)+s,s)\circ\delta^?(\langle i,\lambda,_\rangle.m)\rhd P\overset{i:\lambda}{\rightsquigarrow}(\gamma^{-1}(i),s)\circ m\rhd\lambda.P}\text{ act.}$$

$$a\notin\{\alpha,\bar{\alpha}\}\ \frac{\mathsf{s}\circ m\rhd P\overset{i:\alpha}{\rightsquigarrow}\mathsf{s}'\circ m'\rhd P'}{\mathsf{s}\circ m\rhd P\backslash a\overset{i:\alpha}{\rightsquigarrow}\mathsf{s}'\circ m'\rhd P'\backslash a}\text{ res.}$$

Parallel Group

The rule syn. (resp. $|_{\text{L}}$) can be applied only if $\mathsf{s}_1\perp\mathsf{s}_2$ and $i_1\notin m_2'$, $i_2\notin m_1'$ (resp. $i\notin m_2$).

$$\frac{\begin{array}{c}\mathsf{s}_1\circ m_1[i_1\oplus i_2\leftarrow i_1]\rhd P\overset{i_1:\lambda}{\rightsquigarrow}\mathsf{s}_1'\circ m_1'\rhd P'\\ \mathsf{s}_2\circ m_2[i_2\oplus i_1\leftarrow i_2]\rhd Q\overset{i_2:\bar{\lambda}}{\rightsquigarrow}\mathsf{s}_2'\circ m_2'\rhd Q'\end{array}}{(\mathsf{s}_1,\mathsf{s}_2)\circ[m_1,m_2]\rhd P\mid Q\overset{i_1\oplus i_2:\tau}{\rightsquigarrow}(\mathsf{s}_1',\mathsf{s}_2')\circ[m_1',m_2']\rhd P'\mid Q'}\text{ syn.}$$

$$\frac{\mathsf{s}_1\circ m_1\rhd P\overset{i:\alpha}{\rightsquigarrow}\mathsf{s}_1'\circ m_1'\rhd P'}{(\mathsf{s}_1,\mathsf{s}_2)\circ[m_1,m_2]\rhd P\mid Q\overset{i:\alpha}{\rightsquigarrow}(\mathsf{s}_1',\mathsf{s}_2)\circ[m_1',m_2]\rhd P'\mid Q}\ |_{\text{L}}$$

Sum Group

$$\frac{\mathsf{s}\circ m\rhd P\overset{i:\alpha}{\rightsquigarrow}\mathsf{s}'\circ m'\rhd P'}{\mathsf{s}\circ m +\!\!+_i(\oslash,Q,\mathrm{R})\rhd P\overset{i:\alpha}{\rightsquigarrow}\mathsf{s}'\circ m'\rhd(P'\oslash Q)}\ \oslash_{\text{L}}$$

$$\frac{}{\begin{array}{l}\cap^?(\gamma^{-1}(i)+s,s)\circ\delta^?(\langle i,\lambda_1,(+,\lambda_2.P_2,\mathrm{R})\rangle.m)\rhd P_1\overset{i:\lambda_1}{\rightsquigarrow}\\ \qquad\qquad(\gamma^{-1}(i),s)\circ m\rhd((\lambda_1.P_1)+(\lambda_2.P_2))\end{array}}\ +_{\text{L}}$$

$$\frac{}{\cap^?(\gamma^{-1}(i)+s,s)\circ\delta^?(\langle i,\upsilon,(\sqcap,Q,\mathrm{R})\rangle.m)\rhd P\overset{i:\upsilon}{\rightsquigarrow}(\gamma^{-1}(i),s)\circ m\rhd(P\sqcap Q)}\ \sqcap_{\text{L}}$$

The rules $|_{\text{R}}$, $\oslash_{\text{R}}$, $+_{\text{R}}$ and $\sqcap_{\text{R}}$ can easily be inferred.

Fig. 3. Backward rules of the identified reversible labeled transition system (IRLTS)

Concurrency. To define concurrency in the forward *and backward* identified LTS is easy when both transitions have the same direction: forward transitions will adopt the definition of the identified calculus, and backward transitions will always be concurrent. More care is required when transitions have opposite directions, but the seed provides a good mechanism to define concurrency easily. In a nutshell, the forward transition will be in conflict with the backward transition when the forward identifier was obtained using the identifier pattern(s) that have been used to generate the backward identifier, something we call "being down-stream". Identifying the identifier pattern(s) that have been used to generate an identifier in the memory is actually immediate:

Definition 18. *Given a backward transition* $t : \mathsf{s} \circ m \rhd P \overset{i:\alpha}{\rightsquigarrow} \mathsf{s}' \circ m' \rhd P'$, *we write* ip_t *(resp.* ip_t^1, ip_t^2*) for the unique identifier pattern(s) in* s' *such that* $i \in \mathsf{I}_a$ *(resp.* i_1 *and* i_2 *s.t.* $i_1 \oplus i_2 = i \in \mathsf{I}_p$*) is the first identifier in the stream generated by* ip_t *(resp. are the first identifiers in the streams generated by* ip_t^1 *and* ip_t^2*).*

Definition 19 (Downstream). *An identifier* i *is* downstream *of an identifier pattern* (c, s) *if*

$$\begin{cases} i \in \mathsf{IS}(c, s) & \text{if } i \in \mathsf{I}_a \\ \text{there exists } j, k \in \mathsf{I}_a \text{ s.t. } j \oplus k = i \text{ and } j \text{ or } k \text{ is downstream of } (c, s) & \text{if } i \in \mathsf{I}_p \end{cases}$$

Definition 20 (Concurrency). *Two different coinitial transitions* $t_1 : \mathsf{s} \circ m \rhd P \overset{i_1:\alpha_1}{\longrightarrow} \mathsf{s}_1 \circ m_1 \rhd P_1$ *and* $t_2 : \mathsf{s} \circ m \rhd P \overset{i_2:\alpha_2}{\longrightarrow} \mathsf{s}_2 \circ m_2 \rhd P_2$ *are* concurrent *iff*

- t_1 *and* t_2 *are forward transitions and* $i_1 \perp i_2$ *(Definition 12);*
- t_1 *is a forward and* t_2 *is a backward transition and* i_1 *(or* i_1^1 *and* i_1^2 *if* $i_1 = i_1^1 \oplus i_1^2$*) is not downstream of* ip_{t_2} *(or* $\mathsf{ip}_{t_2}^1$ *nor* $\mathsf{ip}_{t_2}^2$*);*
- t_1 *and* t_2 *are backward transitions.*

Example 6. Re-using the process from Example 5 and adding the memories, after having performed t_1 and t_3, we obtain the process $\mathsf{s} \circ [m_1, m_2] \rhd 0 \mid c$, where $\mathsf{s} = ((2, 2), (3, 2))$, $m_1 = \langle 0, a, (+, b, \mathsf{R}) \rangle$ and $m_2 = \langle 1, \bar{a}, \_ \rangle$, that has three possible transitions:

$$t_1 : \mathsf{s} \circ [m_1, m_2] \rhd 0 \mid c \overset{3:c}{\longrightarrow} ((2, 2), (5, 2)) \circ [m_1, \langle 3, c, \_ \rangle.m_2] \rhd 0 \mid 0$$

$$t_2 : \mathsf{s} \circ [m_1, m_2] \rhd 0 \mid c \overset{1:\bar{a}}{\rightsquigarrow} ((2, 2), (1, 2)) \circ [m_1, \emptyset] \rhd 0 \mid \bar{a}.c$$

$$t_3 : \mathsf{s} \circ [m_1, m_2] \rhd 0 \mid c \overset{0:a}{\rightsquigarrow} ((0, 2), (3, 2)) \circ [\emptyset, m_2] \rhd a + b \mid c$$

Among them, t_2 and t_3 are concurrent, as they are both backward, as well as t_1 and t_3, as 3 was not generated by $\mathsf{ip}_{t_3} = (0, 2)$. However, as 3 is downstream of $\mathsf{ip}_{t_2} = (1, 2)$, t_1 and t_2 are *not* concurrent.

Causal Consistency. We now prove that our framework enjoys causal consistency, a property stating that an action can be reversed only provided all its consequences have been undone. Causal consistency holds for a calculus which satisfies four basic axioms [28]: *Loop Lemma*—"any reduction can be undone"—, *Square Property*—"concurrent transitions can be executed in any order"—, *Concurrency (independence) of the backward transitions*—"coinitial backward transitions are concurrent"— and *Well-foundedness*—"each process has a finite past". Additionally, it is assumed that the semantics is equipped with the independence relation, in our case concurrency relation.

Lemma 3 (Axioms). *For every reachable processes R, R', IRLTS satisfies the following axioms:*

Loop Lemma: *for every forward transition $t : R \xrightarrow{i:\alpha} R'$ there exists a backward transition $t^{\bullet} : R' \xrightarrow{i:\alpha} R$ and vice versa.*

Square Property: *if $t_1 : R \xrightarrow{i_1:\alpha_1} R_1$ and $t_2 : R \xrightarrow{i_2:\alpha_2} R_2$ are two coinitial concurrent transitions, there exist two cofinal transitions $t'_2 : R_1 \xrightarrow{i_2:\alpha_2} R_3$ and $t'_1 : R_2 \xrightarrow{i_1:\alpha_1} R_3$.*

Backward Transitions are Concurrent: *any two coinitial backward transitions $t_1 : R \xrightarrow{i_1:\alpha_1} R_1$ and $t_2 : R \xrightarrow{i_2:\alpha_2} R_2$ where $t_1 \neq t_2$ are concurrent.*

Well-Foundedness: *there is no infinite backward computation.*

We now define the "causal equivalence" [15] relation on traces allowing to swap concurrent transitions and to delete transitions triggered in both directions. The causal equivalence relation is defined for the LTSI which satisfies the Square Property and re-use the notations from above.

Definition 21 (Causal Equivalence). *Causal equivalence, $\sim$, is the least equivalence relation on traces closed under composition satisfying $t_1; t'_2 \sim t_2; t'_1$ and $t; t^{\bullet} \sim \epsilon$ — ϵ being the empty trace.*

Now, given the notion of causal equivalence, using an axiomatic approach [28] and that our reversible semantics satisfies necessary axioms, we obtain that our framework satisfies causal consistency, given bellow.

Theorem 1 (Causal Consistency). *In IRLTS, two traces are coinitial and cofinal iff they are causally equivalent.*

Finally, we give the equivalent to the "unicity lemma" (Lemma 2) for IRLTS: note that since the same transition can occur multiple times, and as backward and forward transitions may share the same identifiers, we can have the exact same guarantee that any transition uses identifiers only once only up to causal consistency.

Lemma 4 (Unicity for IRLTS). *For a given trace d, there exist a trace d', such that $d' \sim d$ and d' contains any identifier at most once, and if a transition in d' has identifier $i_1 \oplus i_2 \in \mathsf{I}_p$, then neither i_1 nor i_2 occur in d'.*

3.3   Links to RCCS and CCSK: Translations and Comparisons

It is possible to work out an encoding of our IRLTS terms into RCCS and CCSK terms [8]. Our calculus is more general, since it allows multiple sums, and more precise, since the identifier mechanism is explicit, but has some drawbacks with respect to those calculi as well.

While RCCS "maximally distributes" the memories to all the threads, our calculus for the time being forces all the memories to be stored in one shared place. Poor implementations of this mechanism could result in important bottlenecks, as memories need to be centralized: however, we believe that an asynchronous handling of the memory accesses could allow to bypass this limitation in our calculus, but reserve this question for future work. With respect to CCSK, our memory events are potentially duplicated every time the $\delta^?$ operator is applied, resulting in a space waste, while CCSK never duplicates any memory event. Furthermore, the stability of CCSK's terms through execution—as the number of threads does not change during the computation—could be another advantage.

We believe the encoding we present to be fairly straightforward, and that it will open up the possibility of switching from one calculus to another based on the needs to distribute the memories or to reduce the memory footprint.

4 Contexts, and How We Do Not Have Congruences yet

We remind the reader of the definition of contexts $C[\cdot]$ on CCS terms P, before introducing contexts $C^I[\cdot]$ (resp. $M[\cdot]$, $C^R[\cdot]$) on identified terms I (resp. on memories M, on identified reversible terms R).

Definition 22 (Term Context). *A context $C[\cdot] : \mathsf{P} \to \mathsf{P}$ is inductively defined using all process operators and a fresh symbol $\cdot$ (the slot) as follows (omitting the symmetric contexts):*

$$C[\cdot] := \lambda.C[\cdot] \mid P \mid C[\cdot] \mid C[\cdot]\backslash\lambda \mid \lambda_1.P + \lambda_2.C[\cdot] \mid P \otimes C[\cdot] \mid P \sqcap C[\cdot] \mid \cdot$$

When placing an identified term into a context, we want to make sure that a well-identified process remains well-identified, something that can be easily achieved by noting that for all process P and seed s, $(\cup^?\cap^?\mathsf{s}) \circ P$ is always well-identified, for the following definition of $\cup^?$:

Definition 23 (Unifier). *Given a process P and a seed s, we define*

$$\cup^?(\mathsf{ip}, P) = \mathsf{ip} \circ P$$

$$\cup^?((\mathsf{s}_1, \mathsf{s}_2), P) = \begin{cases} (\cup^?(\cap_1(\mathsf{s}_1), P)) & \text{if } \mathsf{s}_1 \text{ is not of the form } \mathsf{ip}_1 \\ (\cap_1(\mathsf{s}_1), P) & \text{otherwise} \end{cases}$$

Definition 24 (Identified Context). *An identified context $C^I[\cdot] : \mathsf{I} \to \mathsf{I}$ is defined using term contexts as $C^I[\cdot] = (\cup^?\cap^?\cdot) \circ C[\cdot]$.*

Example 7. A term $(0,1) \circ a + b$, in the identified context $(\cup^?\cap^?\cdot) \circ \cdot \mid \bar{a}$, gives the term $((0,2),(1,2)) \circ a + b \mid \bar{a}$ from Example 5. The term $((0,2),(1,2)) \circ a \mid b$ placed in the same context would give $((0,4),(1,4)),(2,4)) \circ (a \mid b) \mid \bar{a}$.

To study *memory contexts*, we write M for the set of all memories.

Definition 25 (Memory Context). *A memory context $M[\cdot] : \mathsf{M} \to \mathsf{M}$ is inductively defined using the operators and operations of Definitions 13, 14 and 15, an "append" operation and a fresh symbol $\cdot$ (the slot) as follows:*

$$M[\cdot] := [M[\cdot], m] \mid [m, M[\cdot]] \mid e.M[\cdot] \mid M[\cdot].e \mid \delta^? M[\cdot] \mid M[\cdot][j \leftarrow k]$$
$$\mid M[\cdot] +\!\!+_j (o, P, d) \mid \cdot$$

Where $e.m = [e.m_1, e.m_2]$ and $m.e = [m_1.e, m_2.e]$ if $m = [m_1, m_2]$, and $m.e = m'.e.\emptyset$ if $m = m'.\emptyset$.

Definition 26 (Reversible Context). *A reversible context $C^{\mathsf{R}}[\cdot] : \mathsf{R} \to \mathsf{R}$ is defined using term and memory contexts as $C^{\mathsf{R}}[\cdot] = (\cup^? \cap^? \cdot) \circ M[\cdot] \rhd C[\cdot]$. It is memory neutral if $M[\cdot]$ is built using only $\cdot$, $[\emptyset, M[\cdot]]$ and $[M[\cdot], \emptyset]$.*

Of course, a reversible context can change the past of a reversible process R, and hence the initial process O_R to which it corresponds (Definition 17).

Example 8. Let $C^{\mathsf{R}}[\cdot]_1 = [\emptyset, \cdot] \rhd P \mid C[\cdot]$ and $C^{\mathsf{R}}[\cdot]_2 = \delta^?[\cdot] \rhd P \mid C[\cdot]$. Letting $R = (1, 1) \circ \langle 0, a, \_ \rangle \rhd b$, we obtain $C^{\mathsf{R}}[R]_1 = ((1, 2), (2, 2)) \circ [\emptyset, \langle 0, a, \_ \rangle] \rhd P \mid b$ and $C^{\mathsf{R}}[R]_2 = ((1, 2), (2, 2)) \circ [\langle 0, a, \_ \rangle, \langle 0, a, \_ \rangle] \rhd P \mid b$, and we have

$$C^{\mathsf{R}}[R]_1 \overset{0:a}{\leadsto} ((1, 2), (0, 2)) \circ [\emptyset, \emptyset] \rhd P \mid a.b \qquad C^{\mathsf{R}}[R]_2 \overset{0:a}{\leadsto} (0, 1) \circ \emptyset \rhd a.(P \mid b)$$

Note that not all of the reversible contexts, when instantiated with a reversible term, will give accessible terms. Typically, the context $[\emptyset, \cdot] \rhd \cdot$ will be "broken" since the memory pair created will never coincide with the structure of the term and its memory inserted in those slots. However, even restricted to contexts producing accessible terms, reversible contexts are strictly more expressive that term contexts. To make this more precise in Lemma 5, we use two bisimulations close in spirit to Forward-reverse bisimulation [39] and back-and-forth bisimulation [10], but that leave some flexibility regarding identifiers and corresponds to Hereditary-History Preserving Bisimulations [6]. Those bisimulations—B&F and SB&F [6,8]—are *not* congruences, not even under "memory neutral" contexts.

Lemma 5. *For all non-initial reversible process R, there exists reversible contexts $C^{\mathsf{R}}[\cdot]$ such $O_{C^{\mathsf{R}}[R]}$ is reachable and for all term context $C[\cdot]$, $C[O_R]$ and $O_{C^{\mathsf{R}}[R]}$ are not B&F.*

Theorem 2. *B&F and SB&F are not congruences, not even under memory neutral contexts.*

Proof. The processes $R_1 = (1, 1) \circ \langle 0, a, \_ \rangle \rhd b + b$ and $R_2 = (1, 1) \circ \langle 0, a, (+, a.b, \mathsf{R}) \rangle \rhd b$ are B&F, but letting $C^{\mathsf{R}}[\cdot] = \cdot \rhd \cdot + c$, $C^{\mathsf{R}}[R_1]$ and $C^{\mathsf{R}}[R_2]$ are not. Indeed, it is easy to check that R_1 and R_2, as well as $O_{R_1} = (0, 1) \circ \emptyset \rhd a.(b + b)$ and $O_{R_2} = (0, 1) \circ \emptyset \rhd (a.b) + (a.b)$, are B&F, but $O_{C^{\mathsf{R}}[R_1]} = (0, 1) \circ \emptyset \rhd a.((b + b) + c)$ and $O_{C^{\mathsf{R}}[R_2]} = (0, 1) \circ \emptyset \rhd (a.(b + c)) + (a.b)$ are not B&F, and hence $C^{\mathsf{R}}[R_1]$ and $C^{\mathsf{R}}[R_2]$ cannot be either. The same example works for SB&F.

We believe similar reasoning and example can help realizing that *none of the bisimulations introduced for reversible calculi are congruences* under our definition of reversible context. Some congruences for reversible calculi have been studied [5], but they allowed the context to be applied only to the origins of the reversible terms: whenever interesting congruences allowing contexts to be applied to non-initial terms exist is still an open problem, in our opinion, but we believe our formal frame will allow to study it more precisely.

5 Conclusion

We like to think of our contribution as a first sketch enabling researchers to tackle much more ambitious problems. It is our hope that our identified calculus can at the same time help sidestepping some of the implementation issues for reversible protocols [12], and can be re-used for RCCS or CCSK as a convenient base, or plug-in, to obtain distributed and reliable keys or identifiers. We also hope that the probabilistic choice [17]—whose representation requires to either develop an auxiliary relation [17, p. 67], to make the transition system become probabilistic as well [9], or to use Segala automata [44]—will be within the realm of reversible protocols, as its implications and applications could be numerous. The interleaving of the sums—for instance in the mixed choice [21], that offers both probabilistic choice and nondeterministic choice—could then possibly be unlocked and provides opportunities to model and study more complex behavior without leaving the reversible frame.

It is known that CCS is not "universally expressive" [19,20], and we would like to assess how universal the protocol detailed in this paper is. To that aim, careful study of reversible and heterogeneous computing devices will be required, that in turns could shed a new light on some of the questions we left unanswered. Typically, this could lead to the development of "location-aware" calculi, where the distribution of seeds and memory is made explicit, or to make progress in the definition of "the right" structural congruence [7]. Last but not least, interesting declensions of contexts were left out in this study, taking for instance a reversible context $\cdot \rhd P$ that "throws away" the term under study but "steals" its memory.

Acknowledgments. The authors wish to express their gratitude to Ioana Cristescu for asking some of the questions we tried to answer in this paper, to Assya Sellak for suggesting to use (something close to) caktus stacks to represent our memories, and to the reviewers for their interesting observations.

References

1. Abadi, M., Blanchet, B., Fournet, C.: The applied Pi calculus: mobile values, new names, and secure communication. J. ACM **65**(1), 1:1–1:41 (2018). https://doi.org/10.1145/3127586
2. Amadio, R.M.: Operational methods in semantics. Lecture notes, Université Denis Diderot Paris 7, December 2016. https://hal.archives-ouvertes.fr/cel-01422101

3. Arpit, Kumar, D.: Calculus of concurrent probabilistic reversible processes. In: ICCCT, pp. 34–40. ICCCT-2017. ACM, New York, NY, USA (2017). https://doi.org/10.1145/3154979.3155004

4. Aubert, C., Cristescu, I.: Reversible barbed congruence on configuration structures. In: ICE 2015. EPTCS, vol. 189, pp. 68–95 (2015). https://doi.org/10.4204/EPTCS.189.7

5. Aubert, C., Cristescu, I.: Contextual equivalences in configuration structures and reversibility. J. Log. Algebr. Methods Program. **86**(1), 77–106 (2017). https://doi.org/10.1016/j.jlamp.2016.08.004

6. Aubert, C., Cristescu, I.: How reversibility can solve traditional questions: the example of hereditary history-preserving bisimulation. In: CONCUR. LIPIcs, vol. 2017, pp. 13:1–13:24. Schloss Dagstuhl (2020). https://doi.org/10.4230/LIPIcs.CONCUR.2020.13

7. Aubert, C., Cristescu, I.: Structural equivalences for reversible calculi of communicating systems (oral communication). Research report, Augusta University (2020). https://hal.archives-ouvertes.fr/hal-02571597, communication at ICE 2020

8. Aubert, C., Medić, D.: Enabling Replications and Contexts in Reversible Concurrent Calculus (Extended Version), May 2021. https://hal.archives-ouvertes.fr/hal-03183053

9. Baier, C., Kwiatkowska, M.Z.: Domain equations for probabilistic processes. MSCS **10**(6), 665–717 (2000). https://doi.org/10.1017/S0960129599002984

10. Bednarczyk, M.A.: Hereditary history preserving bisimulations or what is the power of the future perfect in program logics. Technical report, Instytut Podstaw Informatyki PAN filia w Gdańsku (1991). http://www.ipipan.gda.pl/~marek/papers/historie.ps.gz

11. Boudol, G., Castellani, I.: Permutation of transitions: an event structure semantics for CCS and SCCS. In: Linear Time, Branching Time and Partial Order in Logics and Models for Concurrency, School/Workshop, Noordwijkerhout, The Netherlands, 30 May–3 June 1988, Proceedings. LNCS, vol. 354, pp. 411–427. Springer (1988). https://doi.org/10.1007/BFb0013028

12. Cox, G.: SimCCSK: simulation of the reversible process calculi CCSK. Master's thesis, University of Leicester (4 2010). https://leicester.figshare.com/articles/thesis/SimCCSK_simulation_of_the_reversible_process_calculi_CCSK/10091681

13. Cristescu, I., Krivine, J., Varacca, D.: A compositional semantics for the reversible p-calculus. In: LICS, pp. 388–397. IEEE Computer Society (2013). https://doi.org/10.1109/LICS.2013.45

14. Cristescu, I., Krivine, J., Varacca, D.: Rigid families for CCS and the π-calculus. In: Theoretical Aspects of Computing - ICTAC 2015. LNCS, vol. 9399, pp. 223–240. Springer (2015). https://doi.org/10.1007/978-3-319-25150-9_14

15. Danos, Vincent, Krivine, Jean: Reversible communicating systems. In: Gardner, Philippa, Yoshida, Nobuko (eds.) CONCUR 2004. LNCS, vol. 3170, pp. 292–307. Springer, Heidelberg (2004). https://doi.org/10.1007/978-3-540-28644-8_19

16. Danos, V., Krivine, J.: Transactions in RCCS. In: Abadi, M., de Alfaro, L. (eds.) CONCUR 2005. LNCS, vol. 3653, pp. 398–412. Springer, Heidelberg (2005). https://doi.org/10.1007/11539452_31

17. Fischer, N., van Glabbeek, R.J.: Axiomatising infinitary probabilistic weak bisimilarity of finite-state behaviours. J. Log. Algebr. Methods Program. **102**, 64–102 (2019). https://doi.org/10.1016/j.jlamp.2018.09.006

18. Frank, M.P., Brocato, R.W., Tierney, B.D., Missert, N.A., Hsia, A.H.: Reversible computing with fast, fully static, fully adiabatic CMOS. In: ICRC, Atlanta, GA, USA, 1–3 December 2020, pp. 1–8. IEEE (2020). https://doi.org/10.1109/ICRC2020.2020.00014
19. van Glabbeek, R.J.: On specifying timeouts. Electron. Notes Theor. Comput. Sci. **162**, 173–175 (2006). https://doi.org/10.1016/j.entcs.2005.12.083
20. van Glabbeek, R.J., Höfner, P.: CCS: it's not fair! - fair schedulers cannot be implemented in ccs-like languages even under progress and certain fairness assumptions. Acta Inform. **52**(2–3), 175–205 (2015). https://doi.org/10.1007/s00236-015-0221-6
21. Goubault-Larrecq, J.: Isomorphism theorems between models of mixed choice. MSCS **27**(6), 1032–1067 (2017). https://doi.org/10.1017/S0960129515000547
22. Graversen, E., Phillips, I., Yoshida, N.: Event structure semantics of (controlled) reversible CCS. In: RC 2018, Leicester, UK, September 12–14, 2018, Proceedings. LNCS, vol. 11106, pp. 102–122. Springer (2018). https://doi.org/10.1007/978-3-319-99498-7_7
23. Hennessy, M.: A distributed Pi-calculus. CUP (2007). https://doi.org/10.1017/CBO9780511611063
24. Hoare, C.A.R.: Communicating Sequential Processes. Prentice-Hall, Hoboken (1985)
25. Krivine, J.: Algèbres de Processus Réversible - Programmation Concurrente Déclarative. Ph.D. thesis, Université Paris 6 & INRIA Rocquencourt (2006). https://tel.archives-ouvertes.fr/tel-00519528
26. Lanese, I., Lienhardt, M., Mezzina, C.A., Schmitt, A., Stefani, J.-B.: Concurrent flexible reversibility. In: Felleisen, M., Gardner, P. (eds.) ESOP 2013. LNCS, vol. 7792, pp. 370–390. Springer, Heidelberg (2013). https://doi.org/10.1007/978-3-642-37036-6_21
27. Lanese, I., Medić, D., Mezzina, C.A.: Static versus dynamic reversibility in CCS. Acta Informatica 1–34 (2021). https://doi.org/10.1007/s00236-019-00346-6
28. Lanese, I., Phillips, I.C.C., Ulidowski, I.: An axiomatic approach to reversible computation. In: FOSSACS 2020, Dublin, Ireland, 25–30 April 2020, Proceedings. LNCS, vol. 12077, pp. 442–461. Springer (2020). https://doi.org/10.1007/978-3-030-45231-5_23
29. Lévy, J.J.: Réductions correctes et optimales dans le lambda-calcul. Ph.D. thesis, Paris 7, January 1978. http://pauillac.inria.fr/~levy/pubs/78phd.pdf
30. Matthews, D.: How to get started in quantum computing. Nature **591**(7848), 166–167, March 2021. https://doi.org/10.1038/d41586-021-00533-x
31. Medić, D., Mezzina, C.A.: Static VS dynamic reversibility in CCS. In: RC 2016. LNCS, vol. 9720, pp. 36–51. Springer (2016). https://doi.org/10.1007/978-3-319-40578-0_3
32. Medić, D., Mezzina, C.A., Phillips, I., Yoshida, N.: A parametric framework for reversible π-calculi. Inf. Comput. **275**, 104644 (2020). https://doi.org/10.1016/j.ic.2020.104644
33. Merro, M., Zappa Nardelli, F.: Behavioral theory for mobile ambients. J. ACM **52**(6), 961–1023 (2005). https://doi.org/10.1145/1101821.1101825
34. Mezzina, C.A., Koutavas, V.: A safety and liveness theory for total reversibility. In: TASE 2017, Sophia Antipolis, France, 13–15 September, pp. 1–8. IEEE (2017). https://doi.org/10.1109/TASE.2017.8285635
35. Milner, R.: A Calculus of Communicating Systems. LNCS, Springer-Verlag (1980). https://doi.org/10.1007/3-540-10235-3

36. Palamidessi, C., Valencia, F.D.: Recursion vs replication in process calculi: Expressiveness. Bull. EATCS **87**, 105–125 (2005). http://eatcs.org/images/bulletin/beatcs87.pdf
37. Perdrix, S., Jorrand, P.: Classically-controlled quantum computation. Electron. Notes Theor. Comput. Sci. **135**(3), 119–128 (2006). https://doi.org/10.1016/j.entcs.2005.09.026
38. Phillips, I., Ulidowski, I.: Reversing algebraic process calculi. In: Aceto, L., Ingólfsdóttir, A. (eds.) FoSSaCS 2006. LNCS, vol. 3921, pp. 246–260. Springer, Heidelberg (2006). https://doi.org/10.1007/11690634_17
39. Phillips, I., Ulidowski, I.: Reversibility and models for concurrency. Electron. Notes Theor. Comput. Sci. **192**(1), 93–108 (2007). https://doi.org/10.1016/j.entcs.2007.08.018
40. Rosenberg, A.L.: Efficient pairing functions - and why you should care. Int. J. Found. Comput. Sci. **14**(1), 3–17 (2003). https://doi.org/10.1142/S012905410300156X
41. Sangiorgi, D.: Introduction to Bisimulation and Coinduction. CUP (2011)
42. Sangiorgi, D., Walker, D.: The Pi-calculus. CUP (2001)
43. Szudzik, M.P.: The Rosenberg-strong pairing function. CoRR abs/1706.04129 (2017)
44. de Visme, M.: Event structures for mixed choice. In: CONCUR. LIPIcs, vol. 140, pp. 11:1–11:16. Schloss Dagstuhl (2019). https://doi.org/10.4230/LIPIcs.CONCUR.2019.11

Reversibility and Predictions

Martin Vassor[✉]

Univ. Grenoble-Alpes, Inria, CNRS, Grenoble Inp, LIG Grenoble, Grenoble, France
martin.vassor@inria.fr

Abstract. This paper analyses the introduction of a non-reversible mechanism in a reversible calculus (called $\Omega\rho\pi$), intended to be used as an oracle which contains persistent memories of previously reversed computation. As a second step, we introduce the notion of weak causal consistency which relaxes the classical causal consistency by allowing the backward semantics not to revert to a previous state, but to a state related to a previous state and we show that $\Omega\rho\pi$ is weakly causally consistent. We finally present a practical application of this calculus.

1 Introduction

Motivations. Reversibility is the ability, for a system, to undo some actions that were previously taken. We can approach this field from various perspectives such as circuit design, quantum algorithms, automaton, etc. In this paper, we are interested in the application of reversibility to concurrent systems. There already exists multiple works in this context, for debugging [4], for fault tolerance [14,18], for biological or chemical modelling [1,2,7,16], or even for reliable concurrent programming abstraction [12].

In concurrent systems, the very notion of reversibility is not trivial. Indeed, since reductions are not deterministic, defining the notion of predecessor is less intuitive. For instance, consider the following CCS process [13]: $a.0 \mid b.0$. There are two possible forward reductions: either $a.0 \mid b.0 \xrightarrow{a} b.0$, or $a.0 \mid b.0 \xrightarrow{b} a.0$, and both reduce to 0: both $a.0$ and $b.0$ are predecessors of 0. Intuitively, reverting to any of those states is acceptable, regardless of the forward sequence.

The standard property of a reversible system is causal consistent reversibility, which captures this intuition. *Causal consistent reversibility* states that a backward reduction can undo an action, provided that its consequences (if any) are undone beforehand.

There are works which intentionally break causal consistent reversibility. Typical applications include reversible calculi to model chemical reactions with catalyst: an example is a reaction between three molecules A, B, and C, where the objective is to bind A and B together. For the reaction to happen, B first have to bind with the catalyst C, to create molecule BC, which can in turn bind with A, to create ABC. Finally, the first binding is reverted, which results in AB and C apart. One can clearly see that such reduction is not causally consistent: the first reaction is reverted while the second holds. Such reversibility is called

S. Yamashita and T. Yokoyama (Eds.): RC 2021, LNCS 12805, pp. 163–181, 2021.
https://doi.org/10.1007/978-3-030-79837-6_10

out-of-causal-order reversibility. Calculi which model such chemical reactions include [16] (which first explicitly mentions *out-of-causal-order reversibility*) and Kuhn and Ulidowski's Calculus of Covalent Bonding [6,7] (in which they distinguish CCB, which is not causally consistent, and CCBs a core calculus which is). [5] compares in detail three out-of-causal-order reversible process calculi, while [15] studies three forms of reversibility (backtracking, causal reversibility, and out-of-causal-order reversibility) in Petri nets.

Breaking causal consistency can also be motivated by practical applications. For instance, in [8], Lanese *et al.* introduce the **croll-π** calculus, which is a reversible π-calculus in which, when a memory is reinstalled in a revert sequence, the original process is replaced by a continuation. Such approach is not causally-consistent, *stricto sensu*[1].

In this paper, we study the relation between algorithms based on *trial and error* and reversibility. An example of such algorithm is a naive consensus algorithm, in which each process tries its own value, and when it receives a smaller value from a peer, it rolls back and tries again with this smaller value. Such algorithm converges toward a state in which all processes agree on the same value.

Informally, we focus on a class of algorithms that behave in four steps: (i) read the current state; (ii) improve it; (iii) store it; and (iv) start over. Among those four steps, only the second depends on the algorithm. Standard reversible process algebra, such as $\rho\pi$, implement the fourth one (or $\text{roll} - \pi$ [9] for explicit rollback control).

In this paper, our goal is to define a calculus which also covers steps (i) and (iii). In particular, the stored state should *not* be reverted during backward execution. Another way to view the mechanism is that processes can *predict* information from the future state of the system. This is the reason why we call the context an *oracle*.

Our second objective is to characterise the reversible nature of such calculus. Intuitively, such calculus is not causally-consistent, since the state of the store is not reverted. Therefore, we relax the notion of causal-consistency by introducing *weak causal consistency*. In a nutshell, weak causal consistency takes as parameter a relation $\mathcal{R}$, and allows backward reduction to reach new states (thus breaking regular causal consistency), under the condition that there exists a related state which is reachable using forward only reduction. In particular, for our application, we are interested in a simulation relation. Taking the identity as the parameter relation, our definition falls back on regular causal consistency. We expect this property to be an intermediate point between strong causal consistency and out-of-causal-order reversibility.

Another interesting aspect of this calculus is that the backward semantics is *partial*, in the sense that its effects are confined to some parts of the term. This notion of partial reversibility is barely discussed in this paper, but we think it is important to explicit it for its potential practical applications.

---

[1] Note that, actually, it still has some sort of causal consistency, in that backward semantics undo the latter messages first. Therefore it is not possible to have an effect without its cause, but the resulting state is not reachable without backward sequence.

Approach. At first, we introduce a calculus (called $\Omega\rho\pi$) based on $\rho\pi$ [10], to which we add two primitives: $\mathtt{inform}\langle\cdot\rangle$ and $\mathtt{forecast}(\cdot) \triangleright \cdot$. These two primitives are used to interact with a context (which we call the oracle): sending on $\mathtt{inform}\langle\cdot\rangle$ stores a process in the context, and receiving from $\mathtt{forecast}(\cdot) \triangleright \cdot$ reads the context. The important aspect of the context is that it is preserved through backward reductions.

Introducing these primitives prevents our calculus to be causally consistent: it is possible to revert to the original configuration, but with a different context. Nonetheless, we still have a notion of consistency: a configuration with an uninitialised context can simulate any context. The second part of this work is to characterise this weaker notion of causal consistency.

We finally conclude with a practical application: we implement a distributed Sieve of Eratosthenes.

Contributions. The main contributions of this papers are: (i) a partially reversible calculus $\Omega\rho\pi$, which adds two primitives to save a process across backward reductions; (ii) the definition of weak causal consistency, which relaxes the usual causal consistency; (iii) a proof that $\Omega\rho\pi$ is weakly causally consistent; and (iv) an application of $\Omega\rho\pi$, which illustrates the capabilities and limitations of the calculus.

Outline. The paper is organised as follow: Sect. 2 introduces informally the $\rho\pi$ calculus, on which $\Omega\rho\pi$ is based, and the notion of simulation which is latter used. Section 3 defines the $\Omega\rho\pi$ calculus. We explain how the calculus relates to $\rho\pi$ and we argue that the oracle behaves as expected. Section 4 is a small section devoted to the introduction of weak causal consistency. Section 5 shows our main result, which is that $\Omega\rho\pi$ is weakly causally consistent. Section 6 contains the application example. Finally, Sect. 7 concludes the paper.

2   Preliminary Considerations

In this first section, we present existing work on which the core of this paper is based. In the first subsection, we informally present $\rho\pi$, a reversible variant of the higher-order π-calculus. In the second subsection, we present the notion of simulation, used in multiple works.

2.1   Informal Introduction to $\rho\pi$

The $\rho\pi$ calculus is a reversible higher-order process calculus, first introduced in [10]. In this section, we informally introduce the $\rho\pi$ calculus, and we refer the interested reader to Lanese's paper for a more detailed presentation.

Terms of the $\rho\pi$ calculus (whose syntax is shown in Fig. 1) are composed of a *configuration*, built up from *threads* and *memories*. Threads are themself composed of a *process* (which is similar to processes of the higher-order π-calculus)) and a *tag*, used as an identifier for the process.

$$
\begin{array}{lll}
\mathcal{P}, \mathcal{Q} & ::= 0 \quad | \quad X \quad | \quad \nu a.P \quad | \quad P \mid Q & \textit{Process} \\
& | \ a\langle P\rangle \quad | \quad a(X) \triangleright P & \\
\mathcal{M}, \mathcal{N} & ::= 0 \quad | \quad \nu u.M \quad | \quad M \mid N \quad | \quad \kappa : P \quad | \quad [\mu; k] & \textit{Configuration} \\
\kappa & ::= k \quad | \quad \langle h, \tilde{h}\rangle \cdot k & \textit{Tag} \\
\mu & ::= \kappa_1 : a\langle P\rangle \mid \kappa_2 : a(X) \triangleright Q & \textit{Memory content}
\end{array}
$$

Fig. 1. Syntax of $\rho\pi$

The basic building blocks of processes are the emission of a message P on a name a (written $a\langle P\rangle$) and the reception of a message on a name a (written $a(X) \triangleright P$). When a message (for instance Q) is received, the free occurrences of X in P are replaced by Q, and the resulting process is assigned a new fresh tag. In addition, upon message exchange, a new memory is created, which contains the state of the two processes prior to the message exchange. Informally, the forward reduction rule is the following:

$$
k_1 : a\langle P\rangle \mid k_2 : a(X) \triangleright Q \twoheadrightarrow \nu k.k : Q\{{}^P/_X\} \mid [k_1 : a\langle P\rangle \mid k_2 : a(X) \triangleright Q; k]
$$

In this forward rule, notice that the memory contains the tag of the resulting process. This allows the backward execution of the configuration, by replacing a process by the relevant memory:

$$
k : P \mid [M; k] \rightsquigarrow M
$$

2.2   State Simulation

Given a set of states $\mathbb{S}$ and a reduction relation $\rightarrow$ over states of $\mathbb{S}$, the notion of simulation, originally defined in [17], formalises the statement "any reduction of state S_1 can be done by state S_2".

Definition 1 (Weak simulation). *Given two states $S_1, S_2 \in \mathbb{S}$, a state S_2 simulates another state S_1 (noted $S_1 \precsim S_2$) if and only if:*

$$
\forall S_1' \cdot S_1 \rightarrow S_1' \Rightarrow \exists S_2' \cdot S_2 \rightarrow^\star S_2' \wedge S_1' \precsim S_2'
$$

where $\rightarrow^\star$ is the reflexive and transitive closure of $\rightarrow$.

Notice that state simulation is reflexive and transitive.

Remark 1. In Sects. 5 and following of this paper, we use a stronger form of simulation in which $S_2 \rightarrow S_2'$ and $S_1 \rightarrow S_1'$ using the same reduction rule.

3   The $\Omega\rho\pi$ Calculus

In this first section, we present the $\Omega\rho\pi$ calculus, which is built on top of the $\rho\pi$ calculus, itself built on top of the higher-order π calculus (H0π).

Processes of HOπ are composed of a multiple sequences of message sending and receiving, with possible name restrictions. The semantics of HOπ is that when a process sends a process P and, simultaneously, a process expects to receive a process (variable X) on the same channel, then the second process replaces free occurances of X by P. The $\rho\pi$ calculus decorates HOπ processes in order to allow reverse executions of message communications. The first subsection of this section informally introduces $\rho\pi$.

In $\Omega\rho\pi$, we decorate $\rho\pi$ configurations with a process. We say a decorated $\rho\pi$ configuration is a *context*. We obtain the semantics of contexts by lifting the $\rho\pi$ semantics to contexts. To interact with the context, we add two primitives inform and forecast (which act as special channels) to write and read the context.

3.1 Syntax

The syntax of the $\Omega\rho\pi$ calculus is given in Fig. 2. Processes are similar to the regular HOπ calculus, with the addition of the inform and forecast primitives. Configurations, tags and memories are similar to those of $\rho\pi$ (up to the addition of the primitives).

Contrary to $\rho\pi$, configurations are not directly executed: there are embedded in a *context*, which annotates the configuration with a process.

$$
\begin{array}{llll}
\mathcal{P}, \mathcal{Q} & ::= 0 \quad | \quad X \quad | \quad \nu a.P \quad | \quad P \,|\, Q & & \textit{Process} \\
& | \, a\langle P \rangle \quad | \quad a(X) \triangleright P & & \\
& | \, \texttt{inform}\langle P \rangle \quad | \quad \texttt{forecast}(X) \triangleright P & & \\
\mathcal{M}, \mathcal{N} & ::= 0 \quad | \quad \nu u.M \quad | \quad M \,|\, N \quad | \quad \kappa : P \quad | \quad [\mu; k] & \textit{Configuration} \\
C & ::= \mathcal{M}|_P & & \textit{Context} \\
\kappa & ::= k \quad | \quad \langle h, \tilde{h} \rangle \cdot k & & \textit{Tag} \\
\mu & ::= \kappa_1 : a\langle P \rangle \quad | \quad \kappa_2 : a(X) \triangleright Q & & \textit{Memory content} \\
& | \, \kappa : \texttt{forecast}(X) \triangleright P & &
\end{array}
$$

Fig. 2. Syntax of $\Omega\rho\pi$. The differences with $\rho\pi$ are highlighted.

Let $\mathbb{C}$ be the set of contexts, $\mathbb{M}$ the set of configurations and $\mathbb{P}$ the set of processes. We let P, Q and their decorated variants range over $\mathbb{P}$; M, N and their decorated variants range over $\mathbb{M}$ and C and its decorated variants range over $\mathbb{C}$. We say that a context C is *initial* when it does not contain memory.

Names $a, b, \ldots$ take their values from $\mathbb{N}$, which does not contains forecast and inform.

As in $\rho\pi$, $\tilde{h}$ denotes a vector of keys.

3.2 Semantics

The semantics of $\Omega\rho\pi$ is defined in two successive parts: first we define the semantics of configurations, as a labelled transition system, then we define the semantics of contexts, using the semantics of configurations. Intuitively, the semantics of configurations acts as the semantics of $\rho\pi$ (up to the required modifications), and the labels of transitions expose the interactions with the oracle. The semantics of contexts simply interprets the labels, updates the oracle accordingly, or constraint the transitions that can be taken by the configurations.

Configuration Semantics. The configuration semantics is defined using two reduction relations (a forward reduction relation $\twoheadrightarrow_c$ and a backward reduction relation $\rightsquigarrow_c$). As usual, we use a structural congruence relation (see Fig. 3), which allows to reorder the processes.

$$M \mid N \equiv N \mid M \qquad (M_1 \mid M_2) \mid M_3 \equiv M_1 \mid (M_2 \mid M_3) \qquad M \mid 0 \equiv M \qquad \nu u.0 \equiv 0$$

$$\nu u.\nu v.M \equiv \nu v.\nu u.M \qquad (\nu u.M) \mid N \equiv \nu u.(M \mid N) \quad u \text{ does not appear free in } N$$

$$M =_\alpha N \Rightarrow M \equiv N \qquad\qquad k : \nu a.P \equiv \nu a.k : P$$

$$k : \left(\prod_{1 \leq i \leq n} P_i \right) \equiv \nu \tilde{h}.\left(\prod_{1 \leq i \leq n} \langle h_i, \tilde{h} \rangle \cdot k : P_i \right) \quad \tilde{h} = \{h_1, \ldots, h_n\}$$

Fig. 3. Structural congruence for $\Omega\rho\pi$ configurations.

We also use an evaluation context (see Fig. 4). Intuitively, an evaluation context is a process with a hole.

$$\mathcal{E} ::= \cdot \mid \nu u.\mathcal{E} \mid M \mid \mathcal{E}$$

Fig. 4. Evaluation context

A relation $\mathcal{R}$ over configurations is *evaluation-closed* if it satisfies the two inference rules in Fig. 5.

$$\frac{M \mathrel{\mathcal{R}} N}{\mathcal{E}[M] \mathrel{\mathcal{R}} \mathcal{E}[N]} \qquad\qquad \frac{M \equiv M' \quad M \mathrel{\mathcal{R}} N \quad N \equiv N'}{M' \mathrel{\mathcal{R}} N'}$$

Fig. 5. Inference rules for evaluation-closed relations.

The configuration semantics is defined as the least evaluation-closed relation that satisfies the rules in Fig. 6.

Reduction rules are heavily based to $\rho\pi$ rules, with the following differences:

$$(\text{C.Fw}) \ \kappa_1 : a\langle P\rangle \mid \kappa_2 : a(X) \triangleright Q \xrightarrow{\tau}_c \nu k.k : Q\{^P/x\} \mid [\kappa_1 : a\langle P\rangle \mid \kappa_2 : a(X) \triangleright Q; k]$$

$$(\text{C.Bw}) \ \nu k.k : P \mid [Q; k] \xrightarrow{\tau}_c Q$$

$$(\text{C.Inf}) \ \kappa : \texttt{inform}\langle P\rangle \xrightarrow{\overline{P}}_c \nu k.k : 0 \mid [\kappa : \texttt{inform}\langle P\rangle; k]$$

$$(\text{C.For}) \ \kappa : \texttt{forecast}(X) \triangleright Q \xrightarrow{P}_c \nu k.k : Q\{^P/x\} \mid [\kappa : \texttt{forecast}(X) \triangleright Q; k]$$

Fig. 6. Reduction rules of $\Omega\rho\pi$ configuration semantics.

- transitions are labeled: reading a process P from the oracle labels the transition with $\overline{P}$, setting the oracle to P labels it with P, and all other transitions are labeled with the special symbol τ; and
- memories created by the modification of the oracle do not contain a receiver process.

Notice that the primitives seemingly act like regular channels.

The two rules (C.Fw) and (C.Bw) correspond to the forward and backward rules of the regular $\rho\pi$ calculus: the former perform the exchange of a message, and creates an associated memory, and the backward rule replace a process by the corresponding memory. Notice that, since those two rules do not interact with the oracle, their label is τ.

Rule (C.Inf) allows a process to update the oracle. Since we are at the configuration level, and therefore the oracle is not visible here, this rule simply reduces to an empty process, and emits a label $\overline{P}$, where P is the new process stored in the oracle.

On the other hand, with rule (C.For), a process $\texttt{forecast}(X) \triangleright Q$ can read a process P from the oracle, and substitute free occurrences of X by P in Q. Since we are at the configuration level, the oracle is not visible, and the process P read is not constrained at this point. Instead, a label P is emitted, which is then used below to constraint the reduction.

Global Semantics. The global semantics is defined using two reduction relations: a forward reduction relation (noted $\rightarrow$) and a backward reduction relation (noted $\rightsquigarrow$), defined according to the reduction rules given in Fig. 7.

Silent configuration transitions are simply lifted to the global semantics (rules G.Fw and G.Bw). If the configuration transition exposes a $\overline{Q}$ label, then the context is updated accordingly (rule G.INFORM). Notice that we require the newly stored process to simulates the previous one, which captures the intuition of refinement of the stored value[2]. On the other hand, for *forecast* labels (P),

---

[2] We could generalize this rule by relaxing the constraint that $Q \precsim P$, by introducing a binary relation of processes $\mathcal{R}$ as parameter and requiring that $\langle P, Q\rangle \in \mathcal{R}$, and then instantiating our semantics with $\precsim$ as $\mathcal{R}$ in this paper. However, the implications

$$(\text{G.Fw}) \ \frac{M \xrightarrow{\tau}_c N}{M|_P \twoheadrightarrow N|_P} \qquad\qquad (\text{G.Bw}) \ \frac{M \xrightarrow{\tau}_c N}{M|_P \rightsquigarrow N|_P}$$

$$(\text{G.Inform}) \ \frac{M \xrightarrow{\overline{Q}}_c N \qquad Q \precsim P}{M|_P \twoheadrightarrow N|_Q}$$

$$(\text{G.Forecast}) \ \frac{M \xrightarrow{P}_c N}{M|_P \twoheadrightarrow N|_P}$$

Fig. 7. Reduction rules of $\Omega\rho\pi$ global semantics.

the corresponding configuration transition is allowed only if the label matches the context (rule G.FORECAST).

We note $\rightarrow$ the semantics of $\Omega\rho\pi$, defined as $\rightarrow = \twoheadrightarrow \cup \rightsquigarrow$. Also, $\rightarrow^*$, $\twoheadrightarrow^*$ and $\rightsquigarrow^*$ are the transitive and reflective closure of $\rightarrow$, $\twoheadrightarrow$ and $\rightsquigarrow$.

A trace is a sequence of transitions $\sigma = t_1; \ldots; t_n$ with $t_i = C_{i-1} \rightarrow C_i$. When C_0 is initial, we call the trace *initial*. When $t_1; \ldots; t_i$ are the only G.INFORM reduction of σ (i.e. if none of $t_{i+1}; \ldots; t_n$ is a G.INFORM reduction), we call σ a *forecast sequence* (t_i is called the *last inform transition* of the sequence). A trace that contains only forward (resp. backward) transitions is called *forward trace* (resp. *backward trace*). We note ϵ for an empty trace. Two traces $t_1; \ldots; t_n$ and $t'_1; \ldots; t'_m$ are said coinitial if $t_1 = C_1 \rightarrow C$ and $t'_1 = C_1 \rightarrow C'$ and cofinal if $t_n = C \rightarrow C_f$ and $t'_m = C' \rightarrow C_f$.

Example. The example in Fig. 8 shows an execution of a $\Omega\rho\pi$ context. The initial context is $c\langle P_1 \rangle \mid c\langle P_2 \rangle$. This context contains two processes to be read on c. The configuration is composed of two threads. The first one (initially with tag k_1) reads the context, and then receives one of the two process on c (due to the non-deterministic semantics, the choice is random), and runs it. Intuitively, it launches one of the process at random. Notice, in particular, that if it rolls back to the initial configuration, an *other* process can be selected during a second attempt. The second process (initially with tag k_2), performs a *definitive* choice. Similarly to the first thread, it selects one of the possible process at random, but contrary to the first thread, it modifies the context to store that choice.

In the example, first k_1 reduces, and first chooses process P_1, which is run (the two first reductions). At this point, if the process rolls back and restarts, it still has the choice (not shown). After, k_2 reads the context, then selects P_2, and finally modifies the oracle (transitions 3, 4 and 5). At this point, the selection

---

of such generalization are not trivial, in particular with respect to the weak causal consistency result presented latter in this paper. Therefore, for the sake of simplicity, we restrict ourself to the restricted definition.

is definitive[3]. A sequence of backward reduction revert the configuration in its initial state, but with the context modified. Now, when the first two reduction are replayed, k_1 has no choice and selects P_2.

3.3 Oracle Soundness

In this subsection, we argue that the oracle behaves as expected: we expect that, looking at a trace, any reduction G.FORECAST that occurs should forecast P, when the previous reduction G.INFORM that occurs in the trace sets the oracle with process P, regardless of any backward reduction in between (or with the initial P if no G.INFORM transition is taken).

More formally, given a trace σ, for any subtrace $\sigma_{ij} = t_i; \ldots; t_j$ of σ with $t_k = M|_P \to N|_Q$ the last inform transition of σ_{ij}, for any $t \in t_{k+1}; \ldots; t_j$, t is either G.Fw, G.Bw or G.FORECAST with context Q.

To begin with, we show that the context does not change, except during G.INFORM transition.

Lemma 1. *Given a trace σ such that the final context is $M|_P$.*
The last G.INFORM reduction (if any) in σ is $N|_Q \twoheadrightarrow N'|_P$.

Proof. By induction on the length of σ. In the case σ is ϵ, then trivially, $Q = P$ and no reduction occurs.

In the case $\sigma = \sigma'; t$. Let $N|_R$ be the final context of the σ' trace. Let t be $N|_R \to M|_P$. We proceed by case analysis of the transition t, the cases G.Fw, G.FORECAST and G.Bw are trivial. If t is G.INFORM, then $t = N|_R \twoheadrightarrow M|_P$, and it is the last G.INFORM transition.

Using this fact, we show that G.FORECAST reductions read the context set by the previous G.INFORM reduction[4].

Lemma 2. *Given a trace $\sigma = t_1; \ldots; t_n$ with $t_i = M|_P \twoheadrightarrow M'|_Q$ being the last G.INFORM reduction of σ, then for any G.FORECAST reduction t in the subtrace $t_{i+1}; \ldots; t_n$, $t = N|_Q \twoheadrightarrow N'|_Q$.*

Corollary 1 (Oracle soundness). *Given a trace σ, for any G.FORECAST reduction $M|_P \twoheadrightarrow M'|_P$, the preceding G.INFORM transition is $N|_Q \twoheadrightarrow N'|_P$.*

4 Weak Causal Consistency

The $\Omega\rho\pi$ calculus is not causally consistent: it is possible to inform the oracle and then go back to the initial configuration (up to context), which is, obviously, not reachable using only forward reductions (see Fig. 9: the modification of the oracle *happens after* —in Lamport terms— the message exchange).

---

[3] Notice that, due to the pending $\langle k_5^1, \tilde{k}_5 \rangle : c\langle P_1 \rangle$ that remains after the choice, if k_1 reduces at this point, when reading c it could actually receive from this pending process. For the sake of simplicity, we ignore this, since that garbage process is cleaned up when k_2 returns in its initial state.

[4] The proof is trivial. Due to length constraints, we omit it.

$k_1 : \texttt{forecast}(X) \triangleright (X \mid c\langle Y\rangle \triangleright Y) \mid k_2 : \texttt{forecast}(X) \triangleright (X \mid c\langle Y\rangle \triangleright \texttt{inform}\langle c\langle Y\rangle\rangle)|_{c\langle P_1\rangle \mid c\langle P_2\rangle}$

$\twoheadrightarrow$ G.FORECAST

$\quad \nu k_3.k_3 : c\langle P_1\rangle \mid c\langle P_2\rangle \mid c\langle Y\rangle \triangleright Y \mid k_2 : \texttt{forecast}(X) \triangleright (X \mid c\langle Y\rangle \triangleright \texttt{inform}\langle c\langle Y\rangle\rangle)$

$\quad \mid [k_1 : \texttt{forecast}(X) \triangleright (X \mid c\langle Y\rangle \triangleright Y); k_3]|_{c\langle P_1\rangle \mid c\langle P_2\rangle}$

$\twoheadrightarrow$ G.Fw

$\quad \nu k_3.\nu\tilde{k_3}.\langle k_3^1, \tilde{k_3}\rangle : c\langle P_1\rangle \mid \nu k_4.k_4 : P_2 \mid k_2 : \texttt{forecast}(X) \triangleright (X \mid c\langle Y\rangle \triangleright \texttt{inform}\langle c\langle Y\rangle\rangle)$

$\quad \mid [k_1 : \texttt{forecast}(X) \triangleright (X \mid c\langle Y\rangle \triangleright Y); k_3] \mid [\langle k_3^2, \tilde{k_3}\rangle : c\langle P_2\rangle \mid \langle k_3^3, \tilde{k_3}\rangle : c\langle Y\rangle \triangleright Y; k_4]|_{c\langle P_1\rangle \mid c\langle P_2\rangle}$

$\twoheadrightarrow$ G.FORECAST

$\quad \nu k_3.\nu\tilde{k_3}.\langle k_3^1, \tilde{k_3}\rangle : c\langle P_1\rangle \mid \nu k_4.k_4 : P_2 \mid \nu k_5.k_5 : c\langle P_1\rangle \mid c\langle P_2\rangle \mid c\langle Y\rangle \triangleright \texttt{inform}\langle c\langle Y\rangle\rangle$

$\quad \mid [k_1 : \texttt{forecast}(X) \triangleright (X \mid c\langle Y\rangle \triangleright Y); k_3] \mid [\langle k_3^2, \tilde{k_3}\rangle : c\langle P_2\rangle \mid \langle k_3^3, \tilde{k_3}\rangle : c\langle Y\rangle \triangleright Y; k_4]$

$\quad \mid [k_2 : \texttt{forecast}(X) \triangleright (X \mid c\langle Y\rangle \triangleright \texttt{inform}\langle c\langle Y\rangle\rangle); k_5]|_{c\langle P_1\rangle \mid c\langle P_2\rangle}$

$\twoheadrightarrow$ G.Fw

$\quad \nu k_3.\nu\tilde{k_3}.\langle k_3^1, \tilde{k_3}\rangle : c\langle P_1\rangle \mid \nu k_4.k_4 : P_2 \mid \nu k_5.\nu\tilde{k_5}.\langle k_5^1, \tilde{k_5}\rangle : c\langle P_1\rangle \mid \nu k_6.k_6 : \texttt{inform}\langle c\langle P_2\rangle\rangle$

$\quad \mid [k_1 : \texttt{forecast}(X) \triangleright (X \mid c\langle Y\rangle \triangleright Y); k_3] \mid [\langle k_3^2, \tilde{k_3}\rangle : c\langle P_2\rangle \mid \langle k_3^3, \tilde{k_3}\rangle : c\langle Y\rangle \triangleright Y; k_4]$

$\quad \mid [k_2 : \texttt{forecast}(X) \triangleright (X \mid c\langle Y\rangle \triangleright \texttt{inform}\langle c\langle Y\rangle\rangle); k_5]$

$\quad \mid [\langle k_5^2, \tilde{k_5}\rangle : c\langle P_2\rangle \mid \langle k_5^3, \tilde{k_5}\rangle : c\langle Y\rangle \triangleright \texttt{inform}\langle c\langle Y\rangle\rangle; k_6]|_{c\langle P_1\rangle \mid c\langle P_2\rangle}$

$\twoheadrightarrow$ G.INFORM

$\quad \nu k_3.\nu\tilde{k_3}.\langle k_3^1, \tilde{k_3}\rangle : c\langle P_1\rangle \mid \nu k_4.k_4 : P_2 \mid \nu k_5.\nu\tilde{k_5}.\langle k_5^1, \tilde{k_5}\rangle : c\langle P_1\rangle \mid \nu k_6.\nu k_7.k_7 : 0$

$\quad \mid [k_1 : \texttt{forecast}(X) \triangleright (X \mid c\langle Y\rangle \triangleright Y); k_3] \mid [\langle k_3^2, \tilde{k_3}\rangle : c\langle P_2\rangle \mid \langle k_3^3, \tilde{k_3}\rangle : c\langle Y\rangle \triangleright Y; k_4]$

$\quad \mid [k_2 : \texttt{forecast}(X) \triangleright (X \mid c\langle Y\rangle \triangleright \texttt{inform}\langle c\langle Y\rangle\rangle); k_5]$

$\quad \mid [\langle k_5^2, k_5\rangle : c\langle P_2\rangle \mid \langle k_5^3, k_5\rangle : c\langle Y\rangle \triangleright \texttt{inform}\langle c\langle Y\rangle\rangle; k_6] \mid [k_6 : \texttt{inform}\langle c\langle P_2\rangle\rangle; k_7]|_{c\langle P_2\rangle}$

$\rightsquigarrow$ G.Bw

$\quad \nu k_3.\nu\tilde{k_3}.\langle k_3^1, \tilde{k_3}\rangle : c\langle P_1\rangle \mid \nu k_4.k_4 : P_2 \mid \nu k_5.\nu\tilde{k_5}.\langle k_5^1, \tilde{k_5}\rangle : c\langle P_1\rangle \mid \nu k_6.k_6 : \texttt{inform}\langle c\langle P_2\rangle\rangle$

$\quad \mid [k_1 : \texttt{forecast}(X) \triangleright (X \mid c\langle Y\rangle \triangleright Y); k_3] \mid [\langle k_3^2, \tilde{k_3}\rangle : c\langle P_2\rangle \mid \langle k_3^3, \tilde{k_3}\rangle : c\langle Y\rangle \triangleright Y; k_4]$

$\quad \mid [k_2 : \texttt{forecast}(X) \triangleright (X \mid c\langle Y\rangle \triangleright \texttt{inform}\langle c\langle Y\rangle\rangle); k_5]$

$\quad \mid [\langle k_5^2, k_5\rangle : c\langle P_2\rangle \mid \langle k_5^3, k_5\rangle : c\langle Y\rangle \triangleright \texttt{inform}\langle c\langle Y\rangle\rangle; k_6]|_{c\langle P_2\rangle}$

$\rightsquigarrow$ G.Bw

$\quad \nu k_3.\nu\tilde{k_3}.\langle k_3^1, \tilde{k_3}\rangle : c\langle P_1\rangle \mid \nu k_4.k_4 : P_2 \mid \nu k_5.k_5 : c\langle P_1\rangle \mid c\langle P_2\rangle \mid c\langle Y\rangle \triangleright \texttt{inform}\langle c\langle Y\rangle\rangle$

$\quad \mid [k_1 : \texttt{forecast}(X) \triangleright (X \mid c\langle Y\rangle \triangleright Y); k_3] \mid [\langle k_3^2, \tilde{k_3}\rangle : c\langle P_2\rangle \mid \langle k_3^3, \tilde{k_3}\rangle : c\langle Y\rangle \triangleright Y; k_4]$

$\quad \mid [k_2 : \texttt{forecast}(X) \triangleright (X \mid c\langle Y\rangle \triangleright \texttt{inform}\langle c\langle Y\rangle\rangle); k_5]|_{c\langle P_2\rangle}$

$\rightsquigarrow$ G.Bw

$\quad \nu k_3.\nu\tilde{k_3}.\langle k_3^1, \tilde{k_3}\rangle : c\langle P_1\rangle \mid \nu k_4.k_4 : P_2 \mid k_2 : \texttt{forecast}(X) \triangleright (X \mid c\langle Y\rangle \triangleright \texttt{inform}\langle c\langle Y\rangle\rangle)$

$\quad \mid [k_1 : \texttt{forecast}(X) \triangleright (X \mid c\langle Y\rangle \triangleright Y); k_3] \mid [\langle k_3^2, \tilde{k_3}\rangle : c\langle P_2\rangle \mid \langle k_3^3, \tilde{k_3}\rangle : c\langle Y\rangle \triangleright Y; k_4]|_{c\langle P_2\rangle}$

$\rightsquigarrow$ G.Bw

$\quad \nu k_3.k_3 : c\langle P_1\rangle \mid c\langle P_2\rangle \mid c\langle Y\rangle \triangleright Y \mid k_2 : \texttt{forecast}(X) \triangleright (X \mid c\langle Y\rangle \triangleright \texttt{inform}\langle c\langle Y\rangle\rangle)$

$\quad \mid [k_1 : \texttt{forecast}(X) \triangleright (X \mid c\langle Y\rangle \triangleright Y); k_3]|_{c\langle P_2\rangle}$

$\rightsquigarrow$ G.Bw

$\quad k_1 : \texttt{forecast}(X) \triangleright (X \mid c\langle Y\rangle \triangleright Y) \mid k_2 : \texttt{forecast}(X) \triangleright (X \mid c\langle Y\rangle \triangleright \texttt{inform}\langle c\langle Y\rangle\rangle)|_{c\langle P_2\rangle}$

$\twoheadrightarrow$ G.FORECAST

$\quad \nu k_3.k_3 : c\langle P_2\rangle \mid c\langle Y\rangle \triangleright Y \mid k_2 : \texttt{forecast}(X) \triangleright (X \mid c\langle Y\rangle \triangleright \texttt{inform}\langle c\langle Y\rangle\rangle)$

$\quad \mid [k_1 : \texttt{forecast}(X) \triangleright (X \mid c\langle Y\rangle \triangleright Y); k_3]|_{c\langle P_2\rangle}$

Fig. 8. Example of a $\Omega\rho\pi$ forward and backward execution. On each line, the part of the term that takes the next transition is coloured in red. The result of the previous transition is coloured in blue on the next line. When the result of the previous transition also takes the next transition, it is coloured in green. (Color figure online)

$k_1 : a\langle P\rangle \mid k_2 : a(X) \triangleright \mathtt{inform}\langle X\rangle|_{P \mid Q}$

$\twoheadrightarrow$ G.Fw

$\quad \nu k_3.k_3 : \mathtt{inform}\langle P\rangle \mid [k_1 : a\langle P\rangle \mid k_2 : a(X) \triangleright \mathtt{inform}\langle X\rangle; k_3]|_{P \mid Q}$

$\twoheadrightarrow$ G.INFORM

$\quad \nu k_3.\nu k_4.k_4 : 0 \mid [k_3 : \mathtt{inform}\langle P\rangle; k_4] \mid [k_1 : a\langle P\rangle \mid k_2 : a(X) \triangleright \mathtt{inform}\langle X\rangle; k_3]|_P$

$\rightsquigarrow$ G.Bw (twice)

$\quad k_1 : a\langle P\rangle \mid k_2 : a(X) \triangleright \mathtt{inform}\langle X\rangle|_P$

Fig. 9. Example of a sequence of reductions which leads to a configuration that can not be reached using only forward reductions.

However, our calculus still exhibits an almost causally consistent behaviour: the embedded configuration is the same and the initial $P \mid Q$ context is *more general* than a specific context P, in the sense that any reduction with a context P can be done by a context $P \mid Q$.

This section formalises this intuition, which we call *weak causal consistency*. In this section, we consider a generic transition system, with a set of states $\mathbb{S}$, equipped with a forward transition relation $\twoheadrightarrow$ and a backward transition relation $\rightsquigarrow$ and a (general) transition relation $\rightarrow = \twoheadrightarrow \cup \rightsquigarrow$.

$\mathcal{R}$-weak Causal Consistency. Given a relation $\mathcal{R} \subseteq \mathbb{S} \times \mathbb{S}$, a reversible system is $\mathcal{R}$-weakly causally consistent is for each state C_f reachable from an initial state C_i, there exists a related state C'_f reachable using only forward transitions. We first define the notion of *initial state* (a state that can only take forward reductions), and we then formalise our notion of weak causal consistency.

Definition 2 (Initial state). *A state C_i is initial (noted $C_i \not\rightsquigarrow$) if and only if there exists no C such that $C_i \rightsquigarrow C$.*

Definition 3 (Weak causal consistency). *A reversible transition system $\Sigma = \langle \mathbb{S}, \twoheadrightarrow, \rightsquigarrow \rangle$ is weakly causally consistent (with respect to $\mathcal{R}$) if and only if:*

$$\forall C_i, C_f \in \mathbb{S} \cdot C_i \not\rightsquigarrow \wedge C_i \twoheadrightarrow^* C_f \Rightarrow \exists C'_f \in \mathbb{S} \cdot C_i \twoheadrightarrow^* C'_f \wedge \langle C'_f, C_f \rangle \in \mathcal{R}$$

This definition is intentionally very broad, depending on the chosen $\mathcal{R}$. In the rest of this paper, we will only consider some particular cases. As we will see in the rest of this paper, we think interesting cases include preorder relations, e.g. simulation relation, or other evaluation-closed relations.

Notice that this definition is close to the definition of reversibility developed by Caires *et al.* in [3] (Definition 3.4).

Remark 2. Notice that if the relation $\mathcal{R}$ we consider is the identity, we fall back on the definition of (strong) causal consistency. Therefore, weak causal consistency is a conservative extension of causal consistency.

5   Weak Causal Consistency of $\Omega\rho\pi$

In this section, we show that $\Omega\rho\pi$ is $\precsim$-weakly causally consistent. We can not show weak causal consistency as causal consistency is usually shown (see for instance the proof of causal consistency of the $\rho\pi$ calculus [10], the details of the proof are shown in Mezzina's thesis [11]), since the loop lemma does not hold in our calculus. Instead, we show the causal consistency in two steps: (i) we show that, if an initial trace σ does not contain G.INFORM reductions, then there exists a coinitial and cofinal forward trace $\sigma_\twoheadrightarrow$, this is shown by relating this particular trace to an equivalent one in $\rho\pi$ and using the causal consistency of $\rho\pi$; (ii) we show that, for every trace σ, there is a coinitial and cofinal trace σ_s free of G.INFORM. A summary of the proof is shown in Fig. 10.

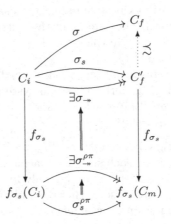

Fig. 10. Summary of the causal consistence proof: for any trace σ (top) from C_i to C_f, it is possible to find a coinitial and cofinal trace σ_s. Aside, we show that any G.INFORM free trace (in particular σ_s) of the $\Omega\rho\pi$ calculus can be played in $\rho\pi$ calculus ($\sigma_s^{\rho\pi}$, bottom left). We introduce a function f_{σ_s} to do the conversion. Since $\rho\pi$ is causally consistent, there necessarily exists an equivalent forward sequence $\sigma_\twoheadrightarrow^{\rho\pi}$ (middle left), which can finally be played instead of σ_g ($\sigma_\twoheadrightarrow$, top left).

5.1   States Simulation

As we have seen in the previous section, weak causal consistency relies on states simulating each other. Hence, we first exhibit some similar states we will rely on in the subsequent sections.

First, a term with P in the context simulates any term composed of the same configuration and a process Q such that $P \precsim Q$ in the context. This is trivial, since $\precsim$ is evaluation closed.

Lemma 3. $\forall M \in \mathbb{M}, P, Q \in \mathbb{P} \cdot P \precsim Q \Rightarrow M|_P \precsim M|_Q$

Also, any $\kappa : \texttt{inform}\langle P \rangle$ simulates $\kappa : 0$. Surprisingly the rule is easy, but not trivial, due to backward reductions.

Lemma 4. $\forall M \in \mathbb{M}, P, S \in \mathbb{P} \cdot M \mid \kappa : \texttt{inform}\langle P \rangle|_S \precsim M \mid \kappa : 0|_S$

Proof. We have to show that, for any C such that $M \mid \kappa : 0|_S \to C$, there exists C' such that $M \mid \kappa : \texttt{inform}\langle P \rangle|_S \to C'$.

We proceed by case analysis on the reduction rule used. Only G.Bw and G.INFORM are not trivial.

G.Bw: From the premisses of G.Bw and C.Bw, $M \mid \kappa : 0 \equiv \nu k.k : P \mid \lfloor Q; k \rfloor$. If κ is independent of k, then the result trivially holds.

If $\kappa = \langle h_i, \tilde{h} \rangle \cdot k$, then $M \mid \kappa : 0 \equiv M' \mid (\nu k.\langle h_j, \tilde{h} \rangle \cdot k : R \mid \langle h_i, \tilde{h} \rangle \cdot k : 0) \mid \lfloor Q; k \rfloor \equiv M' \mid (\nu k.k : R \mid 0) \mid \lfloor Q; k \rfloor$ (notice that it is possible that $\kappa = k$, in which case $R = 0$). Then the backward reduction that occurs is $M' \mid (\nu k.k : R \mid 0) \mid \lfloor Q; k \rfloor|_S \rightsquigarrow M' \mid Q|_S$.

Finally, with the same reasoning, we have $M \mid \kappa : \texttt{inform}\langle P \rangle \equiv M' \mid (\nu k.k : R \mid \texttt{inform}\langle P \rangle) \mid \lfloor Q; k \rfloor$, which can reduce using G.Bw: $M' \mid (\nu k.k : R \mid \texttt{inform}\langle P \rangle) \mid \lfloor Q; k \rfloor|_S \rightsquigarrow M' \mid Q|_S$. The result holds by reflexivity of $\precsim$.

G.Inform: We suppose the $\texttt{inform}\langle \cdot \rangle$ that reduces is $k : \texttt{inform}\langle P \rangle$. In the case it is an other $\texttt{inform}\langle \cdot \rangle$ in M, the result trivially holds.

From the premisses of G.INFORM, $M \mid k : \texttt{inform}\langle P \rangle|_S$ reduces to $M \mid \nu k'.k' : 0 \mid \lfloor k : \texttt{inform}\langle P \rangle; k' \rfloor|_P$ and $P \precsim S$. We have to show that $M \mid \nu k'.k' : 0 \mid \lfloor k : \texttt{inform}\langle P \rangle; k' \rfloor|_P \precsim M \mid k : 0|_S$. Only the case G.FORECAST is relevant.

In that case, according to the premisses of G.FORECAST and C.FOR, $M \equiv M' \mid \kappa : \texttt{forecast}(X) \triangleright Q$. Therefore, $M \mid \nu k'.k' : 0 \mid \lfloor k : \texttt{inform}\langle P \rangle; k' \rfloor|_P$ reduces to $M' \mid \nu k''.k'' : Q\{{}^P/_X\} \mid \lfloor \mu; \kappa \rfloor \mid \nu k'.k' : 0 \mid \lfloor k : \texttt{inform}\langle P \rangle; k' \rfloor|_P$ and, similarly, $M \mid k : 0|_S$ reduces to $M' \mid \nu k.k : Q\{{}^S/_X\} \mid \lfloor \mu; \kappa \rfloor \mid k : 0|_S$. Since $P \precsim S$, $M' \mid \nu k.k : Q\{{}^P/_X\} \mid \lfloor \mu; \kappa \rfloor \mid \nu k'.k' : 0 \mid \lfloor k : \texttt{inform}\langle P \rangle; k' \rfloor|_P \precsim M' \mid \nu k.k : Q\{{}^S/_X\} \mid \lfloor \mu; \kappa \rfloor \mid k : 0|_S$.

Corollary 2. $\forall M \in \mathbb{M}, P, R, S \in \mathbb{P} \cdot R \precsim S \Rightarrow M \mid \kappa : \texttt{inform}\langle P \rangle|_R \precsim M \mid \kappa : 0|_S$

Proof. From Lemmas 3 and 4, $M \mid \kappa : \texttt{inform}\langle P \rangle|_R \precsim M \mid \kappa : 0|_R \precsim M \mid \kappa : 0|_S$. The result holds by transitivity of $\precsim$.

5.2 Causal Consistency of the Traces Without G.INFORM Reductions

When a $\Omega\rho\pi$ trace σ does not contain G.INFORM reduction, there is a one-to-one mapping between the global semantics of $\Omega\rho\pi$ contexts, and the configuration semantics of $\Omega\rho\pi$ configurations. To clarify this paragraph, we will only work with the configuration fragment of $\Omega\rho\pi$.

The configuration semantics is analogous to the regular $\rho\pi$ semantics, except for $\texttt{inform}\langle P \rangle$ and $\texttt{forecast}(X) \triangleright Q$ primitives. Encoding the $\texttt{inform}\langle P \rangle$ primitive in $\rho\pi$ is easy: it acts like an oblivious channel and one just need to add a repeating $\texttt{inform}(X) \rhd 0$ process (and, anyway, since σ does not contain G.INFORM reduction, we could even ignore them).

Encoding the $\texttt{forecast}(X) \rhd Q$ primitive is almost as simple. Since the trace does not contain G.INFORM reduction, the context is constant. Let P be the process it contains. We only need to add enough $\texttt{forecast}\langle P \rangle$. To avoid any problem with the key, we can simply add them under the same key than the forecast. That is, we replace each $\kappa : \texttt{forecast}(X) \rhd Q$, by $\kappa : \texttt{forecast}(X) \rhd Q \mid \texttt{forecast}\langle P \rangle$. Note that this replacement also includes occurrences in memories.

Definition 4. *The function* $[\![M|_R]\!] = [\![M]\!]_R$ *encodes an* $\Omega\rho\pi$ *context into a* $\rho\pi$ *configuration, where* $[\![M]\!]_R$ *is defined in Figs. 11 and 12.*

$$[\![0]\!]_R = 0 \qquad [\![\nu u.M]\!]_R = \nu u.[\![M]\!]_R \qquad [\![M \mid N]\!]_R = [\![M]\!]_R \mid [\![N]\!]_R$$

$$[\![k : P]\!]_R = k : [\![P]\!]_R \qquad [\![[\mu; k]]\!]_R = [[\![\mu]\!]_R; k]$$

Fig. 11. Rules to encode an $\Omega\rho\pi$ configuration into a $\rho\pi$ configuration.

$$[\![0]\!]_R = 0 \qquad [\![X]\!]_R = X \qquad [\![\nu a.P]\!]_R = \nu a.[\![P]\!]_R \qquad [\![P \mid Q]\!]_R = [\![P]\!]_R \mid [\![Q]\!]_R$$

$$[\![a\langle P \rangle]\!]_R = a\langle [\![P]\!]_R \rangle \qquad [\![a(X) \rhd P]\!]_R = a(X) \rhd [\![P]\!]_R$$

$$[\![\texttt{inform}\langle P \rangle]\!]_R = \texttt{inform}\langle [\![P]\!]_R \rangle \mid \texttt{inform}(X) \rhd 0$$

$$[\![\texttt{forecast}(X) \rhd P]\!]_R = \texttt{forecast}(X) \rhd [\![P]\!]_R \mid \texttt{forecast}\langle R \rangle$$

Fig. 12. Rules to encode an $\Omega\rho\pi$ process into a $\rho\pi$ process.

Trivially, ignoring G.INFORM transitions, an encoded $\Omega\rho\pi$ configuration simulates the original configuration, and an $\Omega\rho\pi$ configuration simulates the forward reductions of its encoded counterparts, using only forward rules:

Lemma 5. *For any* $\Omega\rho\pi$ *contexts* C_1 *and* C_2, $[\![C_1]\!] \twoheadrightarrow [\![C_2]\!] \Rightarrow C_1 \twoheadrightarrow C_2$. *If* $C_1 \twoheadrightarrow C_2$ *without a* G.INFORM *reduction, then* $[\![C_1]\!] \twoheadrightarrow [\![C_2]\!]$. *If* $C_1 \rightsquigarrow C_2$, *then* $[\![C_1]\!] \rightsquigarrow [\![C_2]\!]$.

Corollary 3. $\Omega\rho\pi$, *without* G.INFORM *reductions, is causally consistent.*

Proof. Suppose $C_i \rightarrow^* C_f$, for $C_i \not\rightarrow$. Then there exists a $\rho\pi$ reduction $[\![C_i]\!] \rightarrow^* [\![C_f]\!]$.

Since $\rho\pi$ is causally consistent, there exists a forward reduction $[\![C_i]\!] \twoheadrightarrow^* [\![C_f]\!]$. Therefore there exists a forward reduction $C_i \twoheadrightarrow^* C_f$.

5.3   Existence of a Trace Free of G.Inform Reductions

We are given an initial trace $\sigma = t_1; \ldots; t_n$ with C_i the initial configuration. Our goal is to show that there exists a coinitial and cofinal trace $\sigma_f; \sigma_i$ such that σ_f is free of G.Inform reductions. We proceed in two steps: (i) we consider a forecast sequence σ' and we show that we can move the (initial) G.Inform reductions at the end of the trace (see Fig. 13); (ii) we consider an initial trace and we show that we can then move all G.Inform reductions at the end of the trace, by successively pushing the first G.Inform reductions toward the end of the trace.

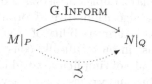

G.Inform

$M|_P \qquad N|_Q$

Fig. 13. Illustration of Lemma 6. If a configuration $M|_P$ reduces to $N|_Q$ using a G.Inform reduction, then the initial configuration simulates the final configuration.

Lemma 6 (Inform removal). $\forall M \in \mathbb{M} \cdot M|_P \rightarrow N|_Q \Rightarrow M|_P \precsim N|_Q$

Proof. Since the transition changes the context, it is a G.Inform transition. Thus, $M = M' \mid \kappa : \mathtt{inform}\langle P \rangle$ and $N = M' \mid \kappa : 0$. From Lemma 4, we have that $M|_P \precsim N|_P$. From the premisses of rule G.Inform, $P \precsim Q$. From Lemma 3, we have that $M|_P \precsim M|_Q$. Finally, from the transitivity of the simulation relation, $M|_P \precsim N|_Q$.

A corollary of this lemma is that for any sequence of reductions from C_i to C_f, it is possible to remove all G.Inform reductions and reach a new C'_f which can simulate C_f.

Corollary 4. *For all initial configuration C_i, for all configuration C_f such that $C_i \rightarrow^* C_f$, there exists a configuration C'_f such that $C_i \rightarrow^* C'_f$ without G.Inform reduction and $C'_f \precsim C_f$.*

Proof. Let $\sigma = t_1; \ldots; t_n$ be the trace of the sequence of reduction $C_i \rightarrow^* C_f$.

By induction on the number of G.Inform reductions in σ. The base case (0 G.Inform reduction in σ) follows from the previous section.

For the inductive case, consider there are n G.Inform reductions in σ, let $t_j = C_{j-1} \rightarrow C_j$ be the first one and $t_k = C_{k-1} \twoheadrightarrow C_k$ the second one. That is, $C_j \rightarrow^* C_{k-1}$ without G.Inform reduction.

From Lemma 6, $C_{j-1} \precsim C_j$, there exists a C'_{k-1} such that $C_{j-1} \rightarrow^* C'_{k-1}$ and $C'_{k-1} \precsim C_{k-1}$. Let σ_1 be the trace of that sequence of reductions. From Remark 1, σ_s does not contain G.Inform reduction.

Also, since $C'_{k-1} \precsim C_{k-1}$, there exists a C'_f such that $C_{k-1} \to^* C'_f$ and $C'_f \precsim C_f$.

Finally, we have $C_i \to^* C'_{k-1} \to^* C'_f$. This sequence contains one less G.INFORM reduction. Thus, from the induction hypothesis, there exists C''_f such that $C_i \to^* C''_f$ without G.INFORM reduction and such that $C''_f \precsim C'_f$.

Finally, from the transitivity of simulation, $C''_f \precsim C_f$.

6   Application: Sieve of Eratosthenes

Presentation. In this section, we informally discuss an example application of the oracle introduced in $\Omega\rho\pi$. This example consists in a distributed implementation of the Sieve of Eratosthenes algorithm to find prime numbers. Despite being quite simple, it shows that partial reversibility of $\Omega\rho\pi$ allows a notion of forward progress, which is not the case in pure causally consistent reversible calculi.

For this example, for the sake of simplicity, we add integers, sets and tuples as primitive values of our calculus, and we assume we have usual primitive functions to manipulate those values.

The Sieve of Eratosthenes is a simple algorithm to find prime numbers under a limit l. This algorithm begins with a set of integers from 2 to l, and iterate over each integers i in the set, removing multiples of i. When a fixpoint is reached, the set contains all prime numbers below l.

In our example, we adapt this algorithm for a distributed setting: instead of iterating over i, we take a second set of integer between 2 and $\lceil\sqrt{l}\rceil$, from which concurrent processes select a local i.

For our example, the oracle contains a tuple of two sets: the first is the set of prime candidates, which we call the *sieve* and the second is the set of possible values for i (which we call *values*). Each thread reads this oracle, selects a possible i and removes its multiples from the sieve. Figure 14 shows an implementation of this distributed variant of the Sieve of Eratosthenes. For the sake of conciseness, we only show a single process, but one could choose an arbitrary number of similar processes. Initially, the oracle contains the two sets $\{2, \dots, l\}$ and $\{2, \dots \lceil\sqrt{l}\rceil\}$. Notice that, once a possible i is tested, it is removed from the set of possible values.

$$k_1 : \mathbf{forecast}(\langle sieve, values \rangle) \triangleright$$
$$\mathbf{let}\ i \in values\ \mathbf{in}$$
$$\mathbf{inform}\langle\langle sieve \setminus \{j | j = k \times i,\ k > 1\}, values \setminus i\rangle\rangle|_{\langle\{2,\dots,l\},\{2,\dots\lceil\sqrt{l}\rceil\}\rangle}$$

Fig. 14. A distributed implementation of the Sieve of Eratosthenes. This implementation has only one process, with tag k_1, but it could contain an arbitrary number of similar processes.

Discussion. The term we show in Fig. 14 is safe, in the sense that when we reach a configuration in which the oracle is $\langle sieve, \emptyset \rangle$, we know that *sieve* contains only prime numbers. However, there is no guarantee that this state is eventually reached. First, as with regular reversible calculi, we can loop in a forward/backward reduction for ever (if the oracle is not updated in between, there is no progress). We ignore this problem since it is common in reversible calculi.

However, the primitives we introduced with the oracle introduce a new problem, which is that forecasts and informs are not atomic: if two receptions are done concurrently, there is a possibility to have a *read–modify–write* inconsistency. The second issue is deeper. To solve it, we would have to introduce standard atomic primitives, such as *compare-and-swap*, to interact with the oracle.

Nonetheless, even with this drawback, this example is interesting. It shows that we have a notion of progress, which can be used to implement standard algorithms for concurrent programming.

7   Conclusion and Future Work

We presented $\Omega\rho\pi$, a reversible calculus in which process can be stored in an *oracle*, which is preserved during backward reductions. This *oracle* is controlled by two primitives which act as two channels `inform` and `forecast`. Until a process is set, any process can be received from the `forecast` primitive (it acts as a random process). Once a process P is sent to the `inform` channel, any message received from the `forecast` channel is that process P (until a new process Q is sent to `inform`) even if the configuration does backward reductions.

Our second main contribution is the definition of a notion of *weak causal consistency*. Weak causal consistency states that for any reachable state, there must exists a similar state reachable using only forward reductions. We think that, in addition to the calculus presented here, this notion of weak causal consistency may be suitable to study other reversible process calculi, for instance those in which backward reductions introduce some garbage which should be ignored.

Future work could improve this paper on two directions.

First, our work can be extended by allowing the process stored in the context to reduce as any other process, following standard HOπ semantics. Thus, terms would have two parts: a reversible part (in the configuration) and a non-reversible side (in the context). Our `forecast` and `inform` primitives would allow processes to cross the boundary between the two sides. On a longer term, we could imagine allowing reversible and non-reversible processes to communicate via standard channels (and removing `forecast` and `inform` channel, which would become useless). Such approach would result in a reversibility confined to some processes, in a globally non-reversible process (or vice-versa).

On the other hand, we could try to relax the simulation constraint in the premisses of rule G.INFORM, which is an important practical limitation. Instead of having a simulation constraint, we could allow a relation $\mathcal{R}$, given as a parameter of the semantics. With sufficient constraints on this relation (typically reflexivity, transitivity and evaluation closure), we could try to prove the weak causal consistency property of $\Omega\rho\pi$ with respect to such $\mathcal{R}$.

Finally, an underlying aspect of this work is to introduce some notion of *progress* in the context of reversible computation. Usually, reversible computation loses this notion by the very nature of the computation: there is an initial configuration, but no final one, as it is always possible to take backward and forward steps; nor any notion of progress, as anything that is done can be undone. Using oracles and contexts as presented in this paper can be used to reintroduce a notion of progress, for instance by having a convergence criterion on the context.

References

1. Berry, G., Boudol, G.: The chemical abstract machine. In: Proceedings of the 17th ACM SIGPLAN-SIGACT Symposium on Principles of Programming Languages, POPL 1990, pp. 81–94 (1989). https://doi.org/10.1145/96709.96717
2. Berry, G., Boudol, G.: The chemical abstract machine. Theoret. Comput. Sci. **96**(1), 217–248 (1992). https://doi.org/10.1016/0304-3975(92)90185-I
3. Caires, L., Ferreira, C., Vieira, H.: A process calculus analysis of compensations. In: Kaklamanis, C., Nielson, F. (eds.) TGC 2008. LNCS, vol. 5474, pp. 87–103. Springer, Heidelberg (2009). https://doi.org/10.1007/978-3-642-00945-7_6
4. Giachino, E., Lanese, I., Mezzina, C.A.: Causal-consistent reversible debugging. In: Gnesi, S., Rensink, A. (eds.) FASE 2014. LNCS, vol. 8411, pp. 370–384. Springer, Heidelberg (2014). https://doi.org/10.1007/978-3-642-54804-8_26
5. Kuhn, S., Aman, B., Ciobanu, G., Philippou, A., Psara, K., Ulidowski, I.: Reversibility in chemical reactions. In: Ulidowski, I., Lanese, I., Schultz, U.P., Ferreira, C. (eds.) RC 2020. LNCS, vol. 12070, pp. 151–176. Springer, Cham (2020). https://doi.org/10.1007/978-3-030-47361-7_7
6. Kuhn, S., Ulidowski, I.: A Calculus for Local Reversibility (2016). https://core.ac.uk/display/191241654
7. Kuhn, S., Ulidowski, I.: Local reversibility in a Calculus of Covalent Bonding (2017). https://core.ac.uk/display/328692337?source=3. Publisher: 'Elsevier BV'
8. Lanese, I., Lienhardt, M., Mezzina, C.A., Schmitt, A., Stefani, J.-B.: Concurrent flexible reversibility. In: Felleisen, M., Gardner, P. (eds.) ESOP 2013. LNCS, vol. 7792, pp. 370–390. Springer, Heidelberg (2013). https://doi.org/10.1007/978-3-642-37036-6_21
9. Lanese, I., Mezzina, C.A., Schmitt, A., Stefani, J.-B.: Controlling reversibility in higher-order Pi. In: Katoen, J.-P., König, B. (eds.) CONCUR 2011. LNCS, vol. 6901, pp. 297–311. Springer, Heidelberg (2011). https://doi.org/10.1007/978-3-642-23217-6_20
10. Lanese, I., Mezzina, C.A., Stefani, J.-B.: Reversing higher-order Pi. In: Gastin, P., Laroussinie, F. (eds.) CONCUR 2010. LNCS, vol. 6269, pp. 478–493. Springer, Heidelberg (2010). https://doi.org/10.1007/978-3-642-15375-4_33
11. Mezzina, C.A.: Reversing execution in Higher-Order Pi. Theses, Université de Grenoble, February 2012. https://tel.archives-ouvertes.fr/tel-00683964
12. Mezzina, C.A.: On reversibility and broadcast. In: Kari, J., Ulidowski, I. (eds.) RC 2018. LNCS, vol. 11106, pp. 67–83. Springer, Cham (2018). https://doi.org/10.1007/978-3-319-99498-7_5

13. Milner, R. (ed.): A Calculus of Communicating Systems. LNCS, vol. 92. Springer, Heidelberg (1980). https://doi.org/10.1007/3-540-10235-3
14. Perumalla, K.S., Park, A.J.: Reverse computation for rollback-based fault tolerance in large parallel systems. Clust. Comput. **17**(2), 303–313 (2013). https://doi.org/10.1007/s10586-013-0277-4
15. Philippou, A., Psara, K.: Reversible computation in petri nets. In: Kari, J., Ulidowski, I. (eds.) RC 2018. LNCS, vol. 11106, pp. 84–101. Springer, Cham (2018). https://doi.org/10.1007/978-3-319-99498-7_6
16. Phillips, I., Ulidowski, I., Yuen, S.: A reversible process calculus and the modelling of the ERK signalling pathway. In: Glück, R., Yokoyama, T. (eds.) RC 2012. LNCS, vol. 7581, pp. 218–232. Springer, Heidelberg (2013). https://doi.org/10.1007/978-3-642-36315-3_18
17. Sangiorgi, D.: Introduction to Bisimulation and Coinduction. University Press, Cambridge (2011). https://doi.org/10.1017/CBO9780511777110
18. Vassor, M., Stefani, J.-B.: Checkpoint/rollback vs causally-consistent reversibility. In: Kari, J., Ulidowski, I. (eds.) RC 2018. LNCS, vol. 11106, pp. 286–303. Springer, Cham (2018). https://doi.org/10.1007/978-3-319-99498-7_20

Theory and Foundations

A Tangled Web of 12 Lens Laws

Keisuke Nakano$^{(\boxtimes)}$ ⓘ

Research Institute of Electrical Communication, Tohoku University, Sendai, Japan
k.nakano@acm.org

Abstract. Bidirectional transformation has played important roles in broad areas, database management, programming language, and model-driven development after Foster et al. revisited view updating problems introduced by Bancilhon and Spyratos. They introduced the concept of (asymmetric) *lens* as a pair of a forward *get* and a backward *put* functions to synchronize a source data and its view consistently. For the *get* and *put* functions to be consistent, they should satisfy several *lens laws* such as the (STRONGGETPUT), (GETPUT), (PUTGET) and (PUTPUT) laws. By combining some of these lens laws, we can represent how consistent a lens satisfying the laws is. Fischer et al. has introduced nine meaningful weaker lens laws to give a "clear picture" of the laws where they show relations among lens laws, for example, that one law implies another and combination of two laws is equivalent to combination of the other three laws. This paper gives more precise relationship among 12 lens laws that have been presented in literature. The relationship makes an intertwined implication diagram like a tangled web. The results can be used for easily verifying the desirable lens laws.

Keywords: Bidirectional transformation · Asymmetric lens laws

1 Introduction

Bidirectional transformation has been called a *lens* after Foster et al. [7] revisited a classic view updating problem introduced by Bancilhon and Spyratos [1]. It has played an important role for maintaining consistency in many fields of applications, database management systems [2,6,16], algebraic data structure interface on programming [13,17], and model-driven software development [4,18,19].

A lens is a pair of a forward function *get* and a backward function *put* which are used for maintaining consistency between two related data, a *source* and a *view*. Let S and V be sets of sources and views. The function $get : S \to V$ generates a view from a given source data typically by extracting a part of the source and arranging it in an appropriate way; the function $put : S \times V \to S$ returns a source for an updated view with assist of the original source because views have less information than the corresponding sources in general.

To define a meaningful bidirectional transformation, two functions, *get* and *put*, that form a lens should relate to each other. The relationship is characterized

S. Yamashita and T. Yokoyama (Eds.): RC 2021, LNCS 12805, pp. 185–203, 2021.
https://doi.org/10.1007/978-3-030-79837-6_11

$$\forall s, s' \in S, \quad put(s, get(s')) = s' \qquad \text{(StrongGetPut)}$$
$$\forall s \in S, \quad put(s, get(s)) = s \qquad \text{(GetPut)}$$
$$\forall s \in S, \forall v \in V, \quad get(put(s, v)) = v \qquad \text{(PutGet)}$$
$$\forall s \in S, \forall v, v' \in V, \quad put(put(s, v), v') = put(s, v') \qquad \text{(PutPut)}$$

Fig. 1. Core lens laws

by equations for these functions called *lens laws*. Figure 1 shows four typical lens laws introduced in [7].

The (StrongGetPut) law requires that a source can always be determined by *put* only with an updated view independently of the original source. Under this law, views are as informative as the corresponding sources. The (GetPut) law is a weaker version of the (StrongGetPut) law. This law requires that *put* returns the same source as original whenever the view has not been updated. The (PutGet) law is about consistency of view updating. This law requires that any updated source by *put* with an updated view yields the same view by *get*. The (PutPut) law is a condition imposed only on the *put* function. This law requires that a source updated twice (or possibly more) by *put* with different views consecutively is the same as one obtained by *put* with the last view.

These core lens laws characterize three practical properties on lenses for meaningful bidirectional transformation: *bijective*, *well-behaved*, and *very-well-behaved*. A bijective lens must satisfy the (StrongGetPut) and (PutGet) laws. A well-behaved lens must satisfy the (GetPut) and (PutGet) laws. A very-well-behaved lens must satisfy the (GetPut), (PutGet) and (PutPut) laws. Programmers defining lenses for bidirectional transformation need to select an appropriate property for lenses according to their purpose and application and check if a defined lens satisfies the corresponding lens laws.

One of the solutions is to use domain-specific languages for bidirectional transformation. Many programming languages have been developed to make it easy to define meaningful lenses under specific lens laws [7,14]. They basically give a solution by either permitting to use limited primitives and their combinations or imposing a strong syntactic restriction to write bidirectional programs. If general-purpose languages are used for bidirectional programming, the conformance to the desirable lens laws should be checked for each program. The problem of checking the conformance is, however, in general undecidable because it involves a kind of functional equalities. This is why many bidirectional programming languages have been proposed, where specific lens laws always hold due to a careful design of the languages.

Fischer et al. [5] have shown that some combinations of weaker lens laws can imply some of the core lens laws. They give a "clear picture" of lens laws by investigating the relationships over the laws shown in Fig. 1 and Fig. 2 minus (PutGetPut), (WeakPutGet), and (Undoability). The resulting relationships show which combination of weaker laws can imply a core law.

$$\forall s \in S, \forall v \in V, \quad put(s, get(put(s, v))) = put(s, v) \quad \text{(WEAKPUTGET)}$$

$$\forall s \in S, \forall v \in V, \quad put(put(s, v), get(put(s, v))) = put(s, v) \quad \text{(PUTGETPUT)}$$

$$\forall s \in S, \forall v \subset V, \quad put(put(s, v), get(s)) = s \quad \text{(UNDOABILITY)}$$

$$\forall s \in S, \forall v \in V, \quad put(put(s, v), v) = put(s, v) \quad \text{(PUTTWICE)}$$

$$\forall s \in S, \exists v \in V, \quad put(s, v) = s \quad \text{(SOURCESTABILITY)}$$

$$\forall s \in S, \exists s' \in S, \exists v \in V, \quad put(s', v) = s \quad \text{(PUTSURJECTIVITY)}$$

$$\forall s, s' \in S, \forall v, v' \in V, \quad put(s, v) = put(s', v') \Rightarrow v = v' \quad \text{(VIEWDETERMINATION)}$$

$$\forall s \in S, \forall v, v' \in V, \quad put(s, v) = put(s, v') \Rightarrow v = v' \quad \text{(PUTINJECTIVITY)}$$

Fig. 2. Other lens laws

Implications among lens laws often help to find their unexpected interaction and give a clear insight to bidirectional transformation. For example, every bijective lens, which satisfies the (STRONGGETPUT) and (PUTGET) laws, is found to be very-well-behaved (that is, to satisfy the (GETPUT), (PUTGET) and (PUTPUT) laws) from the facts that the (PUTGET) law implies (PUTINJECTIVITY) and the conjunction of the (STRONGGETPUT) and (PUTINJECTIVITY) laws implies (PUT-PUT). Fischer et al. introduced several implications to show that a well-behaved lens can be uniquely obtained only from a *put* function as long as *put* satisfies the (PUTSURJECTIVITY), (PUTTWICE) and (PUTINJECTIVITY) laws.

A major goal of this paper is to improve Fischer et al.'s clear picture of lens laws. Specifically, we add three more lens laws, (PUTGETPUT), (WEAKPUTGET) and (UNDOABILITY), which have been introduced for a practical use [3,10–12] and find all Horn-clause-like implications among the 12 lens laws to identify an essence of bidirectional transformation. The contribution of this paper is summarized as follows:

- Relationship among 12 lens laws including the (PUTGETPUT), (WEAKPUTGET) and (UNDOABILITY) laws is investigated and the laws are shown to be classified based on the relation (Sect. 2 and Sect. 3).
- Horn-clause-like formulas among 12 lens laws are shown as many as possible (Sect. 4). They are summarized by a complicated web structure shown in Fig. 3 and Fig. 4.

Related Work. As mentioned earlier, the present work is an improvement of a clear picture of lenses introduced by Fischer et al. [5]. They give only a few implications among lens laws except (WEAKPUTGET) and (UNDOABILITY). This paper covers much more implications some of which are not trivial. Hidaka et al. [11] give a classification to bidirectional transformation approaches including properties like lens laws required for well-behavedness. They just present the properties independently of each other and do not mention anything about their relationship. Stevens [20] gives implications among a few properties of symmetric lenses, in which sources and views are evenly treated and *get* takes two arguments like *put*. Some of the implications she presents hold also for asymmetric ones as shown in this paper. It would be interesting to consider a complete picture similar to ours for symmetric lens laws.

This paper extends the author's short paper [15] in which some implications among 10 lens laws are shown with no completeness. The present paper adds two more laws, (PUTGETPUT) and (WEAKPUTGET), to discuss possible implications among the 12 lens laws and proves completeness for each family of laws.

2   Summary of Lens Laws

We shall give a brief summary to all lens laws in Fig. 2 with tiny examples that may be used for further discussions in this paper.

In the rest of this paper, S and V denote sets of sources and views, respectively. For demonstrating examples of lenses, we will use sets $\mathbb{Z}$, $\mathbb{N}$ and $\mathbb{Q}$ of integers, non-negative integers and rationals, respectively. For $x \in \mathbb{Q}$, $\lfloor x \rfloor$ denotes the largest integer less than or equal to x. We write $x \sqcup y$ to indicate the greatest one among $x, y \in \mathbb{Q}$ and $x \bmod d$ for the remainder after division of $x \in \mathbb{Z}$ by $d \in \mathbb{N} \setminus \{0\}$ where $x \bmod d = x - d \lfloor x/d \rfloor$. Most of the examples presented here may look elaborate so as not to satisfy the other lens laws as far as possible.

2.1   Laws to Relate the *get* and *put* Functions

The six lens laws, (STRONGGETPUT), (GETPUT), (PUTGET), (WEAKPUTGET), (PUTGETPUT), and (UNDOABILITY), involve both the *get* and *put* functions, while the others involve only the *put* function. We start with summarizing the six laws.

The (STRONGGETPUT) law indicates that the source is determined only by the view even though the view has less information than the source in general. If the view is given by *get* with a source, then the source is obtained by *put* independently of the original source. Under this law, the *get* function is left-invertible with the *put* function. For example where $S = V = \mathbb{Z}$, a pair of the *get* and *put* functions defined by $get(s) = 2s$ and $put(s, v) = \lfloor v/2 \rfloor$ satisfies the (STRONGGETPUT) law.

The (GETPUT) law is literally a weakened version of the (STRONGGETPUT) law. Under this law, the source is not changed if the view obtained from the original source is not updated. For example where $S = V = \mathbb{Z}$, a pair of the *get* and *put* functions defined by $get(s) = 2s$ and $put(s, v) = v - s$ satisfies the (GETPUT) law but not the (STRONGGETPUT) law.

The (PUTGET) law requires that all the information in the updated view is reflected to the source so that the same view can be obtained from it. For example where $S = V = \mathbb{Z}$, a pair of the *get* and *put* functions defined by $get(s) = \lfloor s/2 \rfloor$ and $put(s, v) = 2v$ satisfies the (PUTGET) law. A lens is said to be *bijective* if it satisfies the (STRONGGETPUT) and (PUTGET) laws. A lens is said to be *well-behaved* if it satisfies the (GETPUT) and (PUTGET) laws. Note that we only consider the case where all *get* and *put* functions are total. Although the (PUTGET) law has been relaxed for possibly-partial *put* functions in the literature [3,5,7,9], such a case is left for future work.

The (WEAKPUTGET) law is literally a weakened version of the (PUTGET) law. While the (PUTGET) law requires the equality between the view corresponding to the source obtained by an updated view (that is, $get(put(s, v))$) and the updated view (that is, v), the (WEAKPUTGET) law requires the same equality up to the further put operation with the original source. This law is practically important because it allows tentative view updates that may be of an inappropriate form. For example where $S = \mathbb{Z}$ and $V = \mathbb{Z} \times \mathbb{Z}$, a pair of the get and put functions defined by $get(s) = \langle s, s \rangle$ and $put(s, \langle v_1, v_2 \rangle) = v_1$ satisfies the (WEAKPUTGET) law but not the (PUTGET) law. Updating a view into $\langle v_1, v_2 \rangle$ with $v_1 \neq v_2$ breaks the (PUTGET) law because $get(put(s, \langle v_1, v_2 \rangle)) = \langle v_1, v_1 \rangle \neq \langle v_1, v_2 \rangle$.

The (PUTGETPUT) law requires that the (GETPUT) law holds under the condition that the source is in the image of the put function. By replacing s with $put(s, v)$ in the (GETPUT) law, we have the (PUTGETPUT) law. This law has been first introduced by Hu et al. [12] and mentioned in [8] as a law that is required in practical settings. For example where $S = \mathbb{Z} \times \mathbb{Z}$ and $V = \mathbb{Z}$, a pair of get and put functions defined by $get(\langle s_1, s_2 \rangle) = |s_1 - s_2|$ and $put(\langle s_1, s_2 \rangle, v) = (s_2 + |v|, s_2)$ satisfies the (PUTGETPUT) law but not the (GETPUT) law. The source $s = \langle 0, 1 \rangle$ breaks even the (GETPUT) law because $put(s, get(s)) = \langle 1, 2 \rangle \neq s$. This lens breaks the (WEAKPUTGET) law as well.

The (UNDOABILITY) law implies that any source can be recovered with the view obtained from the source itself no matter how source is updated by a different view. For example where $S = V = \mathbb{Z}$, a pair of the get and put functions defined by $get(s) = \lfloor s/2 \rfloor$ and $put(s, v) = 2v - s + 1 + 2 \lfloor s/2 \rfloor$ satisfies the (UNDOABILITY) law. It has been investigated in a few papers [3,9,11][1]. The (UNDOABILITY) law is weaker than the (STRONGGETPUT) law and stronger than the (WEAKPUTGET) law as shown later.

2.2   Laws to Confine the put Function

The last law in Fig. 1 and the last five lens laws in Fig. 2 impose constraints only on the put function. The (PUTPUT) law requires that the source obtained by applying the put functions repeatedly with many views is that obtained by applying put once with the last view. It plays an important role for $state$-$based$ lenses [7,11], that is, the history of updates can always be ignored. For example where $S = V = \mathbb{Z}$, $put(s, v) = 5 \lfloor s/5 \rfloor + (v \bmod 5)$ satisfies the (PUTPUT) law. A lens is said to be $very$-$well$-$behaved$ if it satisfies the (GETPUT), (PUTGET), and (PUTPUT) laws.

The (PUTTWICE) law imposes "idempotency" of the put function applied with the fixed view. This law is obviously a weakened version of the (PUTPUT) law. For example where $S = V = \mathbb{Z}$, $put(s, v) = s \sqcup v$ satisfies the (PUTTWICE) law but violates the (PUTPUT) law).

The (SOURCESTABILITY) law requires every source to be stable for a certain view. Defining the get function that returns the corresponding view for a given

---

[1] In [3], a lens is said to be $undoable$ when not only (UNDOABILITY) but also (PUTGET) hold in our terminology.

source, the pair conforms the (GETPUT) law. For example where $S = V = \mathbb{Z}$, $put(s, v) = sv^2$ satisfies the (SOURCESTABILITY) law for which there are infinitely many choices of the *get* function to have the (GETPUT) law.

The (PUTSURJECTIVITY) law requires literally surjectivity of the *put* function. This law is a weakened version of the (SOURCESTABILITY) law. For example where $S = V = \mathbb{Z}$, $put(s, v) = 2s - 3v$ satisfies the (PUTSURJECTIVITY) law but not the (SOURCESTABILITY) law.

The (VIEWDETERMINATION) law indicates that there is no distinct pair of views that generates the same source by the *put* function. Combining with the (SOURCESTABILITY) law, it guarantees existence and uniqueness of the *get* function to form a well-behaved lens [5]. For example where $S = V = \mathbb{Z}$, $put(s, v) = 2^{|s|}(2v - 1)$ satisfies the (VIEWDETERMINATION) law.

The (PUTINJECTIVITY) law requires literally injectivity of the *put* function for each source fixed. This law guarantees that there is no distinct pair of views that leads the same source for the fixed original source. This law is a weakened version of the (VIEWDETERMINATION) law. The three law combination of (PUTTWICE), (PUTSURJECTIVITY) and (PUTINJECTIVITY) is equivalent to the two law combination of (SOURCESTABILITY) and (VIEWDETERMINATION) [5]. For example where $S = V = \mathbb{Z}$, $put(s, v) = s + v$ satisfies the (PUTINJECTIVITY) law but violates the (VIEWDETERMINATION) law.

3   Three Families of Lens Laws

Lens laws are classified by implication relation among them. As we have seen in the previous section, there are obvious implications between two lens laws, e.g., (STRONGGETPUT) implies (GETPUT), (PUTGET) implies (WEAKPUTGET), and (PUTPUT) implies (PUTTWICE). Investigating all the implications among the 12 lens laws in Fig. 1 and Fig. 2, we will find that the lens laws can be classified into three families, which we call GetPut, PutGet, and PutPut. Every lens law belongs exactly to one family except for the (WEAKPUTGET) law which belongs to the GetPut and PutGet families as we will show later. In this section, all implications between two lens laws are presented with their proofs to classify the laws. It is also shown that there is no other implication between two lens laws by giving counterexamples. In addition, possible implications that involve more than two laws belonging the same family are discussed. In the rest of the paper, we consider Horn-clause-like implications of the form $L_1 \wedge \cdots \wedge L_n \Rightarrow L$ where L_i, L are lens laws. We say that an implication $L_1 \wedge \cdots \wedge L_n \Rightarrow L$ is *derivable* from a set $\mathcal{I}$ of implications if L is obtained by taking an implication closure using $\mathcal{I}$ from $\{L_1, \ldots, L_n\}$. In addition, we assume that the set $\{L_1, \ldots, L_n\}$ is *pairwise incomparable*, that is, none of them can be derived from the others, because the implication is otherwise reduced to that with a smaller n.

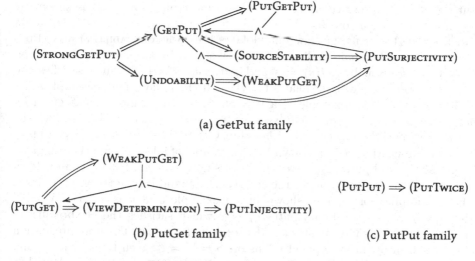

(a) GetPut family

(b) PutGet family   (c) PutPut family

Fig. 3. Three families of lens laws

3.1 GetPut Family

The GetPut family consists of seven lens laws all of which are entailment of the (STRONGGETPUT) law[2]. This family makes an implication web as shown in Fig. 3(a) where a double arrow $\Longrightarrow$ stands for an implication between the two lens laws and a single arrow $\longrightarrow$ from the $\wedge$ symbol stands for an implication from the conjunction of the two lens laws connected with $\wedge$ to the lens law pointed by the arrow head. The (WEAKPUTGET) belongs, conversely to what one would expect from its name, to both the GetPut family and the PutGet family as we will show later.

Every implication in the figure is shown later. Before that, lemmas about non-implications among lens laws are shown, which will be used to disprove the converse of implications. Each of them can be proved by a counterexample.

Lemma 1. The following non-implications hold.

(1-1) (GETPUT) $\not\Longrightarrow$ (WEAKPUTGET)
(1-2) (UNDOABILITY) $\not\Longrightarrow$ (SOURCESTABILITY) $\vee$ (PUTGETPUT)
(1-3) (SOURCESTABILITY) $\not\Longrightarrow$ (PUTGETPUT)
(1-4) (PUTGETPUT) $\wedge$ (WEAKPUTGET) $\not\Longrightarrow$ (PUTSURJECTIVITY)
(1-5)
(PUTSURJECTIVITY) $\wedge$ (WEAKPUTGET) $\not\Longrightarrow$ (PUTGETPUT) $\vee$ (SOURCESTABILITY)
(1-6) (UNDOABILITY) $\wedge$ (GETPUT) $\not\Longrightarrow$ (STRONGGETPUT)
(1-7) (WEAKPUTGET) $\wedge$ (GETPUT) $\not\Longrightarrow$ (UNDOABILITY)

Proof. The non-implication (1-1) is shown by an example of a lens on $S = V = \mathbb{Z}$ given by $get(s) = 2s$ and $put(s, v) = v - s$, which satisfies the (GETPUT) law

---

[2] We prefer a shorter name though it might be called the StrongGetPut family.

but violates the (WEAKPUTGET) law. The non-implication (1-2) is shown by an example of a lens on $S = V = \mathbb{Z}$ given by $get(s) = s$ and $put(s,v) = -s$ satisfies the (UNDOABILITY) law but violates the (SOURCESTABILITY) and (PUT-GETPUT) laws. The non-implication (1-3) is shown by an example of a lens on $S = V = \mathbb{Z}$ given by $get(s) = s$ and $put(s,v) = s + v$, which satisfies the (SOURCESTABILITY) law but violates the (PUTGETPUT) law. The non-implication (1-4) is shown by an example of a lens on $S = \mathbb{Z} \times \mathbb{Z}$ and $V = \mathbb{Z}$ given by $get(\langle s_1, s_2 \rangle) = |s_1 - s_2|$ and $put(\langle s_1, s_2 \rangle, v) = \langle s_2 + |v|, s_2 \rangle$, which satisfies the (PUTGETPUT) and (WEAKPUTGET) laws but violates the (PUTSURJECTIVITY) law. The non-implication (1-5) is shown by an example of a lens on $S = V = \mathbb{Z}$ given by $get(s) = s$ and $put(s,v) = -s$, which satisfies the (WEAKPUTGET) and (PUT-SURJECTIVITY) laws but violates the (PUTGETPUT) and (SOURCESTABILITY) laws. The non-implication (1-6) is shown by an example of a lens on $S = V = \mathbb{Z}$ given by $get(s) = s + 1$ and $put(s,v) = s$ which satisfies the (UNDOABILITY) and (GETPUT) laws but violates the (STRONGGETPUT) law. The non-implication (1-7) is shown by an example of a lens on $S = V = \mathbb{Z}$ given by $get(s) = s$ and $put(s,v) = s \sqcup v$ which satisfies the (WEAKPUTGET) and (GETPUT) laws but violates the (UNDOABILITY) law. $\qquad\square$

Note that two types of entailment of non-implications hold in general: $P \nRightarrow Q$ and $P \Rightarrow R$ entail $R \nRightarrow Q$; $P \nRightarrow Q$ and $R \Rightarrow Q$ entail $P \nRightarrow R$. We will often use them to prove non-implications in the rest of the paper.

Theorem 2. The GetPut family has the following proper implications.

(2-1) (STRONGGETPUT) $\rightleftharpoons\!\!\!\!/$ (GETPUT) $\rightleftharpoons\!\!\!\!/$ (SOURCESTABILITY) $\rightleftharpoons\!\!\!\!/$ (PUTSURJECTIVITY)

(2-2) (STRONGGETPUT) $\rightleftharpoons\!\!\!\!/$ (UNDOABILITY) $\rightleftharpoons\!\!\!\!/$ (PUTSURJECTIVITY)

(2-3) (GETPUT) $\rightleftharpoons\!\!\!\!/$ (PUTGETPUT)

(2-4) (UNDOABILITY) $\rightleftharpoons\!\!\!\!/$ (WEAKPUTGET)

(2-5) (PUTGETPUT) $\wedge$ (PUTSURJECTIVITY) $\rightleftharpoons$ (GETPUT)

(2-6) (SOURCESTABILITY) $\wedge$ (WEAKPUTGET) $\rightleftharpoons\!\!\!\!/$ (GETPUT)

Furthermore, no other implications hold among the GetPut family except for the ones derivable from the implications above.

Proof. First all implications are illustrated without disproving their converse except (2-5).

(2-1) The implications, (STRONGGETPUT) $\Rightarrow$ (GETPUT) and (SOURCESTABILITY) $\Rightarrow$ (PUTSURJECTIVITY) are immediate. The implication (GETPUT) $\Rightarrow$ (SOURCESTABILITY) is shown by taking $get(s)$ as v for (SOURCES-TABILITY).

(2-2) The implication (STRONGGETPUT) $\Rightarrow$ (UNDOABILITY) is immediate. The implication (UNDOABILITY) $\Rightarrow$ (PUTSURJECTIVITY) is obvious by taking $s' = put(s, get(s))$ and $v = get(s)$.

(2-3) The implication (GETPUT) $\Rightarrow$ (PUTGETPUT) is immediate.

(2-4) The implication (UNDOABILITY) $\Rightarrow$ (WEAKPUTGET) is shown by

$$put(s, get(put(s, v)))$$
$$= put(put(put(s, v), get(s)), get(put(s, v))) \qquad \text{by (UNDOABILITY)}$$
$$= put(s, v) \qquad\qquad\qquad\qquad\qquad\qquad \text{by (UNDOABILITY)}.$$

(2-5) The implication (PUTGETPUT) $\wedge$ (PUTSURJECTIVITY) $\Rightarrow$ (GETPUT) is shown by

$$put(s, get(s))$$
$$= put(put(s', v'), get(put(s', v')))$$
$$\qquad\qquad \text{by (PUTSURJECTIVITY) taking } s' \text{ and } v' \text{ such that } put(s', v') = s$$
$$= put(s', v') \quad \text{by (PUTGETPUT)}$$
$$= s \qquad\qquad \text{by assumption on taking } s' \text{ and } v'.$$

The converse is shown by (2-1) and (2-3).

(2-6) The implication (SOURCESTABILITY) $\wedge$ (WEAKPUTGET) $\Rightarrow$ (GETPUT) is shown by

$$put(s, get(s))$$
$$= put(s, get(put(s, v)))$$
$$\qquad\qquad \text{by (SOURCESTABILITY) taking } v \text{ such that } put(s, v) = s$$
$$= put(s, v) \quad \text{by (WEAKPUTGET)}$$
$$= s \qquad\qquad \text{by assumption on taking } v.$$

The skipped converse implications will be disproved together with the latter part of the present statement.

Now we show that no other implications of the form $L_1 \wedge \cdots \wedge L_n \Rightarrow L$ hold with $L_i, L \in \{$(STRONGGETPUT), (GETPUT), (UNDOABILITY), (PUTGETPUT), (WEAKPUTGET), (SOURCESTABILITY), (PUTSURJECTIVITY)$\}$ except for the ones derived from the implications above. Since the set $\{L_1, \ldots, L_n\}$ is pairwise incomparable, the cases of $n \leq 3$ suffice to show the statement.

In the case of $n = 1$, every implication $L_1 \Rightarrow L$ that is unknown from the implications above can be disproved as follows. From (1-1), the cases of (L_1, L) in $\{$(GETPUT), (PUTGETPUT), (SOURCESTABILITY), (PUTSURJECTIVITY)$\} \times \{$(STRONGGETPUT), (UNDOABILITY), (WEAKPUTGET)$\}$ are disproved because of (2-1), (2-3), and (2-4). From (1-2), the cases of (L_1, L) in $\{$(UNDOABILITY), (WEAKPUTGET), (PUTSURJECTIVITY)$\} \times \{$(STRONGGETPUT), (GETPUT), (SOURCESTABILITY), (PUTGETPUT)$\}$ are disproved because of (2-1), (2-2), (2-3), and (2-4). From (1-3), the cases of (L_1, L) in $\{$(SOURCESTABILITY)$\} \times \{$(GETPUT), (PUTGETPUT)$\}$ are disproved because of (2-3). From (1-4), the cases of (L_1, L) in $\{$(WEAKPUTGET), (PUTGETPUT)$\} \times \{$(GETPUT),

(SOURCESTABILITY), (PUTSURJECTIVITY), (UNDOABILITY)} because of (2-1) and (2-2). With a careful observation, we find that all cases are exhausted except the derivable implications.

In the case of $n = 2$, we show that there is no combination (L_1, L_2, L) such that $L_1 \wedge L_2 \Rightarrow L$ holds except for the derivable implications. From our assumption, L_1 and L_2 are incomparable with respect to implication. Thus none of them can be (STRONGGETPUT). In addition, L also cannot be (STRONGGETPUT) because of (1-6) and the other implications. When one of L_1, L_2 is (GETPUT), another should be either (UNDOABILITY) and (WEAKPUTGET), and then all of the cases are either derivable or disproved by (1-7). When one of L_1, L_2 is (UNDOABILITY), another should be (PUTGETPUT) and (SOURCESTABILITY). All cases except for $L = $ (STRONGGETPUT) are derivable because of the known implications. In the remaining cases, we do not need to consider $L = $ (UNDOABILITY) because of (1-7). When one of L_1, L_2 is (PUTGETPUT), another should be (SOURCESTABILITY), (WEAKPUTGET) and (PUTSURJECTIVITY). Those cases with $L \neq $ (STRONGGETPUT), (UNDOABILITY) are either derivable or disproved by (1-4). All of the other cases for $n = 2$ are either derivable or disproved by (1-5).

In the case of $n = 3$, due to the assumption, one of (L_1, L_2, L_3) cannot be (STRONGGETPUT) and (GETPUT). In addition, two of them cannot be selected from (PUTGETPUT), (SOURCESTABILITY), and (PUTSURJECTIVITY) because it is equivalent to the single law (GETPUT). Hence there are no cases needed to be considered.   □

As an immediate corollary of THEOREM 2, the (GETPUT) law is found to have equivalent representations:

$$(\text{GETPUT}) \underset{\Longleftarrow}{\overset{\Longrightarrow}{}} (\text{PUTGETPUT}) \wedge (\text{PUTSURJECTIVITY})$$

$$\underset{\Longleftarrow}{\overset{\Longrightarrow}{}} (\text{PUTGETPUT}) \wedge (\text{SOURCESTABILITY})$$

3.2   PutGet Family

The PutGet family consists of four lens laws all of which are entailment of the (PUTGET) law. This family makes a sequential structure as shown in Fig. 3(b). Every implication in the figure will be later shown in THEOREM 4. First some non-implications are shown as done for the GetPut family.

Lemma 3. The following non-implications hold.

(3-1) (WEAKPUTGET) $\not\Rightarrow$ (PUTINJECTIVITY)
(3-2) (VIEWDETERMINATION) $\not\Rightarrow$ (WEAKPUTGET)

Proof. The non-implication of (3-1) is shown by a lens on $S = V = \mathbb{Z}$ given by $get(s) = s$ and $put(s, v) = s$ which satisfies the (WEAKPUTGET) law but violates the (PUTINJECTIVITY) law. The non-implication of (3-2) is shown by a lens on $S = V = \mathbb{Z}$ given by $get(s) = s + 1$ and $put(s, v) = v$ which satisfies the (VIEWDETERMINATION) law but violates the (WEAKPUTGET) law.   □

The following theorem covers all implications described in Fig. 3(b). Note that the third implication of the theorem is not unidirectional unlike the others.

Theorem 4. The PutGet family has three inclusions.

(4-1) (PUTGET) $\overset{\Rightarrow}{\not\Leftarrow}$ (VIEWDETERMINATION) $\overset{\Rightarrow}{\not\Leftarrow}$ (PUTINJECTIVITY)

(4-2) (PUTGET) $\overset{\Rightarrow}{\not\Leftarrow}$ (WEAKPUTGET)

(4-3) (WEAKPUTGET) $\wedge$ (PUTINJECTIVITY) $\overset{\Rightarrow}{\Leftarrow}$ (PUTGET)

Furthermore, no other implications hold among the PutGet family except ones derivable from the implications above.

Proof. The implications of (4-1) and (4-2) are easy and their converses are disproved later. The bidirectional implication of (4-3) is shown as follows. Suppose that the (PUTINJECTIVITY) and (WEAKPUTGET) laws hold. Then we have $put(s, get(put(s, v))) = put(s, v)$ because of the (WEAKPUTGET) law. This equation implies $get(put(s, v)) = v$ by the (PUTINJECTIVITY) law, hence we have the (PUTGET) law. The converse is immediate from (4-2) and (4-1).

Next, in a way similar to the proof of THEOREM 2, we show that there is no other implication of the form $L_1 \wedge \cdots \wedge L_n \Rightarrow L$ with $L_i, L \in \{(\text{PUTGET}), (\text{WEAKPUTGET}), (\text{VIEWDETERMINATION}), (\text{PUTINJECTIVITY})\}$ except for derivable ones. Since the set $\{L_1, \ldots, L_n\}$ is pairwise incomparable, the cases of $n = 1$ and $n = 2$ suffice to show the statement. In the case of $n = 1$, uncertain combinations of (L_1, L) are either $((\text{WEAKPUTGET}), l)$ or $(l, (\text{WEAKPUTGET}))$ with $l \in \{(\text{VIEWDETERMINATION}), (\text{PUTINJECTIVITY})\}$. None of them satisfy $L_1 \Rightarrow L)$ from (3-1) and (3-2) together with the implications shown above. In the case of $n = 2$, from the assumption, it suffices to consider the statement for $L_1 = (\text{WEAKPUTGET})$ and $L_2 \in \{(\text{VIEWDETERMINATION}), (\text{SOURCESTABILITY})\}$. From the implications above, $L_1 \wedge L_2 \Rightarrow (\text{PUTGET})$ holds, and thus $L_1 \wedge L_2 \Rightarrow L$ is derivable for any L in the PutGet family. Therefore, there are no cases that is needed to be considered when $n = 2$. $\qquad\square$

As an immediate corollary of THEOREM 4, the (PUTGET) law is found to have have equivalent representations:

$$(\text{PUTGET}) \overset{\Rightarrow}{\Leftarrow} (\text{WEAKPUTGET}) \wedge (\text{PUTINJECTIVITY})$$

$$\overset{\Rightarrow}{\Leftarrow} (\text{WEAKPUTGET}) \wedge (\text{VIEWDETERMINATION})$$

3.3   PutPut Family

The PutPut family consists of two lens laws which form a single entailment of the (PUTPUT) law as shown in Fig. 3(c). The implication in this family is shown in the following theorem.

Theorem 5. The PutPut family has the implication (PUTPUT) $\overset{\Rightarrow}{\not\Leftarrow}$ (PUTTWICE).

Proof. The implication (PUTPUT) $\Rightarrow$ (PUTTWICE) is immediate. The converse is shown to be false by a lens on $S = V = \mathbb{Z}$ given by $put(s, v) = s \sqcup v$, which satisfies the (PUTTWICE) law but violates the (PUTPUT) law. $\qquad\square$

3.4   Separation of Three Families

We have seen all possible implications in each family so far. Now we show that the three families are being separated in the sense that there is no implication of the form $L_1 \wedge \cdots \wedge L_n \Rightarrow L$ for lens laws $L_1, \ldots, L_n$ in a family and a law L not belonging to the family.

Theorem 6. No implication of the form $L_1 \wedge \cdots \wedge L_n \Rightarrow L$ holds if $L_1, \ldots, L_n$ belong to a single family that L does not belong to.

Proof. First we show the case of $n = 1$, that is, $L_1 \not\Rightarrow L$ holds for any pair of lens laws L_1, L that do not belong to the same family. Thanks to the known implications inside each family, it suffices to show the non-implication between the strongest law in one family and the weakest law in another, that is,

(6-1) (STRONGGETPUT) $\not\Rightarrow$ (PUTINJECTIVITY) $\vee$ (PUTTWICE)

(6-2) (PUTGET) $\not\Rightarrow$ (PUTGETPUT) $\vee$ (PUTSURJECTIVITY) $\vee$ (PUTTWICE)

(6-3) (PUTPUT) $\not\Rightarrow$ (PUTSURJECTIVITY) $\vee$ (PUTINJECTIVITY)

(6-4) (PUTPUT) $\not\Rightarrow$ (PUTGETPUT) $\vee$ (WEAKPUTGET)

The non-implication (6-1) is shown by a lens on $S = V = \mathbb{Z}$ defined by $get(s) = 2s$ and $put(s, v) = s(v \bmod 2) + \lfloor v/2 \rfloor$ which satisfies the (STRONGGET-PUT) law and violates both the (PUTINJECTIVITY) and (PUTTWICE) laws. The non-implication (6-2) is shown by a lens on $S = V = \mathbb{Z}$ defined by $get(s) = \lfloor s/3 \rfloor$ and $put(s, v) = 1 - (s \bmod 2) + 3v$ which satisfies the (PUTGET) law and violates the (PUTGETPUT), (PUTSURJECTIVITY), and (PUTTWICE) laws. The non-implication (6-3) is shown by a lens on $S = V = \mathbb{Z}$ given by $put(s, v) = 0$, which satisfies the (PUTPUT) law and violates both the (PUTSURJECTIVITY) and (PUTINJECTIVITY) laws. The non-implication (6-4) is shown by a lens on $S = V = \mathbb{Z}$ given by $get(s) = s + 1$ and $put(s, v) = v$ which satisfies the (PUTPUT) law and violates the (PUTGETPUT) and (WEAKPUTGET) law.

In the case of $n \geq 2$, since the set $\{L_1, \ldots, L_n\}$ is pairwise incomparable and all the laws are belong to the same family, only the case with $n = 2$, $\{L_1, L_2\} = \{(\text{GETPUT}), (\text{UNDOABILITY})\}$, needs to be considered because of the known implications for each family. It suffices to show the following non-implication

(6-5) (GETPUT) $\wedge$ (UNDOABILITY) $\not\Rightarrow$ (PUTINJECTIVITY) $\vee$ (PUTTWICE)

since the other combinations have either implication from one to another or an equivalent single law. The non-implication (GETPUT) $\wedge$ (UNDOABILITY) $\not\Rightarrow$ (PUTINJECTIVITY) $\vee$ (PUTTWICE) holds due to (6-1) and the known implications.

□

4   Association Beyond Families

We have seen that lens laws in a single family do not imply any lens law out of the family. In this section, we investigate implications of the form $L_1 \wedge \cdots \wedge L_n \Rightarrow L$

with $n \geq 2$ where L_i and L_j belong to different families for some $i \neq j$. As shown later, we only need implications of $n = 2$ since all the implications with $n \geq 3$ are derivable from them.

First, possible implications of the form $L_1 \wedge L_2 \Rightarrow L$ are studied where L_1 and L belong to the same family and $L \Rightarrow L_1$, and L_2 does not belong to the family. This type of implications indicates that L_1 and L are equivalent under L_2, i.e., $L_1 \wedge L_2 \rightleftarrows L \wedge L_2$. Three implications of this types are found as shown in the following theorem.

Theorem 7. The following unidirectional implications hold.

(7-1) $(\textsc{PutSurjectivity}) \wedge (\textsc{PutTwice}) \underset{\not\Leftarrow}{\Rightarrow} (\textsc{SourceStability})$

(7-2) $(\textsc{PutInjectivity}) \wedge (\textsc{PutTwice}) \underset{\not\Leftarrow}{\Rightarrow} (\textsc{ViewDetermination})$

(7-3) $(\textsc{ViewDetermination}) \wedge (\textsc{PutGetPut}) \underset{\not\Leftarrow}{\Rightarrow} (\textsc{PutGet})$

Proof. Note that each implication has the form $L_1 \wedge L_2 \underset{\not\Leftarrow}{\Rightarrow} L$ where L_2 and L do not belong to the same family. From Theorem 6, we have $L \not\Rightarrow L_2$, which disproves the converse implication. Thereby it suffices to show $L_1 \wedge L_2 \Rightarrow L$ for each item.

(7-1) Suppose that the $(\textsc{PutSurjectivity})$ and $(\textsc{PutTwice})$ laws hold. For $s \in S$, $(\textsc{PutSurjectivity})$ gives $s' \in S$ and $v \in V$ such that $put(s', v) = s$. Then

$$
\begin{aligned}
put(s, v) &= put(put(s', v), v) & put(s', v) &= s \\
&= put(s', v) & \text{by } &(\textsc{PutTwice}) \\
&= s & put(s', v) &= s,
\end{aligned}
$$

hence the $(\textsc{SourceStability})$ law holds.

(7-2) Suppose that the $(\textsc{PutInjectivity})$ and $(\textsc{PutTwice})$ laws hold. If $put(s, v) = put(s', v')$, we have

$$
\begin{aligned}
put(put(s, v), v) &= put(s, v) & \text{by } &(\textsc{PutTwice}) \\
&= put(s', v') & \text{by the assumption} \\
&= put(put(s', v'), v') & \text{by } &(\textsc{PutTwice}) \\
&= put(put(s, v), v') & \text{by the assumption}
\end{aligned}
$$

This equation implies $v = v'$ by the $(\textsc{PutInjectivity})$ law, hence we have the $(\textsc{ViewDetermination})$ law.

(7-3) Suppose that the $(\textsc{ViewDetermination})$ and $(\textsc{PutGetPut})$ laws hold. By the $(\textsc{PutGetPut})$ law, we have $put(put(s, v), get(put(s, v))) = put(s, v)$. Since this equation implies $get(put(s, v)) = v$ by the $(\textsc{ViewDetermination})$ law, we have the $(\textsc{PutGet})$ law.

$\square$

These implications and (2-6) give four equivalence relations in the same family under a lens law belonging to another family, that is,

$$(\text{SourceStability}) \wedge (\text{PutTwice}) \rightleftarrows (\text{PutSurjectivity}) \wedge (\text{PutTwice})$$

$$(\text{ViewDetermination}) \wedge (\text{PutTwice}) \rightleftarrows (\text{PutInjectivity}) \wedge (\text{PutTwice})$$

$$(\text{WeakPutGet}) \wedge (\text{PutGet}) \rightleftarrows (\text{SourceStability}) \wedge (\text{PutGet})$$

$$(\text{PutGetPut}) \wedge (\text{GetPut}) \rightleftarrows (\text{ViewDetermination}) \wedge (\text{GetPut})$$

The following theorem shows an implication where two lens laws in the Get-Put family are involved but, unlike the above ones, the two are not related by inclusion. Nevertheless it leads their equivalence under another lens laws in a different family as we will see later.

Theorem 8 ([3,9]). The implication $(\text{GetPut}) \wedge (\text{PutPut}) \rightleftarrows\kern-1.1em/\;\; (\text{Undoability})$ holds.

Proof. Suppose that the (GetPut) and (PutPut) laws hold. Then we have the (Undoability) law because $put(put(s, v), get(s)) = put(s, get(s)) = s$ holds by applying the (PutPut) and (GetPut) laws. Its converse is disproved by Theorem 6. □

This theorem leads equivalence of the (GetPut) and (Undoability) laws under (PutPut) law as follows:

$(\text{GetPut}) \wedge (\text{PutPut})$
$\Rightarrow (\text{Undoability}) \wedge (\text{PutPut})$ by Theorem 8
$\Rightarrow (\text{Undoability}) \wedge (\text{PutSurjectivity}) \wedge (\text{PutTwice}) \wedge (\text{PutPut})$
                                      by (2-2) and Theorem 5
$\Rightarrow (\text{WeakPutGet}) \wedge (\text{SourceStability}) \wedge (\text{PutPut})$ by (2-4) and (7-1)
$\Rightarrow (\text{GetPut}) \wedge (\text{PutPut})$ by (2-6)

which indicates $(\text{GetPut}) \wedge (\text{PutPut}) \rightleftarrows (\text{Undoability}) \wedge (\text{PutPut})$.

Next, possible implications of the form $L_1 \wedge L_2 \Rightarrow L$ are studied where L_1, L_2 and L belong to different families. Two implications of this type are found.

Theorem 9. The following unidirectional implications hold.

(9-1) $(\text{SourceStability}) \wedge (\text{ViewDetermination}) \rightleftarrows\kern-1.1em/\;\; (\text{PutTwice})$

(9-2) $(\text{StrongGetPut}) \wedge (\text{PutInjectivity}) \rightleftarrows\kern-1.1em/\;\; (\text{PutPut})$

(9-3) $(\text{PutGet}) \wedge (\text{PutGetPut}) \rightleftarrows\kern-1.1em/\;\; (\text{PutTwice})$

(9-4) $(\text{PutGet}) \wedge (\text{PutTwice}) \rightleftarrows\kern-1.1em/\;\; (\text{PutGetPut})$

(9-5) $(\text{PutGetPut}) \wedge (\text{PutPut}) \rightleftarrows\kern-1.1em/\;\; (\text{WeakPutGet})$

Proof. It suffices to simply show these implications since their converses are disproved by THEOREM 6.

(9-1) Suppose that the (SOURCESTABILITY) and (VIEWDETERMINATION) laws hold. By the (SOURCESTABILITY) law, we take v' such that $put(put(s, v), v') = put(s, v)$. The equation implies $v' = v$ by the (VIEWDETERMINATION) law. Then we have

$$
\begin{aligned}
put(put(s, v), v) &= put(put(s, v), v') && \text{by } v = v' \\
&= put(s, v) && \text{by } put(put(s, v), v') = put(s, v)
\end{aligned}
$$

which indicates the (PUTTWICE) law.

(9-2) Suppose that the (STRONGGETPUT) and (PUTINJECTIVITY) laws hold. By the (STRONGGETPUT) law, we have $put(put(s, v), get(put(put(s, v), v'))) = put(put(s, v), v')$. By applying the (PUTINJECTIVITY) law to this equation, we have $get(put(put(s, v), v')) = v'$. Then the (PUTPUT) law holds because

$$
\begin{aligned}
put(put(s, v), v') &= put(s, get(put(put(s, v), v'))) && \text{by (STRONGGETPUT)} \\
&= put(s, v') && \text{by the equation.}
\end{aligned}
$$

(9-3) Suppose that the (PUTGET) and (PUTGETPUT) laws hold. Then the (PUTTWICE) law holds because

$$
\begin{aligned}
put(put(s, v), v) &= put(put(s, v), get(put(s, v))) && \text{by (PUTGET)} \\
&= put(s, v) && \text{by (PUTGETPUT).}
\end{aligned}
$$

(9-4) Suppose that the (PUTGET) and (PUTTWICE) laws hold. Then the (PUT-GETPUT) law holds because

$$
\begin{aligned}
put(put(s, v), get(put(s, v))) &= put(put(s, v), v) && \text{by (PUTGET)} \\
&= put(s, v) && \text{by (PUTTWICE).}
\end{aligned}
$$

(9-5) Suppose that the (PUTGETPUT) and (PUTPUT) laws hold. Then the (WEAKPUTGET) law holds because

$$
\begin{aligned}
put(s, get(put(s, v))) &= put(put(s, v), get(put(s, v))) && \text{by (PUTPUT)} \\
&= put(s, v) && \text{by (PUTGETPUT).}
\end{aligned}
$$

$\square$

Combining all theorems among lens laws presented so far, we can obtain many other implications. For example, the implication (STRONGGETPUT)$\wedge$(PUTGET) $\Rightarrow$ (PUTPUT), which shows that every bijective lens conforms to the (PUTPUT) law, is obtained by

$$
\begin{aligned}
(\text{STRONGGETPUT}) \wedge (\text{PUTGET}) &\Rightarrow (\text{STRONGGETPUT}) \wedge (\text{PUTINJECTIVITY}) && \text{by (4-1)} \\
&\Rightarrow (\text{PUTPUT}) && \text{by (9-2).}
\end{aligned}
$$

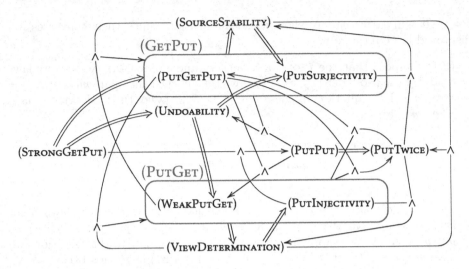

Fig. 4. Implication among lens laws

In addition, the implication (GETPUT) $\wedge$ (PUTGET) $\Rightarrow$ (PUTTWICE), which has been shown in [5], is obtained by

(GETPUT) $\wedge$ (PUTGET)

 $\Rightarrow$ (SOURCESTABILITY) $\wedge$ (VIEWDETERMINATION) by (2-4) and (4-1)

 $\Rightarrow$ (PUTTWICE)   by (9-1).

Similarly, we might have many other implications of the form $L_1 \wedge \cdots \wedge L_n \Rightarrow L$ among lens laws.

All implications shown in this paper give a big web structure among 12 lens laws as shown in Fig. 4, where bidirectional implications, (GETPUT) $\rightleftarrows$ (PUTGETPUT) $\wedge$ (PUTSURJECTIVITY) and (PUTGET) $\rightleftarrows$ (WEAKPUTGET) $\wedge$ (PUTINJECTIVITY), are represented by labelled round squares that contain two laws.

This figure tells not only implications but equalities among lens laws and their conjunctions. For example, the equivalence relation shown in [5, Theorem 2],

$$\text{(SOURCESTABILITY)} \wedge \text{(VIEWDETERMINATION)} \rightleftarrows$$

$$\text{(PUTSURJECTIVITY)} \wedge \text{(PUTTWICE)} \wedge \text{(PUTINJECTIVITY)},$$

can be concluded from this figure by checking that the conjunction of the (SOURCESTABILITY) and (VIEWDETERMINATION) laws entails the (PUTSURJECTIV-ITY), (PUTTWICE), and (PUTINJECTIVITY), and vice versa.

For another example, any lens satisfying the (SOURCESTABILITY), (VIEWDE-TERMINATION), and either (WEAKPUTGET) or (PUTGETPUT) laws can be found to be well-behaved because the figure leads to the (GETPUT) and (PUTGET) laws from the three laws. This holds even when the (PUTINJECTIVITY) law is satisfied instead of (VIEWDETERMINATION).

The web in Fig. 4 is expected to be complete, that is, no implication of the form $L_1 \wedge \cdots \wedge L_n \Rightarrow L$ holds for any lens laws L_i and L except derivable ones from the implications in the web. The completeness is left for future work. What this paper has shown is that the web for each family in Fig. 3 is complete and the three families are separated each other as stated in THEOREM 6.

5   Concluding Remark

A precise relationship among lens laws has been presented. Twelve lens laws which have been introduced in the literature on bidirectional transformation are found to relate to each other, one implies another and a combination of two implies another. The implication graph which shows all the relationship might be helpful to check lens laws and certify properties for a given bidirectional transformation.

The web of lens laws tells us a kind of *duality* among laws. As found from (2-1), (2-3), (2-5), (4-1), (4-2), and (4-3) the GetPut an PutGet families have similar implications among four laws. The (GETPUT), (SOURCESTABILITY), (PUTINJECTIVITY), and (PUTGETPUT) laws in the GetPut family correspond to the (PUTGET), (VIEWDETERMINATION), (PUTSURJECTIVITY), and (WEAKPUTGET) laws in the PutGet family. The implications (2-6), (7-1), (7-3), and (7-2) also strengthen their duality. It would be interesting to investigate even more in detail duality, for example, the counterpart of (STRONGGETPUT) and (UNDOABILITY) in the PutGet family.

Our further goal is to give a "complete picture" of lens laws such that we can derive from it all possible implications of the Horn-clause-like form $L_1 \wedge \cdots \wedge L_n \to L$ with classes $L_1, \ldots, L_n$ and L of lens laws. To achieve the goal, it would be shown that every Horn-clause-like implication that cannot be obtained from the implication graph has a counterexample. The complete picture will help us to understand the essence of bidirectional transformation. In addition, it would be practically helpful to consider the case where *get* and *put* are allowed to be partial. The implication graph might have a different form from the graph in the total case which has been discussed in the present paper.

Acknowledgment. The author thanks Mirai Ikebuchi and anonymous referees for their helpful comments. This work was supported by JSPS KAKENHI Grant Numbers JP17H06099, JP18H04093, and JP21K11744.

References

1. Bancilhon, F., Spyratos, N.: Update semantics of relational views. ACM Trans. Database Syst. **6**(4), 557–575 (1981). https://doi.org/10.1145/319628.319634

2. Bohannon, A., Pierce, B.C., Vaughan, J.A.: Relational lenses: a language for updatable views. In: Vansummeren, S. (ed.) Proceedings of the Twenty-Fifth ACM SIGACT-SIGMOD-SIGART Symposium on Principles of Database Systems, 26–28 Jun 2006, Chicago, Illinois, USA, pp. 338–347. ACM (2006). https://doi.org/10.1145/1142351.1142399

3. Diskin, Z.: Algebraic models for bidirectional model synchronization. In: Czarnecki, K., Ober, I., Bruel, J.-M., Uhl, A., Völter, M. (eds.) MODELS 2008. LNCS, vol. 5301, pp. 21–36. Springer, Heidelberg (2008). https://doi.org/10.1007/978-3-540-87875-9_2

4. Diskin, Z., Xiong, Y., Czarnecki, K.: From state- to delta-based bidirectional model transformations: the asymmetric case. J. Object Technol. 10(6), 1–25 (2011). https://doi.org/10.5381/jot.2011.10.1.a6

5. Fischer, S., Hu, Z., Pacheco, H.: A clear picture of lens laws. In: Hinze, R., Voigtländer, J. (eds.) MPC 2015. LNCS, vol. 9129, pp. 215–223. Springer, Cham (2015). https://doi.org/10.1007/978-3-319-19797-5_10

6. Foster, J.N., Greenwald, M.B., Kirkegaard, C., Pierce, B.C., Schmitt, A.: Exploiting schemas in data synchronization. J. Comput. Syst. Sci. 73(4), 669–689 (2007). https://doi.org/10.1016/j.jcss.2006.10.024

7. Foster, J.N., Greenwald, M.B., Moore, J.T., Pierce, B.C., Schmitt, A.: Combinators for bidirectional tree transformations: a linguistic approach to the view-update problem. ACM Trans. Program. Lang. Syst. 29(3), 17 (2007). https://doi.org/10.1145/1232420.1232424

8. Foster, J.N., Pilkiewicz, A., Pierce, B.C.: Quotient lenses. In: Hook, J., Thiemann, P. (eds.) Proceeding of the 13th ACM SIGPLAN international conference on Functional programming, ICFP 2008, Victoria, BC, Canada, 20–28 Sept 2008, pp. 383–396. ACM (2008). https://doi.org/10.1145/1411204.1411257

9. Foster, N., Matsuda, K., Voigtländer, J.: Three complementary approaches to bidirectional programming. In: Gibbons, J. (ed.) Generic and Indexed Programming. LNCS, vol. 7470, pp. 1–46. Springer, Heidelberg (2012). https://doi.org/10.1007/978-3-642-32202-0_1

10. Hidaka, S., Hu, Z., Inaba, K., Kato, H., Matsuda, K., Nakano, K.: Bidirectionalizing graph transformations. In: Proceeding of the 15th ACM SIGPLAN International Conference on Functional Programming, ICFP 2010, Baltimore, Maryland, USA, 27–29 Sept 2010, pp. 205–216 (2010). https://doi.org/10.1145/1863543.1863573

11. Hidaka, S., Tisi, M., Cabot, J., Hu, Z.: Feature-based classification of bidirectional transformation approaches. Softw. Syst. Model. 15(3), 907–928 (2016). https://doi.org/10.1007/s10270-014-0450-0

12. Hu, Z., Mu, S., Takeichi, M.: A programmable editor for developing structured documents based on bidirectional transformations. In: Heintze, N., Sestoft, P. (eds.) Proceedings of the 2004 ACM SIGPLAN Workshop on Partial Evaluation and Semantics-based Program Manipulation, 2004, Verona, Italy, 24–25 Aug 2004, pp. 178–189. ACM (2004). https://doi.org/10.1145/1014007.1014025

13. Kmett, E.: The Lens library: Lenses, Folds and Traversals (2013). http://lens.github.io

14. Ko, H., Zan, T., Hu, Z.: Bigul: a formally verified core language for putback-based bidirectional programming. In: Proceedings of the 2016 ACM SIGPLAN Workshop on Partial Evaluation and Program Manipulation, PEPM 2016, St. Petersburg, FL, USA, 20–22 Jan 2016, pp. 61–72 (2016). https://doi.org/10.1145/2847538.2847544

15. Nakano, K.: Towards a complete picture of lens laws. In: Proceedings of the Third Workshop on Software Foundations for Data Interoperability (SFDI2019+), Fukuoka, Japan (2019)

16. Nakano, K., Hu, Z., Takeichi, M.: Consistent web site updating based on bidirectional transformation. Int. J. Softw. Tools Technol. Transf. **11**(6), 453–468 (2009). https://doi.org/10.1007/s10009-009-0124-3

17. Pickering, M., Gibbons, J., Wu, N.: Profunctor optics: modular data accessors. Art Sci. Eng. Program. **1**(2), 7 (2017). https://doi.org/10.22152/programming-journal.org/2017/1/7

18. Sasano, I., Hu, Z., Hidaka, S., Inaba, K., Kato, H., Nakano, K.: Toward bidirectionalization of ATL with GRoundTram. In: Cabot, J., Visser, E. (eds.) ICMT 2011. LNCS, vol. 6707, pp. 138–151. Springer, Heidelberg (2011). https://doi.org/10.1007/978-3-642-21732-6_10

19. Stevens, P.: Bidirectional model transformations in QVT: semantic issues and open questions. Softw. Syst. Model. **9**(1), 7–20 (2010). https://doi.org/10.1007/s10270-008-0109-9

20. Stevens, P.: Observations relating to the equivalences induced on model sets by bidirectional transformations. ECEASST **49** (2012). https://doi.org/10.14279/tuj.eceasst.49.714

Splitting Recursion Schemes into Reversible and Classical Interacting Threads

Armando B. Matos[1], Luca Paolini[2] (ID), and Luca Roversi[2(✉)] (ID)

[1] Universidade do Porto, Departamento de Ciência de Computadores, Porto,
Portugal
[2] Università degli Studi di Torino, Dipartimento di Informatica, Turin, Italy
{luca.paolini,luca.roversi}@unito.it

Abstract. Given a simple recursive function, we show how to extract from it a reversible and an classical iterative part. Those parts can synchronously cooperate under a Producer/Consumer pattern in order to implement the original recursive function. The reversible producer is meant to run on reversible hardware. We also discuss how to extend the extraction to a more general compilation scheme.

1 Introduction

Our goal is to compile a class of recursive functions in a way that parts of the object code produced can leverage the promised green foot-print of truly reversible hardware. This work illustrates preliminary steps towards that goal. We focus on a basic class of recursive functions in order to demonstrate its feasibility.

Contributions. Let `recF[p,b,h]` be a recursive function defined in some programming formalism, where `p` is a *predecessor* function, `h` a *step* function, and `b` a *base* function. We show how to compile `recF[p,b,h]` into `itFCls[b,h]` and `itFRev[p,pInv]` such that:

$$\text{recF[p,b,h]} \simeq \text{itFCls[b,h]} \parallel \text{itFRev[p,pInv]} , \tag{1}$$

where: (i) "$\simeq$" stands for "*equivalent to*"; (ii) `itFCls[b,h]` is a classical `for`-loop that, starting from a value produced by `b`, iteratively applies `h`; (iii) `itFRev[p,pInv]` is a reversible code with two `for`-loops in it one iterating `p`, the other its inverse `pInv`; (iv) "$\parallel$" is interpreted as an *interaction* between `itFCls[b,h]` and `itFRev[p,pInv]`, according to a Producer/Consumer pattern, where `itFRev[p,pInv]` produces the values that `itFCls[b,h]` consumes to implement the initially given recursion `recF[p,b,h]`. In principle, `itFRev[p,pInv]` can drive a real reversible hardware to exploit its low energy consumption features.

    In this work we limit the compilation scheme (1) to use: (i) a predecessor `p` such that the value `p(x)-x` is any *constant* Δ_p equal to, or smaller than, `-1`;

© Springer Nature Switzerland AG 2021
S. Yamashita and T. Yokoyama (Eds.): RC 2021, LNCS 12805, pp. 204–213, 2021.
https://doi.org/10.1007/978-3-030-79837-6_12

(ii) recursion functions recF[p,b,h] whose *condition* identifying the base case is x<=0 instead than the more standard x==0; this means that more than one base *non positive* value for recF[p,b,h] exists in the interval $[\Delta_p + 1, 0]$. This slight generalization will require a careful management of the reversible behavior of itFRev[p,pInv] and its interaction with itFCls[b,h] in order to reconstruct recF[p,b,h].

Contents. Sect. 2 sets the stage to develop the main ideas about (1), restricting recF[p,b,h] to a recursive function that identifies its base case by means of the standard condition x==0; this ease the description of how itFRev[p,pInv] and itFCls[b,h] interact. Section 3 extends (1) to deal with recF[p,b,h] having x<= 0, and not x==0, to identify its base case(s); this impacts on how itFRev[p,pInv] must work. In both cases, the programming syntax we use can be interpreted into the reversible languages SRL [3,4] and RPP [4–6], up to minor syntactic details. Section 4 addresses future work.

```
1   Fix recF(x)                                {
2       if    (c(x)) { b(x);            }
3       else         { h(x,recF(p(x))); } }
```

Fig. 1. The recursive function recF.

```
1   /*** Assumption: the inital value of x is 3 */
2   x = p(x)          // ==2
3   x = p(x)          // ==1
4   x = p(x)          // ==0
5   y = b(x)          // ==b(p(p(p(3))))
6   y = h(x,y)        // ==h(p(p(p(3))),b(p(p(p(3)))))
7   x = pInv(x)       // ==pInv(p(p(p(3))))==p(p(3))
8   y = h(x,y)        // ==h(p(p(3)),h(p(p(p(3))),b(p(p(p(3))))))
9   x = pInv(x)       // ==pInv(p(p(3)))==p(3)
10  y = h(x,y)        // ==h(p(3),h(p(p(3))
11                    //        ,h(p(p(p(3))),b(p(p(p(3)))))))
12  x = pInv(x)       // ==pInv(p(3))==3
13  y = h(x,y)        // ==h(3,h(p(3),h(p(p(3))
14                    //        ,h(p(p(p(3))),b(p(p(p(3))))))))
```

Fig. 2. Iterative unfolding recF(3): the bottom-up part.

2   The Driving Idea

Let recF[p,b,h] in (1) have a structure as in Fig. 1 where b(x) is the *base* function, h(x,y) the *step* function, p(x) the *predecessor* x-1, and c(x) the *condition* x==0 to identify a unique base case.

Figure 2 details out h(3,h(p(3),h(p(p(3)), h(p(p(p(3))),b(p(p(p(3)))))))),
unfolding of recF(3). Every comment asserts a property of the values that x or y
stores. Lines 2–4 unfold an iteration that computes p(p(p(3))), which eventually
sets the value of x to 0. Line 5 starts the construction of the final value of recF(3)
by applying the base case of recF, i.e. b(x). By definition, let pInv denote the
inverse of p, i.e. pInv(p(z))==p(pInv(z))==z, for any z. Clearly, in our running
example, the function pInv(x) is x+1. Lines 6–13 alternate h(x,y), whose result y,
step by step, gets closer to the final value recF(3), and pInv(x), which produces
a new value for x.

```
1    s = 0, e = 0, g = 0, w = 0
2    w = w + x;
3    for (i = 0; i<=w; i++)        {
4        if      (x> 0) { g++; }
5        else if (x==0) { e++; }
6        else           { s++; }
7        x = p(x);                 }
8
9    for (i = 0; i<=w; i++)                    {
10       x = pInv(x);
11       if      (x> 0) { g--; y = h(x,y); }
12       else if (x==0) { e--; y = b(x);   }
13       else           { s--;             } }
14   w = w - x;
```

Fig. 3. Iterative itF equivalent to recF.

Let us call itF the code in Fig. 3. It implements recF by means of finite
iterations only. Continuing with our running example, if we run itF here above
starting with x==3, then x==0 holds at line 8, just after the first for-loop; after
the second for-loop y==recF(3) holds at line 14.

The code of itF has two parts. Through lines 2–7 the variable g counts how
many times x remains positive, the variable e how many it stays equal to 0, and
the variable s how many it becomes negative. In this running example we notice
that x never becomes negative, because the iteration at lines 3–7 is driven by the
value of x which, initially, we can assume non negative, and which p(x) decreases
of a single unity. We shall clarify the role of s later. Lines 9–13 undo what lines
2–7 do by executing pInv(x), g--, e--, s--, i.e. the inverses, in reversed order,
of p(x), g++, e++, s++. So the correct values of x are available at lines 12, and
11, ready to be used as arguments of b(x) and h(x,y) to update y as in Fig. 3,
according to the results we obtain by the recursive calls to recF.

Now, let us focus on the main difference between Figs. 4 and 3.

Both x=b(x) and y=h(x,y) at lines 12, and 11 of Fig. 3 are missing from lines
12, and 11 of Fig. 4. Dropping them let Fig. 4 be the *reversible side* of itF; calling
b(x) and h(x,y) in it generates y, which is the result we need, so preventing

```
1  s = 0, e = 0, g = 0, w = 0
2  w = w + x;
3  for (i=0; i<=w; i++)        {
4    if        (x> 0) { g++; } //number of times x is 'g'reater than 0
5    else if (x==0) { e++; } //number of times x is 'e'qual to 0
6    else              { s++; } //number of times x is 's'maller than 0
7    x = p(x);                 }
8
9  for (i=0; i<=w; i++)                                          {
10   x = pInv(x);
11   if        (x> 0) { g--; /* Value of x for h availabe here */ }
12   else if (x==0) { e--; /* Value of x for b availabe here */ }
13   else           { s--;                                   } }
14 w = w - x;
```

Fig. 4. Reversible side of itF.

the possibility to reset the value of every variable dealt with in Fig. 4 to their initial value. This is why we also need a *classical side* of itF that generates y in collaboration with the *reversible side* in order to implement the initial recF correctly.

```
1  /*** Assumption. The value of the input x is available here */
2  /* Inject the current x at line 2 of itFRev to let it start */
3  iterations = /* Probe line 9 of itFRev to get the
4                  number of iterations to execute   */
5  y = b(/* Probe line 14 of itFRev to get the argument */);
6  for (i = 0; i<iterations; i++)                    {
7    y = h(/* Probe line 12 itFRev to get
8           the first argument of h    */ , y); }
```

Fig. 5. Classical side of itF: the consumer itFCls.

The previous observations lead to Fig. 5 which defines the *classical side* itFCls of recF, and to Fig. 6 which defines the *reversible side* itFCRev of recF.

So, here below we can illustrate how itFCls and itFRev synchronously interact, itFRev producing values, itFCls consuming them as arguments of b(x) and h(x,y).

Line 2 of itFCls is the starting point of the synchronous interaction between itFCls and itFRev; its comment:

```
/* Inject the current x at line 2 of itFRev to let it start */
```

describes what, in a fully implemented version of itFCls, we expect in that line of code. The comment says that itFCls injects (sends, puts) its input value x to

```
1   s = 0, e = 0, g = 0, w = 0;
2   x = /* Inject here the value of x at line 2 of itFCls */
3   w = w + x;
4   for (i = 0; i<=w; i++)        {
5      if        (x> 0) { g++; }
6      else if (x==0) { e++; }
7      else            { s++; }
8      x = p(x);                  }
9   /* itFCls probes here g which has the number of iterations */
10  for (i = 0; i<=w; i++)                                      {
11     x = pInv(x);
12     if        (x> 0) { g--; /* itFCls probes here the
13                             first argument value of h */ }
14     else if (x==0) { e--; /* itFCls probes here the
15                             argument value of b        */ }
16     else            { s--;                              } }
17  w = w - x;
```

Fig. 6. Reversible side of `itF` updated to be the producer `itFRev` of the values that the consumer `itFCls` needs.

line 2 of the *reversible side* `itFRev` (cf. Fig. 6). Once `itFRev` obtains that value at line 2, as outlined by:

```
/* Inject here the value of x from line 2 of itFCls */
```

its `for`-loop at lines 4–8 executes.

After line 2, `itFCls` stops at line 3. It waits for `itFRev` to produce the number of times that `itFCls` has to iterate line 7. Accordingly to:

```
/* Probe line 9 of itFRev to get the number of iterations to execute */
```

`itFRev` makes that value available in its variable `g` at line 9:

```
/* itFCls probes here g which has the number of iterations */ .
```

Once gotten the value in `iterations`, `itFCls` proceeds to line 5 and stops, waiting for `itFRev` to produce the argument of `b` which is eventually available for probing at line 14 of `itFRev`.

Once the argument becomes available `b` is applied, and `itFCls` enters its `for`-loop, stopping at line 7 at every iteration. The reason is that `itFCls` waits for line 12 in `itFRev` to produce the value of the first argument of `h(x,y)`. This interleaved dialog between line 7 of `itFCls` and line 12 of `itFRev` lasts `iterations` times.

3   From Recursion to Iteration

We now generalize what we have seen in Sect. 2. Inside (1) we use `recG` of Fig. 7 instead than `recF` of Fig. 1. This requires to generalize Fig. 6.

```
1   Fix recG(x)                        {
2     if (x<=0) { b(x);                }
3     else      { h(x,recG(p(x))); } }
```

Fig. 7. The generic structure of recG.

From the introduction we recall that, given a *predecessor* p(x), we define $\Delta_p = $ p(x)-x, which is a negative value. In this section Δ_p can be any *constant* k <=-1, not only k ==-1; this requires to consider the slightly more general *condition* x<=0 in recG. For example, let p(x) be x-2. The computation of recG(3) is h(3,h(p(3)),h(p(p(3)),b(p(p(3))))))) which looks for the least n of iterated applications of p(x) such that p(...p(3)...)<=0; in our case we have 2== n <3.

Figure 8 introduces itG which generalizes itF in Fig. 3.

The scheme itG iteratively implements any recursive function whose structure can be brought back to the one of recG. We remark that line 1 in Fig. 8 initializes ancillae s, e, g, and w, like Fig. 3 initializes the namesake variables of itF, but line 2 of itG has new ancillae z, predDivX, and predNotDivX.

We also assume an initial *non negative* value for x. The reason is twofold. Firstly, it keeps our discussion as simple as possible, with no need to use the absolute value of x to set the upper limit of every index i in the for-loops that occur in the code. Second, negative values of x would widen our discussion about what a classical recursive function on negative values is and about what its reversible equivalent iteration has to be; we see this as a very interesting subject connected to [1], which is much more oriented than us to optimization issues of recursively defined functions.

We start observing that line 3 of itG sets w to the initial value of x; the reason is that every for-loop, but the one at lines 10–12, has to last x+1 iterations, and x changes in the course of the computation; so, w stores the initial value of x and stays constant from line 4 through line 21. In fact it can change at lines 22–33. We will see why, but w is eventually reset to its initial value 0 at line 36.

With the here above assumptions, given a non negative x, and in analogy to itF, the for-loop at lines 4–8 of itG iterates the application of p(x) as many times as w+1, i.e. the initial value of x plus 1. So, the value of x at line 9 is equal to w+(w+1)*Δ_p which cannot be positive. In particular, all the values that x assumes in the for-loop at lines 4–8 belong to the following interval:

$$I(w) \triangleq [w+(w+1)*\Delta_p, w+w*\Delta_p, \ldots, w+\Delta_p, w] \tag{2}$$

from the least to the greatest; the counters g, e, s say how many elements of $I(x)$ are greater, equal or smaller than 0, respectively. Depending on 0 to belong to $I(x)$ determines the behavior of the reminder part of itG, i.e. lines 10–36.

We distinguish two cases in order to illustrate them.

```
1   s = 0, e = 0, g = 0, w = 0;
2   z = 0, predDivX = 0, predNotDivX = 1;
3   w = w + x; /* x is assumed to be the input */
4   for (i = 0; i <= w; i++)   {
5       if      (x >  0) { g++; }
6       else if (x == 0) { e++; }
7       else             { s++; }
8       x = p(x);                    }
9
10  for (i = 0; i < e; i++)                        {
11      predDivX = predDivX + predNotDivX;
12      predNotDivX = predDivX - predNotDivX; }
13
14  for (j = 0; j < predDivX; j++)             {
15      for (i = 0; i <= w; i++)               {
16          x = pInv(x);
17          if      (x >  0) { g--; y = h(x,y); }
18          else if (x == 0) { e--; y = b(x);   }
19          else             { s--;          }}}
20
21  for (j = 0; j < predNotDivX; j++)                        {
22      w++;
23      for (i = 0; i <= w; i++)                             {
24          x = pInv(x);
25          if      (x >  0) { g--;
26                    x = p(x);
27                    if      (z <  0) {                     }
28                    else if (z == 0) { y = b(x); z++; }
29                    else             { y = h(x,y);   }
30                    x = pInv(x);                           }
31          else if (x == 0) { e--;                   }
32          else             { s--;                 }}
33      w--;                                                 }
34  for (i = 0; i < predNotDivX; i++) {
35      z--;                          }
36  w = w - x;
37  /* y carries the output */
```

Fig. 8. The iterative function itG.

First Case. Let $w \% \Delta_p == 0$, i.e. the integer value Δ_p divides with no reminder the initial value of x that we find in w. So, $0 \in I(x)$, which implies the following relations hold at line 9:

$$e == 1 \qquad\qquad g == -\frac{w}{\Delta_p} \qquad\qquad s == (w+1)-g-e . \qquad (3)$$

```
1   if        (e <  0) {                                                }
2   else if (e == 0) { predDivX = predDivX+predNotDivX;
3                      predNotDivX = predDivX - predNotDivX; }
4   else             {                                                  }
```

Fig. 9. A possible replacement of lines 10–12 in Fig. 8.

Lines 10–12 execute exactly once, swapping `predDivX` and `predNotDivX`. As a remark, we could have well used the `if`-selection in Fig. 9 (a construct of RPP) in place of the `for`-loop at lines 10–12, but we opt for a more compact code.

Swapping `predDivX` and `predNotDivX` sets `predDivX==1` and `predNotDivX==0`, computationally exploiting that Δ_p divides `w` with no reminder: the `for`-loop body at lines 15–19 becomes accessible, while lines 22–33, with `for`-loops among them, do not. Lines 15–19 are identical to lines 10–16 of `itF` in Fig. 4 which we already know to correctly apply `b(x)` and `h(x,y)` in order to simulate the recursive function we start from.

As a Second Case. Let `w%`Δ_p `!= 0`, i.e. the integer value Δ_p divides the initial value of `x` that `w` stores, *but with some reminder*. So, $0 \notin I(x)$, which imply:

$$e\ ==\ 0 \qquad\qquad g\ ==\ -\left\lfloor \frac{w}{\Delta_p} \right\rfloor \qquad\qquad s\ ==\ (w+1)-g-e \qquad (4)$$

hold at line 9. Lines 11–12 cannot execute, leaving `predDivX` and `predNotDivX` as they are: lines 22–33 become accessible and the `for`-loop at lines 15–19 does not. Line 22 increments `w` to balance the information loss that the rounding of `g` in (4) introduces; line 33 recovers the value of `w` when the outer `for`-loop starts. The `if`-selection at lines 25–32 identifies when to apply `b(x)`, which must be followed by the required applications of `h(x,y)`. We know that $0 \notin I(x)$, so `x==0` can never hold. Clearly, `s--` is executed until `x>0`. But the *first* time `x>0` holds true we must compute `b(p(x))`, because the *base* function `b(x)` *must be used the last time* `x` assumes a negative value, *not the first time* it gets positive; lines 26–30 implement our needs. Whenever `x>0` is true, the value of `x` is one step ahead the required one: we get one step back with line 26 and, if it is the first time we step back, i.e. `z==0` holds, then we must execute line 28. If not, i.e. `z!=0`, we must apply the *step* function at line 29. Line 30, restores the right value of `x`. Finally, the `for`-loop at line 34 sets `z` to its initial value.

At this point, in order to obtain the fully reversible version of Fig. 8 we must think of replacing the calls to `h(x,y)` and `b(x)` at lines in 28, and 29 by means of actions that probe the value of `x`, in analogy to Fig. 6, lines 12 and 14. The full details are in [7] which we look as a playground with Java classes that implement Fig. 8 and Fig. 5 as synchronous and parallel threads, acting as a producer and a consumer.

4   Future Work

We have shown that we can decompose every classical recursive function, based on a *predecessor* that decreases every of its input by a constant value, into reversible and classical components that cooperate to implement the original recursive functions under a Producer/Consumer pattern (see (1)).

Firstly, we plan to extend (1) to recursive functions recF based on predecessors p not limited to a constant Δ_p not greater than -1. A predecessor p should be at least such that:

1. Δ_p is not necessarily a constant. For example, Δ_p == -3 on even arguments, and -2 on odd ones can be useful;
2. the predecessor can be an integer division x/k, for some given k>0, like in a dichotomic search, which has k==2.

Secondly, we aim at generalizing (1) to a compiler $[\![\cdot]\!]$:

$$[\![\texttt{p}]\!] = \texttt{some implementation code}$$
$$[\![\texttt{pInv}]\!] = \,![\![\texttt{p}]\!], \text{ i.e. implementation that inverts } [\![\texttt{p}]\!] \qquad (5)$$
$$[\![\texttt{recF[p,b,h]}]\!] = \texttt{itFCls[}[\![\texttt{b}]\!]\texttt{,}[\![\texttt{h}]\!]\texttt{]} \,\|\, \texttt{itFRev[}[\![\texttt{p}]\!]\texttt{,}[\![\texttt{pInv}]\!]\texttt{]}.$$

The domain of $[\![\cdot]\!]$ should be a class R of recursive functions built by means of standard composition schemes, starting from a class of predecessors p1, p2, ...each of which must have the corresponding inverse function p1Inv, p2Inv, ...

In these lines we want to explore interpretations of $\|$ more liberal than the essentially obvious synchronous Producer/Consumer that we implement in [7]. We shall very likely take advantage of parallel discrete events simulators as described in [8,9] in order to get rid of any explicit synchronization between the pairs of reversible-producer/classical-consumer that (5) would recursively generate when applied to an element in R.

We also plan to follow a more abstract line of research. The compilation scheme (5) recalls Girard's decomposition $A \to B \simeq \,!A \multimap B$ of a classical computation into a linear one that can erase/duplicate computational resources. Decomposing recF[p,b,h] in terms of itFCls[b,h] and itFRev[p,pInv] suggests that the relation between reversible and classical computations can be formalized by a linear isomorphism $A^n \multimapinv B^n$ between tensor products A^n, and B^n of A, and B, in analogy to [2]. Then we can think of recovering classical computations by some functor, say γ, whose purpose is, at least, to forget, or to inject replicas, of parts of A^n, and B^n in a way that $(\gamma A^n \to \gamma A^n) \uplus (\gamma A^n \leftarrow \gamma A^n)$ can be their type. The type says that we move from a reversible computation to a classical one by choosing which is input and which is output, so recovering the freedom to manage computational resources as we are used to when writing classical programs.

References

1. Boiten, E.A.: Improving recursive functions by inverting the order of evaluation. Sci. Comput. Programm. **18**(2), 139–179 (1992)

2. James, R.P., Sabry, A.: Information effects. In: Field, J., Hicks, M. (eds.) Proceedings of the 39th ACM SIGPLAN-SIGACT Symposium on Principles of Programming Languages, POPL 2012, 22–28 January 2012, Philadelphia, Pennsylvania, USA, pp. 73–84. ACM (2012)
3. Matos, A.B.: Linear programs in a simple reversible language. Theor. Comput. Sci. **290**(3), 2063–2074 (2003)
4. Matos, A.B., Paolini, L., Roversi, L.: On the expressivity of total reversible programming languages. In: Lanese, I., Rawski, M. (eds.) RC 2020. LNCS, vol. 12227, pp. 128–143. Springer, Cham (2020). https://doi.org/10.1007/978-3-030-52482-1_7
5. Paolini, L., Piccolo, M., Roversi, L.: On a class of reversible primitive recursive functions and its turing-complete extensions. New Gener. Comput. **36**(3), 233–256 (2018)
6. Paolini, L., Piccolo, M., Roversi, L.: A class of recursive permutations which is primitive recursive complete. Theor. Comput. Sci. **813**, 218–233 (2020)
7. Roversi, L., Matos, A., Paolini, L.: Eclipse java project rev2iterrev. https://github.com/LucaRoversi/Rec2IterRev
8. Schordan, M., Oppelstrup, T., Jefferson, D., Barnes, P.D.: Generation of reversible C++ code for optimistic parallel discrete event simulation. New Gener. Comput. **36**(3), 257–280 (2018). https://doi.org/10.1007/s00354-018-0038-2
9. Schordan, M., Oppelstrup, T., Thomsen, M.K., Glück, R.: Reversible languages and incremental state saving in optimistic parallel discrete event simulation. In: Ulidowski, I., Lanese, I., Schultz, U.P., Ferreira, C. (eds.) RC 2020. LNCS, vol. 12070, pp. 187–207. Springer, Cham (2020). https://doi.org/10.1007/978-3-030-47361-7_9

Reversibility of Executable Interval Temporal Logic Specifications

Antonio Cau[1]() , Stefan Kuhn[1] , and James Hoey[2]

[1] School of Computer Science and Informatics, De Montfort University, Leicester, UK
{antonio.cau,stefan.kuhn}@dmu.ac.uk
[2] School of Informatics, University of Leicester, Leicester, UK

Abstract. In this paper the reversibility of executable Interval Temporal Logic (ITL) specifications is investigated. ITL allows for the reasoning about systems in terms of behaviours which are represented as non-empty sequences of states. It allows for the specification of systems at different levels of abstraction. At a high level this specification is in terms of properties, for instance safety and liveness properties. At concrete level one can specify a system in terms of programming constructs. One can execute these concrete specification, i.e., test and simulate the behaviour of the system. In this paper we will formalise this notion of executability of ITL specifications. ITL also has a reflection operator which allows for the reasoning about reversed behaviours. We will investigate the reversibility of executable ITL specifications, i.e., how one can use this reflection operator to reverse the concrete behaviour of a particular system.

Keywords: Interval Temporal Logic · Temporal reflection · Program reversion · Reversible computing

1 Introduction

Formal methods have been used in computer science to verify desirable and undesirable properties of programs. One type of formalism introduced is temporal logic. A temporal logic allows to reason about properties over time, for example "this resource will eventually be freed". In this paper, we are dealing with a particular temporal logic, Interval Temporal Logic (ITL).

Another strand of research is reversibility in computing. This is relevant for reversing the effects of operations, for example if, after having performed a number of operations, proceeding in the desired direction is not possible. This could be because a resource is not available or because a result is outside the allowed range of values. In such cases, a potential strategy is to roll back to a safe state and continue operation from there.

Using the ITL notation (details of which will explained in Sect. 3), a program consisting of two parts could be written as Good;Bad. The semantics (behaviour)

Supported by DMU.

S. Yamashita and T. Yokoyama (Eds.): RC 2021, LNCS 12805, pp. 214–223, 2021.
https://doi.org/10.1007/978-3-030-79837-6_13

of both parts are sequences of states. Good and Bad are arbitrary names indicating sections of the program which worked as expected respectively did not. We now want to reverse the effect of Bad. This would require that we go back to the last state of Good. This can be done by using an operator undo so that we have Good ; Bad ; undo(Bad). This operator must ensure that the last state of Good is the same as the last state of Good ; Bad ; undo(Bad).

We propose a solution for this problem, where we use the reflection operator ^{r}. We show that this reverses the effects of a formula, i.e., reversing the sequence of states of that formula. We also show that it can be applied to any formula that can be specified in ITL. This operator can be used for propositional as well as for first-order logic ITL. Therefore, we have a universal undo operation for these formulae. We distinguish *reflection*, which indicates the possibility to reverse the sequences of states, from *reversibility*. Reversibility indicates that an executable formula, a program, can be reversed.

The outline of the paper is as follows: in Sect. 2 we discuss temporal logic in general and compare ITL with other temporal logics. We also discuss reversibility in general. In Sect. 3 we discuss ITL, i.e., intervals, syntax of basic and derived constructs, and the reflection operator and the semantics of these constructs. In Sect. 4, the notion of executability is formalised and show how this notion can be used together with reflection to reverse the effects of bad computations.

An extended version of this paper can be found on arXiv.org at [3].

2   Background

Temporal logic can be used to describe reactive systems. After some cursory mentions earlier, a first type of temporal logic was presented by N. Prior [13]. Based on this, other types of temporal logic were devised, including (LTL) [8,12]. The main operator of LTL is the until ($\mathcal{U}$) while in ITL it is the chop (;). $f \, \mathcal{U} \, g$ guarantees that g will eventually hold at some future state and that f will continue to hold until then. In ITL, satisfaction of formulas is defined over intervals (sequences of states with at least 1 state) rather than time points which is used in LTL. $f;g$ denotes that the interval can be split into a prefix and a suffix interval in such a way that f holds for the prefix interval and g holds for the suffix interval. So the chop operator corresponds to the sequential composition operator.

There has been increasing interest and research done in reversible computation, for example demonstrated by the COST action IC1405 [14]. We focus on logical reversibility. This is all types of formalisms which allow reversing steps done in order to get back to a previous state of the computation [2].

Any temporal logic models computations over time, and time is generally irreversible, but computations can be reversible, as we have seen. Because of this, it seems a logic extension of temporal logic to introduce a "time reversal", which undoes computations and therefore seemingly reverses time, whereas actual time is progressing. [10] introduced this for ITL.

Reversibility and reflection of logic is related to reversibility of programming languages. Many works have researched the process of reversing executions of traditional programming languages, most of which are typically irreversible as information is lost throughout. One approach to reversing such executions is to save this lost information as a program executes forward and later use it to reconstruct previous states (reflection). This includes the Reverse C Compiler [11] and the works of Hoey and Ulidowski [5,6]. Any irreversible step of an execution is made reversible via this saved information. Execution time and memory usage are crucial aspects of these methods, with a forward execution typically being slower and memory requirements being higher as information is recorded. Such approaches including that described here minimise these overheads sufficiently. This differs from checkpointing approaches, where a snapshot of the state is taken at regular intervals and used to restore to previous positions [11]. Depending on the snapshot frequency, large amounts of information must be recorded and forward re-execution is sometimes required.

A second approach is to use reversible languages such as Janus [7], where any valid program written in such a language can be executed both forward and in reverse. This is comparable to ITL programs whose reflections are executable. Janus relies on the use of increment/decrement operators to ensure no old values of variables are lost, as well as post-conditions that allow correct expression evaluation during a reverse execution. However the challenge of converting programs of a traditional language into that of a reversible language may limit its widespread use.

3   Interval Temporal Logic

Interval Temporal Logic (ITL) is a flexible notation for both propositional and first-order reasoning about periods of time found in descriptions of hardware and software systems [4,15]. Unlike most temporal logics, ITL can handle both sequential and parallel composition and offers powerful and extensible specification and proof techniques for reasoning about properties involving safety, liveness and projected time. Timing constraints are expressible and furthermore most imperative programming constructs can be viewed as formulas in ITL. AnaTempura (available from [4]) provides an executable framework for developing and experimenting with suitable ITL specifications.

3.1   Interval

In this section we revisit the underlying semantic model of Interval Temporal Logic (albeit restricted to the finite case). The key notion of ITL is an *interval*. An interval σ is considered to be a non-empty, finite sequence of states $\sigma_0, \sigma_1 \ldots, \sigma_n$. A state is the union of an integer state State^e which is a mapping from the set of integer variables Var^e to the set of integer values Val, and a Boolean state State^b which is a mapping from the set of propositional variable Var^b to the set of Boolean values Bool. Note: the embedding of ITL in Isabelle/HOL is such that one can use any definable type in Isabelle/HOL as type for an ITL variable. We have restricted the types to just integers and

Boolean in this paper. Let Σ^+ denote the set of all finite intervals with at least 1 state. The length of an interval σ is denoted by $|\sigma|$ and is the number of states minus 1, i.e., an interval with one state has length zero. Let $\sigma = \sigma_0 \sigma_1 \sigma_2 \ldots \sigma_{|\sigma|}$ be an interval then $\sigma_0 \ldots \sigma_k$ (where $0 \le k \le |\sigma|$) denotes a prefix interval of σ, $\sigma_k \ldots \sigma_{|\sigma|}$ (where $0 \le k \le |\sigma|$) denotes a suffix interval of σ, $\sigma_k \ldots \sigma_l$ (where $0 \le k \le l \le |\sigma|$) denotes a sub interval of σ.

3.2   Syntax

We first discuss the basic constructs and then introduce derived constructs.

Syntax of Expressions (Boolean or Integer) in BNF $e ::= z \mid g(e_1, \ldots, e_n) \mid A \mid \text{fin } A \mid \bigcirc A$ where z is a constant, g an operator, and A, $\bigcirc A$ and fin A are temporal variables. Syntax of formulae in BNF $f ::= \text{true} \mid h(e_1, \ldots, e_n) \mid \neg f \mid f_1 \wedge f_2 \mid \exists V \bullet f \mid \text{skip} \mid f_1 ; f_2 \mid f^*$ where h is a Boolean predicate over integer or Boolean expressions, and V is a Boolean or integer variable. The formula skip denotes any interval of exactly two states. The formula $f_1 ; f_2$, where f_1 and f_2 are ITL formulae denotes an interval which is the fusion of two intervals, f_1 holds over the first interval and f_2 holds for the second interval. Fusion will concatenate two intervals in such a way that the last state of the first interval and the first state of the second interval are "fused" together. Fusion is only possible when these states are the same. If these states are not the same the resulting interval does not exist, i.e., is false. The formula f^* where f is an ITL formula denotes the fusion of a finite number of intervals, where for each interval f holds. Zero times fusion will result in an interval with exactly one state irrespective of f, i.e., false* is equal to empty. Temporal variables $\bigcirc V$ and fin V denote the value of variables at a particular point in an interval and are used to specify assignment constructs. The temporal variable $\bigcirc A$ denotes the value of A in the next state. The expression fin A denotes the value of A in the last state. The formula $\exists V \bullet f$ denotes the introduction of a local variable V.

Derived Constructs. The traditional Linear Temporal Logic (LTL) operators $\bigcirc, \Diamond$ and $\square$ are defined as follows: The formula $\bigcirc f \triangleq \text{skip} ; f$ denotes that f holds from the next state. Note that $\bigcirc f$ is different from temporal variable $\bigcirc V$, although the same $\bigcirc$ symbol is used, $\bigcirc f$ is using the $\bigcirc$ symbol on formula f whereas $\bigcirc V$ is using the $\bigcirc$ on a variable V. $\bigcirc f$ itself is a formula whereas $\bigcirc V$ denotes a value. The formula $\Diamond f \triangleq \text{true} ; f$ (sometimes) denotes that there exists a suffix interval for which f holds. The formula $\square f \triangleq \neg \Diamond \neg f$ (always) denotes that for each suffix interval f holds. The formula more $\triangleq \bigcirc \text{true}$ denotes an interval with at least two states. The formula empty $\triangleq \neg \text{more}$ denotes an interval with only one state. Note that no interval will satisfy the formula false. The formula $\overset{\text{w}}{\bigcirc} f \triangleq \text{empty} \vee \bigcirc f$ (weak next) denotes either an interval of only one state or f holds from the next state.

Semantics. We now define the semantics of ITL which is a mapping from the syntactic constructs of Sect. 3.2 and the semantic model (intervals) defined in Sect. 3.1 to values (Boolean or integer). Let $\mathsf{E}[\![\ldots]\!](\ldots)$ be the "meaning" (semantic) function from Expressions $\times \Sigma^+$ to Val and let $\sigma = \sigma_0\sigma_1\ldots$ be an interval. Let $\mathsf{M}[\![\ldots]\!](\ldots)$ be the "meaning" function from Formulae $\times \Sigma^+$ to Bool. The detailed semantics of each basic ITL construct is available from [4]. A first order ITL formula f is satisfiable denoted by $\models f$ if and only if there exists an interval σ such that $\mathsf{M}[\![f]\!](\sigma) = \mathsf{tt}$. A first order ITL formula f is valid denoted by $\vdash f$ if and only if for all intervals σ, $\mathsf{M}[\![f]\!](\sigma) = \mathsf{tt}$.

3.3 Reflection

We now discuss the notion of temporal reflection for ITL formulae as defined in [10]. We first discuss the semantic notion of the reverse of a sequence of states and then discuss the reflection operator and its corresponding semantics.

Let f be a formula, e an expression, and σ be an interval $\sigma_0\ldots\sigma_{|\sigma|}$ then $\mathsf{rev}(\sigma)$ denotes interval reversal and is defined as $\mathsf{rev}(\sigma) \triangleq \sigma_{|\sigma|}\ldots\sigma_0$. f^r denotes temporal reflection of formula f and is defined as $\mathsf{M}[\![f^r]\!](\sigma) \triangleq \mathsf{M}[\![f]\!](\mathsf{rev}(\sigma))$. e^r denotes temporal reflection of expression e and is defined as $\mathsf{E}[\![e^r]\!](\sigma) \triangleq \mathsf{E}[\![e]\!](\mathsf{rev}(\sigma))$.

The Isabelle/HOL ITL library (available from [4]) has defined reflection laws for all basic ITL operators. We need to add a new temporal variable $\ominus V$ to make ITL closed under reflection. The temporal variable $\ominus V$ is the reflection of $\bigcirc V$ and denotes the value of V in the pen-ultimate (previous) state. The formal semantics is as follows: if $|\sigma| > 0$ then $\sigma_{|\sigma|-1}(V)$ else any value from the Val. This leads to the following theorem

Theorem 1. *ITL (extended with $\ominus V$) is closed under reflection.*

4 Executability, Reflection and Reversibility

In this section we will discuss the notion of executability. It is used to determine whether an ITL formula represents a programming construct. We first formalise the notion of forward executability of a formula which corresponds to generating a sequence of states in a particular fashion: we first generate the first state and then generate the next until the final state is generated. This sequence of state constitutes the behaviour of the system described by the formula. We then investigate the reflection of forward executable formula and this requires the introduction of the notion of backward executability. This notion corresponds to generating a sequence of states but now we first generate the final state and then generate the previous state until we generate the first state. This sequence corresponds to the reversed behaviour of the system described by the formula. Forward and backward executability are related by the reflection operator.

4.1 Forward Executability

The intuition of an executable formula (specification) is that it corresponds to a computation, i.e., in our case a sequence of states. Obviously any executable formula needs to be satisfiable. But not every satisfiable formula is executable because we further require it to be "deterministic". We will give a formal definition what we mean by this. The executable formula corresponds to programming constructs. The following definitions are used to determine whether a formula is executable or not. First we define the notion of a value trace of a formula wrt a list of variables. These variables are the "free variables" appearing in f, i.e., f constrains the values of these variables. Note: These definitions and all subsequent theorems have been specified and verified in the Isabelle/HOL [1] system (library available from [4]).

Definition 1. *Let* s *be a state and let* $\bar{v}$ *denote a non-empty list of variables* $v_0, \ldots, v_n$ *and let* $\overline{s(v)}$ *denote the corresponding list of values* $s(v_0), \ldots, s(v_n)$ *of* $\bar{v}$ *in state* s. *Let* Spec *be a formula and* σ *be an interval and* $M[\![Spec]\!](\sigma) = tt$ *then the value trace of* Spec *wrt* $\bar{v}$ *is denoted by* map $(\lambda s.\overline{s(v)})$ σ *and defined as* $\overline{\sigma_0(v)}\, \overline{\sigma_1(v)} \ldots \overline{\sigma_{|\sigma|}(v)}$.

Example 1. The value trace for $A = 0 \land A$ gets $A + 1 \land \Box(B = A * 2)$ wrt (A, B) is $(0, 0)\ (1, 2)\ (2, 4)\ (3, 6)\ (4, 8)\ \ldots$ and it represents how A and B change, A is increased by one and B equals twice A in every state.

The following definition is a constraint on the intervals which satisfy a formula. Only intervals that share a common prefix of the value trace are allowed,

Definition 2. *A formula* Spec *has a common prefix value trace wrt a list of variables* $\bar{v}$ *denoted by* $\ddagger[Spec]_{\bar{v}}$ *if and only if for all intervals* σ *and* σ' *if* $M[\![Spec]\!](\sigma) = tt$ *and* $M[\![Spec]\!](\sigma') = tt$ *and* $|\sigma| \le |\sigma'|$ *then* (map $(\lambda s.\overline{s(v)})$ σ) = (map $(\lambda s.\overline{s(v)})$ $(\sigma'_0 \ldots \sigma'_{|\sigma|})$).

In above definition we compare the value trace corresponding to σ with the prefix (of length $|\sigma|$) of the value trace of corresponding to σ'. The intuition is that the latter is a continuation of the first, i.e., the first value trace is a "beginning" of the latter value trace. The following example illustrates this notion.

Example 2. The following are some formula that have a common prefix value trace.

- $\ddagger[A = 0 \land$ empty$]_A$, there is only one possible value trace 0.
- $\ddagger[A = 0 \land A$ gets $A + 1]_A$, the possible value traces are $0; 0, 1; 0, 1, 2$. Each pair of value traces share a common prefix. The common prefix value trace of pair 0 and $0, 1$ is 0 and of pair $0, 1$ and $0, 1, 2$ is $0, 1$. Note that in the latter pair there is another shared prefix 0 but in the definition it states that we are looking for a prefix that has a length equal to the "smallest" of the two. Note we align on the left.

The following are some formula that have no common prefix value trace.

- not $\ddagger[(A = 0 \lor A = 1) \land$ empty$]_A$, we have two value traces 0 and 1, but they do not share a common prefix.

- not $\ddagger [A = 0 \wedge \mathsf{skip}]_A$, we have for instance value traces $0, 0$ and $0, 1$ but when their length are the same they ought to agree on all values and this does not hold as they disagree in the second state.
- not $\ddagger [\mathsf{skip}]_A$, A does not appear in the formula so values of A are not constrained at all, one has value trace $0, 0$ and $1, 0$ and these do not share a common prefix.

The following theorem states that the combination of satisfiability with the notion of common prefix value trace can be used to determine whether a formula is executable or not, i.e., satisfiable and deterministic.

Theorem 2. *Let* Spec *be a formula and* $\bar{v}$ *be a list of variables. If* $\vDash \mathsf{Spec}$ *and* $\ddagger[\mathsf{Spec}]_{\bar{v}}$ *then for all* $k \geq 0$ $\#\{(\mathsf{map}\ (\lambda s.\overline{s(v)})\ \sigma) \mid \mathsf{M}[\![\mathsf{Spec}]\!](\sigma) = tt\ and\ |\sigma| = k\} \leq 1$.

In above theorem we have that all satisfying intervals of length k will corresponds to at most one value trace.

The notion of common prefix value trace corresponds to the notion of generating a satisfying interval for a formula but it "limits" how this is achieved, i.e., one proceeds in a forward manner by extending at the right and therefore no backtracking will be used. The following definition introduces the notion of forward executability.

Definition 3. *Let* Spec *be a formula and* $\bar{v}$ *a list of variables.* Spec *is forward executable wrt* $\bar{v}$ *denoted by* $\dagger[\mathsf{Spec}]_{\bar{v}}$ *if and only if* $\vDash \mathsf{Spec}$ *and* $\ddagger[\mathsf{Spec}]_{\bar{v}}$.

In Tempura [9], the executable subset of ITL, a formula Spec is rewritten into a normal form $\mathsf{init}\ w_0 \wedge^{\circledcirc} \mathsf{Spec}_0$. The $\mathsf{init}\ w_0$ represents the initial state and $^{\circledcirc} \mathsf{Spec}_0$ represents the behaviour of the system from the next state onward but only if there is a next state. This process is repeated for formula Spec_0, i.e., it is rewritten to $\mathsf{init}\ w_1 \wedge^{\circledcirc} \mathsf{Spec}_1$. This process of rewriting into normal form corresponds to our notion of forward executability. This is expressed in the following theorem.

Theorem 3. *Given formulae* w *and* Spec *and a list of variables* $\bar{v}$. *If* $\dagger[\mathsf{init}\ \mathsf{w} \wedge \mathsf{empty}]_{\bar{v}}$ *and* $\dagger[\mathsf{Spec}]_{\bar{v}}$ *then* $\dagger[\mathsf{init}\ \mathsf{w} \wedge^{\circledcirc} \mathsf{Spec}]_{\bar{v}}$.

In Example 2 we have seen that one needs to be careful in adding constructs that limit the length of an interval. The following theorem gives conditions for which it is safe to do so.

Theorem 4. *Let* Spec_0 *and* Spec_1 *be formula and* $\bar{v}$ *be a list of variables. If* $\vDash \mathsf{Spec}_0 \wedge \mathsf{Spec}_1$ *and* $\ddagger[\mathsf{Spec}_0]_{\bar{v}}$ *then* $\dagger[\mathsf{Spec}_0 \wedge \mathsf{Spec}_1]_{\bar{v}}$.

In this theorem formula Spec_0 ensures that the values for $\bar{v}$ are deterministic and formula Spec_1 is used to put extra constraints on the intervals satisfying Spec_0. The $\vDash \mathsf{Spec}_0 \wedge \mathsf{Spec}_1$ condition ensures that we have at least one such interval. Examples of such Spec_1 are $\mathsf{len}\,(k)$, $\Diamond\,\mathsf{init}\ w$ and $\mathsf{halt}\ w$. On their own these formulae are not forward executable but combined with a forward executable one they will be.

4.2 Backward Executability

We now investigate reversing executable specifications. Reflection relates the notion of prefix intervals with that of suffix intervals. So we need to introduce the "mirror image" of common prefix value traces, i.e. the notion of common suffix value trace.

The following definition is a constraint on the intervals which satisfy a formula. Only intervals that share a common suffix of the value trace are allowed.

Definition 4. *A formula* Spec *has a common suffix value trace wrt a list of variables* $\bar{v}$ *denoted by* $\natural[\text{Spec}]_{\bar{v}}$ *if and only if for all intervals* σ *and* σ' *if* $M[\![\text{Spec}]\!](\sigma) = tt$ *and* $M[\![\text{Spec}]\!](\sigma') = tt$ *and* $|\sigma| \le |\sigma'|$ *then* $(\text{map } (\lambda s.\overline{s(v)})) \sigma) = (\text{map } (\lambda s.\overline{s(v)})) (\sigma'_{|\sigma'|-|\sigma|} \cdots \sigma'_{|\sigma'|}))$.

The following example illustrates this notion.

Example 3. The following are some formula that have a common suffix value trace.

- $\natural[(\text{fin } A) = 0 \wedge \text{empty}]_A$, there is only one value trace 0.
- $\natural[\Box(A = 0)]_A$, the possible value traces are $0; 0, 0; 0, 0, 0$. Each pair of value traces share a common suffix.

The following are some formula that have no common suffix value trace.

- not $\natural[(A = 0 \vee A = 1) \wedge \text{empty}]_A$, we have two value traces 0 and 1, but they do not share a common suffix.
- not $\natural[(\text{fin } A) = 0 \wedge \text{skip}]_A$, we have for instance value traces $0, 0$ and $1, 0$ but when their length are the same they ought to agree on all values and this does not hold as they disagree in the first state.
- not $\natural[\text{skip}]_A$, A does not appear in the formula so values of A are not constrained at all, one has value trace $0, 0$ and $0, 1$ and these do not share a common suffix.

The following lemma states the relationship between common prefix, common suffix and reflection.

Lemma 1. *Let* Spec *be formula and* $\bar{v}$ *be a list of variables then* $\ddagger[\text{Spec}^r]_{\bar{v}}$ *iff* $\natural[\text{Spec}]_{\bar{v}}$ *and* $\natural[\text{Spec}^r]_{\bar{v}}$ *iff* $\ddagger [\text{Spec}]_{\bar{v}}$.

For the notion of satisfiability we have the following lemma.

Lemma 2. *Let* Spec *be a formula then* $(\models \text{Spec}^r)$ *iff* $(\models \text{Spec})$.

The following theorem states that the combination of satisfiability with the notion of common suffix value trace can be used to determine whether a formula is deterministic or not, i.e., is backward executable or not.

Theorem 5. *Let* Spec *be a formula and* $\bar{v}$ *be a list of variables. If* $\models$ Spec *and* $\natural[\text{Spec}]_{\bar{v}}$ *then for all* $k \ge 0$ $\#\{(\text{map } (\lambda s.\overline{s(v)})) \sigma) \mid M[\![\text{Spec}]\!](\sigma) = tt \text{ and } |\sigma| = k\} \le 1$.

The notion of common suffix value trace corresponds to notion of generating a satisfying interval for a formula but it "limits" how this is achieved, i.e., one proceeds in a backward manner. The following definition introduces the notion of backward executability.

Definition 5. *Let* Spec *be a formula and* $\bar{v}$ *a list of variables.* Spec *is backward executable wrt to* $\bar{v}$ *denoted by* $\flat[\text{Spec}]_{\bar{v}}$ *if and only if* $\models$ Spec *and* $\natural[\text{Spec}]_{\bar{v}}$.

In Tempura we have unfortunately no rules for backward execution. But we can define a mirror image of Theorem 3, i.e., the normal form would be fin w $\wedge\ominus$ Spec. So we first generate the last state of the interval and then proceed to determine the previous state if there is any.

Theorem 6. *Given the formulae* w *and* Spec *and list of variables* $\bar{v}$. *If* $\flat[\text{fin w } \wedge$ $\text{empty}]_{\bar{v}}$ *and* $\flat[\text{Spec}]_{\bar{v}}$ *then* $\flat[\text{fin w } \wedge\ominus \text{Spec}]_{\bar{v}}$.

The following theorem is similar to Theorem 4.

Theorem 7. *Let* Spec_0 *and* Spec_1 *be formula and* $\bar{v}$ *be a list of variables. If* $\models \text{Spec}_0 \wedge \text{Spec}_1$ *and* $\natural[\text{Spec}_0]_{\bar{v}}$ *then* $\flat[\text{Spec}_0 \wedge \text{Spec}_1]_{\bar{v}}$.

4.3   Reversing the Effects of Bad Computations

In the introduction we have seen that we are interested in formulae of the form Good ; Bad ; (Bad)^r. We now investigate under which conditions can we forward execute Bad ; Bad^r. The chop operator is non-deterministic if the length of Bad is left unspecified, i.e., generally we have not † [Bad ; Bad^r]$_{\bar{v}}$. However, we can use Theorem 4 to strengthen Bad to Bad $\wedge$ len (k). We similarly strengthen the Bad^r to Bad^r $\wedge$ len (k) in order to ensure that we undone that specific bad computation Bad $\wedge$ len (k). Note that (Bad $\wedge$ len (k))^r is equivalent to Bad^r $\wedge$ len (k), this follows from the reflection laws. The following theorem gives the conditions necessary to "undo" a bad computation.

Theorem 8. *Let* Spec *be a formula and* $\bar{v}$ *be a list of variables. If* $\models$ Spec $\wedge$ len k *and* $\ddagger[\text{Spec}]_{\bar{v}}$ *and* $\natural[\text{Spec}]_{\bar{v}}$ *then* †[(Spec $\wedge$ len (k)) ; (Spec^r $\wedge$ len (k))]$_{\bar{v}}$ *and* $\flat[(\text{Spec}^r \wedge \text{len } (k)) ; (\text{Spec} \wedge \text{len } (k))]_{\bar{v}}$.

Notice that Spec needs to have both a common prefix value trace and a common suffix value trace. In the first case we proceed in a forward manner while in the second case in a backward manner.

5   Conclusion and Future Work

First order ITL is a flexible notation for specifying properties and behaviours of systems. Most imperative programming constructs can be specified by formulae in ITL. We have used the reflection operator for the specification of reversed behaviour of systems. It is shown that ITL is closed under this reflection operator which means that we can specify its reverse for any ITL formula. We have presented an extensive list of reflection laws that help in the construction of the reverse of an ITL formula. We have shown that when an ITL formula is forward and backward executable then one can indeed reverse its behaviour.

Future work consists of adding the backward execution mechanism to the Tempura tool. The reflection and reversal of event-based programs is another area of interest. In an event-based program, a trigger event causes a chain of reactions by a system. The occurrence of a trigger can not be reversed but the reaction by the system can be reversed. However, this reaction might include other triggers that will set off other chains of reactions. Determining this chain of reactions and reversing its effects are some of the challenges that need to be addressed.

References

1. The Isabelle Proof Assistant. https://isabelle.in.tum.de/. Accessed 26 Jan 2020
2. Bennett, C.H.: Logical reversibility of computation. IBM J. Res. Dev. **17**(6), 525–532 (1973)
3. Cau, A., Kuhn, S., Hoey, J.: Executable interval temporal logic specifications. https://arxiv.org/abs/2105.03375 (2021)
4. Cau, A., Moszkowski, B.: The ITL homepage. http://antonio-cau.co.uk/ITL/ (2019). Accessed 26 Jan 2020
5. Hoey, J., Ulidowski, I.: Reversible imperative parallel programs and debugging. In: Thomsen, M.K., Soeken, M. (eds.) RC 2019. LNCS, vol. 11497, pp. 108–127. Springer, Cham (2019). https://doi.org/10.1007/978-3-030-21500-2_7
6. Hoey, J., Ulidowski, I., Yuen, S.: Reversing parallel programs with blocks and procedures. EXPRESS/SOS **2018**, 69–86 (2018)
7. Lutz, C.: Janus: a time-reversible language. A letter to Dr. Landauer (1986). http://tetsuo.jp/ref/janus.pdf
8. Manna, Z., Pnueli, A.: The Temporal Logic of Reactive and Concurrent Systems: Specification. Springer, New York (1992). https://doi.org/10.1007/978-1-4612-0931-7
9. Moszkowski, B.: Executing Temporal Logic Programs. Cambridge University Press, Cambridge (1986)
10. Moszkowski, B.: Compositional reasoning using intervals and time reversal. Ann. Math. Artif. Intell. 175–250 (2013). https://doi.org/10.1007/s10472-013-9356-8
11. Perumalla, K.: Introduction to Reversible Computing. CRC Press, Boca Raton (2014)
12. Pnueli, A.: The temporal logic of programs. In: 18th Annual Symposium on Foundations of Computer Science (sfcs 1977), pp. 46–57, October 1977
13. Prior, A.N.: Diodoran modalities. Philos. Q. **5**(20), 205–213 (1955)
14. Ulidowski, I., Lanese, I., Schultz, U.P., Ferreira, C. (eds.): RC 2020. LNCS, vol. 12070. Springer, Cham (2020). https://doi.org/10.1007/978-3-030-47361-7
15. Zhou, S., Zedan, H., Cau, A.: Run-time analysis of time-critical systems. J. Syst. Archit. **51**(5), 331–345 (2005)

Circuit Synthesis

Efficient Construction of Functional Representations for Quantum Algorithms

Lukas Burgholzer[1(✉)], Rudy Raymond[2], Indranil Sengupta[3],
and Robert Wille[1,4]

[1] Institute for Integrated Circuits, Johannes Kepler University Linz, Linz, Austria
{lukas.burgholzer,robert.wille}@jku.at
[2] IBM Quantum, IBM Research, Tokyo, Japan
rudyhar@jp.ibm.com
[3] Indian Institute of Technology Kharagpur, Kharagpur, India
isg@iitkgp.ac.in
[4] Software Competence Center Hagenberg GmbH (SCCH), 4232 Hagenberg, Austria
https://iic.jku.at/eda/research/quantum

Abstract. Due to the significant progress made in the implementation of quantum hardware, efficient methods and tools to design corresponding algorithms become increasingly important. Many of these tools rely on functional representations of certain building blocks or even entire quantum algorithms which, however, inherently exhibit an exponential complexity. Although several alternative representations have been proposed to cope with this complexity, the *construction* of those representations remains a bottleneck. In this work, we propose solutions for *efficiently constructing* representations of quantum functionality based on the idea of conducting as many operations as possible on as small as possible intermediate representations—using Decision Diagrams as a representative functional description. Experimental evaluations show that applying these solutions allows to construct the desired representations several factors faster than with state-of-the-art methods. Moreover, if repeating structures (which frequently occur in quantum algorithms) are explicitly exploited, exponential improvements are possible—allowing to construct the functionality of certain algorithms within seconds, whereas the state of the art fails to construct it in an entire day.

1 Introduction

Quantum computing promises to outperform classical computers in certain applications. While the theoretical background was already developed in the previous century, it is today that actual physical devices are evolving to a point where first experiments are performed that are suggested not to be easy on a classical computer. However, having hardware without efficient tools to design corresponding algorithms on it certainly presents an unsatisfactory situation. Accordingly, researchers and engineers started to develop methods and tools for important

S. Yamashita and T. Yokoyama (Eds.): RC 2021, LNCS 12805, pp. 227–241, 2021.
https://doi.org/10.1007/978-3-030-79837-6_14

tasks such as synthesis/compilation [1–5], (classical) simulation [6–8], and verification [9–12]—leading to elaborate design flows and tool chains as realized, e.g., by IBM's Qiskit [13], Google's Cirq [14], and Microsoft's QDK [15].

These tools and the corresponding design tasks, however, frequently rely on representations of certain building blocks' functionality or even the functionality of an entire quantum algorithm. This poses a severe challenge since quantum functionality is most generally described by matrices of exponential dimension with respect to the size of the quantum system, i.e., $2^n \times 2^n$ for a system consisting of n qubits (the quantum analogue to bits). To date, industrial tool chains like IBM's Qiskit hardly offer efficient and scaleable solutions for constructing and representing quantum functionality (as witnessed by the evaluations later in Sect. 5).

Fortunately, different approaches have been proposed that try to deal with this complexity, e.g., based on arrays [16–19], tensor networks [20–23], and Decision Diagrams [24–26]. Although we may be able to represent (i.e., store) the overall functionality of certain building blocks or an entire quantum algorithm using these techniques, we may not be able to construct this representation in feasible time—which constitutes a severe bottleneck for many applications in the domain of quantum computing. This is caused by the fact that, even though individual quantum operations typically emit a sparse, tensor product structure, their composition requires subsequent *matrix-matrix* multiplications—leading to a potential decrease in sparsity and/or exploitable structure. Hence, many computations on potentially large intermediate representations have to be conducted in order to construct the overall functional representation.

In this paper, we propose two solutions to overcome this bottleneck—using Decision Diagrams (DDs) as a representative functional description. First, a general solution is presented which can be applied to arbitrary functionality and is based on the idea to conduct as many operations as possible on as small as possible intermediate representations. Besides that, another solution is proposed which explicitly exploits the fact that many quantum algorithms contain repeating structures (e.g., Grover iterations, random walks, etc.). In both cases, the complexity of constructing quantum functionality representations is substantially reduced—in case of the second solution even an exponential improvement is achieved.

Experimental evaluations eventually confirm the resulting benefits. They show that the proposed solutions allow to construct the desired representations several factors faster than with the current state of the art. If additionally repeating structures are exploited, representations for quantum algorithms and building blocks can be constructed in a matter of seconds which, using the current state of the art, could not be constructed in an entire day. The resulting implementation is available as open source at https://github.com/iic-jku/qfr.

The rest of this paper is structured as follows: Sect. 2 reviews the necessary basics on quantum computing and introduces the Quantum Fourier Transform, which will be used as a running example in this paper. In Sect. 3, we show the importance of the considered problem and review the state of the art—

illustrating the current bottleneck. Then, Sect. 4 introduces and describes the proposed solution which, afterwards, is evaluated in Sect. 5. Finally, Sect. 6 concludes the paper.

2   Background

In this section, we briefly review the key concepts of quantum computing as well as a typical building block for quantum algorithms which will serve as an example over the course of this paper. While the respective reviews are kept brief, we refer the interested reader to [27] for a more thorough treatment on quantum computing.

In classical computing, *bits* are used as the smallest computation unit— attaining values from the discrete set $\mathbb{B} = \{0,1\}$. In the field of quantum computing, these discrete values, denoted $|0\rangle$ and $|1\rangle$ using Dirac notation, are chosen as basis elements spanning a two-dimensional complex Hilbert space $\mathbb{H}$. Consequently, the state $|q\rangle$ of a *qubit* (the quantum analogue to the bit) is described by an element of this space, i.e., by a *superposition* of the basis states $|0\rangle$ and $|1\rangle$. More specifically, $|q\rangle = \alpha_0|0\rangle + \alpha_1|1\rangle$ with $\alpha_i \in \mathbb{C}$ such that $|\alpha|^2 = |\alpha_0|^2 + |\alpha_1|^2 = 1$.

A *quantum system* then consists of n qubits $q_0, \ldots, q_{n-1}$ described by the 2^n-dimensional Hilbert space $\mathbb{H} \otimes \cdots \otimes \mathbb{H}$. The state $|q\rangle_n$ of such a system is again described by amplitudes $\alpha_i \in \mathbb{C}$, where $|q\rangle_n = \sum_{i \in \{0,1\}^n} \alpha_i|i\rangle$ with $|\alpha|^2 = 1$. However, the amplitudes α_i of a quantum system are not directly observable. Instead, performing a *measurement* probabilistically collapses the qubits' state to one of the basis states $|i\rangle$ (each with probability $|\alpha_i|^2$).

The state of a quantum system is manipulated through unitary linear transformations $U \colon \mathbb{H} \otimes \cdots \otimes \mathbb{H} \to \mathbb{H} \otimes \cdots \otimes \mathbb{H}$, which are predominantly described by their unitary $2^n \times 2^n$ matrix representations[1] in the computational basis $\{|0\rangle, \ldots, |2^n - 1\rangle\}$. Usually, these *quantum operations* act only on a small subset of a system's qubits. Hence, their matrix representations have a sparse, tensor product structure, where the tensor product of smaller "operation matrices" with identity matrices is formed.

Example 1. Consider a quantum system consisting of $n = 3$ qubits. Then, Fig. 1a, Fig. 1b, and Fig. 1c show a few common quantum operations using their $2^3 \times 2^3$ sparse matrix representations—namely the Hadamard operation as well as the controlled-phase operations S and T, where $\omega = \exp(\frac{2\pi i}{8}) = \sqrt{i}$.

A *quantum algorithm* is described as a sequence of quantum operations applied to a quantum system, i.e., $G = g_0, \ldots, g_{m-1}$ denotes a quantum algorithm consisting of m operations where each g_i is described by a unitary matrix U_i. Since the composition of unitary transformations is again unitary, the functionality of a quantum algorithm may be interpreted as one unitary transformation itself. Consequently, the functionality is described by a unitary matrix U which arises from the *matrix-matrix* multiplication of the individual operation

---

[1] A complex-valued matrix U is unitary if $U^\dagger U = UU^\dagger = \mathbb{I}$, where $U^\dagger$ denotes the conjugate transpose of U and $\mathbb{I}$ the identity matrix.

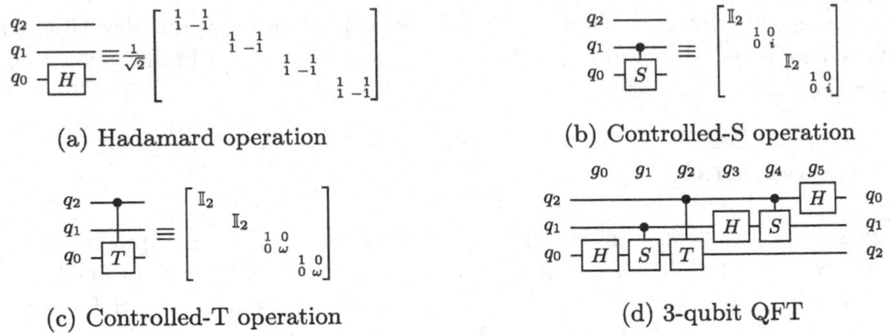

(a) Hadamard operation

(b) Controlled-S operation

(c) Controlled-T operation

(d) 3-qubit QFT

Fig. 1. Common quantum operations and the QFT in a 3-qubit system

matrices U_i, i.e., $U = U_{m-1} \cdots U_0$. Quantum algorithms are usually visualized as *quantum circuit diagrams* where wires indicate the individual qubits and operations (also called *gates*) are placed as boxes on these lines with corresponding identifiers. Time is assumed to progress from left to right.

In the following, quantum algorithms and quantum circuit diagrams will be illustrated by means of the *Quantum Fourier Transform* (QFT) [27]—a well-known building block in many important quantum algorithms. Its most prominent use probably is for period finding in Shor's algorithm for integer factorization [28] and many other group-theoretic problems (see Chapter 5 of [27]), at which exponential speed-ups over the best classical methods are demonstrated. QFT is also used in quantum approximate counting [29], which provides proven polynomial speed-ups over the best classical methods, i.e., Monte-Carlo-type estimators [30]. Such quantum Monte-Carlo algorithms are now popular candidates to achieve quantum advantage with near-term quantum devices [31].

Example 2. Consider a 3-qubit system as already discussed in Example 1. Then, Fig. 1d shows the quantum circuit for the 3-qubit Quantum Fourier Transform consisting of $m = 6$ gates in total. This circuit will be used as a running example for the further discussions throughout this work.

3   Representations for Quantum Algorithms

Working in the domain of quantum computing requires representations of certain building blocks or even entire quantum algorithms. This is evident, e.g., for typical tasks such as:

- *Synthesis/Compilation* [1–5], where an entire quantum algorithm is realized in terms of elementary quantum operations supported by the addressed quantum architecture. Without a proper representation of the algorithm's functionality, no synthesis/compilation approach can work.
- *(Classical) Simulation* [6–8], where a given quantum algorithm is "tested" on a classical machine prior to actual execution on a quantum computer.

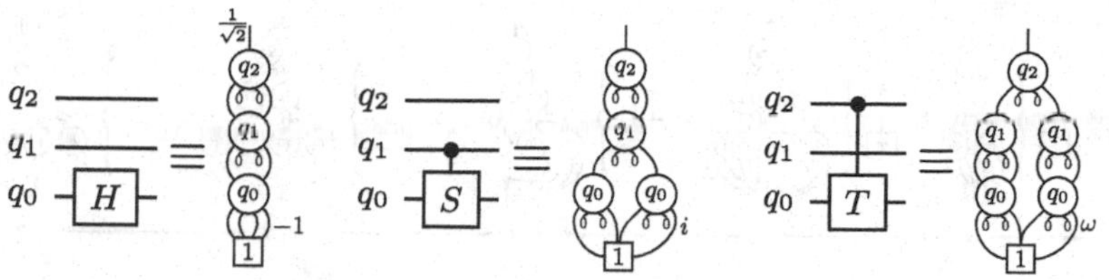

Fig. 2. Decision Diagrams for operations shown in Fig. 1a—1c

While this can be done using consecutive matrix-vector multiplication on the elementary gates, approaches based on *emulation* [32,33], which utilize functional representations of entire building blocks, have been shown to be much more efficient—provided the emulated functionality can be constructed efficiently.

- *Verification* [9–12], where, e.g., for two quantum circuits G and G' it should be checked whether they realize the same function—also referred to as *equivalence checking*. This obviously requires the construction of a functional representation for both functionalities in order to compare them.

In all these cases, having a representation of the considered functionality is essential. The first challenge resulting from that is that quantum functionality in general is described in terms of matrices with exponential size, i.e., for a functionality over n qubits, a matrix U of size $2^n \times 2^n$ results. In previous work, researchers already started to address this challenge, which led to different approaches exploiting certain structural elements of the considered functionality in order to reduce the exponential space complexity of its representation:

- *Array-based approaches* (such as proposed in [16–19]) heavily rely on the sparsity of the involved matrices and try to distribute the workload over several cores of supercomputers, which can often be done efficiently since the *matrix-multiplication* itself is inherently parallelizable.
- *Tensor Networks* (such as proposed in [20–23]) capitalize on the tensor product structure inherent to quantum operations—allowing to decompose the whole matrix into many smaller parts. Their performance typically scales with the degree of entanglement of the considered functionality.
- *Decision Diagrams* (DDs, such as proposed in [24–26]) recursively split the considered functionality into equally sized sub-matrices until only complex numbers remain. By identifying redundancies in these sub-parts and extracting common factors, equal sub-functionality can be shared—frequently leading to a compact representation in terms of directed acyclic graphs with edge-weights.

In the following, we will illustrate those endeavours using Decision Diagrams as a representative. However, the observations and findings discussed in this work apply to the other representations as well.

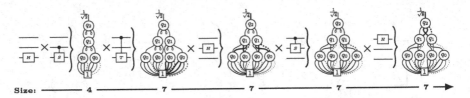

Size: ——————— 4 ——————— 7 ——————— 7 ——————— 7 ——————— 7 ——▶

Fig. 3. State-of-the-art DD composition sequence for 3-qubit QFT (see Fig. 1d)

Example 3. Consider again the quantum operations shown in Fig. 1. Their functionalities can be represented efficiently in terms of Decision Diagrams as shown in Fig. 2. As can be seen, they allow for a rather compact representation (3–5 nodes vs. 8–16 non-zero matrix entries).

Unfortunately, *constructing* those representations for certain building blocks or even entire quantum algorithms can often not be conducted efficiently—even if it is conceptionally simple[2]. In fact, as reviewed in Sect. 2, the functionality of a quantum algorithm (given by a quantum circuit $G = g_0, \ldots, g_{m-1}$) is described by the matrix $U = U_{m-1} \cdots U_0$, with U_i being the matrix corresponding to gate g_i (for $0 \leq i < m$). Hence, since the individual matrices U_i can usually be represented rather efficiently with either of the approaches reviewed above (arrays, tensor networks, DDs), simply conducting multiplications on those representations should allow for an efficient construction of the entire functional representation. But the more quantum operations are multiplied together, the more complex representations result—reducing the sparsity, increasing the degree of entanglement, or eliminating existing redundancies—and, hence, significantly slowing down the construction. Thus, while the multiplication operation itself is realized rather efficiently in general (utilizing, e.g., specialized techniques for sparse chain multiplication), the bottleneck arises from the consequences of consecutive multiplication.

Example 4. Consider again the circuit for the 3-qubit QFT from Fig. 1d. Constructing its functionality requires multiplying the individual representations of all 6 gates. The multiplication of two Decision Diagrams (representing matrices U and V) is recursively broken down into sub-expressions according to

$$\begin{bmatrix} U_{00} & U_{01} \\ U_{10} & U_{11} \end{bmatrix} \cdot \begin{bmatrix} V_{00} & V_{01} \\ V_{10} & V_{11} \end{bmatrix} = \begin{bmatrix} (U_{00}V_{00} + U_{01}V_{10}) & (U_{00}V_{01} + U_{01}V_{11}) \\ (U_{10}V_{00} + U_{11}V_{10}) & (U_{10}V_{01} + U_{11}V_{11}) \end{bmatrix},$$

until only operations on complex numbers remain. That results in a complexity which scales with the product of the number of nodes in the Decision Diagrams

---

[2] The authors want to point out that this construction task is conceptionally different from and should not be confused with the classical simulation of quantum circuits which aims to calculate the resulting state vector for one particular input and not the complete functionality.

to be multiplied. Carrying out all multiplications results in the evolution of representations as shown in Fig. 3[3]. While, as already shown by means of Fig. 2, the functionality of single operations can be represented compactly, the multiplication needed to construct the overall functionality quickly increases the complexity. In fact, after two multiplications, further computations have to be conducted on a representation as large as the final result.

Evaluations on larger examples than the one above confirm that, in many cases, we may be able to represent (i.e., store) the overall functionality of certain building blocks or an entire quantum algorithm (and use it for tasks such as synthesis/compilation, simulation, or verification), but we may not be able to construct this representation in feasible time. This constitutes a severe bottleneck for many applications in the domain of quantum computing.

4   Proposed Approaches

In order to overcome the bottleneck discussed in the previous section, we propose to approach the construction of functional representations for building blocks or entire quantum algorithms with different strategies. We distinguish thereby two use cases: First, a general construction scheme is presented which can be applied for arbitrary functionality. Afterwards, we present a second scheme which is dedicated to repeating structures as they frequently occur in quantum algorithms (e.g., by means of Grover iterations or quantum walks). The resulting schemes allow to speed up the construction of the desired functional representation considerably and even manage to complete the construction where existing methods time out.

4.1   General Scheme

The observations from Sect. 3 show that the bottleneck emerges as a result of a large number of matrix-matrix multiplications on rather large representations. Hence, in order to avoid this, we propose to conduct as many of those multiplications on as small as possible representations, e.g., on the original gate representations. Here, the fact that matrix multiplication is associative comes in handy as it allows to conduct those multiplications in a different order.

More precisely, assume, for sake of simplicity, that the number m of operations of a given building block or quantum algorithm is a power of two, i.e., $m = 2^k$ (for some $k \in \mathbb{N}$). Then, grouping the set of m operations into $m/2$ consecutive pairs, i.e.,

$$(U_{m-1} \cdot U_{m-2}) \cdot \ldots \cdot (U_3 \cdot U_2) \cdot (U_1 \cdot U_0) = U,$$

---

[3] Different edge weights are indicated by dotted ($\equiv$ negative) and/or colored ($\equiv 1, i,$ ω and ω^3) lines. This suffices to illustrate the evolution of the Decision Diagrams' size, i.e., their node count.

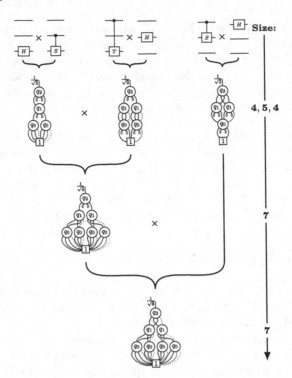

Fig. 4. Proposed approach applied to 3-qubit QFT

and performing the pairwise multiplications $(U_{i+1} \cdot U_i) = U_{i+1,i}$, leaves $m/2 = 2^{k-1}$ factors to be multiplied, i.e.,

$$U_{m-1,m-2} \cdot \ldots \cdot U_{1,0} = U.$$

Recursively applying this idea eventually results in the construction of the full functional representation $U \equiv U_{m-1,\ldots,0}$—requiring a total of k levels of pairwise grouping and multiplication. In case m is not a power of two, in some levels a pair may "degenerate" to a single operation.

Example 5. Consider again the circuit for the 3-qubit QFT from Fig. 1d. Conducting the operations according to the proposed scheme results in the evolution of representations as sketched in Fig. 4. As can be seen, this leads to a much more efficient construction compared to the current state-of-the-art method illustrated before in Example 4: While, thus far, the multiplications resulted in intermediate representations with 4, 7, 7, 7, and 7 nodes (see Fig. 3), now the construction results in Decision Diagrams with 4, 5, and 4 nodes (first level), 7 nodes (second level), as well as 7 nodes (third level). While the total number of operations (as well as the final result) is obviously the same, more matrix-matrix multiplications are conducted on smaller representations. Furthermore, while, for small examples as considered here, this difference might seem negligible, evaluations on larger quantum algorithms show that this change in the order of multiplications has a substantial effect on the efficiency of the construction.

In general, employing the proposed scheme creates a tree-like hierarchy of matrix compositions. In each level $l \in \{0, \ldots, k\}$, at most 2^l operations contribute to a specific group of compositions. As a consequence, the intermediate functionalities during the construction can frequently be represented in a much more compact fashion (since these remain rather compact and/or sparse in many cases)—leading to fewer multiplications involving large representations.

Clearly, associativity of matrix multiplication allows for partitioning schemes beyond pairwise grouping. Determining an optimal partitioning scheme can be related to finding an optimal contraction order of a tensor network (itself an NP-hard problem [34]). In this sense, the proposed scheme can be viewed as one possible heuristic of tackling the contraction problem for quantum circuits.

At a first glance, the proposed scheme merely trades runtime for space: many operations can be conducted on rather small intermediate representations. But, this requires to store a lot more intermediate results when compared to sequential approaches—specifically in the first level of the multiplication hierarchy, where $m/2$ Decision Diagrams have to be stored. However, as those "early" intermediate results correspond to circuits with very low depth, their representations are rather compact and frequently contain redundant subparts that can be shared[4]. Moreover, the proposed approach can be realized using a stack for the intermediate results containing at most $\mathcal{O}(\log m)$ elements at any given time by proceeding in a depth-first fashion.

4.2 Exploiting Repeating Structures

Besides the general scheme proposed above, the made observations and findings can further be tailored to repeating structures in quantum algorithms—allowing for even more improvements in the construction of functional representations. This is described in the following section. To this end, recall that many quantum algorithms rely on repeated building blocks realizing a certain kind of iteration, e.g., Grover's search algorithm [35], Quantum Random Walks [36], Amplitude Estimation [29], or Phase Estimation [37]. Usually this type of algorithms consists of an initialization phase and an iteration phase comprised of multiple (identical) iteration steps. Inspired by emulation techniques [32,33], the current state of the art accelerates the construction of the corresponding functional representation by constructing a single initialization matrix U_{init} followed by *multiple* multiplications with an iteration matrix U_{iter} (which has to be constructed only once), i.e., $(U_{iter} \cdot \ldots \cdot U_{iter}) U_{init} = U$.

This procedure can be drastically improved further by, first, efficiently constructing the individual representations for U_{init} and U_{iter} using the general

---

[4] Decision Diagram packages, e.g., typically employ a unique table where all nodes are stored [26]. Thus, even when multiple different Decision Diagrams are stored concurrently, sharing reduces the memory footprint considerably.

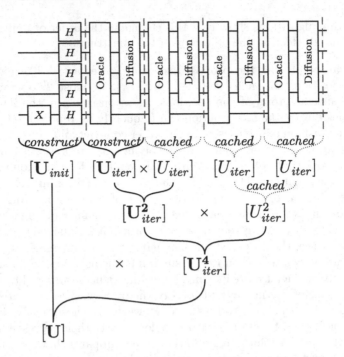

Fig. 5. Proposed strategy applied to Grover's algorithm

scheme proposed in Sect. 4.1 and, then, employing a binary exponentiation scheme for the sequence of multiplications involving U_{iter}. Assume, for sake of simplicity, that the number of iterations N is a power of two, i.e., $N = 2^k$ for some $k \in \mathbb{N}$. Then,

$$\overbrace{(U_{iter} \cdots U_{iter})}^{N} U_{init} = \overbrace{(U_{iter}^2 \cdots U_{iter}^2)}^{N/2} U_{init} = \ldots = U_{iter}^N U_{init} = U.$$

More precisely, once the iteration matrix U_{iter} has been efficiently constructed, it is sufficient to carry out only one multiplication $U_{iter}^{2^l} \cdot U_{iter}^{2^l} = U_{iter}^{2^{l+1}}$ (squaring the current representation) at each level $l \in \{0, \ldots, k-1\}$, since all other multiplications are going to have the same result. As a last step, the initialization matrix U_{init} is multiplied to U_{iter}^N—yielding the desired representation U. Hence, only $k = \log_2(N) + 1$ (instead of N) building block multiplications are required to construct the representation—an exponential reduction. In case N is not a power of two, at most one additional multiplication per level is necessary. Thus, even in this case $\mathcal{O}(\log N)$ building block multiplications are sufficient for the construction. As a matter of fact, this does not just reduce the number of multiplications exponentially, it also avoids many computations on potentially large representations.

Example 6. In order to illustrate the idea we consider an application of Grover's algorithm [35]. The algorithm can be used to search for a specific item in an unstructured set of N items by only querying a given (problem-specific) oracle $\mathcal{O}(\sqrt{N})$ times—a quadratic speed-up over classical methods. To this end, it uses $\log(N) + 1$ qubits and consists of (1) a small initialization phase which puts all qubits into an equal superposition (to be represented by U_{init}) and (2) multiple Grover iterations (to be represented by U_{iter}). A single Grover iteration consists of querying a given oracle and, afterwards, applying the diffusion operator—effectively increasing the probabilities of states matching the search criterion encoded in the oracle.

Now, consider for example the case $N = 16$. This entails $\log(N)+1 = 5$ qubits and approximately $\sqrt{16} = 4$ Grover iterations. By first constructing the matrices U_{init} and U_{iter} (using the scheme described in Sect. 4.1) and, then, applying the approach proposed above, an evolution of representations as shown in Fig. 5 results. Here, it can be seen that, at each level, only a single multiplication has to be carried out (while the other multiplications are functionally equivalent and, hence, can be cached/reused). Thus, only three building block multiplications are required in total, while any sequential approach would need four multiplications. Again, this might look negligible for this small example, but has substantial effect once larger instances are considered.

5   Experimental Evaluations

In order to experimentally evaluate the proposed approaches, we implemented them on top of the publicly-available JKQ-framework [38] which includes the decision diagram package described in [26] and the state-of-the-art construction approach from [24] as reviewed in Sect. 3 and illustrated in Example 4. The resulting implementation has been integrated into the framework and is available at https://github.com/iic-jku/qfr. Afterwards, we used the resulting implementation to construct representations for the functionality of

- the Quantum Fourier Transform, as a representative for a common building block in quantum algorithms such as Shor's algorithm for integer factorization [28],
- Grover's search algorithm [35], as a representative of an algorithm containing repeated building blocks.

All computations have been performed on a machine with an Intel i7-6700K processor and 16 GiB RAM running macOS 11.2. The obtained results have been split into two parts and are shown in Table 1. In all tables, n and m denote the number of qubits and the number of gates, respectively. Furthermore, the runtime (in CPU seconds) as well as the total memory allocation (in GiB) needed to construct the respective representation is listed for

- the current state-of-the-art approach [24],
- the respective proposed techniques, i.e., the general scheme from Sect. 4.1 in Table 1a and the dedicated scheme for repeated structures from Sect. 4.2 in Table 1b.

Table 1. Experimental results

(a) Results for the QFT						(b) Results for Grover's algorithm					
QFT		State of the art [24]		Prop. scheme Sect. 4.1		Grover		State of the art [24]		Prop. scheme 4.2	
n	m	t_{sota}	mem_{sota}	t_{prop}	mem_{prop}	n	m	t_{sota}	mem_{sota}	t_{prop}	mem_{prop}
12	84	0.03	0.07	**0.01**	0.07	12	1741	0.02	0.07	**0.01**	0.07
13	97	0.03	0.07	**0.02**	0.07	13	2614	0.02	0.07	**0.01**	0.07
14	112	0.05	0.08	**0.02**	0.07	14	3991	0.05	0.07	**0.01**	0.07
15	127	0.15	0.09	**0.04**	0.08	15	6076	0.09	0.08	**0.01**	0.07
16	144	0.37	0.09	**0.09**	0.09	16	9105	0.26	0.09	**0.02**	0.07
17	161	1.01	0.10	**0.25**	0.10	17	13686	0.34	0.08	**0.03**	0.07
18	180	3.79	0.11	**1.35**	0.12	18	20467	3.46	0.10	**0.03**	0.07
19	199	10.05	0.16	**3.02**	0.18	19	30572	3.84	0.10	**0.04**	0.07
20	220	14.72	0.20	**4.08**	0.23	20	45541	26.29	0.10	**0.05**	0.08
21	241	21.01	0.23	**7.12**	0.29	21	67558	68.50	0.10	**0.05**	0.08
22	264	27.04	0.27	**10.79**	0.33	22	100079	361.23	0.11	**0.07**	0.09
23	287	33.42	0.31	**13.49**	0.39	23	147960	>24.00 h	—	**0.08**	0.09
24	312	39.83	0.34	**14.58**	0.39	24	218425	>24.00 h	—	**0.12**	0.10
25	337	46.48	0.38	**18.76**	0.43	25	321726	>24.00 h	—	**0.15**	0.12

n: Number of qubits m: Number of gates t: Runtime in CPU seconds [s]
mem: Total memory allocations [GiB]

The results for the QFT, which was used as a running example throughout this paper, clearly show that, compared to the current state of the art, the proposed method manages to construct the algorithm's functionality 3.0× faster on average (and up to 4.2× faster). On the one hand this shows that conducting as many operations as possible on as small as possible intermediate representations indeed pays off. On the other hand, it confirms the discussion from Sect. 4.1 that although the proposed technique requires to store more representations at the same time, possible redundancies/sharing can explicitly be exploited.

Drastic improvements can be achieved for quantum algorithms containing repeated structures for which the dedicated approach from Sect. 4.2 can be used. This is confirmed by the numbers provided in Table 1b: Here, the state-of-the-art method required 6 min to construct a representation for the Grover functionality for $n = 22$ and failed to construct the functionality at all within 24 h for larger instances. In contrast, the proposed approach managed to construct the functionality in *all* these cases within fractions of a second.

In a final series of evaluations, we aimed to compare the proposed techniques to IBM's toolchain Qiskit [13], specifically the CPU backend of the Qiskit Aer *UnitarySimulator* in version 0.7.1 which uses a multi-threaded array-based technique for constructing the functionality of a given circuit. The results for both the QFT as well as the Grover benchmarks are shown in Table 2. Even for moderately sized instances, we observed runtimes more than two orders of magnitude longer when compared to the technique from [24] or the techniques proposed in this paper. In addition, IBM's approach requires exponential amount of memory—leading to memory outs when considering more than 15 qubits while the proposed techniques easily allow to construct the functionality of circuits with more than 20 qubits.

Table 2. Comparison to IBM Qiskit [13]

QFT		IBM qiskit		Grover		IBM qiskit	
n	m	t	mem	n	m	t	mem
12	84	1.80	0.25	10	731	16.70	0.09
13	97	7.90	1.04	11	1 112	98.90	0.19
14	112	36.00	3.92	12	1 741	996.38	0.28
15	127	146.00	15.97	13	2 614	11 336.69	1.03
16	144	—	MemOut	14	3 991	>24.00 h	3.93
17	161	—	MemOut	15	6 076	>24.00 h	15.94
18	180	—	MemOut	16	9 105	—	MemOut
19	199	—	MemOut	17	13 686	—	MemOut

n: Number of qubits m: Number of gates t: Runtime in CPU seconds [s] mem: Total memory allocations [GiB]

6   Conclusion

In this work, we addressed the issue of constructing the functional representation of certain building blocks or even entire quantum circuits. Existing approaches for solving this task are severely limited by the rapidly growing size of intermediate representations during the construction. By conducting as many operations as possible on as small as possible intermediate representations, the solutions proposed in this paper manage to consistently outperform existing approaches— allowing to construct the desired representations several factors faster than with the state of the art. Moreover, in case repeating structures are explicitly exploited, the construction of the representation for certain prominent quantum algorithms can be completed within seconds, whereas state-of-the-art approaches fail to construct it within an entire day. The comparison with IBM's Qiskit has shown that industrial tools for quantum computing are still in their infancy and would greatly benefit from the integration of existing techniques for efficiently constructing functional representations of quantum circuits—and even more so the techniques proposed in this work.

Acknowledgments. This project has received funding from the European Research Council (ERC) under the European Union's Horizon 2020 research and innovation programme (grant agreement No. 101001318). It has partially been supported by the LIT Secure and Correct Systems Lab funded by the State of Upper Austria as well as by the BMK, BMDW, and the State of Upper Austria in the frame of the COMET program (managed by the FFG).

References

1. Niemann, P., Wille, R., Drechsler, R.: Improved synthesis of Clifford+T quantum functionality. In: Design, Automation and Test in Europe, pp. 597–600 (2018)

2. Zulehner, A., Paler, A., Wille, R.: An efficient methodology for mapping quantum circuits to the IBM QX architectures. IEEE Trans. CAD Integrated Circuits Syst. **38**(7), 1226–1236 (2019)
3. Zulehner, A., Wille, R.: Compiling SU(4) quantum circuits to IBM QX architectures. In: Asia and South Pacific Design Automation Conference, Tokyo, Japan, pp. 185–190 (2019)
4. Itoko, T., Raymond, R., Imamichi, T., Matsuo, A., Cross, A.W.: Quantum circuit compilers using gate commutation rules. In: Asia and South Pacific Design Automation Conference, pp. 191–196 (2019)
5. Smith, K.N., Thornton, M.A.: Quantum logic synthesis with formal verification. In: IEEE International Midwest Symposium Circuits System, pp. 73–76 (2019)
6. Zulehner, A., Wille, R.: Advanced simulation of quantum computations. IEEE Trans. CAD Integrated Circuits Syst. **38**(5), 848–859 (2019)
7. Pednault, E., Gunnels, J.A., Nannicini, G., Horesh, L., Wisnieff, R.: Leveraging secondary storage to simulate deep 54-qubit Sycamore circuits. arXiv:1910.09534 (2019)
8. Villalonga, B., et al.: A flexible high-performance simulator for verifying and benchmarking quantum circuits implemented on real hardware. Npj Quantum Inf. **5**(1), 1–16 (2019)
9. Viamontes, G.F., Markov, I.L., Hayes, J.P.: Checking equivalence of quantum circuits and states. In: International Conference on CAD (2007)
10. Yamashita, S., Markov, I.L.: Fast equivalence-checking for quantum circuits. In: International Symposium on Nanoscale Architectures (2010)
11. Burgholzer, L., Raymond, R., Wille, R.: Verifying results of the IBM Qiskit quantum circuit compilation flow. arXiv: 2009.02376 [quant-ph] (2020)
12. Burgholzer, L., Wille, R.: Advanced equivalence checking for quantum circuits. IEEE Trans. CAD Integrated Circuits Syst. **PP**(99), 1 (2021)
13. Aleksandrowicz, G., et al.: Qiskit: an open-source framework for quantum computing, Zenodo (2019)
14. Cirq: A python framework for creating, editing, and invoking Noisy Intermediate Scale Quantum (NISQ) circuits. https://github.com/quantumlib/Cirq
15. Quantum Development Kit, Microsoft. https://microsoft.com/en-us/quantum/development-kit
16. Gutiérrez, E., Romero, S., Trenas, M.A., Zapata, E.L.: Quantum computer simulation using the CUDA programming model. Comput. Phys. Commun. **181**(2), 283–300 (2010)
17. Guerreschi, G.G., Hogaboam, J., Baruffa, F., Sawaya, N.P.D.: Intel Quantum Simulator: A cloud-ready high-performance simulator of quantum circuits. Quantum Sci. Technol. **5**, 034 007 (2020)
18. Jones, T., Brown, A., Bush, I., Benjamin, S.C.: QuEST and high performance simulation of quantum computers. In Scientific Reports (2018)
19. Gheorghiu, V.: Quantum++: a modern C++ quantum computing library. PLOS ONE **13**(12) (2018)
20. Markov, I.L., Shi, Y.: Simulating quantum computation by contracting tensor networks. SIAM J. Comput. **38**(3), 963–981 (2008)
21. Wang, D.S., Hill, C.D., Hollenberg, L.C.L.: Simulations of Shor's algorithm using matrix product states. Quantum Inf. Process. **16**(7), 176 (2017)
22. Biamonte, J.D., Bergholm, V.: Tensor networks in a nutshell (2017). arXiv: 1708.00006
23. Kissinger, A., van de Wetering, J.: PyZX: large scale automated diagrammatic reasoning. Presented Quantum Phys. Logic **318**, 229–241 (2019)

24. Niemann, P., Wille, R., Miller, D.M., Thornton, M.A., Drechsler, R.: QMDDs: efficient quantum function representation and manipulation. IEEE Trans. CAD Integrated Circuits Syst. **35**(1), 86–99 (2016)
25. Wang, S.-A., Lu, C.-Y., Tsai, I.-M., Kuo, S.-Y.: An XQDD-based verification method for quantum circuits. In: IEICE Trans. Fundamentals, pp. 584–594 (2008)
26. Zulehner, A., Hillmich, S., Wille, R.: How to efficiently handle complex values? implementing decision diagrams for quantum computing. In: International Conference on CAD (2019)
27. Nielsen, M.A., Chuang, I.L.: Quantum Computation and Quantum Information. Cambridge University Press, Cambridge (2010)
28. Shor, P.W.: Polynomial-time algorithms for prime factorization and discrete logarithms on a quantum computer. SIAM J. Comput. **26**(5), 1484–1509 (1997)
29. Brassard, G., Høyer, P., Mosca, M., Tapp, A.: Quantum amplitude amplification and estimation. In: Quantum computation and information, ser. Contemp. Math. vol. 305 (2002)
30. Montanaro, A.: Quantum speedup of Monte Carlo methods. Proc. Royal Soc. A, 471 (2015)
31. Rebentrost, P., Gupt, B., Bromley, T.R.: Quantum computational finance: Monte Carlo pricing of financial derivatives. Phys. Rev. A **98**, (2018)
32. Steiger, D.S., Häner, T., Troyer, M.: ProjectQ: an open source software framework for quantum computing. Quantum **2**, 49 (2018)
33. Zulehner, A., Wille, R.: Matrix-Vector vs. matrix-matrix multiplication: potential in DD-based simulation of quantum computations. In: Design, Automation and Test in Europe (2019)
34. Chi-Chung, L., Sadayappan, P., Wenger, R.: On optimizing a class of multidimensional loops with reduction for parallel execution. Parallel Process. Lett. **07**(02), 157–168 (1997)
35. Grover, L.K.: A fast quantum mechanical algorithm for database search. In: Proceedings of the ACM, pp. 212–219 (1996)
36. Douglas, B.L., Wang, J.B.: Efficient quantum circuit implementation of quantum walks. Phys. Rev. A **79**(5), 052 335 (2009)
37. Kitaev, A.Y.: Quantum measurements and the abelian stabilizer problem. Electron. Colloq. Comput. Complex. **3**(3), 22 (1996)
38. Wille, R., Hillmich, S., Burgholzer, L.: JKQ: JKU tools for quantum computing. In: International Conference on CAD (2020)

Finding Optimal Implementations of Non-native CNOT Gates Using SAT

Philipp Niemann[1,2(✉)], Luca Müller[1,2], and Rolf Drechsler[1,2]

[1] Cyber-Physical Systems, DFKI GmbH, Bremen, Germany
{pniemann,lucam,drechsler}@uni-bremen.de
[2] Department of Computer Science, University of Bremen, Bremen, Germany

Abstract. Quantum computer architectures place restrictions on the availability of quantum gates. While single-qubit gates are usually available on every qubit, multi-qubit gates like the CNOT gate can only be applied to a subset of all pairs of qubits. Thus, a given quantum circuit usually needs to be transformed prior to its execution in order to satisfy these restrictions. Existing transformation approaches mainly focus on using SWAP gates to enable the realization of CNOT gates that are not natively available in the architecture. As the SWAP gate is a composition of CNOT and single-qubit Hadamard gates, such methods may not yield a minimal solution. In this work, we propose a method to find an optimal implementation of non-native CNOTs, i.e. using the minimal number of native CNOT and Hadamard gates, by using a formulation as a Boolean Satisfiability (SAT) problem. While straightforward representations of quantum states, gates and circuits require an exponential number of complex-valued variables, the approach makes use of a dedicated representation that requires only a quadratic number of variables, all of which are Boolean. As confirmed by experimental results, the resulting problem formulation scales considerably well—despite the exponential complexity of the SAT problem—and enables us to determine significantly improved realizations of non-native CNOT gates for the 16-qubit IBM QX5 architecture.

1 Introduction

Quantum computers [10] promise to have enormous computational power and, thus, to solve relevant problems significantly faster than their classical counterparts. In recent years, large efforts have been put on their development, but while their mathematical foundations have been widely explored and are mostly quite well understood, the physical realization currently provides the biggest obstacle preventing the widespread use of quantum computers.

While more and more powerful quantum computer architectures have been presented with increasing quantity and quality of the so-called qubits, the basic computational entities in quantum computing, one of the physical constraints that all these architectures have in common is the limited availability of quantum operations/gates. Typically, multi-qubit gates are much harder to realize than

© Springer Nature Switzerland AG 2021
S. Yamashita and T. Yokoyama (Eds.): RC 2021, LNCS 12805, pp. 242–255, 2021.
https://doi.org/10.1007/978-3-030-79837-6_15

single-qubit gates and in many cases there is only one multi-qubit gate natively available, namely the two-qubit controlled-NOT (CNOT) gate. As there are several universal gate libraries consisting of the CNOT gate and single-qubit gates only, e.g. the Clifford+T library [6], this still allows to perform arbitrary quantum computations. However, in various architectures, the CNOT is only available on a small subset of physically adjacent qubit pairs, which can make computations that require CNOT operations on distant qubits quite complex. Fortunately, there are ways to simulate these logical CNOTs at the physical level and transform a quantum circuit that contains non-native CNOTs to a quantum circuit containing only native gates and, thus, being ready for the execution on the targeted quantum architecture.

Many approaches to find efficient CNOT implementations have been suggested, e.g. in [3,4,15,17–19]. The underlying ideas of these solutions are to use so-called SWAP gates in order to swap the qubits which the CNOT is to be applied to, with ones that a CNOT is available for in the specific architecture, or to use templates of pre-computed sequences of native gates. Since the underlying problem has been shown to be NP-complete in [5], it is not surprising that most approaches do not aim to provide minimal solutions. In fact, only [17] aims for solutions with a minimal number of SWAP and Hadamard gates, but SWAP gates themselves are not elementary gates, but need to be realized as cascades of CNOT and Hadamard gates.

In contrast, we propose an algorithm that determines an optimal implementation of arbitrary non-native CNOT gates using any combination of Hadamard gates and CNOT gates that are native to the underlying architecture. To this end, we formulate the problem as an instance of the Boolean Satisfiability (SAT) problem. The algorithm makes use of the planning problem and constructs a propositional formula which, if satisfiable, provides an implementation for a specific CNOT gate. While the SAT problem itself is NP-complete and straightforward representations of quantum states, gates and circuits require an exponential number of complex-valued variables, the crucial trick here is to make use of a dedicated representation borrowed from the stabilizer circuit formalism [2] that requires only a quadratic number of Boolean variables.

Experimental evaluations of some quantum computer architectures show that the resulting problem formulation scales considerably well—despite the exponential complexity of the SAT problem. Our results indicate that SWAP-based approaches indeed do not yield such optimal solutions for many CNOT gates, as the proposed algorithm determined significantly more efficient implementations.

The remainder of this paper is structured as follows. The next section introduces notations and preliminaries needed in this paper. Section 3 discusses the considered problem and related work, followed by Sect. 4 presenting our approach to determining optimal implementations of non-native CNOT gates. Experimental results are presented in Sect. 5. Finally, the paper is concluded in Sect. 6.

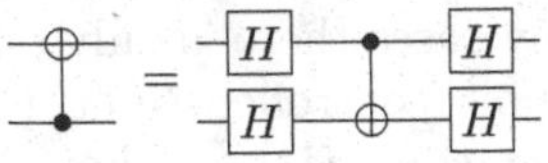

Fig. 1. Swapping control and target of a CNOT using Hadamard gates.

2   Background and Preliminaries

To keep the paper self-contained, this section briefly introduces the basics of quantum computation and the SAT problem.

2.1   Quantum States and Circuits

In contrast to classical bits which can only assume two discrete states, *qubits* can represent any combination of the classical Boolean values 0 and 1. More precisely, the state space of a qubit is a 2-dimensional Hilbert space such that all possible states can be written as $|\psi\rangle = a|0\rangle + b|1\rangle = \binom{a}{b}$ where $|0\rangle, |1\rangle$ denote the computational basis states (associated with the classical Boolean values) and $a, b \in \mathbb{C}$ are complex-valued numbers such that $|a|^2 + |b|^2 = 1$. Analogously, the state space of an n-qubit quantum system has 2^n basis states $(|0\ldots00\rangle, |0\ldots01\rangle, \ldots, |1\ldots11\rangle)$ and the state of such system can be described by a 2^n-dimensional complex-valued vector.

A quantum circuit is a model of quantum computation representing a sequence of quantum operations [10]. Each operation is a unitary transformation and is represented by a quantum gate. The operation of a quantum gate acting on n qubits is uniquely determined by a $2^n \times 2^n$ unitary matrix.

A *stabilizer circuit* is a quantum circuit consisting entirely of gates from the Clifford group which contains controlled-NOT ($CNOT$), Hadamard (H) and Phase (S) gates, represented by the following matrices:

$$CNOT = \begin{pmatrix} 1&0&0&0 \\ 0&1&0&0 \\ 0&0&0&1 \\ 0&0&1&0 \end{pmatrix}, \quad H = \frac{1}{\sqrt{2}}\begin{pmatrix} 1&1 \\ 1&-1 \end{pmatrix}, \quad S = \begin{pmatrix} 1&0 \\ 0&i \end{pmatrix}.$$

A CNOT on two qubits α and β, denoted as CNOT(α, β), performs a NOT operation on the target qubit β if, and only if, the control qubit α is in the $|1\rangle$-state.

Example 1. The left-hand side of Fig. 1 shows the circuit notation of a CNOT. Horizontal lines denote the qubits, the control qubit connection is indicated by a small, filled circle and the target qubit is illustrated by $\oplus$. As shown on the right-hand side, control and target of a CNOT can be swapped by applying Hadamard gates before and after the CNOT gate.

A *stabilizer state* is any quantum state which can be obtained by applying a stabilizer circuit to the initial state $|0\rangle^{\oplus n} = |0\ldots00\rangle$. Stabilizer circuits are not universal, which means that they cannot conduct all quantum computations. Nonetheless, stabilizer circuits are used in quantum error-correction and many other applications (see [10, Section 10.5.1] for more information).

The advantage stabilizer circuits offer is their efficient simulation on a classical computer, according to the Gottesman-Knill theorem. As shown in [2], a stabilizer state on n qubits as described above can be represented by $n(2n + 1)$ binary values, instead of 2^n complex numbers representing the vector which fully describes a quantum state. It can be visualized by a $(2n + 1) \times 2n$ matrix, called *tableau*, containing the Boolean variables $x_{i,j}$, $z_{i,j}$, and r_i for all $i \in \{1, ..., 2n\}$ and $j \in \{1, ..., n\}$ (as shown in Fig. 2).

$$
\begin{pmatrix}
x_{11} & \cdots & x_{1n} & z_{11} & \cdots & z_{1n} & r_1 \\
\vdots & \ddots & \vdots & \vdots & \ddots & \vdots & \vdots \\
x_{n1} & \cdots & x_{nn} & z_{n1} & \cdots & z_{nn} & r_n \\
x_{(n+1)1} & \cdots & x_{(n+1)n} & z_{(n+1)1} & \cdots & z_{(n+1)n} & r_{n+1} \\
\vdots & \ddots & \vdots & \vdots & \ddots & \vdots & \vdots \\
x_{(2n)1} & \cdots & x_{(2n)n} & z_{(2n)1} & \cdots & z_{(2n)n} & r_{2n}
\end{pmatrix}
$$

Fig. 2. Tableau representing a stabilizer state [2]

Applications of quantum gates are conducted by updating these tableau entries in polynomial time by means of the following Boolean formulae:

– For a CNOT from control α to target β:

$$\forall i \in 1, ..., 2n : r_i := r_i \oplus x_{i\alpha} z_{i\beta}(x_{i\beta} \oplus z_{i\alpha} \oplus 1);$$
$$x_{i\beta} := x_{i\beta} \oplus x_{i\alpha}; \; z_{i\alpha} := z_{i\alpha} \oplus z_{i\beta}$$

– For a Hadamard gate on qubit α:

$$\forall i \in 1, ..., 2n : r_i := r_i \oplus x_{i\alpha} z_{i\alpha}; \; x_{i\alpha} := z_{i\alpha}; \; z_{i\alpha} := x_{i\alpha}$$

– For a Phase gate on qubit α:

$$\forall i \in 1, ..., 2n : r_i := r_i \oplus x_{i\alpha} z_{i\alpha}; \; z_{i\alpha} := z_{i\alpha} \oplus x_{i\alpha}$$

This simulation is apparently much more efficient than a matrix-vector multiplication of the state vector with the transformation matrix of the given gate.

2.2 SAT and Planning

The *Boolean Satisfiability Problem*, abbreviated SAT, addresses the following:

Given a Boolean formula ϕ over n variables, does a mapping v from the variables to the Boolean truth values $\{0, 1\}$ exist, such that $\phi(v) = 1$?

Example 2. Consider the following Boolean formula given in Conjunctive Normal Form (CNF):

$$\phi = (a \vee \neg b \vee c) \wedge (\neg a \vee b \vee c) \wedge (\neg a \vee \neg c) \wedge \neg c$$

Because of the last clause $\neg c$, c must be 0 for ϕ to evaluate to 1. This means that the third clause is also 1. We are now left with the sub-formula $(a \vee \neg b) \wedge (\neg a \vee b)$, which is 1 if $a \mapsto 1$ and $b \mapsto 1$, or if $a \mapsto 0$ and $b \mapsto 0$. Thus, ϕ is satisfiable and $v = \{a \mapsto 1, b \mapsto 1, c \mapsto 0\}$ is one mapping that satisfies ϕ.

SAT is an NP-complete problem, as proven by [7] and many reasoning engines have been developed in order to solve SAT for arbitrary Boolean formulae. One application for SAT is the planning problem, which is described in [14]. An instance $\pi = <A, I, O, G>$ of the planning problem consists of the set of state variables A, the initial state I, the operators O and the goal state G. In essence, the problem is to find a sequence of operators that transform a system from an initial state to a defined goal state. It can be expressed as a propositional formula $\phi(t)$, so that ϕ is satisfiable if, and only if, there exists a sequence of actions of length t, so that the system is transformed from the initial state to its goal state. This allows us to conveniently solve the planning problem, by testing ϕ for satisfiability.

3   Considered Problem

Finding optimal implementations for all CNOT gates of a given quantum computer architecture is essential in order to improve the performance of algorithms that are run on said hardware, as every additional gate increases execution time and the probability of errors. If we define the cost of a CNOT gate to be the number t of gates which are native to the architecture that have to be applied in order to realize that gate, we can find an optimal implementation for a particular CNOT by determining the minimum value for t. For available gates like Hadamard gates and native CNOT gates, this cost will obviously be 1, while others will be far beyond that. For instance, the best-known realization of several CNOTs in the IBM QX5 architecture have a cost of more than 50 gates as determined by [3]. One reason this is an important problem is that native/physical CNOTs are only scarcely available in many quantum computer architectures.

Considering IBM's QX5 architecture, which is part of the *IBM Q* project available at [1], only 22 CNOTs are native to the architecture, as illustrated in Fig. 3. More precisely, an arrow between two qubits indicates that the CNOT gate whose control qubit is at the base of the arrow and whose target qubit is at the tip of the arrow is natively available. For instance, CNOT($Q1$, $Q2$), i.e. a CNOT with control on $Q1$ and target on $Q2$ is available on QX5, but not vice versa.

However, there are $\binom{16}{2} \cdot 2 = 240$ logical CNOTs for this 16-qubit system and $\binom{n}{2} \cdot 2$ in the general case of an n-qubit system, which need to be emulated to implement arbitrary quantum algorithms.

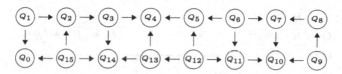

Fig. 3. IBM QX5 architecture.

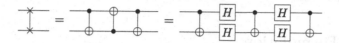

Fig. 4. SWAP gate realized by Clifford group gates.

Existing approaches for the efficient realization of non-native CNOTs have mainly focused on inserting SWAP gates, which are compositions consisting of CNOT and Hadamard gates as shown in Fig. 4. To illustrate this idea, consider the realization of a $CNOT(Q3, Q0)$ in IBM QX5. In order to implement this non-native CNOT, one could simply swap $Q3$ with $Q2$ and $Q2$ with $Q1$ using SWAP gates, transferring the state of $Q3$ to that of $Q1$, then apply the native $CNOT(Q1, Q0)$, and finally undo the SWAPs to restore the original positions of $Q1, Q2$, and $Q3$. However, each SWAP introduces an additional cost of 7 gates (c.f. Fig. 4) resulting in a total cost of $4 \cdot 7 + 1 = 29$ gates, but complete SWAPs may not be required. Almeida et al. [3] identified several movements of control and target qubits which can be realized with reduced costs—resulting in a realization of $CNOT(Q3, Q0)$ using only 20 gates (shown in Fig. 5).

As proven in [5], the underlying problem, like SAT, is NP-complete, which lead the authors of [17] to propose a SAT-based approach for determining the minimal number of SWAP and Hadamard gates given that the Hadamard gates are only used within SWAP gates or to invert the direction of a native CNOT. On the one hand, this limitation simplifies the problem to a purely classical-combinatorial problem and eliminates all aspects of quantum computations. On the other hand, the optimized movements in [3] suggest that it is likely to obtain further reductions if one allows for an unrestricted use of Hadamard and CNOT gates. However, this generalization significantly increases the search space which then also includes quantum circuits realizing true quantum operations and, thus, poses severe obstacles to their representation and the formulation as a SAT problem.

Luckily, CNOT and Hadamard gates do not unleash the full power of quantum computation that would require exponentially large complex-valued vectors and matrices to be dealt with, but only give rise to stabilizer circuits for which the polynomial size *tableau* representation can be employed that consists of Boolean variables only. As we will describe in the next section, this allows to use the planning problem as convenient way to express a quantum circuit as a propositional formula $\phi(t)$ to be solved for satisfiability.

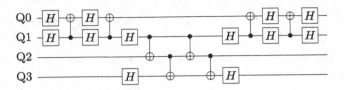

Fig. 5. Realization of CNOT($Q3, Q0$) in IBM QX5 according to [3].

4   SAT Formulation

To determine optimal implementations for non-native CNOTs, we formulate an instance π =$<A, I, O, G>$ of the planning problem and then convert it into a propositional formula $\phi(t)$ for a given number t, as explained in [14]. This formula shall be satisfiable if, and only if, there is a sequence of t native CNOT and Hadamard gates that realizes the desired non-native CNOT.

In the context of the considered stabilizer circuits, the initial state I of the planning problem is an arbitrary stabilizer state $|\psi\rangle$, an operator $o \in O$ represents a single quantum gate and the goal state G is the state $|\psi\rangle$ is transformed to after the application of the non-native CNOT for which we want to find an optimal implementation. The set A of state variables contains all Boolean variables that make up the tableau for a stabilizer state as reviewed in Sect. 2.1, namely x_{ij}, z_{ij}, and r_i for $i = 1, \ldots, 2n$ and $j = 1, \ldots, n$.

With the knowledge of how π can represent a stabilizer circuit in mind, we can now construct ϕ by considering I, O and G individually.

Constructing the Initial State I. The initial state is simply encoded as the conjunction over A^0 in the initial state of the system: $\bigwedge_{a \in A^0} a$. Note that the number in the superscript represents the number of operators which have been applied to the system so far, so A^0 represents the initial state, where no operators have been applied yet, while A^n represents the state after exactly n operators have been applied. For our purposes, the standard initial tableau as defined in [2] is used as the initial state, where $x_{ij}^0 = 1$ if $i = j$ and 0 otherwise, $z_{ij}^0 = 1$ if $i - n = j$ and 0 otherwise and all $r_{ij}^0 = 0$ (c.f. Fig. 6a for the case $n = 2$).

$$\begin{pmatrix} 1\,0 & 0\,0 & 0 \\ 0\,1 & 0\,0 & 0 \\ \hline 0\,0 & 1\,0 & 0 \\ 0\,0 & 0\,1 & 0 \end{pmatrix} \qquad \begin{pmatrix} 1\,1 & 0\,0 & 0 \\ 0\,1 & 0\,0 & 0 \\ \hline 0\,0 & 1\,0 & 0 \\ 0\,0 & 1\,1 & 0 \end{pmatrix}$$

(a) Initial tableau   (b) Goal state for CNOT(1,2)

Fig. 6. Tableaus for initial and goal state for $n = 2$ [2].

Constructing the Operators O. The operators are identified by the effect they have on a given state A to transform it into the successor state A'. These operators are the gates which are natively available in the specific architecture to be used, so while Hadamards may be used on all qubits, only some CNOTs are available. According to [14], any operator o is represented as follows:

$$\tau_o = p \wedge \bigwedge_{a \in A} [(EPC_a(o) \vee (a \wedge \neg EPC_{\neg a}(o))) \leftrightarrow a']$$

where p represents the operator's precondition, which needs to be 1 in order for the operator to be applicable.

For our purposes, the only condition is that a single quantum gate is to be applied by each action. In order to eliminate the possibility of two operators being applied at the same time, let the precondition p of an operator o be $\sigma_o \wedge \bigwedge_{q \in \{O \setminus \{o\}\}} \neg \sigma_q$, where the variable σ_o can later be used to identify which operators have been used, if ϕ is satisfiable.

$EPC_a(o)$ is the effect precondition of o on the state variable a. It corresponds to the formula which, if it evaluates to 1, sets the value of the literal a to 1. Since in our case the operators set a given state variable a to the binary value they evaluate to, we can prove that $\neg EPC_{\neg a}(o) = EPC_a(o)$. To this end, consider the effect the Hadamard gate on a qubit α has on the state variable r_i:
$\forall i \in \{1, ..., 2n\} : r_i := r_i \oplus x_{i\alpha} z_{i\alpha}$.

This means that for an arbitrary but fixed i, we have $EPC_{r_i}(o) = r_i \oplus x_{i\alpha} z_{i\alpha}$ and $EPC_{\neg r_i}(o) = \neg(r_i \oplus x_{i\alpha} z_{i\alpha})$. We can deduce that:

$$\neg(EPC_{\neg r_i}(o)) = \neg(\neg(r_i \oplus x_{i\alpha} z_{i\alpha}))$$
$$= r_i \oplus x_{i\alpha} z_{i\alpha}$$
$$= EPC_{r_i}(o)$$

This obviously also holds for all combinations of operators and state variables other than a Hadamard on qubit α and r_i. With this knowledge we can simplify the formula for τ_o:

$$\tau_o = p \wedge \bigwedge_{a \in A} [(EPC_a(o) \vee (a \wedge \neg EPC_{\neg a}(o))) \leftrightarrow a']$$
$$= p \wedge \bigwedge_{a \in A} [(EPC_a(o) \vee (a \wedge EPC_a(o))) \leftrightarrow a']$$
$$= p \wedge \bigwedge_{a \in A} EPC_a(o) \leftrightarrow a'$$

Note that for all state variables a which are unaffected by an operator o, $EPC_a(o)$ simply corresponds to a, making the given sub-formula for a: $a \leftrightarrow a'$.

Inserting our precondition p, an arbitrary operator o may be encoded as:

$$\tau_o = (\sigma_o \wedge \bigwedge_{q \in \{O \setminus \{o\}\}} \neg \sigma_q) \wedge (\bigwedge_{a \in A} EPC_a(o) \leftrightarrow a')$$

For any given step, the formula for choosing an operator to apply to a state A is represented as:

$$T(A, A') = \bigvee_{o \in O} \tau_o$$

Constructing the Goal State G. The goal state is again encoded as the conjunction over A^t: $\bigwedge_{a \in A^t} a$. This is the tableau state which is created by applying the CNOT to be implemented to the standard initial tableau. Since most entries are 0 in the initial tableau, this reduces to updating

$$x^t_{\alpha\beta} := x^0_{\alpha\beta} \oplus x^0_{\alpha\alpha} = 0 \oplus 1 = 1 \text{ and}$$

$$z^t_{(n+\beta)\alpha} := z^0_{(n+\beta)\alpha} \oplus z^0_{(n+\beta)\beta} = 0 \oplus 1 = 1$$

for a CNOT gate on control qubit α and target qubit β. Figure 6b shows the goal state tableau for the realization of a CNOT on control qubit 1 and target qubit 2 for the standard initial tableau from Fig. 6a.

With all these representations defined, the complete propositional formula is of the following form:

$$\phi(t) = A^0 \wedge \bigwedge_{i=0}^{t-1} T(A^i, A^{i+1}) \wedge A^t$$

where the operators and state variables are super-scripted with the step i they belong to. $\phi(t)$ is satisfiable if, and only if, there is an implementation for the given CNOT using t gates. The operators used are identified by the variables σ; as for each $i \in \{1, \ldots, t\}$ there is only exactly one $\sigma_o{}^i$ for which $\sigma_o{}^i = 1$, the operator used for step i can be identified unambiguously. This means that if $\phi(t)$ is satisfiable, there is a sequence of operators $o^1, \ldots, o^t$ which is an implementation of the CNOT using t quantum gates. In order to determine the cheapest implementation, the minimum value for t such that $\phi(t)$ is still satisfiable has to be found.

A naive approach for finding a minimum t would be to start at $t = 1$ and increment t until $\phi(t)$ is satisfiable. Alternatively, one may take previously suggested minima as an upper bound and decrement t until $\phi(t)$ is no longer satisfiable. In fact, showing that no solution exists for some t implies that no solution exists for any smaller t. This is because the Hadamard and CNOT gates are self-inverse such that two consecutive gates on the same qubit(s) cancel out and do not have an effect to the entire circuit functionality. Thus, proving that no solution exists for t steps directly implies that there is no solution for $t-2$, $t-4$, $t-6$ steps and so on. In order to also cover the remaining cases $t-1$, $t-3$, etc., we allowed an identity operator in the last time step which has no effect to the state tableau.

Table 1. Feasibility study

Control	Target	t	Boolector		Z3	
			Result	Run-time	Result	Run-time
Q1	Q3	3	UNSAT	9.2	UNSAT	1.2
Q1	Q3	4	SAT	14.5	SAT	2.0
Q1	Q4	7	UNSAT	24.2	UNSAT	7.2
Q1	Q4	8	SAT	29.3	SAT	10.0
Q0	Q2	8	UNSAT	28.5	UNSAT	4.0
Q0	Q2	9	UNSAT	37.5	UNSAT	10.7
Q0	Q2	10	SAT	45.0	SAT	16.3
Q0	Q4	17	UNSAT	429.1	UNSAT	141.3
Q0	Q4	18	SAT	355.3	SAT	36.6
Q8	Q13	23	UNSAT	774.0	UNSAT	716.0
Q8	Q13	24	SAT	564.2	SAT	149.8

5   Experimental Results

The algorithm above has been implemented in C++. It takes the number of qubits of the considered architecture, a list of natively available CNOTs, and the CNOT to be implemented as inputs and outputs the resulting instance of the planning problem in the SMT-LIB v2 format [13] which can then be given to any compatible SMT solver. We implemented direct interfaces to Boolector 3.2.1 [12] and Z3 4.8.8 [8]. All experiments were conducted on an Intel Core i5-7200 machine with 32 GB of main memory running Linux 4.15.

5.1   Feasibility Studies

To start with, we performed some feasibility studies to check whether the constructed instances of the planning problem are solvable in reasonable run-time and verify that the obtained quantum circuits indeed realize the desired non-native CNOTs. For this purpose, we used the IBM QX5 architecture and some non-native CNOTs for which a realization with less than 30 native gates was known. The results are provided in Table 1 where the first two columns denote the control and target qubit of the considered non-native CNOT, t denotes the number of steps and the remaining columns denote the outcome (SAT or UNSAT) and run-time in CPU seconds for the two considered SMT solvers Boolector and Z3.

The numbers indicate that for smaller values of t the run-time does not much depend on the result (SAT or UNSAT). For larger values of t, both solvers require significantly more run-time to prove that no solution exists for t steps than to determine one of the possible solutions. But still, the results clearly demonstrate the power of the proposed approach since the search space contains

Table 2. Experimental results for IBM QX5

Qubit	0	1	2	3	4	5	6	7	8	9	10	11	12	13	14	15
0	–	5	10	14	18	28	32	38	54	44	34	30	24	20	10	5
1	1	–	1	4	8	18	22	28	38	54	32	28	22	18	8	10
2	10	5	–	1	4	14	18	24	34	38	28	24	18	14	4	5
3	14	8	5	–	1	10	14	20	30	34	24	20	14	10	1	8
4	18	12	8	5	–	5	8	14	24	28	18	14	8	5	10	12
5	24	18	14	10	1	–	5	10	20	24	14	10	5	10	14	18
6	28	22	18	14	4	1	–	1	10	14	4	1	10	14	20	22
7	38	32	28	24	14	10	5	–	5	8	1	10	14	20	24	32
8	44	38	34	30	20	16	10	1	–	5	4	14	18	24	28	38
9	40	42	38	34	24	20	14	4	1	–	1	10	14	20	24	34
10	34	42	32	28	18	14	8	5	8	5	–	5	8	14	18	28
11	30	32	28	24	14	10	5	10	14	10	1	–	5	10	14	24
12	20	22	18	14	4	1	10	14	18	14	4	1	–	1	4	14
13	16	18	14	10	1	10	14	20	28	24	14	10	5	–	1	10
14	10	12	8	5	10	14	24	28	32	28	18	14	8	5	–	5
15	1	10	1	4	8	18	22	28	38	34	24	20	14	10	1	–

$(22+16)^t$ different possible realizations of native gates to be ruled out in the case of UNSAT. Overall, Z3 solver performed much quicker than Boolector and was solely used for future runs. To verify the correctness of the determined stabilizer circuits, we performed equivalence checking based on QMDDs [11].

5.2 Non-native CNOTs on IBM Q Architectures

Having confirmed the general feasibility and correctness of the proposed approach, we turned to the problem of determining optimal implementations of non-native CNOTs on IBM Q architectures.

For the 16-qubit QX5 architecture, we took the results from [3] as the starting point and iteratively decremented the number of steps until the solver returned UNSAT for some t which, as discussed at the end of Sect. 4, implies that there is no realization with $k \leq t$ gates.

Tables 2 and 3 show the results for all CNOTs in QX5. In both tables, the rows denote the control qubit and the columns denote the target qubit of the CNOT. Each entry in Table 2 represents the cost of the implementation as defined earlier, i.e., the total number of native gates required in order to realize the CNOT, while Table 3 shows the absolute improvement over the best-known constructions from [3]. Note that our cost metric differs from the one used in [3], which expresses the overhead introduced by the implementation, making it less by one in all cases. This difference has been accounted for in Table 3, but should also be considered when comparing Table 2 to the results from [3].

Table 3. Improvements compared to [3]

Qubit	0	1	2	3	4	5	6	7	8	9	10	11	12	13	14	15
0	–	0	1	0	2	2	8	14	8	12	12	12	6	1	1	0
1	–	–	–	0	2	2	8	14	14	8	22	14	8	2	2	1
2	1	0	–	–	0	0	6	12	12	18	18	12	6	0	0	0
3	6	0	0	–	–	1	6	12	12	12	12	12	6	1	–	0
4	8	2	0	0	–	0	0	6	6	6	6	6	0	0	1	2
5	12	8	6	1	–	–	0	1	1	0	0	1	0	1	0	6
6	18	12	6	0	0	–	–	–	1	0	0	–	1	0	6	12
7	18	12	6	0	0	1	0	–	0	0	–	1	6	4	12	12
8	24	18	12	6	6	7	1	–	–	0	0	0	6	12	18	18
9	18	24	18	12	12	6	0	0	–	–	–	1	6	12	12	12
10	12	12	12	6	6	6	0	0	0	0	–	0	0	6	6	6
11	6	12	6	0	0	1	0	1	6	1	–	–	0	1	0	0
12	6	12	6	0	0	–	1	0	6	0	0	–	–	–	0	0
13	7	8	6	1	–	1	6	4	6	0	0	1	0	–	–	1
14	1	2	0	0	1	6	6	6	12	6	6	6	0	0	–	0
15	–	1	–	0	2	2	8	14	14	12	12	12	6	1	–	–

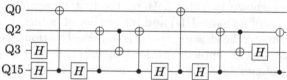

Fig. 7. Implementation of CNOT($Q3, Q0$) as calculated by our algorithm.

Exact minima have been determined for all CNOTs of the QX5 architecture. Overall, there are 67 CNOTs between qubits with a maximum distance of 4 for which the constructions from [3] are indeed optimal, while for 50 CNOTs our approach determined that they can be improved by at least 12 gates. For instance, Fig. 7 shows an optimal realization of CNOT($Q3, Q0$) requiring only 14 gates as compared to the realization from Fig. 5 using 20 gates which was discussed in Sect. 3.

For the 20-qubit Q20 architecture [1], where all CNOTs are available in both directions, we were able to prove the minimality of the construction proposed in [9] using $4 \cdot (d-1)$ CNOTs where d is the distance between control and target.

5.3   Effect on Circuit Transformation

In order to evaluate the impact of the determined improvements on quantum circuit transformation, we considered a suite of benchmarks taken from [16] and

Table 4. Circuit Transformation for IBM QX5

Benchmark		Transformation overhead		
ID	L	[3]	Proposed	Δ
sym6_316	14	3015	2409	−20.10 %
rd53_311	13	3174	2507	−21.01 %
hwb5_53	6	6140	5240	−14.66 %
wim_266	11	6195	5049	−18.50 %
f2_232	8	6319	5198	−17.74 %
rd53_251	8	8976	7134	−20.52 %
cm42a_207	14	9045	7619	−15.77 %
dc1_220	11	10523	8891	−15.51 %
cm152a_212	12	15228	11610	−23.76 %
sym6_145	7	19688	16058	−18.44 %
z4_268	11	23280	18549	−20.32 %
hwb6_56	7	38747	30779	−20.56 %

the naive qubit mapping which maps i-th qubit of the circuit to qubit Qi in the QX5 architecture.

The results are shown in Table 4. Here, the first two columns describe the benchmark in terms of its name (ID) and its number of qubits (L). The next two columns denote the overhead using the original constructions from [3] and the improved/optimal CNOT implementations determined by the proposed approach. The last column lists the relative improvement which is in the range between 10% and 20%.

6   Conclusions

In this work, we proposed a method to determine optimal implementations of non-native CNOTs based on a formulation as a SAT problem. This formulation only becomes possible, since the considered gates (CNOT and Hadamard) are part of the Clifford group library for which a dedicated tableau representation can be employed that only requires $O(n^2)$ Boolean variables. While we restrict to CNOT and Hadamard gates, the approach can steadily be extended to support all Clifford group gates. As confirmed by experimental results, the resulting problem formulation scales considerably well and enabled us to determine significantly improved realizations of non-native CNOT gates for the 16-qubit IBM QX5 architecture, while for Q20 the known construction could be proven to be minimal.

References

1. IBM Q. https://www.research.ibm.com/ibm-q/. Accessed 14 Oct 2020

2. Aaronson, S., Gottesman, D.: Improved simulation of stabilizer circuits. Phys. Rev. A **70**(5) (2004). https://doi.org/10.1103/physreva.70.052328

3. de Almeida, A.A.A., Dueck, G.W., da Silva, A.C.R.: CNOT gate mappings to Clifford+T circuits in IBM architectures. In: International Symposium on Multiple-Valued Logic, pp. 7–12. IEEE (2019). https://doi.org/10.1109/ISMVL.2019.00010

4. Ash-Saki, A., Alam, M., Ghosh, S.: QURE: Qubit re-allocation in noisy intermediate-scale quantum computers. In: Design Automation Conference, pp. 141:1–141:6. ACM, New York (2019)

5. Botea, A., Kishimoto, A., Marinescu, R.: On the complexity of quantum circuit compilation. In: SOCS, pp. 138–142. AAAI Press (2018)

6. Boykin, P., Mor, T., Pulver, M., Roychowdhury, V., Vatan, F.: A new universal and fault-tolerant quantum basis. Inf. Process. Lett. **75**, 101–107 (2000). https://doi.org/10.1016/S0020-0190(00)00084-3

7. Cook, S.A.: The complexity of theorem proving procedures. In: Symposium on Theory of Computing, pp. 151–158 (1971)

8. de Moura, L., Bjørner, N.: Z3: an efficient SMT solver. In: Ramakrishnan, C.R., Rehof, J. (eds.) TACAS 2008. LNCS, vol. 4963, pp. 337–340. Springer, Heidelberg (2008). https://doi.org/10.1007/978-3-540-78800-3_24

9. Nash, B., Gheorghiu, V., Mosca, M.: Quantum circuit optimizations for NISQ architectures. Quantum Sci. Technol. **5**(2), 025010 (2020)

10. Nielsen, M.A., Chuang, I.L.: Quantum Computation and Quantum Information: 10th Anniversary Edition. Cambridge University Press (2010). https://doi.org/10.1017/CBO9780511976667

11. Niemann, P., Wille, R., Miller, D.M., Thornton, M.A., Drechsler, R.: QMDDs: efficient quantum function representation and manipulation. IEEE Trans. CAD **35**(1), 86–99 (2016). https://doi.org/10.1109/TCAD.2015.2459034

12. Niemetz, A., Preiner, M., Biere, A.: Boolector 2.0. J. Satisf. Boolean Model. Comput. **9**(1), 53–58 (2014). https://doi.org/10.3233/sat190101

13. Ranise, S., Tinelli, C.: The Satisfiability Modulo Theories Library (SMT-LIB). www.SMT-LIB.org (2006)

14. Rintanen, J.: Planning and SAT. In: Handbook of Satisfiability, vol. 185, pp. 483–504 (2009)

15. Siraichi, M.Y., Santos, V.F.d., Collange, S., Pereira, F.M.Q.: Qubit allocation. In: International Symposium on Code Generation and Optimization, CGO 2018, Vienna, pp. 113–125. ACM (2018). https://doi.org/10.1145/3168822

16. Wille, R., Große, D., Teuber, L., Dueck, G.W., Drechsler, R.: RevLib: an online resource for reversible functions and reversible circuits. In: International Symposium on Multiple-Valued Logic, pp. 220–225 (2008)

17. Wille, R., Burgholzer, L., Zulehner, A.: Mapping quantum circuits to IBM QX architectures using the minimal number of SWAP and H operations. In: Design Automation Conference, pp. 142:1–142:6. ACM (2019)

18. Zhou, X., Li, S., Feng, Y.: Quantum circuit transformation based on simulated annealing and heuristic search. IEEE Trans. CAD 1 (2020). https://doi.org/10.1109/TCAD.2020.2969647

19. Zulehner, A., Paler, A., Wille, R.: An efficient methodology for mapping quantum circuits to the IBM QX architectures. IEEE Trans. CAD **38**(7), 1226–1236 (2019). https://doi.org/10.1109/TCAD.2018.2846658

Fast Swapping in a Quantum Multiplier Modelled as a Queuing Network

Evan E. Dobbs[1], Robert Basmadjian[2], Alexandru Paler[1,3(✉)], and Joseph S. Friedman[1]

[1] University of Texas at Dallas, Richardson, TX 75080, USA
[2] Clausthal University of Technology, 38678 Clausthal-Zellerfeld, Germany
[3] Transilvania University, 500036 Brașov, Romania

Abstract. Predicting the optimum SWAP depth of a quantum circuit is useful because it informs the compiler about the amount of necessary optimization. Fast prediction methods will prove essential to the compilation of practical quantum circuits. In this paper, we propose that quantum circuits can be modeled as queuing networks, enabling efficient extraction of the parallelism and duration of SWAP circuits. To provide preliminary substantiation of this approach, we compile a quantum multiplier circuit and use a queuing network model to accurately determine the quantum circuit parallelism and duration. Our method is scalable and has the potential speed and precision necessary for large scale quantum circuit compilation.

Keywords: Quantum circuit · Queuing network · Parallelism

1 Introduction

Compilation of quantum circuits has been investigated from different perspectives. Only recently, with the advent of NISQ devices, did compilation methods start to address optimality in the context of large scale circuits and hardware topology constraints. One of the first works presenting a systematic method to evaluate the performance of running a circuit compiled to a particular qubit layout was [7] – it discusses ancilla qubit factories, interconnects and logical computation units. The quantum arithmetic as a distributed computation perspective was presented in [9]. The analogy between quantum circuits and communication networks has been presented for error-corrected CNOT circuits in [8]. Some recent works on gate parallelism during compilation investigate how the same device can be shared for multiple circuits [11], and how edge-coloring and subgraph isomorphism are related to the parallel scheduling of gates [6]. Organizing qubits into specialized regions has been analyzed for ancillae by [5]. Exact and not scalable methods for the computation of optimal SWAP circuit depths have been introduced by [14].

This work is motivated by the need to determine automatically, as fast and precise as possible the *average* SWAP circuit depth when compiling to an arbitrary hardware layout (not necessary a regular 3D one like in the following). To

© Springer Nature Switzerland AG 2021
S. Yamashita and T. Yokoyama (Eds.): RC 2021, LNCS 12805, pp. 256–265, 2021.
https://doi.org/10.1007/978-3-030-79837-6_16

the best of our knowledge, this is the first work in which the optimal SWAP depth is predicted in order to support the circuit compiler. At the same time, no work treated a complete circuit as a network of queues. We present a proof of concept and investigate the feasibility of using queuing networks – we use the analogy between SWAP depth and input-output mean response time.

We report preliminary results after testing our approach by compiling a multiplier [10] to a 3D hardware layout. Most quantum devices have 1D or 2D qubit layouts, and 3D (e.g. neutral atom devices and photonic quantum technologies) is not considered viable in the short-term. However, for the purpose of this work, we chose a 3D qubit layout because we assumed that: a) routing the qubits in 3D may shorten the resulting depth; b) it is difficult for automated compilation methods; c) it is useful for developing novel compilation heuristics.

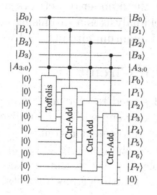

Fig. 1. The multiplication circuit from [10] consists of three steps: 1) the Toffoli gates, 2) a sequence of controlled addition circuits; 3) the SWAP circuits occurring between every controlled addition. The third step is not illustrated.

We treat our circuit as a network of single element queues inter-connecting input and output queues. The multiplier has a highly regular structure, and we chose to compile the circuit manually. The circuit can be divided into three steps:

1. a one-time application of Toffoli gates,
2. repeated controlled-additions on subsets of the qubit register, and
3. setting up for the next controlled-addition step (which occurs between every controlled addition).

The goal is to determine how the coordinates (e.g. 2D or 3D) and properties of the queues influence the compilation result. The SWAP depth of a (sub-)circuit depends not only on the qubit layout but also on the structure of the previous (sub-)circuits. We propose to use queuing network parameters (e.g. arrival rate of the queues) to capture these aspects.

In the following, in order to build the intuition behind the formal approach, we start by compiling the multiplier of Muñoz-Coreas et al. [10] to a 3D lattice of qubits. Qubit queues are conveniently placed next to the adder. The queues are storing ancillae and partial product qubits. After compiling the controlled-additions to 3D, the third step of the multiplier has a constant SWAP depth of 5 gates – irrespective of the number of qubits involved in the multiplication. All qubits were swapped in parallel without delaying (*blocking*) each other.

We will not describe how we compiled the first two steps of the multiplier. It suffices to say that we used known Toffoli gate decompositions that have a 3D-like Clifford+T decomposition, and we exploited the ripple-carry structure of the controlled addition circuits.

Afterwards, we compare the prediction obtained from the queuing network analysis with our manually compiled and optimized circuit. We formalize the queuing network model of the circuit and perform a closed-form analysis to illustrate the feasibility of our approach. The analysis method has a polynomial complexity that depends on the number of network nodes. Finally, we conclude that queuing network model analysis is a promising approach towards the compilation and optimization of quantum circuits, and we formulate future work.

2   The Multiplication Circuit

The structure in Fig. 2 is designed to efficiently implement a multiplier [10] in a 3D nearest-neighbor environment with a minimized SWAP gate depth. By creating a single structure to implement a controlled-adder and connecting this circuit to queues within which the qubit registers are stored, the total number of qubits necessary to implement the circuit is kept small, while the SWAP depth in the third step of the multiplier has a constant depth of 5 for any n-bit multiplication.

There are four queues in the structure (cf. Fig. 1 and Fig. 2): The top left queue, which stores used control qubits from the B register, the top right queue, which stores calculated product bits from the P register, the bottom-most queue which stores unused qubits from the P register (all initialized to $|0\rangle$), and the queue in the final cube which stores unused control qubits from the B register. At the beginning of the calculation the top two queues are empty and the bottom two queues hold their corresponding values.

Note that the A register is the only register not stored in a queue; this is because all of the A qubits are used for every controlled addition step, so they are stored in constant positions along the structure. Additionally, the first n P qubits and the first B qubit begin the computation already placed throughout the structure as opposed to beginning in the queues, and at the end of the computation the last n P qubits and the final B qubit are stored in the structure, so at no point do any queues hold every qubit in a register. It should also be noted that when a register is referred to as 'empty' that means it is filled with ancilla initialized to $|0\rangle$. This is so that when a qubit is added to the queue it can swap with such an ancilla which is necessary for the next step in the computation.

Gates are initially performed in the topmost cube, followed by the one below it and so on until the necessary gates have been applied to the bottom-most cube.

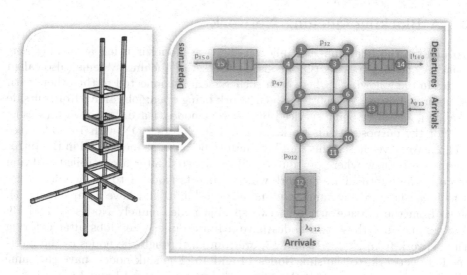

Fig. 2. Mapping of multiplier circuit to an open queuing network of $N = 15$ nodes. (LHS) The 3D qubit layout where the quantum circuit is mapped to; there are four queues (two gray, one yellow and a red one) connected to the cuboid-like 3D layout; (RHS) The QN with 15 nodes, out which 4 have a finite buffer size, whereas the others (only circles with numbers 1 till 11) have a capacity of 1 (e.g. buffer size of zero). For some of the transitions, their corresponding probability p_{ij} is shown. Jobs from outside arrive only at Nodes 12 and 13, and depart from Nodes 14 and 15.

Due to the uncompute step, gates are then applied in the opposite direction, beginning with the bottom-most cube and moving up to the top-most cube, at which point a single controlled-addition step is complete. More importantly, after each controlled-addition step a single value from both the B and P queues will have moved from the bottom queues into the structure, and another value from the B and P queues will have moved from within the structure into their corresponding top queues.

The qubits are initially positioned to implement the first step of the multiplier, then SWAP gates are applied to prepare for repeated applications of the second and third steps. After the application of the first step a single qubit from both the P and B registers moves forward into the structure from the bottom queues, and a single qubit from both registers also moves out from the structure into the top queues in a manner identical to the end of each controlled addition step.

For each moment in the calculation, every qubit value can swap with a single neighboring qubit. In this structure, there are three positions which only have two neighbors, $n - 2$ positions with three neighbors, and every other position has four neighbors. So the majority of qubits can move in one of four different directions at each moment, or choose not to move.

3   A Blocking Queuing Network

To analyze the quantum multiplier circuit, we model it using a queuing network. A queuing network (QN) consists of a set of queuing systems (also called *nodes* in the following), where each such system is connected to the others with some probabilities. We consider the network being open: jobs arrive from outside (*source*), and after being serviced by different nodes, leave the network (*sink*).

For the purpose of this work, we use a small, open QN with 15 nodes (see Fig. 2). We have chosen this simple structure because, as mentioned in the Introduction, we knew where our qubits will be located after a controlled addition circuit. The intermediate network which connects Nodes 1 to 11 includes nodes which can hold at any time only one job (no buffer and have a capacity of 1). Jobs from the outside arrive at two specific nodes namely Nodes 12 and 13. We assume that those two nodes have a finite buffer size. Jobs after entering the network from Nodes 12 and 13, are routed, through the nodes of the intermediate network, to the sink Nodes 14 and 15. The sink nodes, have the same characteristics in terms of buffer size as the source Nodes 12 and 13.

SWAP gate parallelism implies that qubit paths are independently running through the hardware layout, but that the paths are not blocking at intersections: a qubit does not need to wait for another qubit to cross a node (there are no bottlenecks). In order to model qubit swapping, we use a blocking queuing network. If the target nodes, to which the job needs to be transmitted after being serviced by a queuing system i, are full, then the job at i is blocked until one of the target nodes becomes free to process this job.

3.1   Modeling the Network

The open network model uses the following parameters: (1) The number of nodes of the network N, (2) routing (or transition) probability p_{ij} of jobs from node i to j, (3) probability p_{0i} that arriving job enters the QN at node i, (4) probability p_{i0} that job leaving node i also leaves the QN such that $p_{i0} = 1 - \sum_{j=1}^{N} p_{ij}$, (5) arrival rate λ_{0i} of jobs from the outside to node i such that the overall arrival rate to QN is given by $\lambda = \sum_{i=1}^{N} \lambda_{0i}$. The parameters determine the QN model and, for example, the arrival rate λ_i for each node i can be derived using the traffic equation such that $\lambda_i = \lambda_{0i} + \sum_{j=1}^{N} p_{ji}\lambda_j$.

This mathematical formulation allows us to carry out a closed-form analysis (see below) for the steady-state probabilities. Our objective is to obtain the state probability vector $\pi = [\pi_1, ..., \pi_{15}]$ such that $\sum_{i=1}^{15} \pi_i = 1$. Obtaining a closed-form solution for such a network consisting of 15 nodes with each node having at least 3 states (as we will see later) is not trivial: the state space size explodes to 14 million (i.e. 3^{15}) states!

Therefore, we chose a product-form queuing network (PFQN) approach. Such networks consist of a special type of nodes only, where the underlying state-space does not have to be generated for evaluation:

$$\pi(S_1, S_2, ..., S_N) = \frac{1}{G}[\pi(S_1) * \pi(S_2) * \cdots * \pi(S_N)]$$

where G is a normalization constant, and S_i is the specific state of node i. We adopt the Jackson network model for PFQN, where in order to calculate the steady-state probability of the whole network, it suffices to calculate the marginal probability of each node:

$$\pi(S_1, S_2, ..., S_N) = \pi_1(S_1) * \pi_2(S_2) * \cdots * \pi_2(S_N) \tag{1}$$

3.2   Modeling the Nodes

The nodes of the circuit network are of two types: boundary and non-boundary. Boundary nodes are where jobs arrive (Nodes 12 and 13) or leave (Nodes 14 and 15) the network. Non-boundary nodes belong to the intermediate network (Nodes 1 till 11). All nodes are of the type M/M/1-FCFS: arrival and service processes are [M]arkovian (e.g. inter-arrival and service times are exponentially distributed), each node consists of one server, and jobs are processed in first-come-first-served (FCFS) fashion [2].

The difference between the boundary and non-boundary nodes is that the former have a capacity of K, and the latter have a capacity of one. Thus, the nodes are either M/M/1/K-FCFS or M/M/1/1-FCFS systems.

To model and analyze a node (queuing system) named i, the following parameters are required: (1) The different states S_i that the system can have, (2) the arrival and service rates of jobs λ_i and μ_i respectively, (3) the number of servers m_i, and the size of the buffer K_i in case of a finite capacity queuing systems. In this paper, the considered state-space of each queuing system is discrete and the timing convention is continuous. These parameters are used to generate a continuous-time Markov chain (CTMC). The CTMC allows us to produce the square generator matrix Q which presents the transition rates between two states l and m of the queuing system i under study, such that the diagonal elements of the matrix $q_{ll} = -\sum_{m,m \neq l} q_{lm}$.

A closed-form solution (see below) is obtained by solving a set of linear global balance equations originating from $\pi_i * Q_i = 0$, where π_i is the vector of the steady-state probabilities $\pi_i(l)$ such that $\sum_l \pi_i(l) = 1$ for a given queuing system i and its states l.

3.3   Non-boundary Nodes

We describe the states and the transitions of the non-boundary M/M/1/1-FCFS nodes. Since these nodes have a capacity of one and only a single server, then upon arrival of a new job to this node while its server is busy, this new job cannot be buffered. To model and analyze the behavior of a job-blocking queuing system, we model the states as a two-dimensional tuple of binary values.

Figure 3 shows all the possible states as well as their transitions and the corresponding rates. The (0,0) is for the empty system. Upon the arrival of a new job with an arrival rate of λ_i, the system transitions from state (0,0) to (1,0). This indicates that there is a single job at the node i and that the job is being serviced by a single server. After service, there are two possible transitions: (0,0)

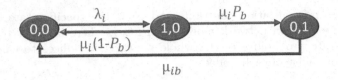

Fig. 3. A Markov chain for non-boundary nodes: three different states and the transitions. The first and second dimensions of each state denote the number of jobs at the service and if the job is blocked (1/0 = True/False).

or (0,1). The former case happens when the serviced job can leave the queuing system i and enter the next neighboring one j in the network without being blocked by j. Consequently, the corresponding system i becomes idle again and in (0,0) with the service rate of $\mu_i(1 - P_b)$, where P_b is the probability that the job after being serviced will be blocked by its neighboring node.

The transition from (1,0) to (0,1) indicates that the job after being serviced with a service rate of μ_i will be blocked by its neighbor with a probability P_b. The transition from (0,1) to (0,0) models the possibility of the blocked job at the queuing system i to leave it and enter one of its neighboring nodes j. This happens because one of the queuing system i's neighbors can now process the job. The queuing system i becomes idle again, and this transition happens with a rate of μ_{ib} (i.e. the unblocking rate of the jobs). The steady-state probability for a full system in a finite capacity M/M/1/K-FCFS [4] is Eq. 2.

$$\pi_i(K) = \rho_i^K \frac{1 - \rho_i}{1 - \rho_i^{K+1}}, \text{ where } \rho_i = \frac{\lambda_i}{\mu_i} \tag{2}$$

3.4   Closed-Form Analysis

We focus on a single job running through the network, but assume that the job can take exclusive ownership of a node (see Fig. 3). To determine the mean response time of a an arbitrary job running between source and sink, we consider that there is a non-zero probability of each node to be blocked at some point by some other job that took exclusive ownership of it.

Performing a general analysis is a complex task. We make simplifying assumptions and tune some of the parameters to the circuit we would like to compile. First, we assume that $\rho_i = 1$, Eq. 2. The result is that $\pi_i(K) = \frac{1}{K+1}$, and considering that the non-boundary nodes are of type M/M/1/1-FCFS, it leads to the conclusion that the probability of any neighboring node j of a another node i being full (e.g. $\pi_j(1)$) is 50%. We can derive the worst case blocking probability P_b of a job as the probability that the next hop of j neighboring nodes is full: $P_b = \sum_j p_{ij}\pi_j(1) = 0.5$.

Second, we have to determine the rate at which jobs arrive in the queues at nodes 12 and 13. The multiplication circuit consists of three steps (see Introduction), and herein our goal is to determine the SWAP duration during the last step. Therefore, we need to select values for λ_{12}, and λ_{13} which reflect the structure of the previous two steps. After systematic trials necessary to select values which reflect the gate depths of the previous two steps, we arrive at $\lambda = \lambda_{12} + \lambda_{13} = 0.15 + 0.1 = 0.25$.

We use the PFQN to calculate the marginal probabilities of each node in the intermediate network. We used SHARPE [13] to calculate the steady-state probabilities from Table 2 with respect to the CTMC from Fig. 3 and the parameters from Table 1. The utilization $\rho_i = 1 - \pi_i(0,0)$, and the mean number of jobs $\bar{K}_i$ is the sum of the steady-state probabilities of $(1,0)$ and $(0,1)$. We observe that all the nodes are occupied for more than 79.5% (e.g. $\pi_i(0,0) < 20.5\%$) of the time, and have blocked jobs between 60% and 69% (e.g. $\pi_i(0,1)$) of the time.

The mean response time $\bar{T}_i$ is computed using Little's law [3] which is the ratio between the mean number of jobs $\bar{K}_i$ to the arrival rate. The mean number of jobs in the network is $K = \frac{\sum_{i=1}^{11} \bar{K}_i}{11} = 0.831$. We calculate a mean response time of $\bar{T} = \frac{K}{\lambda} = 3.324$. This result confirms that our depth 5 SWAP circuit is close to the predicted optimal depth.

4   Discussion

Our method estimates average SWAP depths using a circuit modeled as a network of queuing systems. In a nutshell, the average SWAP depth indicates intuitively for a packet (i.e. qubit) the number of steps it takes to traverse a network between *any* pair of source and destination queues. There may be additional constraints that the packet has to obey: for example, it should move between a predetermined pair of queues (i.e. this the case for the qubits that arrive and exit given queues). The value we observed in the previous Sect. 3.3, is for a packet that moves between *any pair of queues*. The best value of 5 SWAPs is when moving between a specific pair of queues.

We assumed that *a single job traverses the network at a time*, but the fact that *the nodes are blocking* seems to be a good model for multiple non-blocking SWAP qubit paths. Using the PFQN we observe that more than 3 hops are required on average to traverse from one of the source nodes to one of the sink nodes. This is not surprising and for the simple 3D layout that we have been using could have been determined by visual inspection: there are two source-sink routes, one of 5 hops and another one of 3 hops.

Our small example shows that the arrival rates at the source queues influence the optimality of the average SWAP depth estimation. Our approach can prove valuable with respect to look-ahead compilation heuristics. Compilation speedups and cost improvements may be achieved by tuning queue parameters without being forced to consider the existing movement constraints. We showed in [12] how queuing theory can be used for predicting when to start and stop T-gate distillations. Similar look-ahead scheduling techniques can be applied to the source queues (e.g. Nodes 12 and 13 in Fig. 2).

Our procedure can be generalized. Similar approaches are used for modeling latency times and delays in communication networks [1]. In this work we focused

Table 1. The parameter values to compute the steady-state probabilities

Node #	1	2	3	4	5	6	7	8	9	10	11
λ_i	0.94	0.94	0.936	0.88	1.644	1.596	1.02	1.6	1.18	1.42	0.86
μ_i	1	1	1	1	1	1	1	1	1	1	1
μ_{ib}	0.136	0.136	0.13	0.144	0.17	0.142	0.124	0.173	0.175	0.195	0.143

Table 2. The steady-state probabilities and the calculated performance metrics.

Node #	1	2	3	4	5	6	7	8	9	10	11
$\pi_i(0,0)$	0.185	0.185	0.181	0.203	0.135	0.121	0.163	0.138	0.18	0.165	0.205
$\pi_i(1,0)$	0.174	0.174	0.169	0.178	0.219	0.194	0.166	0.221	0.213	0.234	0.178
$\pi_i(0,1)$	0.641	0.641	0.65	0.619	0.646	0.685	0.671	0.641	0.607	0.601	0.617
ρ_i	0.815	0.815	0.819	0.797	0.867	0.8783	0.837	0.862	0.82	0.835	0.795
$\bar{K}_i$	0.815	0.815	0.819	0.797	0.867	0.8783	0.837	0.862	0.82	0.835	0.795
$\bar{T}_i$	0.867	0.867	0.875	0.906	0.527	0.550	0.821	0.539	0.695	0.588	0.924

solely on multiplication circuits because these are building blocks of larger practical algorithms. The scale of those circuits is not a limiting factor: thousands of qubits (nodes) should be within the reach of PFQN methods. This work has been mostly to showcase and test the potential of our idea, and leave for future work the extension of our method to larger circuit instances.

5   Conclusion

We presented empiric evidence that a simple blocking PFQN can be used to model and predict the depth of SWAP circuits resulting during the compilation of circuits. The closed-form analysis method has a polynomial complexity, because it is based on solving a set of linear equations for π_i and per node there are only three states in the CTMC for intermediate network nodes.

The precision of our queuing network model is influenced by the arrival rates at the source queues. We did not model the correlations between sub-circuits, and leave this for future work. Another significant parameter is the per node probability of $(0,0)$.

Queuing networks may be a useful approach towards steering the automated compilation of very large scale quantum circuits to arbitrary (irregular) qubit layouts. Future work will focus on automatically modeling queue arrival rates and benchmarking larger and more diverse types of qubit layouts.

References

1. Balsamo, S.: Product form queueing networks. In: Haring, G., Lindemann, C., Reiser, M. (eds.) Performance Evaluation: Origins and Directions. LNCS, vol. 1769, pp. 377–401. Springer, Heidelberg (2000). https://doi.org/10.1007/3-540-46506-5_16

2. Basmadjian, R., de Meer, H.: Modelling and analysing conservative governor of DVFS-enabled processors. In: Proceedings of the Ninth International Conference on Future Energy Systems, pp. 519–525. e-Energy 2018. Association for Computing Machinery, New York (2018). https://doi.org/10.1145/3208903.3213778
3. Basmadjian, R., Niedermeier, F., de Meer, H.: Modelling performance and power consumption of utilisation-based DVFS using M/M/1 queues. In: Proceedings of the Seventh International Conference on Future Energy Systems. e-Energy 2016. Association for Computing Machinery, New York (2016). https://doi.org/10.1145/2934328.2934342
4. Bolch, G., Greiner, S., de Meer, H., Trivedi, K.S.: Queueing Networks and Markov Chains: Modeling and Performance Evaluation with Computer Science Applications, 2nd edn. WileyBlackwell, Hoboken (2006)
5. Ding, Y., et al.: SQUARE: strategic quantum ancilla reuse for modular quantum programs via cost-effective uncomputation. In: 2020 ACM/IEEE 47th Annual International Symposium on Computer Architecture (ISCA), pp. 570–583 (2020). https://doi.org/10.1109/ISCA45697.2020.00054
6. Guerreschi, G.G., Park, J.: Two-step approach to scheduling quantum circuits. Quantum Sci. Technol. 3(4), 045003 (2018)
7. Isailovic, N., Whitney, M., Patel, Y., Kubiatowicz, J.: Running a quantum circuit at the speed of data. ACM SIGARCH Comput. Archit. News 36(3), 177–188 (2008)
8. Javadi-Abhari, A., et al.: Optimized surface code communication in superconducting quantum computers. In: Proceedings of the 50th Annual IEEE/ACM International Symposium on Microarchitecture, pp. 692–705 (2017)
9. Meter, R.V., Munro, W., Nemoto, K., Itoh, K.M.: Arithmetic on a distributed-memory quantum multicomputer. ACM J. Emerg. Technol. Comput. Syst. (JETC) 3(4), 1–23 (2008)
10. Muñoz-Coreas, E., Thapliyal, H.: Quantum circuit design of a t-count optimized integer multiplier. IEEE Trans. Comput. 68(5), 729–739 (2018)
11. Niu, S., Todri-Sanial, A.: Enabling multi-programming mechanism for quantum computing in the nisq era. arXiv preprint arXiv:2102.05321 (2021)
12. Paler, A., Basmadjian, R.: Clifford gate optimisation and t gate scheduling: using queueing models for topological assemblies. In: 2019 IEEE/ACM International Symposium on Nanoscale Architectures (NANOARCH), pp. 1–5 (2019). https://doi.org/10.1109/NANOARCH47378.2019.181305
13. Trivedi, K.S., Sahner, R.: Sharpe at the age of twenty two. SIGMETRICS Perform. Eval. Rev. 36(4), 52–57 (2009). https://doi.org/10.1145/1530873.1530884
14. Wille, R., Lye, A., Drechsler, R.: Optimal swap gate insertion for nearest neighbor quantum circuits. In: 2014 19th Asia and South Pacific Design Automation Conference (ASP-DAC), pp. 489–494 (2014). https://doi.org/10.1109/ASPDAC.2014.6742939

OR-Toffoli and OR-Peres Reversible Gates

Claudio Moraga[1,2(✉)]

[1] Faculty of Computer Science, Technical University of Dortmund, Dortmund, Germany
claudio.moraga@udo.edu
[2] Department of Informatics, Technical University "Federico Santa María", Valparaíso, Chile

Abstract. The paper introduces new Toffoli and Peres reversible gates, which operate under disjunctive control, and shows their functionality based on the Barenco et al. quantum model. Both uniform and mixed polarity are considered for the controls. Rewriting rules are presented, which provide a reduction of the number of gates and quantum cost of reversible (sub) circuits using standard Toffoli or Peres gates. It is shown that in most cases a reduction in the number of CNOT gates is obtained, which is convenient when mapping reversible circuits to IBM-QX quantum computers.

Keywords: Reversible gates · OR gates · Rewriting rules

1 Introduction

One of the earliest contributions to the development of reversible/quantum circuits is due to T. Toffoli [16, 17], who proposed a functionally complete controlled reversible circuit, that soon became known as "Toffoli gate", distinguishing two control bits and a target bit, preserving the control bits and inverting the target bit when the conjunction of the control bits became true. This reversible gate has intensively been used ever since and has received several "extensions", like multi-controlled Toffoli gates and their decomposition as V-shaped cascades of elementary Toffoli gates and ancillary bits [5], a quantum realization model [5]. mixed polarity controlled Toffoli gates [14], and Clifford-T realizations [2, 3] as well as mappings to the IBM QX quantum computers [1, 3]. Together with the Toffoli gate, the NOT gate and CNOT (the controlled NOT gate), are basic universal components of reversible circuits.

The realization of minimal (irreversible) binary circuits is NP-complete [18]. Due to the constraints imposed by reversibility, like no feedback and no fan-out of gates, the synthesis of minimal reversible/quantum circuits is NP-hard [12]. The synthesis of reversible/quantum circuits is, therefore, mostly based on heuristics (see e.g. the surveys [4, 13]). A fast transformation based synthesis system is presented in [15]. Post-processing optimization of circuits has been applied, mainly using Templates [11] and rewriting rules [14].

In the present paper Toffoli gates with disjunctive control [7, 8] will be disclosed, including mixed polarity. Similarly, for the case of Peres reversible gates. These gates will be simply called OR-Toffoli and OR-Peres gates. Rewriting rules will be developed for the post-processing of circuits, allowing to replace, when applicable, sub-circuits based on classical reversible gates by simpler circuits including OR- reversible gates.

© Springer Nature Switzerland AG 2021
S. Yamashita and T. Yokoyama (Eds.): RC 2021, LNCS 12805, pp. 266–273, 2021.
https://doi.org/10.1007/978-3-030-79837-6_17

2 Formalisms

Definition 1: A disjunct controlled Toffoli gate has the following behavior: the target bit will be inverted iff the *disjunction* of the binary control signals is true, i.e. if any or both control bits have the value 1. The gate remains inhibited if *both* controls have the value 0 and behaves as an identity.

Its symbol, its quantum model under positive polarity, (similar to the Barenco *et al.* [5] model) and its specification matrix [7, 8] are shown in Fig. 1, where the connection between a control bit and the target inverter is represented by a triangular symbol ▼, (in black when the expected control signal is 1), which is close to the disjunction sign $\bigvee$ of the Mathematical Logic. In the classical reversible gates, which are activated under conjunctive control, the connection between a control bit and the target is represented by a black dot if the activating control signal has the value 1 or a white dot if the activating control signal has the value 0 [14]. The same color assignment will be used in the case of OR-reversible gates. In what follows, as a matter of fairness, the quantum model will be called Barenco model. This model shows that the OR-Toffoli gate, as the classical Toffoli gate, has a quantum cost of 5. In the Barenco model, the matrix specification of the $\mathbf{V}$-gate is the square root of the matrix specification of the NOT gate [5]. Therefore $\mathbf{V} \cdot \mathbf{V} = $ NOT.

It is simple to see in the Barenco model of Fig. 1 that if c_1 has the value 1, ("c_1 is 1"), and c_2 has the value 0, ("c_2 is 0"), the first $\mathbf{V}$-gate will become active, and the second one will be inhibited, thus behaving as the identity. Furthermore, c_1 will activate the CNOT gates, producing a "local 1" that will activate the third $\mathbf{V}$-gate. Finally, the cascade of the two active $\mathbf{V}$-gates produce the expected NOT behavior. (Notice that the last CNOT gate only recovers the original value of c_2).

In the case that c_1 is 0 and c_2 is 1, the first $\mathbf{V}$-gate and the CNOT gates will be inhibited, whereas the second and the third $\mathbf{V}$-gates will be activated and their product will produce the expected NOT behavior.

Finally, if both c_1 and c_2 are 1, the two first $\mathbf{V}$-gates become activated and produce the expected NOT behavior. Since the CNOT gates will also become activated by c_1 they will produce a local 0 by negating c_2, inhibiting the third $\mathbf{V}$-gate.

It is simple to see that if both c_1 and c_2 are 0, then all gates will be inhibited.

This analysis clearly shows that the OR-Toffoli gate becomes active, when the *disjunction* –(OR)– of the control signals is *true*. Furthermore, the target line of its Barenco model contains only $\mathbf{V}$-gates, whereas in the case of classical Toffoli gates the target line contains two $\mathbf{V}$-gates and one adjoint $\mathbf{V}$-gate [5].

Figure 2 shows OR-Toffoli gates under mixed polarity, where if a 0 control signal is meant to be effective, then a white triangle will be placed on the control line, in analogy to the "white dots" of the conjunctive case (see e.g. [14]). The "=" sign in Fig. 2 refers to the functionality, not to the structure of the gates. Furthermore, the Barenco type of quantum models only illustrate the functionality of the gates. Prevailing "quantum technologies" may not necessarily support negative control of elementary quantum gates.

The gates of Fig. 2 become active when at least one of the controls is effective, i.e. when a white triangle is driven by 0 or a black triangle is driven by 1. The gates become inhibited, when *both* controls are ineffective.

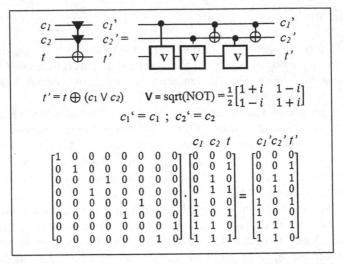

Fig. 1. Symbol, Barenco quantum model, and matrix specification of the basic disjunct controlled Toffoli gate.

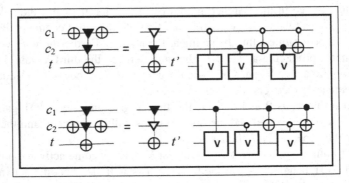

Fig. 2. OR-Toffoli gates with mixed polarity and their Barenco functional quantum models.

As mentioned earlier, the role of the last CNOT gate of the Barenco models is the recovering of the initial value of c_2, but it does not affect the target output. If this gate is deleted, the target will not be affected, but the output at the middle qubit will change. It is simple to conclude that the modified gate has the behavior of a Peres gate [10], or more precisely, that of an OR-Peres gate. Details of the OR-Peres gate, including mixed polarity, may be found in [9], available from the author upon request.

Still an important structural aspect of OR-Toffoli gates has to be considered: the scalability, i.e. the possibility of building multicontrolled OR-Toffoli gates. A direct realization of an OR-Toffoli gate with 3 controls adapted from [8] is shown in Fig. 3, where the boxes on the target line represent **W**-gates. **W** equals the fourth root of NOT:

$$W = \frac{1}{2}\begin{bmatrix} 1 + i^{1/2} & 1 - i^{1/2} \\ 1 - i^{1/2} & 1 + i^{1/2} \end{bmatrix}$$

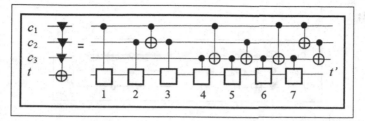

Fig. 3. Direct realization of an OR-Toffoli gate with 3 controls: $t' = t \oplus (c_1 \vee c_2 \vee c_3)$

Table 1. Proof of correctness of the circuit of Fig. 3:

$c1$	1	0	1	0	1	0	1
$c2$	0	1	1	0	0	1	1
$c3$	0	0	0	1	1	1	1
Active gates	1, 3 5, 7	2, 3 6, 7	1, 2 5, 6	4, 5 6, 7	1, 3 4, 6	2, 3 4, 5	1, 2 4, 7

From Table 1 it becomes apparent that for any combination of control signals such that $c_1 \vee c_2 \vee c_3 \neq 0$, four W-gates will be active and their cascade –(product)– will generate the expected 3-controlled NOT behavior. If all three control signals have the value 0, then the OR-Toffoli gate will be inhibited.

3 Rewriting Rules

Rewriting rules comprise indications on how to move gates within a circuit and replace sub-circuits with simpler ones. (See e.g. [14]). Templates [11] comprise pairs of sub-circuits, where one has the inverse functionality of the other. (Their cascade leads to an identity). The simpler will be used.

In the case of OR-Toffoli gates, most rewriting rules may be obtained based on construction, considering that $x \bigvee y = x \oplus y \oplus xy = x \oplus \bar{x} y = y \oplus x \bar{y}$ and also that $x \bigvee y = \overline{\bar{x}\bar{y}}$. This is shown in Fig. 4, which, as the basic straight forward rewriting rule, must be read according to the arrows.

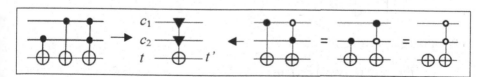

Fig. 4. Basic straightforward rewriting rules:

$$\overline{\bar{c}_1 \bar{c}_2} = c_2 \oplus c_1 \bar{c}_2 = c_1 \oplus \bar{c}_1 c_2 = c_1 \vee c_2; \ c_1 \oplus c_2 \oplus c_1 c_2 = c_1 \vee c_2$$

Rule 1:

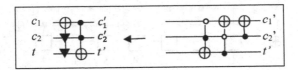

Proof of equivalence:

$$c_1' = c_1 \oplus (c_2 \vee t) = c_1 \oplus c_2 \oplus t \oplus c_2 t = c_1 \oplus c_2 \oplus \bar{c}_2 t; \, c_2' = c_2$$

$$t' = t \oplus c_1' c_2 = t \oplus (c_1 \oplus c_2 \oplus \bar{c}_2 t) \, c_2 = t \oplus c_1 c_2 \oplus c_2 = t \oplus \bar{c}_1 c_2$$

However, if both sides of $t' = t \oplus \bar{c}_1 c_2$ are multiplied by $\bar{c}_2$, then.

$$\bar{c}_2 t' = \bar{c}_2 t \text{ and } c_1' = c_1 \oplus c_2 \oplus \bar{c}_2 t'$$

The circuit based on an OR-Toffoli gate and a classical Toffoli gate gives the simpler realization, where a CNOT gate is no longer needed.

Rule 2:

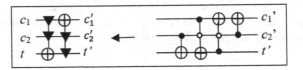

Proof of equivalence:

$$t' = t \oplus (c_1 \vee c_2) = t \oplus c_1 \oplus c_2 \oplus c_1 c_2 = t \oplus c_2 \oplus c_1 \bar{c}_2$$

$$c'_1 = c_1 \oplus (t' \vee c_2) = c_1 \oplus t' \oplus c_2 \oplus t' c_2 = c_1 \oplus c_2 \oplus t' \bar{c}_2$$

Rule 3:

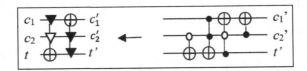

Proof of equivalence:

$$t' = t \oplus (c_1 \vee \bar{c}_2) = t \oplus c_1 \oplus \bar{c}_2 \oplus c_1 \bar{c}_2 = t \oplus \bar{c}_2 \oplus c_1 c_2$$

$$c_1' = c_1 \oplus (t' \vee c_2) = c_1 \oplus t' \oplus c_2 \oplus t' c_2 = c_1 \oplus c_2 \oplus t' \bar{c}_2$$

Rule 4:

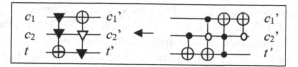

Proof of equivalence:

$$t' = t \oplus (c_1 \vee c_2) = t \oplus c_1 \oplus c_2 \oplus c_1 c_2 = t \oplus c_2 \oplus c_1 \bar{c}_2$$

$$c_1' = c_1 \oplus (t' \vee \bar{c}_2) = c_1 \oplus t' \oplus \bar{c}_2 \oplus t' \bar{c}_2 = c_1 \oplus \bar{c}_2 \oplus t' c_2$$

Rule 5:

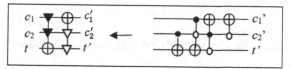

Proof of equivalence:

$$t' = t \oplus (c_1 \vee c_2) = t \oplus c_1 \oplus c_2 \oplus c_1 c_2 = t \oplus c_2 \oplus c_1 \bar{c}_2; c_2' = c_2$$

$$c_1' = c_1 \oplus (\bar{t'} \vee \bar{c}_2) = c_1 \oplus \bar{t'} \oplus \bar{c}_2 \oplus \bar{t'} \bar{c}_2 = c_1 \oplus \bar{c}_2 \oplus \bar{t'} c_2$$

Rule 6:

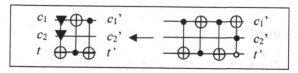

Proof of equivalence: Let $t_0 = t \oplus (c_1 \vee c_2) = t \oplus c_1 \oplus c_2 \oplus c_1 c_2$

$$c_1' = t_0 \oplus c_1 = t \oplus c_1 \oplus c_2 \oplus c_1 c_2 \oplus c_1 = t \oplus \bar{c}_1 c_2; t' = t_0 \oplus c_1' = c_1;$$

Notice that in the circuit at the right the first three CNOT gates swap c_1 and t.
Further rules may be found in [9].

These few rewriting rules obviously do not cover all possible simplifications, but should be considered as motivating examples offering new possibilities for post-processing of prevailing Toffoli circuits. Notice that in these rewriting rules, all the OR-circuits not only require less gates than the classical ones, but they also require less CNOT gates, what will be positive in the context of processing in IBM/QX quantum computers, where there is a limited number of so-called native CNOT gates in fixed positions [1, 3].

Example: The benchmark "mod5d1" has the following specification. A 5×5 reversible circuit should be designed, where the input 5-tuple $b_4b_3b_2b_1b_0$ represents the binary coding of the integers 0, 1, 2,..., 31. For this sequence of input integers, the coded output should be [**0**, **1**, 3, 2, 5, 4, 7, 6,..., 27, 26, 29, 28, **30, 31**], i.e. the integers 0, 1, 30 and 31 should be preserved at the output and the remaining even integers should be swapped with the corresponding next odd integers. It is simple to see that only the b_0 bit will be affected. It is known [19] that an optimal solution is the following:

$$b_0' = b_0 \oplus [(b_4 \oplus b_2) \vee (b_3 \oplus b_1)].$$

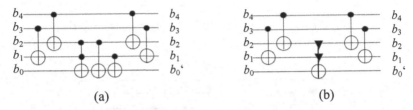

(a)   (b)

Fig. 5. (a) Classical solution [19], (b) Solution with an OR-Toffoli gate.

Notice that the realization with an OR-Toffoli gate saves two CNOT gates.

A next step may be the study of OR-gates at the level of their Clifford + T models. This can rather easily be done taking advantage of the existence of Clifford + T gates with optimal T-count of 7 and optimal T-depth of 4 for the realization of $t \oplus c_1\bar{c}_2$ and for the realization of a classical Toffoli gate [2]. Adding at the input side of the first gate a CNOT gate controlled by c_2 realizes a Clifford + T OR-Toffoli (recall Fig. (4)) and adding at the output side of the Toffoli gate a CNOT gate controlled by c_1 produces an OR-Peres gate.

4 Closing Remarks

OR-Toffoli and OR-Peres gates have been presented and their functionality introduced, based on an adapted Barenco model for the classical Toffoli gate. A possible way of using these gates to improve existing reversible/quantum Toffoli circuits in form of rewriting rules, is discussed. Prevailing circuits may be improved with the rewriting rules by reducing the number of gates –(particularly CNOT gates)- and quantum cost. An example of the realization of a benchmark is given; Others may be found in [6]. Finally, a possible Clifford-T realization of OR-Toffoli and OR-Peres gates with minimum T-count, based on circuits presented in [2] is suggested, which may be considered when optimized circuits are mapped to an IBM-QX quantum computer.

References

1. Abdessaied, N., Amy, M., Soeken, M., Drechsler, R.: Technology mapping of reversible circuits to Clifford+T quantum circuits. In: Proceedings of 2016 46th International Symposium on Multiple-Valued Logic (ISMVL), pp. 150–155. IEEE Press (2016)

2. Amy, M., Maslov, D., Mosca, M., Roetteler, M.: A meet-in-the-middle algorithm for fast synthesis of depth-optimal quantum circuits. IEEE Trans. Comput.-Aided Des. Integr. Circ. Syst. **32**, 818–830 (2013)
3. de Almeida, A.A.A., Dueck, G.W., da Silva, A.C.R.: Efficient realization of Toffoli and NCV circuits for IBM QX architectures. In: Thomsen, M.K., Soeken, M. (eds.) Reversible Computation. LNCS, vol. 11497, pp. 131–145. Springer, Cham (2019). https://doi.org/10.1007/978-3-030-21500-2_8
4. Cheng, C.S., Singh, A.K.: Heuristic synthesis of reversible logic – a comparative study. Theor. Appl. Electr. Eng. **12**(3), 210–225 (2014)
5. Barenco, A., et al.: Elementary gates for quantum computation. Phys. Rev. A **52**, 3457–3467 (1995)
6. Hadjam, F.Z., Moraga, C.: RIMEP2. evolutionary design of reversible digital circuits. ACM J. Emerg. Technol. Comput. Syst. **11**(3), 1–23 (2014)
7. Moraga, C.: Hybrid GF(2) – boolean expressions for quantum computing circuits. In: De. Vos, A., Wille, R. (eds.) Reversible Computation. LNCS, vol. 7165, pp. 54–63. Springer, Heidelberg (2012). https://doi.org/10.1007/978-3-642-29517-1_5
8. Moraga, C.: Using negated control signals in quantum computing circuits. Facta Universitatis, Ser. Electron. Energetics **24**(3), 423–435 (2011)
9. Moraga, C.: Reversible gates with disjunctive control. Research Report 875, Faculty of Computer Science, Technical University of Dortmund (2021)
10. Peres, A.: Reversible logic and quantum iComputers. Phys. Rev. **32**(6), 3266–3276 (1985)
11. Rahman, M., Dueck, G.W.: An algorithm to find quantum templates. In: Proceedings of IEEE Congress on Evolutionary Computation, pp. 623–629. IEEE Press (2012)
12. Rahul, I., Loff, B., Oliveira, I.C.: NP-hardness of circuit minimization for multi-output functions. In: Proceedings of 35th Computational Complexity Conference (CCC 2020). Schloss Dagstuhl-Leibniz-Zentrum für Informatik (2020)
13. Saeedi, M., Markov, I.L.: Synthesis and optimization of reversible circuits – a survey. Comput. Surveys, arXiv 1110.2574v1
14. Soeken, M., Thomsen, M.K.: White dots do matter: rewriting reversible logic circuits. In: Dueck, G.W., Miller, D.M. (eds.) Reversible Computation. LNCS, vol. 7948, pp. 196–208. Springer, Heidelberg (2013). https://doi.org/10.1007/978-3-642-38986-3_16
15. Soeken, M., Dueck, G.W., Miller, D.M.: A fast symbolic transformation based algorithm for reversible logic synthesis. In: Devitt, S., Lanese, I. (eds.) Reversible Computation. LNCS, vol. 9720, pp. 307–321. Springer, Cham (2016). https://doi.org/10.1007/978-3-319-40578-0_22
16. Toffoli, T.: Reversible computing. Tech. memo MIT/LCS/TM-151, MIT Lab for Computer Science (1980)
17. Toffoli, T.: Reversible computing. In: de Bakker, J., van Leeuwen, J. (eds.) Automata, Languages and Programming. LNCS, vol. 85, pp. 632–644. Springer, Heidelberg (1980). https://doi.org/10.1007/3-540-10003-2_104
18. Wegener, I.: The Complexity of Boolean Functions. John Wiley and Sons, New York (1987)
19. Wille R., et al.: www.revlib.com. (2008)

Author Index

Printed in the United States
by Baker & Taylor Publisher Services